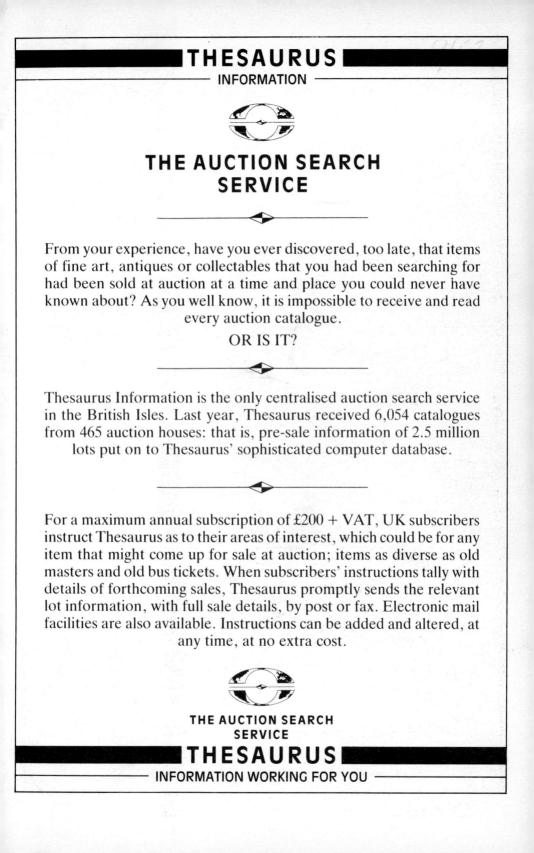

MILLER'S
Collectables
PRICE GUIDE

MILLER'S COLLECTABLES PRICE GUIDE 1994/95

Compiled, edited and designed by
Miller's Publications
The Cellars, High Street
Tenterden, Kent TN30 6BN
Telephone: 0580 766411

Compiled and edited by
Judith & Martin Miller

General Editor: Robert Murfin
Editorial & Production Co-ordinator: Sue Boyd
Editorial Assistants: Sue Montgomery, Marion Rickman, Jo Wood
Production Assistants: Gillian Charles, Helen Burt
Design: Stephen Parry, Jody Taylor, Darren Manser
Photographic Co-ordinator and Advertising Executive: Elizabeth Smith
Display Advertisements: Sally Marshall, Liz Warwick
Index compiled by: DD Editorial Services, Beccles
Additional photography: Ian Booth, Robin Saker

First published in Great Britain in 1994
by Miller's
an imprint of Reed Consumer Books Limited
Michelin House, 81 Fulham Road
London SW3 6RB
and Auckland, Melbourne, Singapore and Toronto

A CIP catalogue record for this book is
available from the British Library

ISBN 1-85732-338-6

Bromide output: The Final Word, Tonbridge, Kent
Illustrations: G. H. Graphics, St. Leonards-on-Sea
Colour origination: Scantrans, Singapore
Printed and bound in England by William Clowes Ltd,
Beccles and London

MILLER'S
Collectables
PRICE GUIDE

Consultants
Judith and Martin Miller

General Editor
Robert Murfin

1994-95
(Volume VI)

KEY TO ILLUSTRATIONS

Each illustration and descriptive caption is accompanied by a letter code. By reference to the following list of Auctioneers (denoted by *) and Dealers (•), the source of any item may be immediately determined. In no way does this constitute or imply a contract or binding offer on the part of any of our contributors to supply or sell the goods illustrated, or similar articles, at the prices stated. Advertisers in this year's directory are denoted by (†).

A • Alma Gallery Ltd, 29 Alma Vale Road, Bristol. Tel: 0272 237157

AA • Ambeline Antiques, By George Antique Centre, St. Albans, Herts. Tel: 0727 53032 & 081 445 8025

AAM • Anything American (Chris Pearce), 33-35 Duddenhill Lane, London NW10. Tel: 081 451 0320

AAR * Amersham Auction Rooms, 125 Station Road, Amersham, Bucks. Tel: 0494 729292

AAV * Academy Auctioneers & Valuers, Northcote House, Northcote Avenue, Ealing, London W5. Tel: 081 579 7466

ABS • Abstract, 58-60 Kensington Church Street, London W8. Tel: 071 376 2652

ACA •† Acorn Antiques, Sheep Street, Stow-on-the-Wold. Tel: 0451 831519

AG * Anderson & Garland (Auctioneers), Marlborough House, Marlborough Crescent, Newcastle-upon-Tyne Tel: 091 232 6278

AGM • The Button Museum, Kyrle Street, Ross-on-Wye, Hereford & Worcs. Tel: 0989 66089

AH * Andrew Hartley, Victoria Hall, Little Lane, Ilkley, W. Yorks. Tel: 0943 816363

AHL • Adrian Hornsey Ltd, Three Bridge Mill, Twyford, Bucks. Tel: 0296 738373

AI • Antiques & Interiors, 22 Ashford Road, Tenterden, Kent. Tel: 0580 765462

AJ •† A. J. Partners, Stand J28, Gray's In The Mews, Davies Mews, London W1. Tel: 071 629 1649

AL •† Ann Lingard, Ropewalk Antiques, Ropewalk, Rye, East Sussex. Tel: 0797 223486

ALL * Allen & Harris, Bristol Auction Rooms, St. John's Place, Apsley Road, Clifton, Bristol, Avon. Tel: 0272 737201

AMH •† Amhurst Antiques, 23 London Road, Riverhead, Kent. Tel: 0732 455047.

ANX • Alan Wood, Annexe Antiques, 33 The Pantiles, Tunbridge Wells, Kent. Tel: 0892 547213

AOS • Antiques on the Square, Church Stretton, Shropshire. Tel: 0694 724111.

APO • Apollo Antiques Ltd., The Saltisford, Birmingham Road, Warwick. Tel: 0926 494746

ARE • Arenski, Stand 107, Gray's Antique Market, 58 Davies Street, London W1 Tel: 071 499 6824

ASA • AS Antiques & Decorative Arts, 26 Broad Street, Pendleton, Salford 6, Manchester. Tel: 061 737 5938

ASB •† Andrew Spencer Bottomley, The Coach House, 173A Huddersfield Road, Thongsbridge, Holmfirth, Huddersfield, Yorks. Tel: 0484 685234

B * Boardman, Station Road Corner, Haverhill, Suffolk. Tel: 0440 703784

BAf • Books Afloat, 66 Park Street, Weymouth, Dorset, DT4 7DE.

BAN • Banking Memorabilia, P.O. Box 14, Carlisle. Tel: 06974 76465

BAT • Bartlett St Antique Centre, Bartlett St, Bath, Avon.

BCO • British Collectables, 1st Floor, 9 Georgian Villas, Camden Passage, Islington, London N1. Tel: 071 359 4560

BER • Douglas Berryman, Bartlett Street Antiques Centre, Bath, Avon. Tel: 0225 446841

BGA • By George Antique Centre, 23 George Street, St. Albans, Herts. Tel: 0727 53032

BIB • Erivvin Biberger, Bartlett St Antique Centre, Bath, Avon.

BIR • Birchall's, Cotebrook, Tarporley, Cheshire, CW6 9DY. Tel: 0829 760754

BKK • Bona Knick-Knacks, 19 Princesmead, Farnborough, Hants. Tel: 0252 372188/544130

BKS * Robert Brooks (Auctioneers) Ltd, 81 Westside, London SW4. Tel: 071 228 8000

Bon * Bonhams, Montpelier Galleries, Montpelier Street, London SW7. Tel: 071 584 9161

BRK • Breck Antiques, 762 Mansfield Road, Nottingham. Tel: 0602 605263

BWA • Bow Well Antiques, 103 West Bow, Edinburgh. Tel: 031 225 3335.

BWe * Biddle & Webb of Birmingham, Ladywood Middleway, Birmingham. Tel: 021 455 8042

C * Christie, Manson & Woods Ltd, 8 King Street, St James's, London SW1. Tel: 071 839 9060

C(S) * Christie's Scotland Ltd, 164-166 Bath Street, Glasgow. Tel: 041 332 8134

CA •† Crafers Antiques, The Hill, Wickham Market, Suffolk. Tel: 0728 747347

CAG * Canterbury Auction Galleries, 40 Station Road West, Canterbury, Kent. Tel: 0227 763337

CAI • Cain Antiques, Littleton House, Littleton, Nr. Somerton, Somerset. Tel: 0458 72341

CAT •† Catto Animation, 41 Heath Street, London NW3. Tel: 071 431 2892

CB • Christine Bridge Antiques, 78 Castlenau, London SW13. Tel: 081 741 5501

CC • Collectable Costume, The Great Western Antique Centre, Bartlett Street, Bath. Tel: 0225 428731

CCC •† The Crested China Co., The Station House, Driffield, E. Yorks. Tel: 0377 47042

CD • The China Doll, 31 Walcot Street, Bath, Avon. Tel: 0225 465849

ChL • Chelsea Lion, Steve Clark. Tel: 081 658 1599

CK •† Claire Kinloch, Bulmer House, The Green, Sedlescombe, East Sussex. Tel: 0424 870364

CNY * Christie, Manson & Woods International Inc, Park Avenue, New York, NY 10022, USA. Tel: (212) 546 1000 (including Christie's East)

COB •† Cobwebs, 78 Northam Road, Southampton. Tel: 0703 227458

COL • Collectables, PO Box 130, Chatham, Kent. Tel: 0634 828767

CS •† Christopher Sykes Antiques, The Old Parsonage, Woburn, Bucks. Tel: 0692 402962

CSK *† Christie's (South Kensington) Ltd, 85 Old Brompton Road, London SW7. Tel: 071 581 7611

DAB • Danby Antiques, York. Tel: 0904 415280

DaD * David Dockree, 224 Moss Lane, Bramhall, Stockport Cheshire. Tel: 061 485 1258

DAN • Andrew Dando, 4 Wood Street, Queen Square, Bath, Avon. Tel: 0225 422702

DAV •† Davies Antiques, 44a Kensington Church St, London W8. Tel: 071 937 9216

DEL • Ann Delores, Bartlett Street Antique Centre, Bath, Avon.

DHo • Derek Howard, The Original Chelsea Antiques Market, 245/253 King's Road, London SW3. Tel: 071 352 4113

DID • Didier Antiques, 58-60 Kensington Church Street, London W8. Tel: 071 938 2537 & 0836 232634

DMT • David Martin-Taylor Antiques, 56 Fulham High Street, London SW6.

DN * Dreweatt Neate, Donnington Priory, Donnington, Newbury, Berks. Tel: 0635 31234

DP • David Payne, Bartlett Street Antiques Market, 9 Bartlett Street, Bath, Avon. Tel: 0225 330267

DUN •† Richard Dunton, 920 Christchurch Road, Boscombe, Bournemouth, Dorset. Tel: 0202 425963

EB • E. Brook, Smith Street Antique Centre, Warwick. Tel: 0926 497864

EGR • Frances Baird, The Anchorage, Wrotham Road, Culverstone, Meopham, Kent.

ELR * Eadon Lockwood & Riddle, 411 Petre Street, Sheffield. Tel: 0742 618000

F * Francis Fine Art Auctioneers, The Tristar Business Centre, Star Industrial Estate, Partridge Green, Horsham, Sussex. Tel: 0403 710567

FMN •† Forget Me Not Antiques (Heather Sharp), By George Antique Centre, 23 George Street, St. Albans, Herts. Tel: 0727 53032 & 0923 261172

G&CC •† Goss and Crested China Ltd, 62 Murray Road, Horndean, Hants. Tel: 0705 597440

GA • Garry Atkins, 107 Kensington Church St, London W8. Tel: 071 727 8737

GAK * G. A. Key, 8 Market Place, Aylsham, Norwich, Norfolk. Tel: 0263 733195

GAZ • Gazelles, 31 Northam Road, Southampton. Tel: 0703 235291 & 780798

GBL • Gregory, Bottley & Lloyd, 13 Seagrave Road, London SW6. Tel: 071 381 5522

GH * Giles Haywood, The Auction House, St. John's Road, Stourbridge, W. Midlands. Tel: 0384 370891

GHA •† Garden House Antiques, 116-118 High Street, Tenterden, Kent. Tel: 0580 763664

GIL * Gildings, Roman Way, Market Harborough, Leics. Tel: 0858 410414

GKR •† GKR Bonds Ltd, PO Box 1, Kelvedon, Essex. Tel: 0376 71711

GRF • Grange Farm Ltd, Grange Farm, Tongham, Surrey. Tel: 0258 2993/2804

GSP * Graves, Son & Pilcher, 71 Church Road, Hove, Sussex. Tel: 0273 735266

HAL •† John & Simon Haley, 89 Northgate, Halifax, W. Yorks. Tel: 0422 822148

HAY • Hayloft Woodwork, Box Dept, 3 Bond St, Chiswick, London W4. Tel: 081 747 3510

HB •† Harrington Bros, The Chelsea Antique Market, 253 King's Road, London SW3 Tel: 071 352 5689 & 1720.

HCH * Hobbs & Chambers, Market Place, Cirencester. Tel: 0285 4736

HDS * HY Duke & Son, 40 South Street, Dorchester, Dorset. Tel: 0305 265080

HEG • Stuart Heggie, 58 Northgate, Canterbury, Kent. Tel: 0227 470422

HER • Heritage Antiques, Unit 14, Georgian Village, Camden Passage, London N1. Tel: 071 226 9822

HEW •† Muir Hewett, Halifax Antiques Centre, Queen's Road Mills, Queen's Road/ Gibbet Street, Halifax, W. Yorks. Tel: 0422 366657

HEY • Heyford Antiques, 7 Church Street, Nether Heyford, Northampton. Tel: 0327 40749

HOW • Howards Antiques, 10 Alexandra Road, Aberystwyth, Dyfed. Tel: 0970 624973

HSS * Henry Spencer & Sons, 20 The Square, Retford, Notts. Tel: 0777 708633.

IS • Ian Sharp Antiques, 23 Front Street, Tynemouth. Tel: 0491 641349

JAC • John & Anne Clegg, 12 Old Street, Ludlow, Shropshire. Tel: 0584 873176

JBB • Jessie's Button Box, Great Western Antique Centre, Bartlett Street, Bath, Avon. Tel: 0225 310388

JMC • J. & M. Collectables. Tel: 0580 891657

JMG • Jamie Maxtone Graham, Lyne Haugh, Lyne Station, Peebles, Scotland. Tel: 07214 304.

JO •† Jacqueline Oosthuizen, The Georgian Village & 23 Cale Street, Chelsea, London, SW3. Tel: 071 352 6071

KAC • Kensington Antique Centre, 58-60 Kensington Church Street, London W8. Tel: 071 376 0425

KOH • Koh I Noor Antiques, 150 High Street, Bushey, Herts. Tel: 081 950 6260/071 359 4560

L * Lawrence Fine Art, South Street, Crewkerne, Somerset.Tel: 0460 73041

LB •† The Lace Basket, la East Cross, Tenterden, Kent. Tel: 0580 763923

LBL • Laurance Black Ltd. Antiques of Scotland, 45 Cumberland Street, Edinburgh. Tel: 031 557 4545

LIO • Lion's Den, 31 Henley Street, Stratford-upon-Avon, Warwicks. Tel: 0789 415802.

LL • Linen & Lace, (Jo Watson & Maggie Adams), The Great Western Antique Centre, Bartlett Street, Bath. Tel: 0225 310388

LR • Leonard Russell, 21 King's Avenue, Mount Pleasant, Newhaven, E. Sussex. Tel: 0273 515153

LRG * Lots Road Galleries, 71 Lots Road, London SW10 0RN. Tel: 071 351 7771

LT * Louis Taylor Auctioneers & Valuers, Britannia House, 10 Town Road, Hanley, Stoke on Trent. Tel: 0782 214111

LW * Lawrences Auctioneers, Norfolk House, 80 High Street, Bletchingley, Surrey. Tel: 0883 7433232

MAP • Marine Art Posters, 42 Ravenspur Road, Bilton, Hull. Tel: 0482 874700 & 815115

MAW * Thos Mawer & Son, The Lincoln Saleroom, 63 Monks Road, Lincoln. Tel: 0522 524984

MCA * Mervyn Carey, Twysden Cottage, Benenden, Cranbrook, Kent. Tel: 0580 240283

Mit * Mitchells, Fairfield House, Station Road, Cockermouth, Cumbria. Tel: 081 952 2002

MJW • Mark J. West, Cobb Antiques Ltd, 39a High Street, Wimbledon Village, London SW19. Tel: 081 946 2811

MofC • Millers of Chelsea Antiques Ltd, Netherbrook House, 86 Christchurch Road, Ringwood, Hants. Tel: 0425 472062

MR * Martyn Rowe, The Truro Auction Centre, Calenick Street, Truro, Cornwall Tel: 0872 260020

MRT • Mark Rees Tools, Barrow Mead Cottage, Rush Hill, Bath. Tel: 0225 837031

MSW * Marilyn Swain, Westgate Hall, Westgate, Grantham. Tel: 0476 68861

MUR •† Murray Cards (International) Ltd, 51 Watford Way, Hendon Central, London NW4. Tel: 081 202 5688

MW • Mary Wellard, Stand 165, Gray's Antique Market, Davies Street, London W1.

NCA • New Century Antiques, 69 Kensington Church Street, London W8 Tel: 071 376 2810

ND *† Nock Deighton, Livestock & Auction Centre, Tasley, Bridgnorth, Shropshire Tel: 0746 762666

NM • Nick Marchant, Bartlett St Antiques Centre, Bartlett St, Bath, Avon. Tel: 0225 310457

NP •† Neville Pundole, PO Box 6, Attleborough, Norfolk. Tel: 0953 454106

OCA • The Old Cinema, 160 Chiswick High Road, London W4. Tel: 081 995 4166

OD • Offa's Dyke Antique Centre, 4 High Street, Knighton, Powys, Wales. Tel: 0547 528635

ONS * Onslow's Metrostore, Townmead Road, London SW6. Tel: 071 793 0240

OO •† Pieter Oosthuizen, De Verzamelaar, Georgian Village, Camden Passage, London N1. Tel: 071 359 3322/376 3852

ORI •† Oriental Gallery, 1 Digbeth St, Stow-on-the-Wold, Glos. Tel: 0451 830944

OTC •† Old Telephone Company, The Old Granary, Battle Bridge Antiques Centre, Nr. Wickford, Essex. Tel: 0245 400601

P * Phillips, Blenstock House, 101 New Bond Street, London W1. Tel: 071 629 6602

P(O) * Phillips, 39 Park End Street, Oxford. Tel: 0865 723524

P(S) * Phillips, 49 London Road, Sevenoaks, Kent. Tel: 0732 740310

PAR •† Park House Antiques, Park Street, Stow-on-the-Wold, Nr Cheltenham, Glos.

PC Private Collection

PCh * Peter Cheney, Western Road Auction Rooms, Western Road, Littlehampton, Sussex. Tel: 0903 722264 & 713428

POW •† Sylvia Powell Decorative Arts, 28 The Mall, Camden Passage, London N1. Tel: 071 354 2977/081 458 4543.

PSA • Pantiles Spa Antiques, 6 Union House, Eridge Road, Tunbridge Wells, Kent. Tel: 0892 541377

PSC • Peter and Sonia Cashman, Bartlett Street Antique Centre, Barlett Street, Bath, Avon. Tel: 0225 310451

RAM • Ram Chandra, Grays Portobello, 138 Portobello Road, London W8. Tel: 081 740 0655

RBA •† Roger Bradbury Antiques, Church Street, Coltisfoot, Norfolk. Tel: 0603 737444

RdeR • Rogers de Rin, 76 Hospital Road, Paradise Walk, London SW3. Tel: 071 352 9007

REL • Relic Antiques at Brillscote Farm, Lea, Malmesbury, Wilts. Tel: 0666 822332

RID * Riddetts of Bournemouth, 26 Richmond Hill, Bournemouth, Dorset. Tel: 0202 555686

RMV • Radio Memories & Vintage Wireless, 203 Tankerton Road, Whitstable, Kent. Tel: 0227 262491

ROS * Rosbery's, The Old Railway Booking Hall, Crystal Palace Station Road, London SE19. Tel: 081 778 4024

ROW • Rowena Blackford at Penny Lampard's Antique Centre, 31-33 High Street, Headcorn, Kent. Tel: 0622 890682 & 861360

RWB • Roy W. Bunn Antiques, 34-36 Church Street, Barnoldswick, Colne, Lancs. Tel: 0282 813703

S * Sotheby's, 34-35 New Bond Street, London W1. Tel: 071 493 8080

S&S * Stride & Son, Southdown House, St John's Street, Chichester. Tel: 0243 782626

S(NY) * Sotheby's New York, 1334 York Avenue, New York, NY 10021. Tel: 212 606 7000

S(S) * Sotheby's Sussex, Summers Place, Billingshurst, W. Sussex. Tel: 0403 783933

SAD • Old Saddlers Antiques, Church Road, Goudhurst, Kent. Tel: 0580 211458

SBA • South Bar Antiques, Digbeth Street, Stow-on-the-Wold, Glos. Tel: 0451 30236

SCR •† The Scripophily Shop, Britannia House, Grosvenor Square, London W1. Tel: 071 495 0580

SER •† Serendipity, 168 High Street, Deal, Kent. Tel: 0304 369165/366536

Sim * Simmons & Sons, 32 Bell Street, Henley-on-Thames, Oxon. Tel: 0491 591111

Som • Somervale Antiques, 6 Radstock Road, Midsomer Norton, Bath, Avon. Tel: 0761 412686

SPI * Spink, 5, 6 & 7 King Street, St. James's, London SW1Y 6QS. Tel: 071 930 7888

SRA *† Sheffield Railwayana Auctions, 43 Little Norton Lane, Sheffield, Yorks. Tel: 0742 745085 & 0860 921519

SUF * Suffolk Sales, Half Moon House, High Street, Clare, Suffolk. Tel: 0787 277993

SWO * Sworders, G. E. Sworder & Sons, 15 Northgate End, Bishops Stortford, Herts. Tel: 0279 51388

TED •† Teddy Bears of Witney, 99 High Street, Witney, Oxon. Tel: 0993 702616

TER • Terrace Antiques, 10 & 12 South Ealing Road, London W5. Tel: 081 567 5194/567 1223

TP •† Tom Power, The Collector, Alfie's Antique Market, 13-25 Church Street, London NW8. Tel: 081 883 0024

TRU • The Trumpet, West End, Minchinhampton, Glos. Tel: 0453 883027

TS • Tim's Spot, Ely St. Antique Centre, Stratford-upon-Avon, Warwicks. Tel: 0789 297496

TTM • The Talking Machine, 30 Watford Way, London NW4. Tel: 081 202 3473

TVA • Teme Valley Antiques, 1 The Bull Ring, Ludlow, Shropshire. Tel: 0584 874686.

VB •† Variety Box, 16 Chapel Place, Tunbridge Wells, Kent. Tel: 0892 31868 & 21589

VH • Valerie Howard, 131e Kensington Church Street, London W8. Tel: 071 792 9702

VS *† T. Vennett-Smith, 11 Nottingham Road, Gotham, Nottingham. Tel: 0602 830541

W * Walter's, No. 1 Mint Lane, Lincoln. Tel: 0522 525454

WA • Windmill Antiques, 4 Montpellier Mews, Harrogate, Yorks. Tel: 0423 530502 & 0845 401330

WAB • Warboys Antiques, Old Church School, High Street, Warboys, Cambridge. Tel: 0487 823686

WAL *† Wallis & Wallis, West Street Auction Galleries, Lewes, E. Sussex. Tel: 0273 480208

WEL • Wells Reclamation & Co., The Old Cider Farm, Coxley, Nr Wells, Somerset Tel: 0749 77087/77484

WIL * Peter Wilson, Victoria Gallery, Market Street, Nantwich, Cheshire. Tel: 0270 623878

WL * Wintertons Ltd, Lichfield Auction Centre, Wood End Lane, Fradley, Lichfield, Staffs Tel: 0543 263256

WW * Woolley & Wallis, The Castle Auction Mart, Castle Street, Salisbury, Wilts Tel: 0722 321711

ZEI • Zeitgeist, 58 Kensington Church Street, London W8. Tel: 071 938 4817

ZKF •† Peggy Davis Ceramics, 28 Liverpool Road, Stoke-on-Trent. Tel: 0782 48002

CONTENTS

INTRODUCTION

The antiques trade at last seems to be shrugging off the recession and most dealers and auctioneers seem quietly confident that the worst is over. Collectables continue to be a growing and exciting area, with bargain-priced treasures still being discovered at boot fairs or in attics, and new, sometimes surprising, objects rapidly acquiring collectable status.

Ceramics are as popular as ever with collectors. Art Nouveau and Art Deco prices have levelled off somewhat, but prices for Victorian pieces appear to be on the increase, especially for Staffordshire pottery - but beware, as reproductions abound, especially of figural subjects. Many of these have been made from the original mould, so particular attention should be paid to colours, crispness of moulding and gilding. If in doubt, consult an auctioneer or reputable dealer.

The toy and doll market remains strong. Interest is growing in Celluloid dolls, particularly Action Man and also in Sindy and Barbie. As with all dolls and toys their value will be enhanced if they are in good condition and preferably still in their original box.

The biggest sports scoop of the year was the sale of three Henry Cooper's Lonsdale Challenge belts for approximately £48,000. Golfing items continue to sell well and other sporting collectables and equipment are becoming increasingly popular. Look out for skiing equipment as prices maybe on their way up.

Perhaps more than ever, this year the market has been strongly influenced by fashion and the media, in particular geological specimens have shown a resurgence in interest on a scale unprecedented since the Victorian period, thanks almost entirely to the launch of Stephen Speilberg's film, *Jurassic Park*. In fact, the amazing hype surrounding this film pushed prices up to such an extent that some fossilized dinosaur eggs sold for over £50,000, whereas a pistol owned and used by the famous outlaw Jesse James failed to make its reserve at auction, although at one time such an item would have been certain to inspire fierce competition.

Still on a topical note, to celebrate the 300th anniversary of the Bank of England in 1994, we have included a selection of bank notes. Although we all endeavour to collect money, the 'error' notes are of special interest, so check your change!

Other items shown for the first time include Tibetan jewellery and, believe it or not, lunch boxes, one of the newest and most exciting categories of collectables.

In fact, the speed at which new items gain collectable status has led many collectors to speculate on what the newest craze might be. This year, we have introduced a new section, 'Collectables of the Future' see page 432. Our favourites for 1994 are undoubtedly the adorable cuddly animals used in the Electricity Board's *Creature Comforts* television campaign. If you think you know what next year's hottest collectable might be, let us know, and the best answer will win a free copy of *Miller's Collectables Price Guide* every year until the year 2000!

Happy hunting - as ever!

Judith H. Miller

ACKNOWLEDGEMENTS

The publishers would like to acknowledge the great assistance given by our consultants.

BOOKS: **Peter Harrington,** Harrington Bros. The Chelsea Antique Market, 253 King's Road, London SW3.

BOXES: **Janet Manson,** Hayloft Woodwork, Box Dept., 3 Bond Street, Chiswick, London W4 1QZ.

CERAMICS:
BESWICK
BEATRIX POTTER: **Diana Callow,** B.C.C., P.O. Box 1793, Gerrards Cross, Bucks.

MEISSEN ANIMALS: **Hugh Davies,** Davies Antiques, 44A Kensington Church Street, London W8.

NANKING CARGO: **Roger Bradbury,** Church Street, Coltishall, Norfolk.

EPHEMERA: **Trevor Vennett-Smith, FRICS, FSVA, CAAV,** 11 Nottingham Road, Gotham, Nottingham.

PAPER MONEY: **Trevor Jones,** Banking Memorabilia, P.O. Box 14, Carlisle.

STANHOPES: **Douglas Jull,** 7 Cissbury Drive, Findon Valley, Worthing BN14 UDT.

AERONAUTICA

A mahogany panelled four-section screen, with carved RFC wings and 3 aerial photographs of St. Quentin dated 1918, each section 72 by 24in (182.5 by 61.5cm). **£525-575** *CSK*

A bronze figure of a pilot, on marble plinth base, c1930, 19½in (49.5cm) high. **£700-750** *CSK*

A crêpe paper napkin, printed in colours with the programme of the Blackpool Flying Meeting, Oct. 18-23, 1909, 14 by 13in (35.5 by 33cm). **£160-180** *CSK*

A BOAC plastic refreshment tray, c1960. **£30-35** *COB*

A section of the fin from a Heinkel He 111, showing signs of .303 bullet damage and signed by the pilot, 27in (69cm) square. **£600-625** *CSK*

A silver plated white metal commemorative plaque, signed Emil Monier, 19¾in (50cm) high. **£1,600-1,700** *CSK*

An RAF sector clock, fusee movement, dated 1941, 18½in (47cm) diam. **£1,000-1,100** *CSK*

A pair of decorative stands made from part of a wooden aeroplane propeller and a brass flying boat propeller, c1920. **£400-450** *MofC*

A Royal Flying Corps standard, 67 by 100in (170 by 254cm). **£125-150** *CSK*

Aviation Art

Caudron Racing Monoplane, watercolour with pencil heightened with white, French School, 20thC, 13 by 17¼in (33 by 44cm).
£150-170 *CSK*

Original artwork for Profile and other publications.
£160-180 *CSK*

After Melliers, 'Aviation' 1896, pen and ink and bodycolour, 15 by 40¾in (38 by 103.5cm).
£225-250 *CSK*

A Luftwaffe pattern binocular telescope No. 2545, with Luftwaffe embossed markings, 41½ by 10in (105 by 25cm).
£700-725 *CSK*

Original artwork for Profile and other publications, by A. Sturgess and others, featuring Messerschmidt Me 262 and others.   **£130-150** *CSK*

Frederick Searle, Supermarine Spitfire, black ink and watercolour heightened with white, signed, 11¼ by 17¾in (29 by 45cm).
£280-300 *CSK*

Aviation Ephemera

Frank Wootton, the De Havilland Enterprise, a proposal for an advertisement, oil on board, 15 by 25in (38 by 63.5cm).
£580-620 *CSK*

Charles C. Dickson, a KLM poster, lithograph in colours, dated 1926, 19in (48.5cm) square, framed and glazed.
£350-380 *CSK*

An advertising brochure for aircraft propellers, c1930.
£15-20 *COB*

A Swedish Air Lines poster, Beckman, Aerotransport, lithograph in colours, 39 by 24½in (99 by 62cm).
£700-750 *CSK*

Anonymous, Army Aviation Manoeuvre poster, 21¾ by 12½in (55.5 by 32cm).
£200-225 *CSK*

Production of this rare poster was commissioned before the armistice.

A collection of aviation books including Monke & Winter 'Pilot and Plane', and others.
£50-60 *CSK*

Charles Livingston Bull, a poster depicting the American eagle guarding a squadron of fighters, 28¼ by 18½in (72 by 47cm).
£40-45 *CSK*

A Boeing SST colour brochure, and 6 other aircraft brochures.
£40-45 *CSK*

Models

A flying scale model of a Swedish Thulin bi-plane, with fabric covered wooden airframe, c1920, 53½in (136cm) wingspan.
£450-475 *CSK*

A silver plated bronze model of the Supermarine S6B, signed Chailey under the tail plane, 8½ by 9½in (21.5 by 24cm).
£1,100-1,300 *CSK*

A flying scale model of the Hawker Fury, with fabric and metal covered wooden airframe, finished in the pre-war livery of No. 43 Sqn RAF 'The Fighting Cocks', 91in (231cm) wingspan.
£1,900-2,100 *CSK*

A hallmarked sterling silver model of a Handley Page 0-100, 18in (45.5cm) wingspan.
£3,200-3,400 *CSK*

Presented to Lt. P. T. Rawlins DSC RNVR after the flight to Constantinople and the bombing and sinking of the Turkish destroyer 'Goeben' Nov 1917, and thence by descent. Lt. Rawlins lost his life on 25.6.1919 when the Tarrant Triplane he was test flying at Farnborough crashed.

A flying scale model of the De Havilland DH 83 Fox Moth, with wood and fabric covered airframe, 54in (137cm) wingspan.
£480-500 *CSK*

A collection of 4 stylised wood and metal monoplanes, largest 19in (48cm) wingspan.
£200-225 *CSK*

A flying scale model of the Gloster Gladiator II, with fabric covered wooden airframe, finished in No. 1 Sqn RAF livery, 55½in (141cm) wingspan.
£725-750 *CSK*

A flying scale model of an Etrich Taube 2 seat monoplane, with fabric and wood covered wooden airframe, 61½in (156cm) wingspan.
£500-525 *CSK*

A flying scale model of a Messerschmidt Bf109, with wooden airframe, 78in (198cm) wingspan.
£550-575 *CSK*

A flying scale model of the De Havilland Fox Moth DH 86 A, with fabric and wood covered airframe, 87in (221cm) wingspan.
£2,200-2,400 *CSK*

A carved wood display model of the Avro Lancaster, 52¼in (133cm) wingspan.
£60-70 *CSK*

A flying scale model of a Sopwith Pup, with fabric covered wooden airframe, finished in the RFC camouflage of No. 46 Sqn RFC at Izel-Le-Hameau 1917, 97in (246.5cm) wingspan.
£1,900-2,100 *CSK*

A flying scale model of the Gloster Gladiator, with fabric and wood covered wooden airframe, finished in RAF camouflage for No. 615 Sqn, 55½in (141cm) wingspan.
£700-750 *CSK*

Photographs

A private photograph album containing a quantity of WWI period US air service and other photographs. **£170-190** *CSK*

A collection of 18 gelatin silver photographic prints, c1907-1909. **£375-400** *CSK*

Uniforms

A pair of RFC pattern officer's leather boots, with spurs and chamois leather lined canvas storage bags, approx. size 9½. **£800-825** *CSK*

A US Aero service captain's tunic, breeches, garrison cap, leather boots and spurs. **£420-450** *CSK*

A US Aero service tunic. **£125-150** *CSK*

A US Aero Service uniform, comprising a garrison cap, tunic with captain's rank badges, a Sam Browne, and cavalry twill breeches. **£425-450** *CSK*

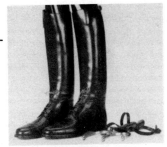

An RFC Lieutenant's uniform, comprising a tunic, a Sam Browne belt, breeches, and a pair of leather boots. **£130-150** *CSK*

Zeppelins & Airships

A collection of Zeppelin memorabilia. **£550-580** *CSK*

A Zeppelin timetable, 1934. **£50-60** *COB*

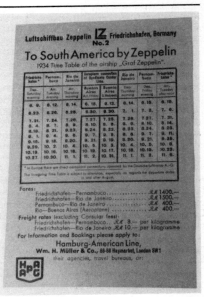

AUTOMOBILIA

The BOC Stirling Moss Golden Helmet trophy.
£900-950 *CSK*

The helmet and goggles worn by Stirling Moss when he won the British Grand Prix, at Aintree in 1957, finished in gold, perspex display case and inscription.

A chromium plated Irish Motor Racing Club badge, and a selection of enamelled lapel badges.
£190-210 *CSK*

Grosser Preis von Europa - Nurburgring 1954, a coloured enamel brass plaque, and IX Grande Premio de Portugal, Porto 1960, a painted metal plaque. **£120-140** *CSK*

Sir Malcolm Campbell, a menu from the dinner in his honour held at the Dorchester Hotel, London, on March 10th 1933, autographed by Campbell, and others.
£280-310 *CSK*

XXXVeme Rallye Automobile Monte Carlo, a coloured enamel plaque, 24 Heures du Mans 1956', and 2 lapel badges, XIIe Tour de Corse 1967 and Coupe des Alpes.
£185-200 *CSK*

A Rolls Royce red label radiator grille, c1920. **£425-450** *WIL*

A motor car interior vanity set, by G. Keller, 8in (20.5cm) wide.
£1,500-1,600 *CSK*

An Austin Motor Company poster, lithograph in colours, 30 by 40in (76 by 101.5cm), and a quantity of other Austin publicity posters.
£375-400 *CSK*

A bronze study of Tazio Nuvolari on his Alfa Romeo P3, by Gordon Chism, 14½in (37cm) long.
£1,200-1,300 *CSK*

Photographs

A selection of autographed portrait photographs, including Stirling Moss driving his H.W.M., Duncan Hamilton, John Heath and Stirling Moss and Graham Hill on the rostrum after winning the 1962 German Grand Prix.
£250-275 *CSK*

A collection of photographic and other material relating to Gunnar Nilsson, the late Swedish Grand Prix driver.
£210-230 *CSK*

CROSS REFERENCE
Ephemera
  Autographs ⟶ p190

A colour photograph of a Bugatti Type 59 at Prescott Hill Climb, 1939, 17 by 20in (43 by 51cm), framed and glazed.
£120-140 *BKS*

A collection of original pre-war photographs of racing drivers.
£100-110 *BKS*

A collection of 90 photographs, by Maxwell Boyd, mid-1950s, 7 by 9in (17.5 by 22.5cm) and larger.   **£350-375** *CSK*

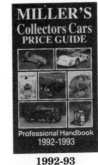

An autographed portrait photograph of Mike Hawthorn below a photograph of Hawthorn driving a Ferrari in the Ulster Trophy 1953 and an autographed photograph of Bobbie Baird.
£210-230 *CSK*

An album of early black and white photographs of Mercedes Benz interest.   **£65-75** *CSK*

ARTS & CRAFTS

The Arts and Crafts movement traces its roots back to the Aesthetic Movement of the last quarter of the 19thC. The main style was the incorporation of the ideals of medieval hand craftsmanship to the machine age.

Many guilds were founded to practise these traditional crafts, probably the most famous was Charles Ashbee's Guild of Handicraft in 1888. These guilds flourished until manufacturers, notably Liberty & Co, were able to produce ranges of goods that looked handmade but were in fact mass produced.

Several guilds did survive indeed the Cotswold School of furniture design is still in existence today.

Art Nouveau, again directly descended from the Aesthetic Movement, dominated French design in the latter years of the 19thC and became firmly established in the UK and America by Edwardian times.

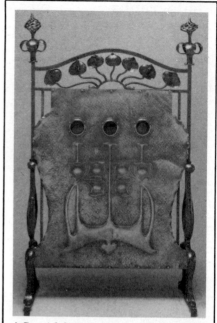

A Scottish hammered wrought iron, copper, brass and glazed ceramic fire screen, c1900, 25½in (65cm) wide. **£3,000-3,250** *S(NY)*

An enamelled copper plaque by Mabel Burras, signed lower right, 5½ by 3in (14 by 8cm), framed and glazed. **£360-380** *P*

An Irish cigarette box, by West & Sons, Dublin, 1906, 7½in (19cm) wide. **£270-290** *HSS*

Art Nouveau

A Guild of Handicraft electroplated serving dish and cover, 5½in (14cm) high. **£350-375** *C*

A painted oak pipe holder, 15½in (39cm) wide. **£150-200** *APO*

A copper hot water can, late 19thC. **£90-100** *GAK*

A pair of German preserve pots,
5in (13cm) high, with spoons
and blue glass liners, maker's
mark for H. Meyer & Co.,
Berlin.
£850-900 *P*

A wrought iron vase, attributed
to Nick Frères, c1910.
£2,000-2,500 *ABS*

An Orivit gilt candelabra, 1902,
14in (35.5cm).
£400-500 *ZEI*

CROSS REFERENCE
Candlesticks ⟶ p64

A German circular shallow
bowl, designed in the manner of
Van de Velde, crown and
crescent marks, maker's mark
for Körner & Proll, Berlin, 9½in
(24cm) wide.
£1,600-1,700 *P*

A brass belt, c1900, 27in (69cm)
long.   **£60-75** *OCA*

ART DECO

For a further selection of
Art Deco, please refer to
*Miller's Collectables
Price Guide*, Volume V,
pp30-32, available from
Millers Publications.

A games set with leather lid,
c1925, 9½in (24cm) diam.
£150-170 *CA*

A spelter figurine, on marble
base, bow missing, c1920.
£120-150 *ROW*

A white metal and enamel
buckle.
£25-45 *ASA*

BAMBOO

A telescope, 63in (160cm) long, on a stand.
£1,200-1,300 *AL*

A plant stand, new top, 31in (79cm) high.
£60-65 *AL*

A table, new top, 28in (71.5cm) high. **£45-50** *AL*

A screen, 30in (76cm) high.
£80-85 *AL*

A set of shelves, 22in (56cm) wide. **£80-85** *AL*

BELLS

A Victorian brass counter bell, with onyx base.
£30-40 *NM*

A hand painted metal bell, 3in (8cm) high. **£15-18** *AMH*

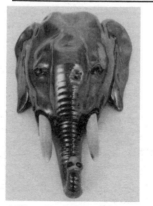

A Victorian brass and ivory elephant bell, 6⅜in (16.5cm) high. **£500-600** *ARE*

A Victorian table bell made with shells, 5½in (14cm) high.
£80-95 *AMH*

BICYCLES

An Ordinary bicycle, with metal spoked canvas/rubber tyred wheels, c1880, leading wheel 50½in (128cm), rear 17½in (44.5cm) diam.
£1,300-1,500 *CSK*

A Velocipede bicycle, with wooden spoked wheels and metal tyres, c1870, leading wheel 36in (91.5cm), rear 29½in (75cm) diam.
£1,900-2,000 *CSK*

BIRDCAGES

A child's tricycle, with wooden spoked wheels and metal tyres, front wheel mounted pedals, one missing, 19thC, leading wheel 21½in (54.5cm) diam, rear wheels 19in (48cm) diam.
£675-725 *CSK*

A metal birdcage, 20in (51cm) high.
£75-95 *MofC*

A singing bird in a cage, with gilded base, clockwork movement, 19thC, 21in (53cm).
£1,500-1,600 *LW*

A metal and wood birdcage with glass windows, 36in (92cm) wide.
£450-500 *REL*

BOOKS

Old books are valued according to condition, rarity and the presence or absence of engraved illustrations. The binding should be tight, all pages and illustrations intact and the cover bright and unsoiled. Twentieth century books often have a dust jacket which, at least in post-war books, should be present and in good condition.

Travel and guide books continue to be popular collector's items. Those books printed before 1850 are particularly sought after for their engravings but as a result many books were 'broken' and the engravings sold off separately. This sad practice unfortunately increases the rarity of untampered with books and hence their value. The list of plates at the beginning or end of a book will help to confirm the books completeness.

Colonization in the latter half of the 19thC opened the world to travel and exploration. Travel books that emerged at this time were richly illustrated with highly decorative covers designed to attract the 'armchair' traveller. Similarly 20thC travel and guide books are adorned with colourful photographic illustrations and maps, all of which serve to make this an expanding field of collectables.

A selection of children's books, published by Hodder & Stoughton, c1914, 2¼in (6cm) wide.
£5-15 each *WAB*

The Passionate Quest, paperback novel, 1943.
£1-2 *COL*

Hansel and Gretel, limited edition illustrated by K. Nielson, signed by the artist, 1 vol.
£1,300-1,400 *WIL*

Five Weeks in a Balloon, by Jules Verne, 19thC, 5in (13cm) wide.
£4-6 *ROS*

CROSS REFERENCE
Aeronautica ⟶ p15

East of Malta, West of Suez, one of a series, 1939.
£2-3 *COL*

Travel Books

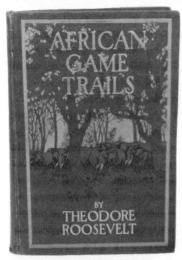

African Game Trails, by
Theodore Roosevelt, 1st Edition,
published by Charles Scribner's
& Sons, c1910, 9¾ x 7in (24.5 by
18cm).
£90-120 *HB*

Burma, painted and described
by R. Talbot-Kelly, signed, 246
of limited edition of 300, 75 full
colour illustrations, published
by Adam & Charles Black,
London, 1905, 8¾in (22cm) wide.
£150-200 *HB*

Voyage of The Challenger, The
Atlantic, Vol. I, by Sir Wyville
Thompson, published by
Macmillan & Co, London 1877,
9 by 6½in (22.5 by 16.5cm).
£140-180 *HB*

A complete set of The Voyages of Captain Cook,
8 volumes, bound in full contemporary calf twin
coloured label and gilt, 11½ by 9½in (29.5 by 24cm).
£10,000-12,000 *HB*

*With the publication of the first 2 voyages and his
dramatic death in Hawaii, Cook (1728-79) became
a national hero. So eagerly awaited was his
account of his 3rd voyage that it was sold out on
the 3rd day after publication. Although the
published price was £4.14s.6d. as much as 10
guineas was offered by would-be purchasers.*

Under the Syrian Sun, by A. C. Inchbold, 2 volumes, published by Hutchinson & Co, 1906, 9½ by 6¾in (24.5 by 17cm).
£60-90 *HB*

Embassy to China, by Sir George Staunton, 2 volumes of text and a folio of 44 copper engraved maps, plans and views, printed by W. Bulmer & Co. for G. Nicol, London, 1798. **£1,400-1,800** *HB*
Very little was known of China at this time.

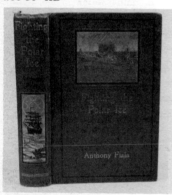

Fighting the Polar Ice, by Anthony Fiala, illustrations from photographs by the author, 1st English edition, published by Hodder & Stoughton, 1907.
£90-120 *HB*

French Pictures, drawn with pen and pencil by the Rev Samuel Green D.D., published by The Religious Tract Society, 1865, 11 by 8in (28 by 20cm).
£20-30 *HB*

Spain, by Gustave Doré, published by Bicker & Son, 1 Leicester Square, London 1881, 13¾ by 10¾in (35 by 27cm).
£120-150 *HB*

Paris, by Mortimer Menpes, text by Mortimer Menpes, No. 79 of limited edition of 500, published by Adam & Charles Black, 1909, 8¾in (22cm) wide.
£120-150 *HB*

Italian Pictures, drawn with pen and pencil by the Rev. Samuel Manning,, published by The Religious Tract Society, c1865. **£30-45** *HB*

Tallis's Illustrated London, 4 volumes, in commemoration of The Great Exhibition, 1851, 8 by 5in (20 by 12.5cm). **£90-120** *HB*

Swiss Pictures, drawn with pen and pencil by the Rev Samuel Manning LL.D., The Religious Tract Society, 56 Paternoster Row, 65 St Paul's Churchyard & 164 Piccadilly, c1860. **£25-40** *HB*

A Series of Travel Books, Baedeker's Switzerland, 1900, 6½ by 4½in (16.5 by 11.5cm). **£15-20** *HB*

Egypt, by Prof. G. Ebers, 2 volumes, 1st edition, 15 by 12in (38 by 31cm). **£120-150** *HB*

Unbeaten Tracks in Japan, by Mrs Bishop, published by George Newnes Ltd, 1901, 9¾ by 7in (24.5 by 17.5cm). **£30-45** *HB*

BOTTLES

Costumes des Peuples du Levant, Recueil de Cent Estampes, representing different costumes including Greece and Turkey, by M. de Ferriol. **£3,500-4,500** *HB*

A green glass Burgundy wine bottle, 13½in (34cm) high. **£30-40** *MofC*

A green glass Burgundy wine bottle, 21in (53.5cm) high. **£70-85** *MofC*

A green glass Burgundy wine bottle, 18in (46cm) high. **£70-85** *MofC*

BOXES

Boxes come in many shapes and sizes. Constructed from almost any wood, they can be lavishly decorated with brass and pearl inlays, marquetry, parquetry, painting veneer or plain finish.

Their uses are as varied as their shapes and designs. They can be containers for jewellery and perfume, music boxes for entertainment, puzzle boxes with secret compartments or even cigarette dispensers.

Smaller boxes in good condition are still readily available at affordable prices and can be found at most car boot sales, antique and flea markets. Larger boxes, although beautiful, are too expensive to be considered collectable.

Whatever your period preference, from Victoriana, Art Deco or the sixties, you will be able to find boxes with appeal to use as a basis for gathering and building an increasingly valuable and stylish collection.

An inlaid box, with key, early 20thC, 10in (25cm) long.
£20-30 *HAY*

An oak box, c1930, 10¼in (25.5cm) long.
£18-20 *HAY*

A silver and tortoiseshell box, Birmingham 1922.
£85-100 *WIL*

An olive wood box, from Jerusalem, 20thC, 3¼in (8cm) long.
£8-10 *HAY*

A walnut box inlaid with abalone and mother-of-pearl, 20thC, 4¼in (11cm) long.
£25-30 *HAY*

A brass box, 9in (23cm) diam.
£75-85 *MofC*

A carved wooden box with lid, shaped as a shoe, Swiss, 20thC, 7in (17.5cm) long.
£15-18 *HAY*

CROSS REFERENCE
Treen ⟶ p463

A carved wooden box inlaid with ivory, Indian, 20thC, 5in (12.5cm) long.
£25-28 *HAY*

A wooden box with divisions inside for perfume bottles, Odeurs carved on lid, French, 20thC, 5in (12.5cm) long.
£25-28 *HAY*

A birch wood box, c1945, 4½in (11.5cm) long.
£8-10 *HAY*

An inlaid wooden box, c1920, 7½in (19cm) long.
£15-18 *HAY*

A beech box with bone handle, c1920, 7in (17.5cm) long.
£16-20 *HAY*

A wrought iron deed box stand containing 4 boxes with pull down fronts, one inscribed in gilt Mme. Sarah Bernhardt, 67½ by 23in (171 by 59cm).
£850-900 *HDS*

A pine wood box, the lid decorated with roses, early 20thC, new escutcheon.
£12-15 *HAY*

A sycamore wood box, the lid decorated with roses, Victorian.
£20-25 *HAY*

An ebony rouge pot, 20thC, 1in (3cm) high.
£10-12 *HAY*

An inlaid box with yacht on lid, Japanese, c1920, 6in (15cm) long.
£10-12 *HAY*

A turned rosewood seal box, c1930, 1¾in (5cm) diam.
£10-15 *HAY*

An inlaid wooden box, c1930, 6in (15cm) long.
£15-20 *HAY*

An Edwardian carved and hand painted wooden box, Swiss, 5in (12.5cm) long.
£18-20 *HAY*

An oak pot with a chrome handle, c1920, 5in (13cm) diam.
£12-18 *HAY*

A 6-sided black painted wooden box, c1960, 3in (7.5cm) wide.
£2-5 *HAY*

An oak pot, 20thC, 3¼in (8cm) diam.
£10-12 *HAY*

An Egyptian inlaid box, 20thC, 5½in (13.5cm) long.
£15-20 *HAY*

An almond wood pot, c1930, 3½in (9cm) diam.
£12-15 *HAY*

A brass box, c1880, 8½in (21cm) long.
£75-85 *MofC*

A mahogany book box with concealed compartments, Edwardian, 6¼in (15.5cm) long.
£25-28 *HAY*

Book Boxes

A Victorian rosewood book box with secret entrance, in the form of a Bible with inlaid cross, 2¾in (7cm) long.
£30-35 *HAY*

A mahogany book box with concealed opening, c1900, 3¾in (9cm) long.   **£15-20** *HAY*

A Japanese secret book box, with concealed lock and key, 20thC, 4½in (11cm) long.
£15-20 *HAY*

A pokerwork book box, with concealed drawer, 20thC, 4in (10cm) long.
£12-20 *HAY*

An Indian wood pop-up cigarette dispenser, inlaid with bone, c1960, 5½in (14cm) wide.
£15-20 *HAY*

A Chinese black lacquer book box, decorated in Chinkin technique, probably from Fuzhou, c1913, 4in (10cm) long.
£15-20 *HAY*

Cigarette Boxes

An oak inlaid cigarette dispenser, c1925, 6in (15cm) long.
£30-35 *HAY*

An inlaid veneered pop-up cigarette dispenser, c1930, 7in (17.5cm) wide. **£20-25** *HAY*

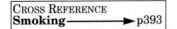

CROSS REFERENCE
Smoking ——————➤ p393

A Japanese pop-up birdie radio cigarette dispenser, 20thC, 5in (12.5cm) high.
£30-40 *HAY*

A mahogany pyramid topped cigarette dispenser, with pull out drawer in plinth, c1930, 5in (12.5cm) wide.
£25-30 *HAY*

An inlaid cigarette box, French, c1925, 6½in (16cm) long.
£20-25 *HAY*

A wooden tobacco jar, c1920-50, 3¾in (9cm) diam.
£15-20 *HAY*

A Japanese cigarette dispenser, inlaid with a Scottie dog, with ash tray, 20thC, 4in (10cm) long.
£25-30 *HAY*

A Japanese pop-out cigarette dispenser, with inlaid veneered Scottie dog, c1930.
£25-35 *HAY*

A Japanese push button fan-out cigarette dispenser, with inlaid veneered Scottie dog, c1925, 4¾in (12cm) wide.
£25-30 *HAY*

A wooden barrel cigarette box, 20thC, 3¼in (8cm) high. **£10-15** *HAY*

An olive wood cigarette case from Jerusalem, 20thC, 3½in (9cm) long.
£8-10 *HAY*

A Japanese lacquer and metal push button pecking bird cigarette dispenser, c1930, 7in (17.5cm) high.
£45-50 *HAY*

A Japanese matchbox dispenser, with sliding front, 20thC, 5½in (14cm) high.
£20-30 *HAY*

A carved cigarette box with inset oval coin from Netherlands, Japara, Java carved on back, probably by prisoner-of-war, 5½in (14cm) long. **£18-20** *HAY*

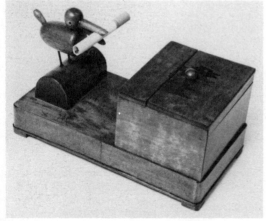

A wooden cigarette box inlaid with Military Police George VI, 6in (15cm) long.
£20-25 *HAY*

A Japanese wooden pecking bird cigarette dispenser, c1930, 7in (17.5cm) long.
£25-30 *HAY*

A Japanese veneered Scottie dog cigarette dispenser, c1930, 4in (10cm) square.
£25-30 *HAY*

Drinking Boxes

A Georgian satinwood cased travelling decanter set, with rosewood and shell inlay, 13in (33cm) long.
£850-900 *GAK*

A Victorian burr walnut and rosewood crossbanded travelling liquor set, inlaid with brass.
£1,000-1,100 *GAK*

CROSS REFERENCE
Drinking ⟶ p174

Games Boxes

A Waddington's cardboard playing card box of Lexicon, shaped as a book, c1930.
£5-10 *HAY*

A boxed game of Roulette, c1900-30, 10¾in (27cm) long.
£20-25 *HAY*

A Japanese lacquer playing card box, c1930, 4⅜in (11cm) long.
£18-20 *HAY*

A Mauchline ware black lacquer playing card box, Victorian, 4⅜in (11cm).
£25-30 *HAY*

A boxed wooden spinning top, 20thC, 1½in (4cm) diam.
£10-15 *HAY*

A playing card box with novelty opening, 20thC, 5in (12.5cm) long.
£15-20 *HAY*

A decorated lacquer playing card box, with drawers for packs of cards, c1930, 4in (10cm) high.
£18-20 *HAY*

A wooden box of Tiddleywinks, with pictorial cover, Bavarian, c1935, 5in (12.5cm) long.
£15-20 *HAY*

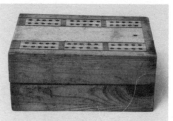

An inlaid cribbage board box, early 20thC, 5½in (14cm) long.
£15-20 *HAY*

A wooden travelling chess box, 1960s, 4½in (11cm) long.
£10-15 *HAY*

An inlaid cribbage board box, early 20thC, 5½in (14cm) long.
£15-18 *HAY*

CROSS REFERENCE
Toys
  Games ⟶ p447

A fruitwood box of draughts, c1920, 6⅓in (16cm) long.
£20-25 *HAY*

A wooden box of Lotto with pictorial cover, German, c1925, 8⅓in (21cm).
£15-20 *HAY*

Japanese Boxes

A Japanese inlaid puzzle box, 20thC, 6in (15cm) long.
£30-35 *HAY*

A Japanese box with concealed inlaid drawers, 20thC, 6in (15cm) long.
£25-30 *HAY*

A Japanese lacquer pot, c1930, 4⅓in (11cm) diam.
£10-12 *HAY*

A Japanese lacquer tea caddy
and lid, c1940-50, 4½in (11cm).
£18-20 *HAY*

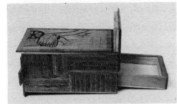

A Japanese
inlaid puzzle
box, 20thC,
6in (15cm)
long.
£20-30 *HAY*

A Japanese
lacquer box,
20thC,
5½in (14cm)
long.
£10-12 *HAY*

A Japanese inlaid box, with key,
20thC, 11½in (29cm) long.
£18-20 *HAY*

Jewellery Boxes

A Regency satinwood jewellery
box, c1820.
£700-900 *WA*

An ebony jewellery box, with velvet lining, c1920,
5 1/2 in (14cm) long.
£15-18 *HAY*

A boulle jewellery box.
£500-550 *SWO*

Musical Boxes

An inlaid musical box, possibly
Italian, c1945, 5½in (14cm).
£15-18 *HAY*

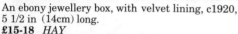

CROSS REFERENCE
Musical Jugs ──▶ p116

Pokerwork Boxes

A circular woven pokerwork
pot, 20thC, 5in (12.5cm) diam.
£15-20 *HAY*

A pokerwork playing card box,
c1910, 6in (15cm).
£20-25 *HAY*

Paint Boxes

A Regency paint box, decorated with an oval coloured
engraving of a mythological scene highlighted in gilt,
containing blocks of paint and glass bottles, inscribed
R Ackerman... at his Repository of Arts,
15in (38cm) long. **£325-350** *HDS*

An inlaid Japanese
paint brush holder
and box containing
water and spirit
pots, 20thC.
£15-18 *HAY*

A painted pokerwork powder
bowl, with puff, c1910, 4¾in
(12cm) diam.
£12-15 *HAY*

**For a further selection
of paint boxes and
artist's palettes, please
refer to *Miller's
Collectables Price Guide
Vol IV, pp337-340*,
available from Millers
Publications.**

A painted pokerwork box, 20thC, 4½in (11cm) diam. **£10-12** *HAY*

Pill Boxes

A decorated horn pill box, with early bicycling engraving, c1816, 3in (8cm) diam. **£250-275** *S*

Stamp Boxes

An Edwardian carved stamp box, Swiss, 3in (8cm) long. **£20-25** *HAY*

An Edwardian carved stamp box, Swiss, 2 1/4 in (6cm) long. **£20-25** *HAY*

A gilt brass box and cover with relief portrait of Admiral Lord Nelson, 19thC, 2¾in (7cm) diam. **£160-175** *GAK*

An enamel pill box, with blue ground, floral panels decorated in gilt, French, 2in (5cm) diam. **£280-300** *AAV*

Trinket Boxes

A Victorian papier mâché egg shaped trinket box. **£20-30** *KOH*

A Victorian trinket box, the lid inset with a finely carved mother-of-pearl plaque, signed Rosenthal and Jacob, London 1885, 5½in (14cm) long. **£725-750** *CSK*

Work Boxes

A rosewood and mother-of-pearl inlaid work box, with 2 doors enclosing 3 drawers, one fitted as a writing slope with glass ink bottles, early 19thC, 13½in (34cm) high.
£550-650 *AH*

A mahogany brass bound lap desk, 19thC, 14in (35.5cm) long.
£125-150 *GAK*

A mahogany writing box, with shell inlay and brass carrying handles, c1800.
£400-600 *WA*

Writing Boxes

A Regency boulle work writing box, with drawer, 10in (25cm) long.
£400-450 *HDS*

A Regency rosewood and boulle work writing box, with single exterior drawer, 12in (30.5cm) long.
£750-800 *HDS*

BUCKETS

A pair of George III mahogany brass bound plate buckets, with part lead lined interiors, stamped MORGAN, 14½in (37cm) high.
£2,500-2,600 *C*

A copper brewer's bucket, with steel handle, plaque reads W. Reeves & Son, London SW10, Brewers Appliances, 12in (31cm) high.
£200-220 *PAR*

A Georgian mahogany brass bound plate bucket, c1780, 16in (41cm) high.
£1,100-1,200 *JAC*

MAKE THE MOST OF MILLERS

Condition is absolutely vital when assessing the value of any item. Damaged pieces appreciate much less than perfect examples. However, a rare, desirable piece may command a high price even when damaged.

BUCKLES & CLASPS

An Oriental hinged clasp, 12in (31cm).
£90-100 *JBB*

A Japanese red cloisonné butterfly clasp, 3in (8cm).
£65-70 *JBB*

An Oriental cloisonné flower clasp.
£60-65 *JBB*

A Japanese cloisonné butterfly clasp, c1880, 3in (8cm).
£180-195 *JBB*

A turquoise and jasper clasp, 2in (5cm).
£35-40 *JBB*

A silver clasp, London 1906, 3½in (9cm).
£80-85 *JBB*

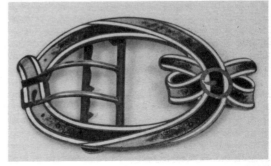

A white metal and enamel belt buckle.
£30-40 *ASA*

A Chinese silver dragon clasp, 3½in (9cm). **£70-75** *JBB*

A Victorian silver plated horseshoe pattern clasp, 3½in (9cm). **£45-50** *JBB*

A silver plated Connemara marble clasp, 13½in (34cm). **£50-55** *JBB*

An Art Deco white metal, enamel and glass buckle, c1930. **£10-20** *ASA*

CROSS REFERENCE
Art Deco ——————▶ p23

A cinnabar clasp, 2in (5cm). **£45-50** *JBB*

A Satsuma porcelain clasp, 3in (8cm). **£70-80** *JBB*

BUTTONS

Three Barbola handmade buttons, c1930. **50p-£1 each** *AGM*

A selection of shipping buttons. **50p-£2 each** *AGM*

A selection of early police buttons. **£1-5 each** Standardised Crown. **10p-£1 each** *AGM*

Four buttons depicting childrens TV characters; Sooty, Muffin the Mule, The Flowerpot Men and Noddy. **5p-10p each** *AGM*

Six inlaid
papier
mâché
buttons,
c1860.
£80-90 *JBB*

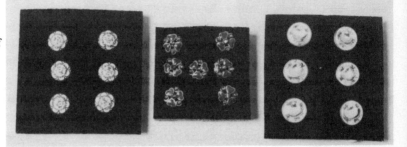

Three boxes of
Victorian
miniature
floral enamel
buttons.
**£30-40 each
set** *JBB*

Ten Victorian
steel/brass
buttons, boxed.
£25-35 *JBB*

Military

Two early Volunteer
Regiment buttons.
£10-15 each *AGM*

Six County Regiments buttons.
50p-£1 each *AGM*

CROSS REFERENCE
Militaria ⟶ p308

Six County Regiments buttons.
50p-£1 each *AGM*

Three naval buttons, early
19thC.
£5-10 each *AGM*

Sporting

A gentleman's sporting button, worn on country attire in late 19thC.
50p-£2 *AGM*

A gentleman's sporting button, late 19thC.
50p-£2 *AGM*

CROSS REFERENCE
Sport ──────────→ p399

A Georgian button, The Archers of Chevy Chase.
£5-10 *AGM*

A selection of cricket clubs' buttons.
£1-5 each *AGM*

A selection of rowing clubs' buttons.
50p-£2 each *AGM*

A selection of various archery clubs buttons.
£1-5 each *AGM*

BUTTONHOOKS

A shoe horn and buttonhook, London 1889, 12½in (32cm) long.
£130-140 *AMH*

Buttonhooks have been a regular feature in previous issues of *Miller's Collectables Price Guides*, available from Millers Publications.

Eight Rowing Clubs' buttons.
50p-£2 each *AGM*

CAMERAS & OPTICAL EQUIPMENT
Cameras

A Vega folding book style camera, with black metal case, simple lens and internal magazine, Swiss, c1900.
£725-775 *S*

A 13 by 10½mm folding bellows camera, with removable mahogany struts, silk bellows and brass bound lens, rack and pinion focusing, brass lens cap, probably French, c1880.
£440-480 *S*

An Anschütz press camera, focal plane shutter, with case and dark slides, 1900, case 12 by 8in (30.5 by 20cm).
£85-100 *HEG*

An Etui patent camera, with Schneider Compur shutter, c1930.
£60-80 *HEG*

A Lancaster Instantograph camera, half plate view, brass barrel lens, c1892, 10in (25cm) long.
£150-180 *HEG*

A Ernemann Ermanox camera, with Anastigmat Ernostar f2 10cm lens, carrying strap and 8 single metal slides in maker's fitted leather case, German, c1925, 1¾ by 2½in (4½ by 6cm).
£1,250-1,450 *S*

A quarter-plate mahogany body falling plate camera, brass bound Choroskop lens, mounted on a T-P roller blind shutter.
£120-140 *CSK*

An H. Antoine 'La Pochette' folding portable camera, black leather covered body with Som Berthot Perigraphe Series IV f14 12cm lens, c1900, 12½ by 17cm.
£1,200-1,400 *S*

A Dubroni, France, 4cm diam. No. 1 camera, with an amber glass 'bottle' and Lachenal lens, c1860.
£3,800-4,000 *S*

A Gerschel 'The Mosaic' camera, leather covered wood body, 9 exposures with lens, Bausch & Lomb Junior shutter, Cardon & Rey retailer's label, French, early 20thC, 7¼ by 5⅗in (18 by 14cm).
£1,500-1,600 *S*

A Bakelite Rajah No. 6 folding camera, introduced 1929, 6¾in (17cm) high.
£20-25 *HEG*

One of the earliest Bakelite cameras.

A W. Tyler, Birmingham, Pocket Tit-Bit camera, with rotary shutter, 2½ by 3¾in (6½ by 9cm).
£350-380 *CSK*

A Super Ikonta 530 camera, 120 film, c1934-37.
£75-85 *HEG*

A Purma Special camera, 127 film, 3 speed focal plane shutter controlled by gravity, camera with plastic lenses, with leather case and filter, English, c1930.
£25-30 *HEG*

A James A. Sinclair & Co. Ltd, London Una hand and stand camera, with polished wood interior, black leather bellows, Taylor, Taylor & Hobson Cooke Aviar Series II 5¼in f4.5 lens, 2½ by 3¾in (6 by 9cm), NS Accurate shutter, in maker's fitted leather case, with a tripod in leather case.
£600-650 *CSK*

A George Houghton & Son, London, rollfilm The Sanderson Roll Film camera, with polished wood interior, red leather bellows and a Beck-Steinheil Convertible Orthostigmat Series II No. 3a 5½in lens in a Volute shutter.
£250-275 *CSK*

A G.A. Krauss 'Peggy' 35mm camera, with Tessar f3.5 5cm lens, German, early 1930s.
£325-350 *S*

A Plasmat, Berlin 120-rollfilm Roland camera with an Anastigmat f/3.5 75mm lens and Prontor II shutter, in maker's box.
£330-350 *CSK*

An Ernemann aerial camera, No. F.K. I I559, green painted metal body with Tessar f4.5 25cm lens, focal plane shutter, German, c1915.
£1,100-1,200 *S*

A Berning 'Luftwaffe Robot' 35mm camera, with Tele-Xenar f3.8 7.5 cm lens, together with a Robot I with Tessar f2.8 3cm lens, German, early 1940s.
£440-480 *S*

A Merlin cast metal subminiature camera, crackle enamel finish, c1936, 2in (5cm) wide.
£45-50 *HEG*

An E. Krauss, France, 34 x 21mm 'Le Photo-Revolver' camera, with black metal body, helical focusing lens, trigger, folding sportsfinder, black leather covered magazine, quantity of plates and maker's carrying pouch, c1920.
£1,400-1,500 *S*

An Eastman Kodak No. 6 outfit camera, with Graphic 6½ by 8½in Rapid Rectilinear lens set in an Auto shutter, American, early 20thC.
£550-600 *S*

A Wrayflex camera, with original box and care instructions, c1950.
£100-120 *HEG*

This was the only commercially successful English made 35mm camera.

A Berning & Co, Germany, 35mm Robot Royal model III camera, with a Schneider Xenar f2.8 38mm lens, in maker's ever ready case and instruction booklet.
£375-400 *CSK*

An R.A. Goldman, Austria, 7 by 7in mahogany and brass studio camera, brass bound Dallmeyer portrait lens, with rack and pinion focusing and aperture for Waterhouse stops, angle adjustment and studio stand, 23in (60cm) long.
£900-950 *S*

A Pignons Dummy Alpha Reflex 6c 35mm camera, with dummy Kern Macro Switar f1.8 50mm lens, Swiss, 1960s.
£350-360 *S*

An Ensign Full View simple box camera, c1952, 4in (10cm) high.
£10-12 *HEG*

A Zeiss Ikon Dummy 35mm Contax I camera, German, mid-1930s.
£1,100-1,300 *S*

A Hasselblad 500C 'Space Replica' 6 x 6cm camera, with Planar f2.8 80mm lens and roll film back, Swedish, c1970.
£380-400 *S*

A W. Kunik, Germany, Petie Vanity outfit, comprising a 16mm Petie camera, in chrome and red covered body with powder compact, lipstick holder and film holder, in maker's box.
£480-520 *CSK*

A Pignons S.A., Switzerland, 35mm Alpa-Reflex 'luxus' camera, blue leather body covering and an Angenieux Alitar 50mm f1.8 lens.
£440-480 *CSK*

A black German Minox B Camera, with Complan 15mm f3.5 lens,
£280-320 *CSK*

A 35mm 'no name' Contax type camera, with an 8M f2 50mm lens, in maker's ever ready case.
£280-320 *CSK*

Cinematographic Cameras

A Reulos and Goudeau, France, 'Mirographe' 21mm camera, leather covered body with hand turned mechanism, barrel shutter and simple lens, with one magazine and 2 winding handles, c1900.
£2,800-3,200 *S*

The Mirographe used an unusual film with notched edges.

A hand crank ciné camera, with wooden body, brass fittings, internal claw mechanism and a brass bound lens.
£225-250 *CSK*

A Pathé 35mm camera, leather covered body with hand turned mechanism and film counter, French, c1910.
£400-425 *S*

Canon

A Canon Camera Co Inc, Japan, 35mm 7 camera, with a Canon 50mm f0.95 lens and Canon Flash V2 in case.
£750-780 *CSK*

> **FURTHER READING**
> *An Age of Cameras,* Edward Holmes, 1974.

A Pathé 35mm camera, leather covered body with Ruo Kino f2.5 5cm lens, intermittent claw mechanism, disc shutter, film counter and externally mounted magazines, French, c1905.
£750-800 *S*

A Canon Camera Co. Inc., Japan, 35mm IIf camera, with Canon 50mm f1.8 lens and instructions, in maker's box, with leather ever ready case, and a Canon Flash Unit model Y and accessories. **£700-750** *CSK*

Detective Cameras

A box form camera, with leather covered wooden body, integral changing bag, possibly French, c1900, 2½ by 3¼in (6 by 8cm).
£525-550 *S*

A Buisson, France, box form camera, with polished mahogany case, c1880, 3 by 4¾in (9 by 12cm).
£600-650 *S*

A half-plate boxform falling plate detective camera, with a brass bound Taylor, Taylor & Hobson Cooke Series III lens, roller blind shutter, black stamped Miller's Patent No. 12,669 and label W. H. Tomkinson, Photographic Dealer, 81 Dale Street, Liverpool.
£300-330 *CSK*

T. Miller was granted British Patent No. 12,669 of 13 August 1890 for a design of detective camera, change-boxes, shutters and roller slides.

A German box form camera, the mahogany body with brass lens with rotary diaphragm, pull string shutter and plate counter, c1890, 3½ by 4¾in (9 x 12cm).
£300-350 *S*

A L'Eclair twin lens box form camera, mahogany body with removable front section, rotary shutter, brass lenses with rack and pinion focusing and pill box stop and internal magazine, French, c1880s, 3 by 4¾in (9 by 12cm).
£580-620 *S*

A Watson & Son camera, with black leather covered case, English, and a quarter-plate mahogany and brass field camera with an aluminium Perken, Son & Rayment Optimus lens, mid-1880s.
£440-460 *S*

A box form camera, with mahogany body, brass bound lens with pull string rotary shutter and one Waterhouse stop, carrying handle, probably French, c1880, 2½ x 3¾in (6½ by 9cm).
£100-120 *S*

A Suter magazine camera, the leather covered wood body with Sutter lens, iris diaphragm and internal magazine containing 12 single metal sheets, Swiss, c1890, 3½ by 4¾in (9 x 12cm).
£520-550 *S*

An 'Edison', Germany, box form camera, the mahogany body with integral changing bag and 12 single metal slides, early 20thC, 3½ by 4¾in (9 by 12cm).
£275-300 *S*

The Edison company never made cameras as such, and it was common practice in those days to use the name 'Edison' on various products to give them added credence.

Eastman Kodak

A Brownie camera No. 2A, with original box, c1918.
£35-45 *HEG*

A 16mm Ciné Kodak Special camera, with a Kodak Anastigmat f2.7 15mm lens, a Kodak Anastigmat f1.9 25mm lens, a Ciné Kodak telephoto f4.5 6in lens, a Kodak Anastigmat f2.7 102mm lens, a Ciné Kodak telephoto f4.5 3in lens and instruction booklet How to Use the Ciné Kodak Special, in a case.
£525-575 *CSK*

Three Kodak Brownie cameras in original boxes, No. 2A, 2 and 1.
£130-150 *CSK*

A No. 4 folding Kodak camera, with internally contained rollfilm holder and brass bound lens in a sector shutter.
£750-800 *CSK*

A No. IA Pocket Kodak Series II camera, with green leather case.
£140-160 *P(O)*

Leica

A black Leica M2 camera, with a chrome Leica-Meter MC.
£1,300-1,400 *CSK*

A Swedish Army Leica IIIg with black finish, and a chrome finish Elmar F2.8 5cm lens, with triple crown insignia, German, 1960. **£4,800-5,000** *S*

125 of these black finish IIIg cameras were produced for the Swedish Army in 1960.

A Leica II camera, with non-factory bronzed metal body, skin covering and a non-factory black Leitz Elmar f3.5 50mm lens, in maker's leather case.
£350-370 *CSK*

A Leica If camera, with red dial and an Elmar f3.5 3.5cm lens, German, 1951.
£500-525 *S*

A Leica Compur camera, with an Elmar f3.5 50mm lens set into a rim set Compur shutter and indented mushroom shaped release, German, 1930.
£4,250-4,500 *S*

A Leica II dummy camera, German, c1935.
£750-775 *S*

A Leica II camera, with a single speed MOOLY Leica-Meter, German, 1936.
£625-650 *S*

A Leica IIIc camera, the back engraved Luftwaffen-Eigntum, with an Elmar f3.5 5cm lens, German, 1941-42, lens 1940.
£2,600-2,800 *S*

A Leica IIIg camera, with maker's instructions, German, 1957.
£650-675 *S*

A Leica M3 doublewind camera, with a Leitz Summicron 5cm f2 lens, and Leica-Meter MC, in maker's leather ever ready case.
£700-750 *CSK*

A Leica I camera, with an Elmar f3.5 50mm lens, German, c1926.
£1,100-1,200 *S*

A Leica I Model C camera, with a matched Elmar f3.5 50mm lens, German, 1930.
£1,800-1,900 *S*

A Leica M2 camera, with a Leica-Meter MR, Summicron f2 50mm lens, and another, and a Hektor f4.5 13.5cm lens, German, 1961.
£1,300-1,400 *S*

A Leica IIIc camera, No. 437750 with a Leitz Summarit 5cm f1.5 lens.
£300-330 *CSK*

A Leica III dummy camera, with a SCNOO manual winder, German, c1935.
£750-775 *S*

A Leica IIIf camera, black dial with a Leitz Elmar 5cm f3.5 lens, in maker's leather ever ready case, and a Leitz Summar 5cm f2 lens, German.
£350-375 *CSK*

A Leica 250FF Reporter camera, converted to a GG, with an Elmar f3.5 50mm lens, internal take-up spool and film cassette, German, 1934-36. **£3,800-4,000** *S*

A Leitz replica Ur-Leica camera, German, 20thC.
£330-350 *S*

These replicas of Oscar Barnack's original prototype Leica of 1912-13 were made at the Wetzlar factory by apprentices. It is believed only 30 to 40 were made.

A Leica Ic camera, converted to a 750 Reporter camera, scratch built, German, c1949-50.
£750-775 *S*

A Leicaflex chrome camera, with a Leitz Summicron-R f2 50mm lens, in maker's ever ready case.
£440-460 *CSK*

A Leica IIIc camera, with red shutter blind, German, 1940.
£500-525 *S*

'Le Photosphère'

A Compagnie Francaise de Photographie camera, the metal bodied camera with hemispherical shutter, late 1880's, 3¾ by 4¾in (9 by 12cm).
£600-625 *S*

A cased Compagnie Francaise de Photographie, Le Photosphère camera, the metal bodied camera with hemispherical shutter, in original leather covered wood casing, late 1880s, 3¾ by 4¾in (9 by 12cm).
£850-900 *S*

A Compagnie Francaise de Photographie, Le Photosphère camera, the metal body with an E. Krauss Anastigmat-Zeiss f8 12mm lens, hemispherical shutter, spirit levels, late 1880s, 3¾ by 4¾in (9 x 12cm).
£1,800-1,900 *S*

Panoramic Cameras

A Mutoscope & Film Co., Al Vista 4B Panoramic camera, with swinging lens and 5 vanes, American, c1905.
£240-260 *S*

An Eastman Kodak No. 3A panoramic camera, with swinging Zeiss Tessar f6.8 13cm lens, 1926-28.
£350-375 *S*

A Krasnogorsk 35mm Horizont panoramic camera, with an OF-28P f2.8 28mm lens and removable viewfinder, Soviet, c1968.
£325-350 *S*

Rolleiflex

A Franke and Heidecke, Braunschweig, 120 rollfilm tele- Rolleiflex camera, with a Heidosmat f4 135mm viewing lens and a Carl Zeiss Sonnar f4 135mm taking lens in a Synchro-Compur shutter, and a Rolleinar 0.7.
£1,650-1,750 *CSK*

A panoramic camera, with swinging lens and iris diaphragm, French, early 20thC, 7 by 2in (17.5 by 5.5cm).
£350-375 *S*

A Rolleiflex 120 rollfilm dummy
camera, with magazine back
and a Rollei HFT Planar f2.8
80mm lens, German.
£350-375 *CSK*

Spy Cameras

A Franke and Heidecke,
Braunschweig, 120 rollfilm
Rolleiflex TLR camera, with a
Heidosmat f2.8 75mm viewing
lens and a Schneider Xenar f3.5
75mm taking lens, in a Synchro
Compur shutter.
£220-240 *CSK*

A Franke and Heidecke,
Braunschweig, Rolleiflex 2.8f
camera, with a Heidosmat f2.8
80mm viewing lens, and a Carl
Zeiss Planar f2.8 80mm taking
lens, in a Synchro-Compur
shutter, 2½in (6cm) square.
£480-500 *CSK*

A Houghtons Ltd, London, Ticka
watch camera, with swinging
viewfinder and instruction
booklet, in maker's box.
£420-440 *CSK*

A John C. Hegelein, New York,
1¾in diameter nickel metal body
The Watch Camera, with
collapsible 7 section metal tube,
shutter and meniscus lens, with
removable wood body.
£20,000-22,000 *CSK*

A Stirn 1¾in Concealed Vest
Camera, with circular nickeled
body, lens and 6 position
exposure counter, in maker's
fitted mahogany box, American,
c1890.
£2,150-2,250 *S*

*This is the second known
example of the Hegelein watch
camera and is the most complete
example having the removable
plate holder. The Hegelein
watch camera was loosely based
on the British Lancaster watch
camera. It was the subject of US
Patent no. 624142 of 7th August
1894 and was marketed by
Anthony from August 1895 when
it was priced at $5.00.*

A Möller Cambinox combined
binocular camera, with Jdemar
f3.5 90mm lens and 7 by 33
binoculars, in a box, German,
mid-1950s.
£1,600-1,700 *S*

Stereoscopic Cameras

An Excelsior 14 by 18cm tailboard camera, the mahogany body with brass and nickel plated parts, lenses set in a pneumatic shutter, English, c1900.
£440-460 *S*

A Jules Richard, France, 35mm Homeos camera, with metal body and guillotine shutter, lacks lenses, c1915.
£1,000-1,100 *S*

An English 20 by 12cm box form camera, the mahogany body with a pair of brass bound lenses, rack and pinion focusing, green leather bellows and removable ground glass panel, late 1880s.
£400-425 *S*

A Destot-pattern camera, the mahogany body with twin 'spreading' tailboard section, each for a single 2¾ by 5in (7 by 12.5cm) plate, rack and pinion focusing, brass bound lenses, Waterhouse stops and removable front panels with pulley operated hinged 'cap', French, 20thC.
£2,250-2,500 *S*

Dr. Destot's camera was discussed in a number of issues of the bulletin of the French Photographic Society in 1901.

A Leroy, France, 6 by 13cm Le Stéréo Panoramique camera, with a pair of Darlot Planigraphe f1.9 81mm lenses and panoramic or stereoscopic option, c1910.
£325-350 *S*

A Mackenstein 17 by 9cm tailboard camera, with polished mahogany body, brass bindings, dual spirit levels, twin brass bound lenses, shutter and removable ground glass screen, French, late 19thC.
£600-625 *S*

A Franke & Heidecke, Germany, 6 by 13cm Heidoscop camera, with a Zeiss Sucher-Triplet f4.2 7.5cm viewing lens and a pair of Tessar f4.5 7.5cm taking lenses, with magazine back, c1930.
£375-400 *S*

A Coronet 3D stereo 127 film camera, with mottled plastic case, c1953.
£40-60 *HEG*

A Realist stereo camera, 1952.
£160-180 *HEG*

Tailboard Cameras

A front folding 13 by 18cm camera, the mahogany body with nickel plated fittings and a nickel bound Arwin Rectilinge No. 2 lens, French, early 20thC.
£500-550 *S*

Tropical Cameras

A tropical 8½ by 11cm folding strut camera, the polished teak body with brass bindings, tan leather bellows, viewing hood and Zeiss Tessar f4.5 15cm lens, with film pack, in fitted leather case, French, early 20thC.
£425-450 *S*

Zeiss

A Carpentier, France, 12cm square wet plate camera, with mahogany body, brass bound lens with rack and pinion focusing and aperture for Waterhouse stops, signed Derogy Fr., No. 15392, Brevete, Paris & Londres, late 19thC.
£575-600 *S*

A Continental pattern, 18 by 12cm mahogany and brass camera, with a large Darlot portrait lens No. 35968 set in a roller blind shutter, French, c1900.
£275-300 *S*

A Contessa-Nettel 8½ by 11cm Deck-Rullo tropical camera, teak body with tan leather bellows, nickel plated metal parts and a Triotar f3.5 15cm lens, with magazine back, German, c1920.
£275-300 *S*

An Ikon Contaflex 35mm twin lens Reflex camera, with Sucher-Objectiv f2.8 8cm viewing lens and a Sonnar f1.5 5cm taking lens, 1930s.
£1,050-1,150 *S*

A Kenngott 6½ by 9cm tropical Phönix camera, with polished teak body, tan leather bellows, gold plated metal parts, Zeiss Tessar f4.5 12cm lens in a Compur shutter, German, mid-1920s.
£325-350 *S*

A Contax IIa 35mm camera, and a Carl Zeiss, Jena Sonnar f1.5 5cm lens No. 1826790.
£160-180 *CSK*

This camera bears no manufacturer's name. The quality of the top plate suggests Russian manufacture.

Lenses

A Voigtländer brass bound No. 7A Portrait-Euryscope lens, German, with one Waterhouse stop and screw mount, c1860, 10½in (27cm) long.
£150-170 *S*

An Elmar stereo f3.5 35mm lens, German, c1940.
£3,750-4,000 *S*

It is believed only 32 stereo Elmars were produced, and none were ever offered commercially.

A Jamin brass bound lens, France, with dual rack and pinion focusing, with brass lens cap, c1860, 12⅝in (32cm) long.
£300-330 *S*

A Leitz brass bound Summar f4 250mm lens, German, probably early 20thC.
£220-240 *S*

A rigid Summar f2 5cm lens, German, 1933.
£500-540 *S*

A Goerz Hypergon Doppel Anastigmat Series X 150mm lens, with rotating vane, mounted on lensboard, German, c1911.
£1,800-1,900 *S*

A Thambar screw mount f2.2 9cm lens, with centre spot filter, reversible lens hood and back cap, German, 1938.
£1,300-1,400 *S*

A screw mount 'Fat Bodied' Elmar f4 9cm lens, with lens cap, and an Elmar f4 9cm lens, with lens cap, German, c1931.
£330-360 *S*

A Telyt screw mount f4.5 20cm lens, with reversible lens hood, German, 1956.
£180-200 *S*

A screw mount Summarex f1.5 8.5cm lens, with reversible lens hood, German, 1951.
£440-480 *S*

A screw fit Elmar 10.5cm f6.3 lens, with reversible lenshood and front and back caps.
£700-725 *CSK*

Optical Equipment & Toys

An Adam de Colmar projection microscope, in mahogany case with 3 specimen slides in fitted mahogany case, French, 14½in (37cm) wide.
£1,000-1,100 *S*

An International Mutoscope Reel Co, mutoscope, the red painted metal body with viewing hood, winding handle, electric illuminant, coin mechanism, top flash and reel Silk Stockings, American, early 20thC, 74in (188cm) high.
£1,300-1,400 *S*

An International Mutoscope Reel Co, mutoscope, the coin-operated mechanism with photo reel depicting The Dance of the Seven Veils, blue painted metal case, American, early 20thC, 74in (188cm) high.
£1,250-1,350 *S*

A brass bound 2 draw camera lucida with prism, collapsing into an integral wooden box.
£200-225 *CSK*

A Cinématographe toy, with paper covered cardboard body, French, early 20thC.
£350-375 *S*

An Ernst Planck, Germany, metal body episcope, with hinged subject holder, 2 chimneys and brass bound lens.
£280-300 *CSK*

A 10in diam. cardboard body zoetrope drum, with applied chromolithograph label and 6 coloured picture strips.
£450-475 *CSK*

Camera Obscuras

A brass bound camera obscura head, with internal prism and mounting flange, English, c1880, 5in (14cm) high
£575-600 *S*

A tinplate camera obscura, hand painted in marbled black with gilt lining, hinged viewing hood and brass feet, 2⅛in lens, French, c1905, 6in (15cm) high.
£380-400 *S*

A brass bound camera obscura head, with internal prism and mounting flange, English, c1860, 6in (16.5cm) high.
£400-425 *S*

Kaleidoscopes

A Magic Pictures box-form kaleidoscope, the green paper covered box with wood eyepiece, kaleidoscopic lens, possibly English, mid-19thC, 11in (28cm) long.
£550-575 *S*

A tinplate camera obscura, hand painted in 2 tone green, hinged viewing hood, 1¾in lens, German, c1905, 4in (10cm) high. **£460-480** *S*

A kaleidoscope, the mauve paper covered tube with metal ends, probably French, late 19thC, 9⅜in (24cm) long.
£150-160 *S*

A Bloch kaleidoscope, metal body with wood end section, capstan turning wheel and coloured glass pieces, with turned wooden stand, French, early 20thC, 15in (38cm) long.
£750-775 *S*

A mechanical kaleidoscope, red leather covered tube with wood eyepiece, ½in lens, French, c1880, 6¼in (16cm) long.
£625-650 *S*

Lithophanes

A pair of 6⅛ by 8¼in lithophane panels, one depicting the baby Moses, the other showing his discovery by Pharoah's daughter, French, 19thC, 11 by 9½in (28 by 24cm).
£440-480 *S*

A 4 by 5⅛in coloured lithophane panel, showing a couple in an art gallery, French, 19thC, 9 by 10½in (22.5 by 27cm).
£200-225 *S*

A 5⅜in (13.5cm) diameter lithophane shade, with 4 scenes of flirting couples, stamped L.H. 46, French, 19thC.
£250-275 *S*

Magic Lanterns

A mahogany and brass magic lantern, the brass bound lens with rack and pinion focusing, now with electric illuminant, English c1890.
£250-275 *S*

A Jean Schoenner magic lantern, the spherical brass body with spirit illuminant, on wooden base, in maker's carrying case, German, c1900.
£900-950 *S*

A Carette & Co, Germany, metal body upright lantern with red painted body, integral spirit burner, lens, chimney, in maker's fitted box.
£375-400 *CSK*

A J. Ganz Pinagascop magic lantern, the brass body and brass bound lens with rack and pinion focusing, integral slide carrier with electric illuminant, Swiss, c1900, 26¼in (67cm) high. **£1,000-1,100** *S*

A tropical magic lantern, with teak body, brass bindings, extending front, lens, electric illuminant, access door, with 35 wood mounted slides, English, early 20thC.
£625-650 *S*

Peep Boxes

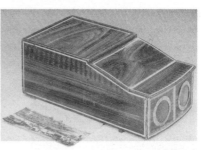

A stained pine double peep box, with applied paper stringing, two 2½in lenses, French, 2nd quarter 19thC, 19¾in (50cm) long.
£1,350-1,450 *S*

A stained pine peep box, the body with applied paper stringing, 1½in lens and hinged top section, together with 4 views, French, late 19thC, 14in (35cm) long.
£800-850 *S*

A double peep box, the mahogany cabinet of rectangular section inset at the front with double lens apertures, probably French, late 18thC, 33in (84cm) high.
£950-1,000 *S*

A collection of 6 peep views, English, French and German, 1820-1860.   **£1,800-2,000** *S*

Stereoscopes

A mahogany body Claudet pattern stereoscope, and a pair of brass bound lenses.
£200-220 *CSK*

A mahogany bodied pedestal stereoscope, with twin eyepieces, French, 19thC, 47in (120cm) high.
£250-270 *S*

A wood body pedestal combined stereoscope and photograph viewer with fixed lenses.
£250-275 *CSK*

A green leather covered Magic Stereoscope, by Negretti & Zambra, London. **£820-840** *CSK*

Viewers

A Kinora viewer, with hand-turned mechanism, English, c1910.   **£675-700** *S*

A Lumière clockwork motor moving picture viewer, the mahogany case with viewing hood, French, early 20thC. **£2,100-2,300** *S*

A Bonds Ltd, London, Kinora viewer, with wood body, hand cranked, metal lens shade and maker's plate.
£525-575 *CSK*

A Kinora-type viewer, the cast iron viewer with adjustable magnifying lenses, probably English, c1910.   **£720-740** *S*

A Bonds Ltd, London, Kinora viewer, hand cranked, the metal viewing hood and maker's label, on a wood base, with 8 Kinora reels.   **£800-850** *CSK*

CANDLE EXTINGUISHERS

A Worcester French Cook candle extinguisher, c1897, 2¼in (6cm) high.   **£145-165** *CA*

Photographic Miscellaneous

The Pistol Flashmeter, used in early photography.
£15-25 *WAB*

A Kodak Film display lithograph, printed in colours, c1920, 16¾ by 22in (42.5 by 56cm).
£280-320 *CSK*

Candle Extinguishers have been a regular feature in previous issues of *Miller's Collectables Price Guides,* available from Millers Publications.

CANDLESTICKS

A pair of George V silver mounted candlesticks, Birmingham 1910, 9in (22.5cm). **£220-240** *GAK*

A brass chamber stick, c1880, 7in (17.5cm) diam.
£40-45 *NM*

A copper chamber stick with snuffer, 8in (20cm) high.
£50-60 *NM*

A pair of Tudric beaten pewter candlesticks, 9½in (24cm) high.
£400-425 *WIL*

A copper candle holder, 6in (15cm) diam.
£30-35 *NM*

A bronze candlestick, c1775, 11in (28cm) high.
£160-170 *SAD*

A pair of Victorian wooden candlesticks, 9in (22.5cm) high.
£20-28 *SAD*

A pair of French bronze candelabras, c1900, 26in (66cm) high. **£1,200-1,500** *CAI*

CARD CASES

An ivory and mosaic card case, c1879, 4 by 3in (10 by 7.5cm).
£40-45 *SAD*

Card Cases have been a regular feature in previous issues of *Miller's Collectables Price Guides*, available from Millers Publications.

A Victorian mosaic puzzle note case, c1879. **£20-25** *SAD*

A Picturesque Tour Along The River Ganges and Jumna in India, with 24 coloured views, a map and vignettes, 1884, 16 by 13in (41 by 33cm).
£2,500-3,500 *HB*

English Scenery, with 120 chromo views, published by T. Nelson & Son, 1889.
£150-200 *HB*

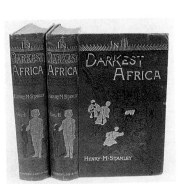

In Darkest Africa, first edition, two volumes, with 150 illustrations, published by Sampson, Low & Co, 1890, 9 by 6in (22.5 by 15cm).
£90-120 *HB*

Scenery, Costumes and Architecture, chiefly on the Western Side of India, first edition, by Capt. Robert Melville Grindlay, published by Rudolph Ackermann, Strand, London 1826.
£3,000-4,000 *HB*

An illustrated Hardy Bros Anglers' Guide, published 1934.
£30-35 *F*

Greece, first edition, one of a series of 96, painted by John Fulleylove, described by J.A. McClymont and published by A. & G. Black, 1906.
£90-120 *HB*

Royal Residences, first edition, 3 volumes, containing 100 fine hand-coloured aquatints, by William Henry Pyne, published by Cassell & Co. Ltd, 1819.
£3,500-4,500 *HB*

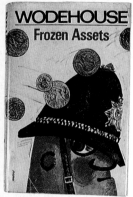

Frozen Assets, first edition, by P.G. Wodehouse, published by Herbert Jenkins, 1964. **£25-30** *HB*

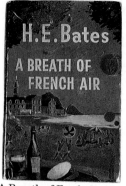

A Breath of Fresh Air, first edition, by H. E. Bates, published by Michael Joseph, 1959. **£25-30** *HB*

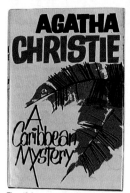

A Caribbean Mystery, first edition, by Agatha Christie, published for the Crime Club, by Collins, 1964. **£20-25** *HB*

Cocktail Time, first edition, by P.G. Wodehouse, published by Herbert Jenkins, London, 1958, slightly creased. **£60-85** *HB*

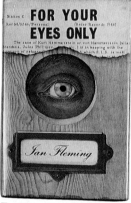

For Your Eyes Only, first edition, by Ian Fleming, published by Jonathan Cape, London, 1960. **£80-85** *HB*

Stiff Upper Lip, Jeeves, first edition, by P.G. Wodehouse, published by Herbert Jenkins, 1963. **£55-60** *HB*

Billy Bunter Afloat, first edition, by Frank Richards, 1957, 7½ by 5in (18.5 by 13cm). **£25-30** *HB*

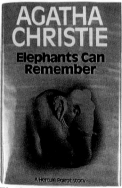

Elephants Can Remember, first edition, by Agatha Christie, published for the Crime Club by Collins, 1972. **£20-25** *HB*

A High Wind in Jamaica, first edition, by Richard Hughes, published by Chatto & Windus, 1929. **£55-60** *HB*

A Japanese parquetry cigarette dispenser, c1930s, 5in (12.5cm) high. **£25-35** *HAY*

A Victorian burr walnut dressing case, fitted with cut glass and gilt metal containers, the lid with gilt metal mounted mirror and 4 classical plaques. **£1,600-1,700** *AAV*

A hand painted box, probably 1920s, 7in by 4½in (17.5cm by 11cm)
£20-30 *HAY*

An Edwardian painted pokerwork powder bowl, 3½in (9cm) high.
£12-15 *HAY*

A Russian pokerwork box, with peasant scene, possibly c1930s.
£10-20 *HAY*

A Japanese inlaid box, 1920s 4½ by 3⅜in (11 by 8.5cm).
£8-10 *HAY*

A Brazilian mahogany box, inlaid with a palm tree scene, 1960s, 7 by 5in (17.5 by 12.5cm) .
£15-20 *HAY*

A Japanese numbers game box, 1920s, 3¾in (9cm) square.
£15-20 *HAY*

A European painted pokerwork box, 1930s-1940s.
£10-15 *HAY*

A Japanese puzzle box, with a secret drawer, c1930s, 6 by 4in (15 by 10cm).
£30-40 *HAY*

A set of Victorian wooden building blocks in pictorial box, 12 by 8in (30.5 by 20cm).
£35-45 *HAY*

A sycamore box, with hand painted African scene, 1940s, 5 by 4in (12.5 by 10cm) **£30-40** *HAY*

A tortoiseshell and enamel singing bird box, the painted enamel oval cover painted with alpine scene, the bird rotating, flapping its wings, opening its beak and wagging its tail, 4in by 2½in (9.7 by 6cm). **£1,600-1,700** *C*

A wooden box containing postage scales, inscribed 'Weigh it and see', 1930s, 5 by 4in (12.5 by 10cm). **£25-30** *HAY*

A Victorian shell box, 9 by 7in (22.5 by 17.5cm). **£95-110** *ARE*

A tortoiseshell sewing box, inlaid with mother-of-pearl, c1820, 9 by 6in (23 by 15cm). **£1,200-1,500** *CAI*

A child's decorated money box, with key, 1930s, 3in (7.5cm) high. **£20-25** *HAY*

A church collection box, from Chiswick Baptist Church, 1930s, 5¾ by 3⅜in (14 by 9cm). **£7-10** *HAY*

A Russian pokerwork box, decorated with a picture of a sleigh ride, c1930s, 8in (20cm) square. **£20-30** *HAY*

A Japanese puzzle box, c1930s, 3¼ by 4½in (8.5 by 11cm). **£25-35** *HAY*

A Beswick figure of Miss Moppet, modelled by Arthur Gredington, introduced 1954. **£60-70** *PC*

A Beswick figure of Mrs. Ribby, from The Pie and the Patty Pan, modelled by Arthur Gredington, introduced 1951. **£70-80** *PC*

A Beswick figure of Benjamin Bunny, 1st version modelled by Arthur Gredington, introduced 1948. **£130-145** *PC*

A Beswick figure of Peter Rabbit, modelled by Arthur Gredington, introduced 1948. **£55-65** *PC*

A figure of Samuel Whiskers, from the Roly Poly Pudding, by Arthur Gredington, 1948. **£55-65** *PC*

A group of Beswick figures of Flopsy, Mopsy and Cottontail, modelled by Arthur Gredington, introduced 1954. **£60-70** *PC*

A Beswick figure of Mrs. Rabbit, modelled by Arthur Gredington, introduced 1951, remodelled early 1970s. **£120-150** *PC*

A Beswick figure of Jemima Puddle-Duck, modelled by Arthur Gredington, introduced 1948. **£55-65** *PC*

A Beswick figure of Hunca Munca, from The Tale of Two Bad Mice, modelled by Arthur Gredington, introduced 1951. **£60-70** *PC*

A Beswick figure of Squirrel Nutkin, introduced 1948. **£50-65** *PC*

A Beswick figure of Tommy Brock, from the Tale of Mr. Tod, modelled by Graham Orwell, introduced 1955. **£100-125** *PC*

A Beswick figure of Foxy Whiskered Gentleman, from the Tale of Jemima Puddle-Duck. **£60-70** *PC*

A Beswick figure of The Old Woman Who Lived in a Shoe, from Appley Dapply's Nursery Rhymes, modelled by Colin Melbourne, introduced 1959. **£55-65** *PC*

A Brannam vase, c1894,
10in (25cm) high.
£180-200 *NCA*

A Brannam vase, c1886,
7in (17.5cm) high.
£125-150 *NCA*

A Chelson childrens' 6 place setting tea
service, produced 1900-1915, marked, plate
6in (15cm), cup 2¼in (5.5cm) high.
£350-450 *ARE*

A commemorative mug for the
Coronation of King Edward
VIII, designed by Dame Laura
Knight, 3in (7.75cm) high.
£50-65 *ARE*

A golliwog Ragtime
pattern plate, by Joan
Allen, 9½in (23.5cm)
diam.
£100-145 *ARE*

A highly decorative Brannam
jug, 3½in (9cm) high.
£30-40 *NCA*

A terracotta bust of Lord
Roberts, signed by K. T.
Pratt, c1900, 15½in (39cm)
high.
£300-350 *OO*

A 60th anniversary
commemorative plate of the
reign of Emperor Franz Joseph of
Vienna, beehive mark, c1908, 8in
(20cm) diam. **£275-300** *BCO*

A moulded china jardinière,
commemorating 60 years of the reign
of Queen Victoria.
£90-100 *MAW*

A basalt loving
cup, Captain
Cook, limited
edition, 1970,
8in (20cm)
high.
£200-250 *TP*

A Doulton Series Ware commemorative plate, Primitive Methodists Connexion, c1910, 10½in (26.5cm) diam.
£80-100 *HER*

A Royal Doulton Santa Claus mug, with candy stripe handle, D6793.
£150-160 *F*

A Doulton Series Ware plate, Proverbs - Golf, 1902-14, 10½in (26.5cm) diam.
£150-200 *HER*

A Doulton Series Ware plate, H.M.S. Lion, c1914-18, 10½in (26.5cm) diam.
£70-90 *HER*

A collection of Royal Doulton Santa Claus mugs, with various style handles.
£45-160 each *F*

An oil lamp, Doulton, Burslem, c1885, 22½in (57cm) high.
£350-450 *POW*

A Doulton Series commemorative plate, Victory and Peace, c1919, 10½in (26cm) diam.
£100-120 *HER*

A Boer War commemorative wall plaque, with Lord Roberts, General French and Lieutenant Colonel Baden Powell, 9in (22.5cm) diam.
£100-120 *OO*

A Doulton Series Ware plate, the centre decorated with a Canadian maple tree, c1936-39, 10½in (26.5cm) diam.
£70-90 *HER*

A Doulton Series Ware plate,
Vines and Leaves, 1937-39, 10½in
(26.5cm) diam.
£80-100 *HER*

A Doulton Series Ware
plate, Flora and Fauna,
c1920, 10½in (26.5cm) diam.
£40-50 *HER*

A Doulton vase, Wiltshire
Moonrakers, c1906-38, 7¾in
(19cm) high.
£150-200 *HER*

A Doulton Series Ware plate,
Flora and Fauna, c1934,
10½in (26.5cm) diam.
£45-50 *HER*

A Doulton bone china jug, The
Jackdaw of Rheims, from The
Ingoldsby Legends, c1906-30,
7¼in (18cm) high.
£130-150 *HER*

A Doulton Series Ware plate,
Flora and Fauna, c1934,
10½in (26.5cm) diam.
£45-50 *HER*

A Doulton Series Ware plate,
Fishing, designed by Isaac
Walton, c1901-38, 10½in (26.5cm)
diam.
£100-125 *HER*

A Doulton Series Ware plate,
Windsor Castle, c1911, 10½in
(26.5cm) diam.
£40-50 *HER*

A Doulton Canterbury
Pilgrims jug, c1909-33,
4¾in (12cm) high.
£50-75 *HER*

A Doulton Dogberry's tobacco jar, with lid, c1906-28, 6¼in (15.5cm) high.
£150-200 *HER*

A Doulton Lambeth vase, by Frank Butler, c1895.
£500-600 *POW*

A Doulton Lambeth jardinière, by Frank Butler, 10½in (26cm) high.
£1,100-1,300 *POW*

A Doulton Lambeth faience jardinière, unrecorded artist, c1890, 10in (25cm) high.
£350-450 *POW*

A Royal Doulton bulldog figure, in WWI uniform and steel helmet, No. 662746, 8in (20cm) long.
£160-180 *PCh*

A Doulton Lambeth jug, with silver rim, by Florence Barlow, c1885, 9½in (23.5cm).
£750-850 *POW*

A pair of Doulton Lambeth vases, by Eliza Simmance, c1891, 11in (28cm) high.
£1,200-1,400 *POW*

A Royal Doulton vase, by Eliza Simmance, c1914, 9½in (23.5cm) high.
£300-400 *POW*

A Royal Doulton vase, by Winnie Bowstead, c1922, 7in (17.5cm) high.
£100-150 *POW*

A Longwy bowl, French, c1925, 13in (33cm) diam.
£900-1,000 *POW*

A Keramic vase, Belgium Art Pottery, c1929, 16in (41cm) high.
£800-900 *POW*

A Royal Doulton Dickens Ware bowl, David Copperfield, 8in (20cm) diam.
£60-75 *PCh*

A Keramic vase, Belgium Art Pottery, c1930, 16¼in (41cm) high.
£900-1,000 *POW*

A Royal Doulton posy bowl and vase, c1920, vase 7½in (18.5cm) high, bowl 5in (12.5cm) wide.
£55-65 each *POW*

A Gouda vase, made for Liberty & Co, c1922, 5¾in (14cm) high. **£80-100** *OO*

A Gouda pot, with lid, Riouw design, 6in (15cm) high. **£90-100** *OO*

A Gouda vase, Golden Net design, c1924, 7½in (18.5cm) high. **£75-100** *OO*

A Gouda vase, Princess design, from the Ivora factory, 4¾in (12cm) high. **£60-70** *OO*

A Gouda jug, Madeleine design, Royal Factory, c1920, 7½in (18.5cm) high. **£90-100** *OO*

A Gouda bowl, Rhodian design, c1923, 10½in (26.5cm) diam. **£100-110** *OO*

A Gouda candlestick, Grotius design, c1929, 10¾in (27cm) high. **£60-65** *OO*

A Gouda vase, Lolette design, c1924, 4in (10cm) high. **£40-50** *OO*

A Gouda Export Range jug, Damascus design, c1920, 6¼in (16cm) high. **£125-150** *OO*

A Gouda vase, Dagman design, c1920, 5¾in (14cm) high. **£80-90** *OO*

l. A Gouda night light, Matapan design, c1920, 11in (28cm) high. **£180-200**
r. A Schoonhoven factory night light, c1920, 3¾in (9cm) high. **£30-35** *OO*

A Mason's Ironstone inkstand, c1820, 4½in (11cm) diam.
£250-350 *CAI*

A Mason's Ironstone miniature teapot, c1820, 2½in (6cm).
£250-350 *CAI*

A Mason's Ironstone jug, with orange scale ground, c1820, 9¾in (24cm) high.
£300-330 *MJW*

A pair of Mason's Ironstone candlesticks, c1820, 3½in (8.5cm) high.
£400-500 *CAI*

A Mason's Ironstone scent bottle, c1826, 4½in (11cm) high.
£120-200 *CAI*

A Mason's Ironstone miniature chamberstick, c1820, 1½in (3.5cm) high.
£250-300 *CAI*

A Mason's Ironstone pen holder, 8in (20cm) long.
£250-300 *CAI*

A pair of Mason's Ironstone jardinières, c1840, 5in (12.5cm) high.
£650-750 *CAI*

A set of 7 graduated Mason's Ironstone jugs, c1840, 4 to 10⅛in (10 to 26cm) high.
£1,600-1,800 *CAI*

A Mason's Ironstone pot pourri, c1820, 5in (12.5cm) high. **£200-300** *CAI*

A pair of Mason's Ironstone vases, c1810, 4in (10cm) high. **£150-250** *CAI*

A Meissen panther and leopard fighting, painted in underglaze colours, first modelled by Rudolf Löhner in 1912, No. C 229, 14in (36cm) long. **£3,000-3,500** *DAV*

A Meissen toucan, painted in overglaze colours, first modelled by Paul Walther in 1924, signed, 18½in (47cm) high. **£6,000-8,000** *DAV*

Two Meissen guinea fowl, painted in underglaze colours, first modelled by Paul Walther in 1909, No. Z 155, signed, 15½in (39cm). **£2,500-3,500** *DAV*

A Meissen antelope, painted in underglaze colours, first modelled by Paul Walther in 1911 No. B 218, 7⅓in (18.5cm) high. **£2,200-2,800** *DAV*

Two Meissen desert foxes, painted in underglaze colours, first modelled by Otto Pilz in 1907, No. F 257, 5⅜in (14cm) high. **£600-900** *DAV*

A Meissen leopard and cubs, first modelled by Otto Pilz in 1911, No. B 206, signed on base O. Pilz, 8¼in (20.5cm) high. **£2,500-3,500** *DAV*

A Meissen leopard attacking a zebra, first modelled by Otto Pilz in 1911 No. B 252, signed, 12¼in (31cm) high. **£2,500-3,500** *DAV*

A Meissen fox, first modelled by Paul Walther in 1906, No. X 170, 9¾in (24cm) long. **£500-800** *DAV*

l. Two Meissen tigers, modelled by R. Löhner in 1912, No. B 298, 13⅓in (34cm) long. **£3,000-4,000** *DAV*

r. Two Meissen bears, first modelled by Eric Hösel, c1905, No. V 111, 7in (17.5cm) high. **£800-1,200** *DAV*

A pair of spill vases, possibly Minton, c1820, 4¾in (12cm) high.
£800-900 *AMH*

A Meissen polar bear and cub, painted in underglaze colours, first modelled by W. Zugel in 1906, No. X 147, signed on base, 6½in (16cm) high. **£2,000-2,500** *DAV*

A Meissen tiger with kill, painted in underglaze colours, first modelled by Otto Jarl in 1903, No. U 123, signed on base Otto Jarl, 1903.
£3,000-4,000 *DAV*

Two Minton Secessionist vases, c1902, 9½in (23.5cm) high.
£180-220 each *POW*

A Minton Sessionist vase, c1902, 13in (33cm) high.
£220-300 *POW*

A Meissen figure, Cupid and Knife Sharpener, 19thC, damaged.
£130-140 *PCh*

A Minton toilet jug and bowl set, attributed to Christopher Dresser, bowl 15in (38cm) diam, jug 12in (30.5cm) high. **£380-400** *NCA*

A Meissen elephant and rider, painted in underglaze colours, first modelled by Paul Walther in 1905, No. W 148, 11in (28cm) high.
£2,500-3,500 *DAV*

A New Hall lustreware fruit bowl, 9½in (23.5cm) diam.
£50-95 *AOS*

A Japanese Imari plate, with design on reverse, c1890, 8¼in (21cm) diam.
£65-75 *TER*

A Japanese Imari plate, the centre with stylised landscape, 8¾in (22cm) diam.
£45-55 *TER*

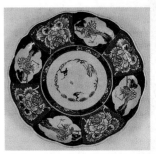

A Japanese Imari plate, with stork design, c1890, 8½in (21cm) diam.
£60-70 *TER*

A pair of Japanese Imari plates, with stencilled centre, 8½in (21cm) diam.
£90-100 *TER*

A Japanese Imari plate, with landscape design, c1890, 8¾in (22cm) diam. **£70-80** *TER*

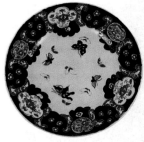

A Japanese Imari plate, with butterflies, c1910, 8½in (21cm) diam.
£60-70 *TER*

A Japanese Imari plate, with stencil design, c1890, 8½in (21.5cm).
£65-75 *TER*

A Japanese Imari plate, with flower decoration, c1890, 8¾in (22cm) diam. **£45-55** *TER*

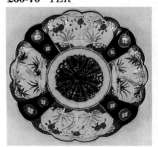

A Japanese Imari plate, c1910, 8½in (21cm) diam.
£45-55 *TER*

A Japanese Imari plate, decorated with money bags and purses, design on reverse, 8½in (21cm) diam.
£75-85 *TER*

A Japanese Imari plate, decorated with stylised rabbits, c1890, 8½in (21cm) diam. **£60-70** *TER*

A Japanese Imari plate, with flowers and bird decoration, 8¾in (22cm) diam. **£60-70** *TER*

A Japanese Imari plate, c1890, 12in (30.5cm) diam.
£150-165 *TER*

A Japanese Imari plate, with design on the reverse, c1890, 12in (30.5cm) diam.
£170-180 *TER*

A Vung Tau Cargo vase, c1690, 4½in (11cm).
£450-500 *RBA*

A Japanese Imari plate, inferior quality, 8in (20cm) diam.
£35-40 *TER*

A pair of Fukagawa Imari bottle vases, late 19thC, 6in (15cm) high.
£275-300 *ORI*

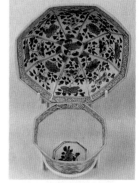

A Vung Tau Cargo tea bowl and saucer, c1690, saucer 5in (12.5cm) diam.
£350-400 *RBA*

A Nanking Cargo vomit pot, Peony Pattern, 4¾in (12cm) diam.
£1,200-1,500 *RBA*

l. A Japanese Imari vase, late 19thC, 5in (12.5cm) high.
£75-80 *ORI*

A Nanking Cargo tea bowl and saucer, Blue Pine Tree Pattern, c1750.
£150-185 *RBA*

A Nanking Cargo blue and white milk jug, c1750, 6in (15cm) diam.
£750-950 *RBA*

l. A Fukagawa Imari plate, with enamel decoration, late 19thC, 8¼in (21cm) diam.
£100-120 *ORI*

CERAMICS

The collectable ceramics market continues to prove both popular and consequently reasonably steady, price wise.

This year we have focused, on the following subjects; that perennial favourite, Victorian blue and white china, Meissen animals and birds are featured in depth. This is a very exciting but neglected area of Meissen, and sometimes, with research and shrewd buying, bargains can still be found. We have re-examined the Nanking Cargo to detail how well these glorious pieces have stood up price wise, since their rescue from the sea.

We have devoted several pages to another collecting favourite - Staffordshire china, notably religious figures and Staffordshire dogs. Items which are included in this issue but have been featured in past volumes are cross referenced.

The Ceramics section is organised alphabetically by factory or collecting areas, e.g. Beswick, cats & dogs, Clarice Cliff. Finally, please remember that values are seriously affected by condition, damage and check very closely for evidence of repair especially on the more expensive items.

Two frogs, 2½in (6.5cm) wide, *l.* a Thuringian copy, c1890, **£100-150** *DAN* *r.* Meissen, c1860 **£250-300** *DAN*

A white glazed dove, by J. Adnet, Adnet Factory impressed mark, 19¼in (49cm) high. **£350-450** *POW*

A Budt blue dove, c1920, 8in (20cm) high. **£125-135** *POW*

Animals

A pair of Victorian cats, c1870, 4in (10cm) high. **£300-400** *DAN*

CROSS REFERENCE
Staffordshire Pottery————▶ p124

A Continental figure of a cat, 20thC. **£150-160** *WIL*

A faience seated lion, 18thC, feet restored, 5¼in (13.5cm) wide. **£100-125** *GA*

A bone china swan, c1850, 3in (8cm) wide. **£60-70** *DAN*

A porcelain elephant, possibly by Karlovar, c1950, 6½in (16.5cm) high. **£80-100** *KAC*

A monkey's head water jug, French, 19thC, 8in (20cm) high.
£35-40 *TRU*

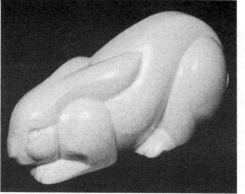

A crackle glaze rabbit, by Charles Lemanceau, c1925, 13in (33.5cm) wide.
£300-350 *POW*

An earthenware figure of a monkey, with agate body, and green glaze, probably Wrexham pottery, feet chipped, 19thC, 7in (18cm) high.
£90-110 *OD*

CROSS REFERENCE
Staffordshire
Dogs ⎯⎯⎯⎯➤ p125

A lid in the form of a dog with kennel, Dutch, dated 1798, 3½in (9cm) high.
£100-150 *GA*

A toad, possibly Portuguese, c1845, 11in (28cm) wide.
£300-400 *DAN*

Ashworth

A water lily pattern jug, c1805, 12¼in (31cm) high.
£650-700 *VH*

A porcelain cat, possibly by Belvedere, c1950, 5½in (14cm) high.
£70-90 *KAC*

Barge Ware

A barge ware kettle, 1809, 8½in (21.5cm) high.
£75-85 *TER*

For a further selection of Barge Ware, please refer to *Miller's Collectables Price Guide, Vol V, p115,* available from Millers Publications.

Belleek

Two jardinières, 1st period,
l. **£800-850.**
r. **£650-700** *PC*

A Ring cup and saucer with raised decoration of roses and convolvulus, 1st period marks, top maroon, bottom orange. **£200-225** *PC*

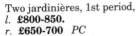

A Hexagon tea set, 2nd period, comprising: cup and saucer tinted with butterscotch and gilded. **£120-130**
Teapot, tinted pink. **£110-130**
2 cream jugs. **£40-50 each** *PC*

A collection of 1st period Institute items, gilded, plate 6in (15cm) diam. **£70-80**
Sugar bowl with pink pattern. **£60-70**
Breakfast cup and saucer, pink pattern. **£170-180** *PC*

Beswick

In this section, which deals with Beatrix Potter figures, the prices given are for the first versions only, with a Beswick gold backstamp on the base.

Several models have been produced over the years in different versions. To avoid confusion, in this book the estimated price for the first version only, in perfect condition, will be given. This is the version which will naturally be the most expensive and also the hardest to find. Rarity is one of the factors which controls price and contributes to the vast differences which can be found in the prices asked, and those realised at auctions. *Duchess with the Pie* is an exception, as the model was introduced after the gold backstamps had been discontinued.

In August 1989 the John Beswick backstamp was discontinued and replaced with the Royal Albert stamp. Current models are available only as Royal Albert figures and these can be found in normal retail outlets.

A collection of animals, including: a Shire horse, Highland cattle, cows, calves, sheep, lambs and pigs, some damaged, printed and painted marks, horse 5¼in (13.5cm) high. **£1,200-1,300** *CSK*

- The Beswick factory was founded by John Beswick at Gold Street, Longton, Staffordshire, and produced earthenwares from c1936.
- Early wares not marked, later wares printed marks as shown.

A pottery figure of a horse and rider, 10in (25cm) high. **£80-90** *GAK*

CROSS REFERENCE
Colour Section ⟶ p69

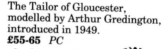

A collection of figures, Rupert Bear and his friends. **£425-450** *F*

BESWICK
ENGLAND

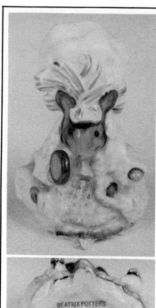

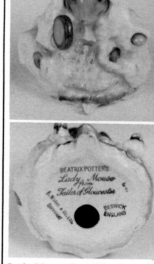

The Tailor of Gloucester, modelled by Arthur Gredington, introduced in 1949. **£55-65** *PC*

Appley Dapply, from Appley Dapply's Nursery Rhymes by Beatrix Potter, modelled by Albert Hallam, introduced in 1971. **£125-140** *PC*

Lady Mouse from The Tailor of Gloucester, modelled by Arthur Gredington, introduced in 1950. **£55-65** *PC*

A collection of figures, comprising camel, 2 parakeets, lion, tiger, dove, elephant, pheasant, Sabrina's Sir Richard, and a turkey, printed factory marks. **£550-575** *CSK*

Mrs Tiggy-Winkle, modelled by Arthur Gredington, introduced in 1948.
£60-70 *PC*

The pattern on her dress changed during 1970.

FURTHER READING
John Beswick and Royal Albert Beatrix Potter Figures, edited by Louise Irvine, published by UK International Ceramics.

The Duchess from The Pie and The Patty Pan, modelled by Graham Tongue, introduced 1979, discontinued 1982.
£85-100 *PC*

Blue and White

A Leeds Pottery Italian Scenery pattern dish, unmarked, c1820, 14in (36cm) wide.
£175-200 *CA*

A dessert dish, Hospitality pattern, possibly Spode shape, c1820, 9in (22.5cm) wide.
£120-140 *CA*

A Victorian platter, Asiatic Pheasant pattern, 13¼in (34cm) diam.
£30-35 *AA*

This pattern was made from Victorian times until 1920.

A dish, The Villagers pattern, marked Turner, maker unknown, c1820, 9½in (24cm) square.
£120-140 *CA*

A Davenport child's potty, Fisherman series, marked, c1820, 5in (12.5cm) diam.
£120-150 *CA*

CROSS REFERENCE
Children's Ceramics ──────▶ p91

An oval footbath, slight crack.
£700-725 *MR*

A dish, The Beemaster pattern, 8½in (21.5cm) wide.
£150-175 *CA*

The Beemaster pattern was based on a watercolour entitled 'Swarm of Bees, Autumn', by George Robertson, 1742-88, commonly attributed to Wm. Adams but no known marked examples exist.

A plate, The Winemakers pattern, c1820, 9¾in (24.5cm) diam.
£150-175 *CA*

A gin bottle, with Eton College pattern, by George Phillip of Longport, c1825, 8in (20cm) high.
£140-160 *CA*

A blue and white mug, Boy Piping pattern, c1820, 4¼in (11cm) high.
£130-150 *CA*

A chestnut dish and stand, possibly Spode Greek pattern, c1810, 9¼in (23cm) wide.
£185-220 *CA*

A pickle leaf dish, with Piping Shepherd pattern, c1810.
£75-100 *CA*

A mug, transfer printed with fishing, horse riding and walking scenes, maker unknown, c1810, 4¾in (12cm) high.
£135-150 *CA*

A Davenport plate, The Villagers pattern with pierced border, c1815, 7in (17.5cm) diam.
£135-165 *CA*

A sauce tureen, Goldfinch pattern, adapted from a Thomas Bewick wood engraving, c1820, 9¼in (23cm) wide.
£175-200 *CA*

A blue and white mug, decorated with the London Royal Liverpool Mail Train, maker unknown, c1830, 3¼in (8cm) high.
£150-175 *CA*

The subject featured can often increase the desirability of a piece; for example, this mug could well be collected by a railway enthusiast. Other desirable subjects would include fishing, golf, or any sport, transport, especially ballooning, and political commemorative ware.

A Davenport boordarloue, with Muliteer pattern, c1820, 9½in (23cm) wide. **£150-200** *CA*

This was made for ladies who found the vicar's sermon too long.

A doll's tureen, showing Benjamin Franklin Flying His Kite, maker unknown, lid missing, c1830, 4½in (11.5cm) wide. **£25-30** *CA*

A tea bowl, Tea Party pattern, c1810, 1¾in (4.5cm) high. **£35-40** *CA*

A tankard, from the Shipping Series, c1820, 5¼in (13cm) high. **£130-150** *CA*

A Victorian blue and white cream jug, 5in (12.5cm) high. **£50-55** *OCA*

A black and white transfer pattern tea bowl and saucer, cup 1¾in (4.5cm) high. **£75-95** *CA*

A tea bowl and saucer, marked Semi China, c1820, cup 2¼in (6cm) high. **£85-95** *CA*

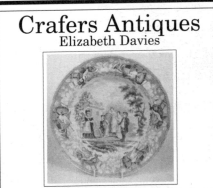

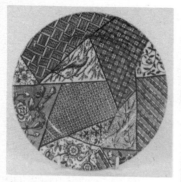

A pair of Victorian blue and white plates, 7½in (19cm) diam.
£18-25 *OCA*

An Edwardian Shredded Wheat dish, Abbey pattern, by Geo. Jones & Sons, marked, 6in (15cm) wide.
£15-25 *CA*

A transfer decorated platter, with The Durham Ox and John Day, early 19thC, 22in (56cm) wide.
£950-1,000 *DaD*

A Victorian blue transfer printed plate, with 'Are You Well, Sir - Not Very', badly damaged, 5in (12.5cm) diam.
£35-45 if perfect *CA*

FURTHER READING
The Dictionary of Blue and White Printed Pottery, 1780-1880, Vol I & II, by A. W. Coysh & R. K. Henry Wood, published by the Antique Collectors Club.

A transfer printed plate, possibly by Joshua Heath, c1780, 9in (22.5cm) diam.
£30-40 *OD*

A blue and white cereal and dessert plate set, by the Empire Porcelain Co, c1928, dish 6in (15cm) diam.
£25-35 *OCA*

Two ladles with silver bands:
top: with view of the Imperial Park at Gehol, Davenport, c1810, 12in (31cm) long.
bottom: maker unknown, c1815, 11in (28.5cm) long.
£75-80 each *CA*

A dish, The Returning Woodman pattern, impressed Brameld mark, c1806-26, 15¾in (40cm) wide.
£175-200 *CA*

Book Ends

A plate, Pastoral Scene pattern, by Edward and George Phillips, c1825, 9¾in (24.5cm) diam.
£100-125 *CA*

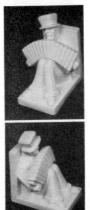

Two Victorian book ends, coloured in pastel pink, yellow and blue, c1885, 6in (15cm) high.
£50-55 *ROW*

Two Robj crackle glaze book ends, French, c1930, 8in (20cm) high.
£300-350 *POW*

Two Guillemin factory crackle glaze squirrel book ends, French, c1920, 9¼in (23cm) high.
£300-400 *POW*

Brannam

- C. H. Brannam Ltd produced earthenwares at the Litchdon Pottery, Barnstaple, Devon, from about 1879.
- Marks consisted of incised letters C. H. BRANNAM, sometimes dated and BARUM (the Roman name for Barnstaple).

A slipware vase, red body with white slip, signed C. H. Brannam, Barum, N. Devon, dated 1881, 15½in (39cm).
£550-600 *P*

At this early date it is highly plausible that C. H. Brannam himself threw and decorated this piece.

CROSS REFERENCE
Contemporary Ceramics ⟶ p95

A slipware vase, red body overlaid with white slip, signed C. H. Brannam, Barum, N. Devon, dated 1881, 15in (38.5cm).
£750-800 *P*

Bretby

A Bretby plaque, c1910, 13¾in (35cm).
£120-140 *TER*

For a further selection of Bretby, please refer to *Miller's Collectables Price Guide, Vol V, p84,* available from Millers Publications.

- Bretby Art Pottery was a partnership formed during the early 1880s by William Tooth (Linthorpe Art Pottery) and William Ault.
- Factory was atWoodville, near Burton-on-Trent, Derbyshire.
- Products marked as shown. The World 'ENGLAND' was added from c1891.
- William Ault left the partnership in 1886. The company became Tooth and Co from the 1920s.

A Bretby jardinière, c1896, 41in (104cm) high.
£360-410 *ACA*

Burleigh

A matched pair of Burleigh hand painted canoes, c1930, 8½in (21cm).
£80-100 *BKK*

A pair of Burleigh hand painted lupin vases, c1930, 8in (20cm).
£120-140 *BKK*

Burmantofts

l. & r. A pair of faience lustre candlesticks, coloured plum and pale blue, impressed BF monogram, and numbered 2219, 9in (22.5cm).
£150-175
c. A faience lustre plate, in matt plum gold against blue olive ground, impressed Burmantofts Works, The Leeds Fireclay Co. Ltd, England, monogram appears as JW, 10⅓in (26cm) diam.
£250-275 *P*

CROSS REFERENCE
Contemporary Ceramics ⟶ p95

Carlton Ware

A cloisonné bowl, with Carlton Cloisonné Ware mark, 1892, 9in (22.5cm) diam.
£380-420 *BKK*

A Carlton Ware chinoiserie pattern ginger jar and cover, inscribed, mark to base.
£280-300 *P*

A pair of early pseudo cloisonné handpainted vases, with W & R mark, c1899, 3in (7.5cm).
£110-130 *BKK*

A Guinness toucan table lamp, with original printed shade, printed factory marks, 16¼in (41cm) high.
£350-375 *CSK*

- Produced since 1890 at the Carlton Works at Stoke-on-Trent.
- Art Pottery produced during the 1920s; household domestic wares very heavily Art Deco influenced.
- Particularly famous for Guinness advertising figures and animals.
- Later marks sometimes feature previous name Wiltshaw & Robinson Ltd.

A Carlton Ware bowl, c1930, 4½in (11cm) diam.
£35-45 *FMN*

A charabanc, manufactured for H. W. Bradbury Pratt, British Empire Exhibition, 5½in (13.5cm) long.
£65-75 *OCA*

CROSS REFERENCE
Tins, Signs & Advertising ——▶ p440

A Carlton Ware vase, c1860, 18in (46cm).
£600-800 *CAI*

An apple blossom yellow cress dish and stand, c1934.
£35-38 *BKK*

A hand painted ovoid dish, c1936.
£15-20 *BKK*

Three wall mounted pottery toucans, in black, yellow and orange enamels, inscribed 'My Goodness - My Guinness', 6½ to 10in (16 to 25cm).
£130-150 *WIL*

Children's and Nursery Ware

A Walt Disney tea set, teapot 3in (7.5cm) high.
£75-80 *BAT*

A satirical nursery set, c1930,
7½in (19cm) diam.
£60-80 *BAT*

A football pattern cup and
saucer.
£10-12 *BGA*

A Victorian birthday jug, colour
transfer printed, 8¼in (20cm).
£45-55 *FMN*

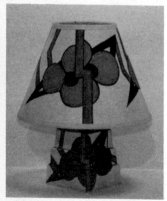

A set of 6 hand painted fairy
tale plates, German, c1970.
£80-100 *BIB*

A Humpty Dumpty mug and
plate, Brixham Pottery, Devon,
plate 5in (12.5cm) diam.
£10-15 *BAT*

Clarice Cliff

- **Originally Clarice Cliff worked for Arthur J. Wilkinson (Ltd.)**
- **Produced designs for Newport Pottery marked as below from 1938.**

An Autumn pattern plate, dated
May 1931, 7in (17.5cm) diam.
£140-160 *BKK*

A lamp base in orange flower
pattern, shape No. 391, with
original bayonet fitting and flex,
c1932, with later matching
shade, base 3½in (9cm) high.
£400-440 *BKK*

A Marguerite pattern
sugar sifter.
£225-250 *AOS*

A pair of hand painted jugs,
c1930, 7½in (18.5cm).
£140-160 *BKK*

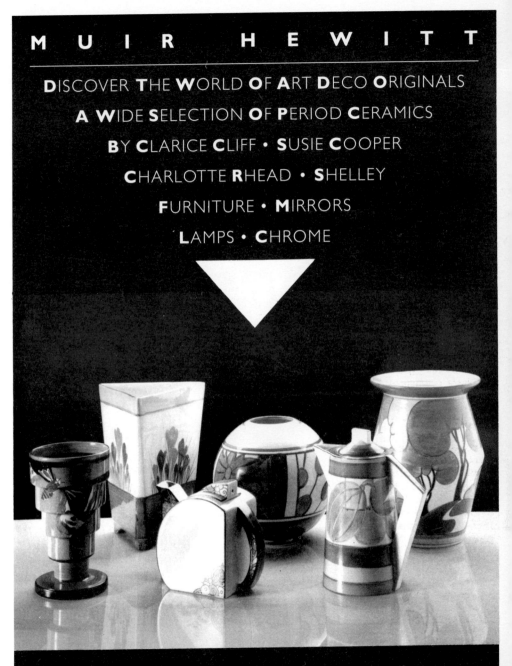

A Sungay pattern bowl, c1932, 7½in (19cm) diam.
£100-120 *BKK*

A Geometric jug, with early mark, c1928, 5in (13cm). **£180-200** *BKK*

A Bizarre pattern bowl.
£45-60 *COB*

For a further selection of Clarice Cliff, please refer to *Miller's Collectables Price Guide, Vol V, pp88-90,* available from Millers Publications.

A selection of Clarice Cliff comprising: a Fantasque 19-piece part teaset in Secrets Orange pattern.
£740-780
A ribbed wall charger in Original Crocus pattern, 18in (44.5cm) diam.
£480-520
A Fantasque 5-bar toast rack in Farmhouse pattern.
£175-185
A cylindrical preserve jar and cover.
£200-225
A pair of conical salt and pepper casters in Forest Glen pattern.
£170-180
A Bizarre conical sugar sifter in Blue Crocus pattern.
£380-420 *ALL*

A black My Garden pattern vase, c1934, 7½in (18.5cm).
£140-160 *BKK*

Coalport

A Coalport plate, with hand painted panels of birds and flora, mid-19thC, 9in (23cm) diam.
£150-170 *WIL*

A Coalport hand painted jug, c1820, 7in (18cm) high.
£350-375 *AMH*

An Autumn Crocus pattern beehive jam pot, c1932, 3in (7.5cm). **£80-90** *BKK*

A 35-piece enamel painted tea service, 3 cups repaired, c1825, teapot 6½in (16cm) high.
£650-700 *SWO*

CROSS REFERENCE
Tea Sets ⟶ p132

Contemporary Ceramics
Deidre Burnett

A Coalport mug, c1815, 4in (10cm) high.
£350-450 *LIO*

A porcelain double rimmed bowl, by Deidre Burnett, eroded mouth, brown with golden edge, impressed DB seal, 7½in (18.5cm) diam. **£225-250** *Bon*

Shoji Hamada

A stoneware bowl, olive green with 3 beige splashes, 6in (15cm) diam.
£900-1,000 *Bon*
Exhibited in New York 1988.

A stoneware vase, khaki glaze with 3 floral motifs, c1965, 7¾in (19cm) high, with signed wooden box.
£2,000-2,200 *Bon*

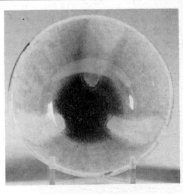

A stoneware vase, tenmoku glaze with 3 finger wipe designs, the textured collar green, 8¾in (22cm) high, with signed wooden box and orange cloth.
£1,900-2,000 *Bon*

Barbara and Michael Hawkins

A ceramic bowl, 'Red Flames', c1992, 9in (22.5cm) diam.
£40-60 *A*

Two ceramic pebble pots, by Barbara and Michael Hawkins, c1992. **£35-50 each** *A*

A vase, by Barbara and Michael Hawkins, c1992, 12in (30.5cm) high. **£45-55** *A*

A bottle, with fish and gold leaf decoration, by Barbara and Michael Hawkins, c1992, 8½in (21cm) high. **£50-60** *A*

A John Dory gold lustre bowl, by Barbara and Michael Hawkins, c1992, 6in (15cm) high. **£100-130** *A*

Dame Lucie Rie

A white stoneware bowl, by Dame Lucie Rie, the rim with manganese runs, impressed LR seal, 6½in (16cm) wide. **£750-800** *Bon*

A porcelain bowl, by Dame Lucie Rie, with brown manganese glaze, plain dished centre and turned foot, impressed LR seal mark. **£2,500-2,800** *P*

This piece was purchased from the potter in 1969.

A flower vase, by Barbara and Michael Hawkins, c1992, 10½in (26cm) high. **£60-70** *A*

A stoneware vase, by Dame Lucie Rie, with pink and blue volcanic glaze, impressed LR seal, c1982, 10¾in (27cm) high. **£1,200-1,300** *Bon*

Gabrielle Koch

An earthenware bowl, by Gabrielle Koch, burnished dark brown and deep orange, incised Gabrielle Koch, 6in (15cm) diam. **£180-200** *Bon*

A stoneware bowl, by Dame Lucie Rie, with grey and pink pitted glaze, impressed LR seal, c1980, 5½in (14cm) diam. **£5,200-5,500** *Bon*

Exhibited at Victoria & Albert Museum, 1982.

Mary Rogers

A Studio Pottery vase, by Mary Rogers, with incised decoration, 1960s, 3in (8cm) high.
£80-120 *DID*

Nichola Theakston

John Ward

A stoneware pot, by John Ward, vertical graduations of green and white, impressed JW seal, 7½in (19cm) high.
£280-300 *Bon*

> CROSS REFERENCE
> **Contemporary
> Ceramics** ⟶ p95

A terracotta sculpture of a wildebeest, by Nichola Theakston, c1992.
£400-450 *A*

> CROSS REFERENCE
> **Ceramic Animals** ➝ p81

Crown Devon

A Crown Devon plaque, painted with Highland cattle in a landscape, c1915, 7 by 9½in (17.5 by 24cm).
£450-500 *TVA*

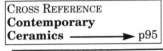

CROWN···
···DEVON
MADE IN ENGLAND
"TRADE MARK"

A Crown Devon Fieldings vase, blue background, early 1930s, 9in (22.5cm).
£250-300 *GAZ*

Susie Cooper

A Susie Cooper Polka Dot hand painted 15-piece coffee set, c1950.
£85-95 *BKK*

Copeland

A mug, c1885, 2¾in (7cm) high.
£50-60 *CA*

Inscribed on base, 'A piece of antiquity painted on the wall adjoining the kitchen of Winchester College', published by Wm. Savage Winchester.

A Crown Devon Leaping Hart early electric coffee percolator, c1934, 11in (28cm) high.
£30-40 *BKK*

Cruets

An egg cup and cruet set, c1920.
£25-30 *BGA*

A Continental cruet,
Edwardian, 6in (15cm) wide.
£18-25 *BGA*

Doulton

A Doulton 'Jewel' plate,
Midland Photo Keramic
Famous Musician Series,
'Joachim', c1897, 9in (22.5cm)
diam.
£80-100 *HER*

Worcester also made these.

A Doulton jug, with lions, by
Hannah and Lucy Barlow,
c1883, 9¼in (23cm) high.
£400-450 *HER*

Derby

A Derby porcelain flower seller
candle holder, sconce replaced,
patch marks, c1765, 11½in
(29cm) high.
£1,000-1,250 *BRK*

A pair of Samson's Derby
porcelain figures, 6¾in (17cm)
high. **£280-300** *P(S)*

A Derby dolphin ewer cream
boat, painted by the Cotton
Stem painter, c1760, 3in
(7.5cm) high.
£600-665 *TVA*

A Royal Crown Derby vase,
painted and gilt, printed mark
for 1891 and red numerals, 10in
(25cm) high.
£200-225 *MSW*

> **FURTHER READING**
> *Derby Porcelain*, by J.
> Twitchett.

A Royal Doulton porcelain
plaque, by Leslie Johnson, 7 by
9in (17.5 by 22.5cm).
£680-700 *LT*

A Doulton vase, Goats and Ponies, by Hannah Barlow, c1900, 12in (30.5cm) high.
£550-650 *HER*

A Royal Doulton figure 'Collinette', HN1999, 7½in (19cm) high.
£180-200 *WIL*

A Doulton cheese dish, in Haystacks design, coloured green and ochre, c1925, 10in (25cm) wide.
£80-120 *HER*

A Royal Doulton figure, 'Phyllis', HN1420, 9in (23cm) high.
£180-200 *WIL*

A Royal Doulton figure of Harlequin, 1957-69, 7½in (19cm) high.
£120-140 *TRU*

A pair of Doulton
Art Nouveau vases,
18in (46cm) high.
£350-380 *WIL*

Two jugs, c1930, 9in (22.5cm) high.
l. Shakespeare. **£60-80**
r. Gallant fishers. **£70-90** *TP*

A Royal Doulton hand painted
Art Deco pattern plate, c1936,
10½in (26cm) diam.
£70-75 *BKK*

A Doulton flambé Peruvian
penguin, by Fred Moore,
c1930, 8¾in (22cm) high.
£350-400 *HER*

A Doulton Eglington
Tournament green jug, c1839,
6in (15cm) high.
£70-100 *HER*

*The Tournament, held at
Eglington Castle, Ayrshire 1839,
was watched by 100,000 people
in pouring rain. These jugs
were produced in 3 colours.*

A pair of Doulton Burslem Blue
Flow plaques, 13⅓in (34cm) diam.
£650-675 *LT*

A Doulton flambé fox, c1930,
9½in (24cm) high.
£200-250 *HER*

A Doulton Zodiac plate, made
for Batchelors Foods, limited
edition 500, 1980, 10⅓in (26cm)
diam.
£40-50 *HER*

A Friar of Orders Gray 1733
wall mask, 1936-40.
£500-700 *TP*

CROSS REFERENCE
**Tins, Signs &
Advertising** ⟶ p440

A Doulton tyg, by Hannah Barlow, c1880, 7in (17.5cm) high.
£400-500 *HER*

A Royal Doulton, 'Nelson' commemorative loving cup, No. 245 of an edition of 600, signed by H. Fenton, verse on base, 10in (25cm) high.
£420-450 *GAK*

A Doulton Series Ware corset jug, Morrison pattern, yellow and black, c1920, 8¼in (21cm) high.
£100-125 *HER*

Fairings

'Welsh Spinning Party', 6in (15cm) high.
£40-60 *BRK*

'Happy Father', by Elbogen, German, c1900, 3½in (9cm) high.
£75-85 *TER*

'Shall we sleep first or how' German Script, 3¾in (9cm).
£50-60 *BRK*

Foley

A Foley blue pattern trio, rib shape, c1888.
£35-50 *AJ*

A Foley scalloped shape trio, c1900.
£35-45 *AJ*

'Last in bed to put out the light', 3in (8cm) high.
£30-50 *BRK*

Goldscheider

A Goldscheider figure, wearing a maroon dress and shoes, signed and impressed Dakon, further signature on base, 10in (25cm) high.
£1,800-1,900 *AG*

Goss & Crested China

- **Crested China was produced by many factories between about 1880 and 1940.**
- **Most famous main manufacturers were Arcadian, Carlton, Grafton, Shelley and Willow Art.**
- **Goss factory started producing Parian Ware in 1858.**

Goss China

A vase, decorated with Flags of the Allies, 2¾in (7cm) high.
£25-30 *BGA*

A bust of Georgiana Jewitt.
£1,700-1,900 *G&CC*

A parian bust of Sir Walter Scott, 1st period, c1870, 5½in (14cm) high.
£45-55 *TVA*

A figure of St John's Font, Barmouth.
£360-380 *G&CC*

A Wembley lion, c1924, 4in (10cm) wide.
£150-175 *CCC*

A Goss Blackpool crest, c1880, 6in (15cm) high.
£180-220 *CCC*

A bust of Mary, Queen of Scots.
£220-230 *G&CC*

A sheep, c1925, 4in (10.5cm) wide.
£200-250 *CCC*

'Joan', c1930, 5in (13cm) high. **£200-250** *CCC*

A Menai Bridge basket, c1870, 5½in (14cm) high.
£300-350 *CCC*

A Saxony lifeboatman.
£12-15 *G&CC*

A boot black, c1873, 8¼in (21cm) high.
£300-350 *CCC*

A Goss 'Window in Thrums' nightlight, c1920, 5¼in (5.5cm) wide.
£300-350 *CCC*

A selection of Goss cottages.
£75-85 each *CCC*

A posy basket.
£230-260 *G&CC*

A Blackpool lion, c1910, 4½in(11cm) wide.
£60-65 *CCC*

A Goss Art Deco styled vase, c1928, 8in (20cm) high.
£230-250 *CCC*

Crested China

An Arcadian WWI tank, c1916, 4¾in (12cm) high.
£500-550 *CCC*

A Shelley Scottish soldier,c1920, 4½in (11.5cm) high.
£100-125 *CCC*

An Arcadian figure of Stowmarket Memorial Gates,c1920, 6in (15cm) wide.
£100-150 *CCC*

A collection of vehicles:
l. An Arcadian tank, 4¼in(11cm) wide. **£18-24**
l.c. A Shelley armoured car, 4½in (11.5cm) wide. **£50-70**
r.c. A Willow ambulance, 3½in (8cm) wide. **£25-35**
r. An Arcadian ambulance, 3¾in (9cm) wide. **£25-35** *CCC*

l. to r: A Gemma cow creamer, c1920, 5in (12.5cm) wide
£30-35
A Carlton bull, c1920, 4½in (11cm) wide. **£90-115**
A Willow pony, c1920, 5¼in (13cm) wide. **£30-40**
An Arcadian donkey, c1920, 5in (12cm) wide. **£45-55** *CCC*

A Carlton saloon car.
£60-65 *G&CC*

A Botolph figure of St. Paul's, c1920, 5in (13cm) high.
£38-48 *CCC*

A Grafton bomb thrower, c1916, 5½in (13.5cm) high.
£250-275 *CCC*

An Arcadian Scottish soldier, c1916, 5¼in (13.5cm) high.
£200-250 *CCC*

A Crown Devon car, Douglas, Isle of Man, c1920, 6¼in (16cm) wide.
£700-750 *CCC*

A Leadbeater Art figure, c1920, 6in (15.5cm) high.
£190-225 *CCC*

A West Pier, Brighton, plate, German, c1890, 10in (25cm) diam.
£25-30 *CCC*

Gouda

Three Gouda vases:
l. Ali design, 3½in (9cm) high.
£25-30
c. Limpo design, c1929, 3in (8cm) high.
£25-30
r. Magda design, Regina factory, c1930, 3¼in (9cm) high.
£30-35 *OO*

A Gouda vase, Regina factory, Rosario design, c1930, 6¼in (16cm) high.
£40-50 *OO*

A Gouda ashtray, Regina factory, Rosario design, c1930, 4¾in (12cm) high.
£35-40 *OO*

A Gouda chamberstick, Ripo design, c1923, 5in (12.5cm) diam.
£50-60 *OO*

A Gouda jug, in Iris design, c1928, 9in (23cm).
£80-90 *OO*

A Gouda chamberstick, Zolher design, c1931, 5in (13cm) diam.
£40-50 *OO*

Two Gouda ashtrays:
l. Collier design, c1924. **£20-25**
r. Danier design, c1924, 4¼in (11cm).
£30-35 *OO*

A Gouda vase, made for Liberty & Co, c1922, 3¼in (8cm).
£40-45 *OO*

A Dutch Rembrandt pottery vase, c1926, 11in (28cm) high.
£250-280 *OO*

A Gouda pottery inkwell, Tokyo design, c1925, 3½in (9cm) high.
£80-90 *OO*

A Gouda pottery vase, Amphora factory, Chrijsant design, c1925, 4¼in (11cm) high.
£80-100 *OO*

A Gouda pottery Dutch shoe ashtray, made for a company named Hoekstri, c1925, 5½in (14cm) wide.
£30-35 *OO*

A Gouda vase, Bacalar design, c1930, 7in (17.5cm) high.
£60-70 *OO*

Gray

A pair of A. E. Gray vases.
£60-80 *OCA*

These vases were selected by Queen Mary at the British Industries Fair, March 13th, 1918, for the Red Cross Bazaar, Hanley, on May 14th, 1918.

Ironstone Ware

A Hicks & Meigh pot pourri jar, with lid and inside cover, c1822-31, 25in (63.5cm) high.
£3,500-4,000 *MJW*

CROSS REFERENCE
Mason's Ironstone ———➤ p107

Lustreware

A pair of religious plaques, c1870, 8½in (21.5cm) wide.
£40-50 *TER*

Linthorpe

- **Linthorpe pottery was produced at Middlesbrough, Yorks, between 1879-1889.**
- **Simple block lettered impressed mark - LINTHORPE (sometimes with the outline of a vase).**
- **Christopher Dresser designed works had an incised, impressed or painted signature.**

A pottery ewer, designed by Christopher Dresser, the red body covered with a streaked milky-green/brown glaze, factory mark, facsimile Dresser signature, HT monogram for Henry Tooth, numbered 502, 21in (53cm).
£400-425 *P*

CROSS REFERENCE
Contemporary Ceramics ———➤ p95

A pottery dish, designed by Christopher Dresser, painted with white chrysanthemums on a brown ground, impressed Linthorpe, facsimile signature and HT for Henry Tooth and BL monogram for painter, 11½in (29cm) diam.
£160-180 *P*

Majolica

A George Jones fish dish and cover, with a salmon lying on a leaf moulded ground, pink interior, numbered 2764 in black, hairline crack to tail, 15¼in (39cm) wide.
£2,250-2,500 *HSS*

A fish teapot, in blue, yellow, green and brown, spout chipped, 6½in (16.5cm) high.
£100-120 *Bon*

Mason's

A Mason's Ironstone china vase, with mazarine blue and gilded butterflies and flowers decoration, c1815, 8in (20cm).
£330-340 *VH*

An Ironstone hall vase, restored, c1835-40, 37in (94cm) high.
£1,600-1,650 *VH*

A vase, c1815-20, 19½in high.
£750-780 *VH*

- **C. J. Mason patented his 'Ironstone China' in 1813.**
- **If the Mason's Mark features the word 'Improved', it indicates manufacture after about 1840.**

Meissen

Two figures with jugs, c1860, 8½in (21cm) high.   **£1,700-1,800** *AMH*

A tureen and cover, with crown finial, cross swords mark in underglaze blue and incised B136, late 19thC, 10in (25.5cm) wide.
£4,750-5,000 *HSS*

A group of a lady and a gallant with a lamb and a dog, c1860, 8in (20cm) high.
£1,750-1,850 *AMH*

A pair of figures of children bearing grapes, c1870, 6in (15cm) high.
£1,600-1,700 *AMH*

Coins

A Meissen donation medal, 20thC, 1½in (4cm) diam.
£10-20 *DAN*

A Meissen commemorative medallion, Augustus Rex mark and factory mark, by Johann Friedrich Böttger, 1719, 2½in (6.5cm) diam.
£20-40 *DAN*

A set of Meissen coins, c1920 and 1921. **£60-100** *DAN*

3000 sets were minted as emergency money during the 1920s. They were never legal tender, but the 1921 coins were admitted as legal tender within Saxony. Some were designated 'Collectors Items' only. A boxed set of coins originally cost 50 marks and had gold edges, because their predecessors were gold coins. In 1921 40,000 complete sets were minted, made of Böttger stoneware.

Animals

At the Meissen factory a new age of porcelain modelling dawned under the leadership of Erich Hösel, chief designer from 1903.

Many of the animals and birds produced during the next 20 years were decorated with underglaze painting. This proved to be a difficult technique, as the paint applied to the biscuit porcelain, which was then fired at very high temperatures, could not withstand the heat. A new range of colours had to be developed which could withstand the high temperatures.

Paul Walther was the most important of the new wave of modellers of Meissen animal and bird figures. Others include Erich Hösel, Otto Pilz, Otto Jarl, Rudolf Löhner and Max Esser.

A collared bear, painted in underglaze colours, model No. V106, 4in (10cm) high.
£400-600 *DAV*

First modelled by Erich Hösel c1905.

A monkey, painted in underglaze colours, model No. W141, 3in (7.5cm) high.
£300-500 *DAV*

A silver fox, painted in underglaze colours, model No. V189, 10in (25cm) wide.
£1,000-1,500 *DAV*

First modelled by Erich Hösel c1905.

A bison, painted in underglaze colours, signed on base E. Hösel 02, model No. V101, 7½in (19cm) wide.
£2,000-2,500 *DAV*

First modelled by Erich Hösel in 1902.

A kangaroo, painted in underglaze colours, model No. Y107, 4¼in (11cm) high.
£500-700 *DAV*

A polar bear, painted in underglaze colours, model No. T181, 21in (53cm) wide.
£3,500-4,500 *DAV*

First modelled by Otto Jarl in 1903.

A lion cub, painted in underglaze colours, modelled by Paul Walther, c1905, 4in (10cm) high.
£400-600 *DAV*

An elephant, painted in underglaze colours, model No. D227, c1914, , 7½in (19cm) high.
£2,000-2,500 *DAV*

A bear, unpainted, model No. H256, signed on base M. Esser, 1924, 10½in (26.5cm) high.
£2,000-2,500 *DAV*

First modelled by Max Esser in 1924.

A mandrill baboon, painted in underglaze colours, model No. X143, 9in (22.5cm) high.
£1,500-2,000 *DAV*

First modelled by Otto Pilz in 1907.

A wild boar, painted in underglaze colours, signed on base Hartung '99, model No. S133, 10in (25cm) high.
£2,500-3,500 *DAV*

A kangaroo, painted in underglaze colours, model No. Y105.
£500-700 *DAV*

First modelled by Bochmann in 1908.

Birds

An owl perched on 2 books, painted in underglaze colours, signed Jarl on the book, model No. U177.
£400-700 *DAV*

First modelled by Otto Jarl in 1904.

A group of 3 owls, painted in underglaze colours, by Paul Walther, model No. W143, 1905, 6½in (16.5cm) high.
£700-1,000 *DAV*

A stork, painted in underglaze colours, model No. W149, c1905, 8½in (21.5cm) high.
£800-1,200 *DAV*

A duck, painted in underglaze colours, model No. Y116, 3½in (9cm) wide.
£300-500 *DAV*

First modelled by Paul Walther in 1906.

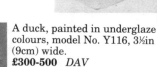

Two falcons, painted in underglaze colours, model No. X185, 12½in (32cm) high.
£2,500-3,000 *DAV*

A pelican, painted in underglaze colours, model No. W142, 6¼in (16cm) high.
£600-900 *DAV*

First modelled by Paul Walther in 1905.

A bird with grapes, painted in overglaze colours, model No. F283, signed on base PW, 12¾in (33cm) high.
£2,200-2,800 *DAV*

First modelled by Paul Walther in 1920.

A parrot, painted in underglaze colours, model No. E278, signed on base PW, 11in (28cm) high.
£1,800-2,300 *DAV*

A sea eagle, painted in underglaze colours, model No. X181, 16½in (42cm) high.
£1,500-2,000 *DAV*

First modelled by Paul Walther in 1907.

A cockatoo, painted in underglaze colours, signed on base PW, model No. Y117, 12¼in (31cm) high.
£2,000-2,500 *DAV*

First modelled by Paul Walther in 1908.

A toucan on a tray, painted in underglaze colours, model No. A204, c1909, 11in (28cm) high.
£2,500-3,000 *DAV*

Two parakeets, painted in underglaze colours, model No. E277, signed on base of tree PW, 13in (33.5cm) high.
£2,500-3,000 *DAV*

A mandarin duck standing on an egg shaped box, painted in underglaze colours, model No. Y129, 5½in (14cm) high.
£300-500 *DAV*

First modelled by Paul Walther in 1908.

A toucan, painted in underglaze colours, model No. Z188, 12½in (32cm) high.
£1,800-2,300 *DAV*

First modelled by Paul Walther in 1909.

A cockatoo, painted in overglaze colours, model No. G297, signed on base PW, 18in (46cm) high.
£4,000-5,000 *DAV*

First modelled by Paul Walther in 1922.

A great crested grebe, painted in underglaze colours, model No. B272, 6in (15cm) high.
£1,800-2,200 *DAV*

First modelled by Paul Zeiller in 1911.

A mandarin duck, painted in overglaze colours, model No. G259, 15in (38cm) high.
£3,000-4,000 *DAV*

An ostrich, painted in underglaze colours, model No. B249, signed on base PW, 6½in (16.5cm).
£800-1,200 *DAV*

First modelled by Paul Walther in 1911.

A mandarin duck, painted in underglaze colours, model No. Y129, 4in (10cm) high.
£300-500 *DAV*

First modelled by Paul Walther in 1908.

A hen pheasant, painted in overglaze colours, model No. G269, signed on base L. C. Paul Walther, 19¼in (50.5cm) high.
£4,000-6,000 *DAV*

First modelled by Paul Walther in 1921.

A bird with sunflowers, painted in overglaze colours, model No. F284, signed on base PW, 11½in (29.5cm) high.
£2,200-2,800 *DAV*

A parakeet, painted in underglaze colours, model No. F228, signed on base of tree PW, 11¾in (30cm) high.
£2,000-2,500 *DAV*

Cats

A cat, painted in overglaze colours, c1905. **£800-1,200** *DAV*

A cat, painted in underglaze colours, model No. U172, c1904, 4in (10cm) high.
£1,000-1,500 *DAV*

A spaniel, painted in underglaze colours, model No. V157, c1905, 8½in (21.5cm) wide.
£1,200-1,800 *DAV*

Dogs

A group of setters, painted in underglaze colours, model No. U164, signed on base Jarl, 10¾in (27cm) wide.
£1,200-1,800 *DAV*

An Alsatian, painted in underglaze colours, model No. V188, 7⅛in (18cm) wide.
£1,000-1,500 *DAV*

A collie, painted in underglaze colours, model No. V110, 4in (10cm) high.
£800-1,200 *DAV*

First modelled by Erich Hösel c1905.

A seated pointer, painted in underglaze colours, model No. U120, signed on base PW, 3¼in (8cm) high.
£700-1,000 *DAV*

First modelled by Paul Walther in 1904.

A French bulldog, painted in underglaze colours, model No. V134, 6in (15cm) high.
£800-1,200 *DAV*

First modelled by Erich Hösel c1903.

A seated spaniel, painted in underglaze colours, model No. V158, c1905, 13½in (34.5cm) high.
£5,000-7,000 *DAV*

A sitting silver fox, painted in underglaze colours, model No. V147, 7½in (19cm) high.
£1,000-1,500 *DAV*

A group of Italian greyhounds, painted in underglaze colours, model No. A236, signed on base O. Pilz, 9¾in (24.5cm) high.
£1,800-2,300 *DAV*

First modelled by Otto Pilz in 1909.

A spaniel lying down, painted in underglaze colours, model No. V155, c1905, 7in (18cm) wide.
£1,200-1,800 *DAV*

A bulldog, painted in underglaze colours, model No. V128, c1905, 2½in (6.5cm) high.
£500-800 *DAV*

Martin Brothers

- **Robert Wallace, Walter, Edwin and Charles Martin produced Studio Stoneware between 1873 and 1914.**
- **Factories at Fulham and Southall, London.**
- **Wares marked with signature and place of manufacture.**

A stoneware bird, with removable head, signed on neck and base R.W. Martin & Bros, London & Southall, dated 3-1901, 12¼in (31cm) high.
£5,750-6,250 *P*

A stoneware miniature bird, with removable head, signed on neck R. W. Martin, on base Martin London, and 96, 2½in (5.5cm).
£360-380 *P*

A stoneware bird, signed on neck and near base Martin Bros, London & Southall, 8in (20cm).
£900-950 *P*

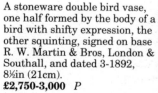

A stoneware miniature bird, with removable head, signed on neck Martin, and on the base Martin & Bros, London and dated 96.
£380-400 *P*

A stoneware double bird vase, one half formed by the body of a bird with shifty expression, the other squinting, signed on base R. W. Martin & Bros, London & Southall, and dated 3-1892, 8½in (21cm).
£2,750-3,000 *P*

Minton

A blue and a crackleglaze tan polar bear, c1920, 5½in (14cm). **£200-225 each** *POW*

A porcelain mastiff, c1835, 5in (12.5cm) wide. **£350-400** *DAN*

CROSS REFERENCE
Ceramic Animals ➞ p81

A Minton toilet jug, bowl and soap dish, manufactured for Mortlock, late 19thC. **£40-50** *GAK*

A Secessionist jug, designed by John Wadsworth and Leon V. Solon, printed factory marks, No.11, dated code for 1902, 14in (35.5cm). **£260-280** *P*

A parian figure of 'Miranda', 15in (38cm) high. **£200-225** *WIL*

Miniature Ceramics

A Royal Crown Derby kettle and vase, Old Derby Witches pattern, the kettle c1911, 3in (7.5cm). **£350-425**
Vase shape No. 465, c1916. **£150-215** *TVA*

Moorcroft

A William Moorcroft salt glazed vase, c1935, 10in (25cm). **£700-750** *NP*

A William Moorcroft Spring Flowers design teapot, c1945, 5in (12.5cm). **£340-380** *NP*

A Moorcroft/MacIntyre Lilac pattern pot, c1902, 3½in (9cm) high. **£350-400** *NP*

- **William Moorcroft worked from 1898 at the MacIntyre & Co factory in Staffordshire.**
- **Examples marked Moorcroft Burslem are post-1913.**
- **Walter Moorcroft continued making pottery in the traditional Moorcroft style with an initialled mark.**
- **Modern wares also have a printed mark 'Moorcroft Made In England'.**

A Moorcroft/MacIntyre Aurelian pattern urn shaped vase, c1898, 7in (17.5cm) high.
£360-390 *NP*

A Moorcroft dish, waving corn design, 8in (20cm) diam.
£440-480 *WIL*

A Moorcroft vase, designed by Sally Tuffin in Bramble design, c1990, 10in (25cm) high.
£225-250 *NP*

A Moorcroft/MacIntyre Alhambra pattern miniature box and cover, c1903, 2¼in (5.5cm) high.
£450-500 *NP*

A Moorcroft Clematis design charger, with a flambé glaze, c1955, 13in (33cm) diam.
£350-400 *NP*

An Anemone pattern vase, 1993, 11in (28cm).
£180-220 *NP*

A Moorcroft Pomegranate pattern bowl, on a Liberty pewter base, c1920, 8in (20cm) diam.   **£350-400** *P*

A selection of Moorcroft powder blue tableware, 1913-1963.
£5-95 each *NP*

Moustache Cups

A German moustache cup and saucer, c1895, cup 3½in (9cm) diam. **£60-70** *TER*

An exceptionally large moustache cup and saucer, cup 5in (12.5cm) diam. **£100-125** *TER*

Musical Jugs

Nanking Cargo

CROSS REFERENCE
Toby Jugs ──────▶p133

The Nanking Cargo sunk in 1752. It was not until the Spring of 1985 that it was discovered and brought to the surface. During April and May of the following year Christies Amsterdam auctioned the contents. There was great concern within the Antiques trade that the market would be flooded, however, prices below demonstrate what a good investment these pieces have proved to be. An illustration of the label that was adhered to genuine pieces by Christies Amsterdam is shown below.

A Batavian blue and white Peony pattern bowl, with brown exterior, c1750, 6½in (16cm) diam. **£250-350** *RBA*

CROSS REFERENCE
Colour Section ──▶ p145

A musical Toby Jug, plays Auld Lang Syne, 9in (23cm) high. **£150-200** *PC*

An Imari pattern tea bowl and saucer, Bamboo and Pine pattern, some pattern has been washed away. **£150-250** *RBA*

An enamelled Imari pattern teapot, c1750, 5½in (14cm) high. **£400-450** *RBA*

A soup tureen and cover, Lattice Fence pattern, interior painted with peony sprays, lot 3501, c1750, 9½in (23.5cm). **£5,500-6,500** *RBA*

A Provincial blue and white dragon plate, c1750, 7¾in (19.5cm) diam. **£100-120** *RBA*

A Provincial blue and white bowl, with flowersprays around an unglazed biscuit interior, c1750. **£100-120** *RBA*

> **FURTHER READING**
> *The Hatcher Porcelain Cargoes,*
> by Colin Sheaf and Richard
> Kilburn, published by Phaidon-
> Christies.

A selection of tea bowls
comprising:
l. Pagoda Riverscape pattern,
2¼in (6cm) diam.
c. A Batavian bowl, with brown
exterior, Bamboo and Peony
pattern inside, 2¾in (7cm) diam.
r. Blue Pine Tree pattern, 2½in
(6.5cm) diam.
£45-95 each *RBA*

Above: A blue, white and Imari
bowl, Scholar on Bridge pattern,
lot No. 2702, 7¼in (18cm) diam.
Below: As above, but the sea
has washed away the scholar
and some of the pattern.
£300-350 each *RBA*

New Hall

Oriental Ceramics

A hand painted lustre vase,
c1928, 8in (20cm) high.
£25-30 *BKK*

An Imari bowl, the centre
decorated with a building and
figures in a mountainous river
landscape, 9⅝in (24.5cm).
£200-225 *GAK*

A Ming blue and white
porcelain dish, 13¾in (35cm)
diam.
£550-575 *HCH*

An Imari charger, panels
decorated in traditional
terracotta and underglazed
blue, late 19thC, 15¼in (39cm).
£225-250 *WIL*

A Chinese porcelain
figure of a dignitary,
seal mark of Ch'ien
Lung, old damage,
19thC, 12½in
(32cm) high.
£680-700 *P(S)*

A Chinese blue and white
porcelain ewer, 12¾in
(33cm) high.
£7,800-8,000 *HCH*

A Chinese famille rose dish,
14¼in (36cm) diam.
£525-575 *WIL*

A Japanese
earthenware vase,
Meiji period, red seal
mark to base,
8in (20cm) high.
£440-460 *WIL*

A pair of Chinese blue and white floor vases, decorated with scrolling dragons and lotus flowers in underglaze blue, neck repaired, early 19thC, 38in (96.5cm) high.
£1,200-1,300 *GIL*

A pair of Chinese Export meat plates, Qianlong period, one damaged, 17⅜in (45cm).
£350-375 *GAK*

A Japanese hand painted bowl, with bright blue background, 1920s, 3in (7.5cm) square.
£8-10 *ROW*

An Arita/Imari vase, decorated in blue, rust and gilt, the lid with brass finial, cracked and damaged, late 18thC, 24in (61cm). **£650-675** *GAK*

Pilkington's

- Pilkington's Tile & Pottery Co. Ltd, of Clifton Junction, Nr Manchester, Lancs, produced earthenwares and lustre and glazed finishes.
- Art Pottery produced from about 1897-1938 and from c1948-57.

A Kinkozan caddy, with inner lid and outer cover, seal and paper marks, 3in (8cm) high.
£1,300-1,400 *GSP*

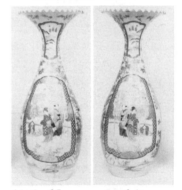

A pair of Japanese porcelain vases, both with damaged rims, 31in (79cm) high. **£380-400** *P(S)*

Parian Ware

A parian ware figure, Cupid Betrayed, 17¼in (44cm) high.
£580-620 *W*

later mark c1948-57

A Pilkington's Royal Lancastrian bowl, by Richard Joyce, decorated with a man on a horse, 11in (28cm) wide. **£500-700** *ASA*

A Pilkington's Royal Lancastrian lustre vase, 10⅝in (27cm) high.
£425-450 *WIL*

Pin Boxes

A selection of pin boxes, 3 to 6in
(7.5 to 15cm) high.
£50-75 each *BRK*

A Victorian porcelain hand
painted trinket pot, with a goat
seated on a fetta cheese, 2¼in
(5.5cm) high.
£40-50 *FMN*

A Poole Pottery vase, pattern
No. 213, 10in (25.5cm) and
water jug, pattern No. 309,
8in (20cm) high.
£175-325 each *GAK*

Poole Pottery

- **Poole Pottery Ltd, was set up
  officially in 1963 after changing its
  name from Carter Stabler & Adams.
  It had been known unoffically as
  Poole Pottery since 1914.**
- **Blue-bird design on vases, bowls
  and jugs became their hallmark.**
- **Certain lines of pottery are rare but
  overall it is presently underrated
  on the antiques market.**

A Poole Studio Pottery brown/
black wall plate, 10½in (26cm)
diam. **£25-35** *OCA*

A Poole Pottery vase, Blue Bird
pattern, c1930, 10in (25cm) high.
£160-170 *BKK*

CROSS REFERENCE
Colour Section ──► p146

Three Poole Studio Pottery
stamped pieces, probably
Morris and Sydenham, c1960.
l. **£140-160**
c. **£340-360**
r. **£130-150** *NCA*

A Poole Studio Pottery vase,
probably Jefferson and
Sydenham, Studio marks.
£430-450 *NCA*

A Poole Pottery presentation
bowl, Festival of Britain 1951,
17in (43.5cm) diam.
£450-480 *P*

*Probably designed by Claude
Smale, this piece would have
been part of the small output of
presentation pieces granted to
the pottery under licence during
festival year, and possibly
unique in representing the town
of Poole itself.*

Pot Lids

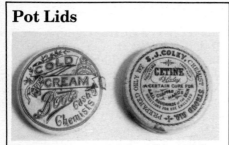

Two monochrome printed pot lids, 19thC.
£5-10 *TRU*

**Pot Lids have been a
regular feature in
previous issues of *Miller's
Collectables Price Guides*,
available from Millers
Publications.**

Prattware

A Prattware two-handled
comport, with green acorn
border, marked, c1860, 12in
(30.5cm).
£100-200 *HEY*

Quimper

A Virgin and child, marked with
painted enamels, c1890, 12½in
(32cm).
£160-180 *VH*

Radford Ware

A hand
painted tree
design
vase, c1935.
£60-75
OCA

Ribbon Plates

A ribbon plate, with transfer
print of The Esplanade,
Sheerness, mauve border and
gilt edge, 8½in (21cm) diam.
£10-15 *OCA*

*The Decoration was enhanced
by threading ribbons through
the pierced border of the plate.*

**For a further selection of
Ribbon Plates, please
refer to *Miller's
Collectables Price Guide,
Volume IV, pp122-123*.**

Royal Dux

A Royal Dux style tinted
bisque porcelain figure,
some damage,
20in (51cm) high.
£150-200 *HCH*

A sweetmeat dish, shaped as
lily leaf, with female attendant,
glazed in green, gold and pink,
8in (20cm).
£225-250 *GAK*

A Royal Dux cockatoo, c1935,
8in (20cm) high.
£20-25 *OCA*

A porcelain figure of
a girl feeding ducks,
14in (35.5cm).
£275-300 *GAK*

A selection of Royal Dux figures:
l. **£450-475**
c. **£270-290**
r. **£400-425** *SUF*

An Art Nouveau figure of a
ram, blue and gilt decorated,
6¾in (17cm) high.
£90-100 *PCh*

Royal Winton

A Royal Winton cup and
sandwich server, Victorian.
£25-35 *AOS*

Shelley

A Brighton armorial trio, dainty
white shape, from 1897.
£35-85 *AJ*

A Wildflower pattern trio, c1950.
£20-35 *AJ*

A miniature cup and saucer,
mid-20thC.
£25-85 *AJ*

A Snowdonia armorial jug,
c1920, 5in (12.5cm)
£20-25 *AJ*

A pair of Blue Dragon
pattern vases,
6¾in (17cm).
£140-150 *TS*

A mould, with
crayfish pattern
and plain
exterior, 1920s.
£35-85 *AJ*

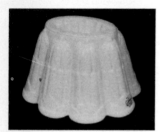

A Lomond shape trio, pattern No. 11614, c1928.
£25-45 *AJ*

A 15-piece coffee set, c1950.
£85-225 *AJ*

A Mode shape 16-piece coffee service, pattern No. 11792, c1931.
£300-350 *BKK*

A Carlton jelly mould, c1922.
£15-65 *AJ*

A Maytime pattern teapot, milk jug and sugar bowl, 1930s.
£65-95 *AJ*

A Queen Anne trio, 1926-1940.
£35-75 *AJ*

A figure of a child golfer, designed by Mabel Lucie Attwell, 6in (15cm).
£350-375 *LT*
This piece is a factory second.

Three Moresque pattern vases, No. 8718, c1930.
£45-95 *AJ*

A painted bone china pixie figure, in blue romper suit with pink wing buds, designed by Mabel Lucie Attwell, printed factory marks, No. LA29, 3in (7.5cm) high.
£300-325 *CSK*

A coffee can and saucer, Yellow Bubbles pattern, c1918.
£25-30 *AJ*

A Mode coffee cup and saucer, Horn of Flowers pattern No. 11774/4, c1932.
£45-65 *AJ*

A Coventry armorial jug, c1920s.
£20-25 *AJ*

CROSS REFERENCE
Crested China ⟶ p102

A trio, Mode shape.
£100-120 *HEW*

A figure of a young girl,
designed by Mabel Lucie
Attwell, damaged, 5¾in (14cm).
£460-480 *LT*

A Vogue trio, Red J pattern No.
11739, 1930-32.
£80-130 *AJ*

A figure of a Chinese
boy with a basket of
flowers, badly
damaged.
£650-675 *LT*

A hand painted nursery tea set,
designed by Mabel Lucie
Attwell, signed, duck teapot
6½in (16cm), mint condition,
c1930.
£1,100-1,200 *BKK*

A figure of a young girl
with a pet dog, designed
by Mabel Lucie Attwell,
poor quality.
£250-270 *LT*

A Mode shape trio, c1930-32.
£80-120 *AJ*

Shorter Ware

Shorter Ware has been a
regular feature in
previous editions of
*Miller's Collectables Price
Guides,* available from
Millers Publications.

A Shorter Ware fish dish, 14½in
(37cm) long.
£20-25 *OCA*

Slipware

A slipware dish, 18thC, 13in (33.5cm) wide.
£450-500 *JAC*

A slipware water carrier, c1800, 14in (36cm) high.
£75-105 *SAD*

Staffordshire Pottery

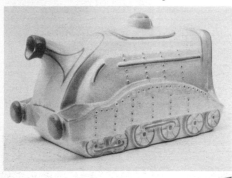

A novelty teapot in the of shape of a locomotive, 9¼in (23cm) wide.
£225-250 *WIL*

A pair of porcelain dessert plates, probably Daniel, hand painted with flowers, cobalt blue and gilt border, both cracked, 8in (20cm) diam.
£70-80 *WIL*

Spode

A shaped dish, decorated with blue and white transfer print, Forest Landscape II, c1800, 7in (17.5cm) square.
£55-60 *OD*

FURTHER READING
Spode's Willow Pattern & Other Designs after the Chinese, by Robert Copeland, published by Studio Vista, Christies, 1979. *Spode,* by Leonard Winter, published by Barrie & Jenkins. *Spode Printed Ware,* David Drakard & Paul Holdway, published by Longman, 1983. *Spode & Copeland Marks,* by Robert Copeland, published by Studio Vista, London, 1993.

CROSS REFERENCE
Colour Section ——▶p150

Animals

A pearlware lion, tail restored, c1800.
£850-1,000 *GA*

A pair of lions, 19thC, 11in (28cm) wide.
£150-165 *ACA*

CROSS REFERENCE
Miniature Ceramics ——▶p114

A pony, c1870, 4¼in (11cm) high.
£120-150 *DAN*

A pair of donkeys, 19thC, 9½in (24cm) high.
£450-500 *ACA*

Two hens on nests, 19thC, 9in (23cm) wide.
£200-225 each *ACA*

CROSS REFERENCE
Ceramic Animals ➤ p81

Dogs

A dalmation with black spots, c1830-35, 3½in (8.5cm) wide.
£250-350 *DAN*

Cow Creamers

A cow creamer, 19thC, 6in (15cm) wide. **£150-175** *ACA*

A Yorkshire cow creamer, 19thC, 7in (18cm) wide.
£200-225 *ACA*

A poodle, 19thC, 3in (7.5cm) wide. **£55-65** *ACA*

A lurcher, 19thC, 5½in (13.5cm) high.
£180-210 *ACA*

A poodle, 19thC, 3½in (8.5cm) high.
£40-50 *ACA*

A pekinese, c1900, 8in (20cm) wide.
£80-95 *ACA*

A pair of red and white dogs, 19thC, 4½in (11cm) high.
£100-120 *ACA*

A pair of black and white dogs, 19thC, 10in (25cm) high.
£160-185 *ACA*

A pair of poodles, c1880, 4in (10cm) high.
£120-140 *JO*

Four red and white dogs, 19thC, largest 10in (25cm) high.
£55-110 each *ACA*

A poodle, the base decorated with gilt, c1840, 3½in (8cm) high. **£100-120** *DAN*

A cupid with a rust and white decorated dog, on a blue base, c1845, 6in (15cm) high.
£230-250 *JO*

A poodle with a top hat, c1830, 5in (12.5cm) high.
£180-200 *JO*

A pair of poodle groups, on blue bases, 5¼in (13cm) high.
£500-520 *JO*

A pair of red and white dogs, with glass eyes, 19thC, 14in (36cm) high.
£180-200 *ACA*

A pair of lustre dogs, with separate front legs, 19thC, 9½in (24cm) high.
£200-225 *ACA*

A dalmation with brown spots, c1830-35, 3¼in (8cm) wide.
£250-350 *DAN*

A dog and child, c1850, 5in (12.5cm) high.
£200-220 *JO*

A greyhound pen holder, 19thC, 5in (12.5cm) wide.
£100-110 *ACA*

A pen holder, with poodles on a blue, green and rust base, 3in (7.5cm) wide.
£100-120 *JO*

A hound and hare, on a blue base, c1830-35, 4in (10cm) wide.
£200-220 *JO*

Figures

Home, a Staffordshire figure, 19thC, 11in (28cm) high.
£80-110 *ACA*

A Staffordshire figure of a boy with the Lamb of God, 19thC, 7½in (19cm) high.
£100-145 *ACA*

A pair of Staffordshire figures of Royal children, seated on recumbent spaniels, c1845, 6½in (16cm) high.
£900-1,000 *RWB*

A clock group modelled with Wellington, mounted in full military uniform, above moulded base with clock face, hairlines and wear, 19thC, and Napoleon, similarly depicted, 20thC, with 2 plaster of Paris moulds from which the model of the Napoleon was drawn, wear and chips, 19th/20thC.
£350-450 *CSK*

A Staffordshire figure
of a girl catching birds,
c1845, 7½in (19cm)
high.
£120-135 *RWB*

A Staffordshire figure
of Shakespeare,
19thC, 8in (20cm)
high.
£100-125 *ACA*

A Staffordshire figure,
c1810, 7½in (19cm)
high.
£150-175 *ACA*

A pair of Staffordshire figures of
Victoria and Albert, 19thC, 6in
(15cm) high.
£200-250 *ACA*

A pair of Staffordshire
equestrian figures of
Generals Havelock
and Campbell,
c1857,
9in (23cm) high.
£450-500 *RWB*

A Staffordshire figure
of a bagpiper, c1820,
9in (23cm) high.
£150-175 *ACA*

A Staffordshire group,
modelled as Mr Harwood
and Miss Rosa Henry in
their roles of Selim and
Zuleika in The Bride of
Abydos, repaired, c1847,
7¾in (19cm) high.
£480-520 *CSK*

Old Age, a Staffordshire
figure, c1810, 7in
(18cm) high.
£150-200 *ACA*

A Staffordshire group,
Queen Victoria with
Prince Albert, c1845,
7in (17.5cm) high.
£230-260 *RWB*

A Staffordshire figure of a huntsman, 19thC, 11in (28cm) high.
£400-450 *ACA*

A Staffordshire figure of Chaucer, with book and scroll, 19thC, 12½in (32cm) high.
£250-270 *PCh*

The Victory, in under and overglaze colours, c1856, 14¼in (36cm) high.
£2,000-2,250 *ANX*

A Staffordshire group of a child being rescued by its mother from an eagle's nest, after a painting by George Dawe, c1855, 16in (41cm) high.
£280-320 *RWB*

Pepper Pots

A Staffordshire pepper pot man, 19thC, 5in (12.5cm) high.
£50-55 *ACA*

A Staffordshire pepper pot man, 19thC, 6in (15cm) high.
£75-85 *ACA*

A Staffordshire pepper pot man, 19thC, 6in (15cm) high.
£75-85 *ACA*

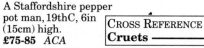

CROSS REFERENCE
Cruets ⟶ p98

A Staffordshire pepper pot policeman, 19thC, 6in (15cm) high.
£100-110 *ACA*

Religious Figures

A Staffordshire figure of St. Mark, Walton, c1820, 7in (17.5cm) high.
£400-500 *JO*

Three Staffordshire figures of Faith, Hope and Charity, by Obadiah Sherratt, in lilac, green and beige, c1830, 7¾ to 9½in (19.5 to 24cm) high.
£2,000-2,200 *JO*

A Staffordshire figure of St. Peter, early 19thC, 9in (23cm) high. **£150-200** *ACA*

A Staffordshire group of Joseph and Mary, 19thC, 9½in (24cm) high.
£100-135 *ACA*

The Widow of Zarpeth and Elijah, c1800, 11in (28cm) high. **£900-1,000** *JO*

A Staffordshire group of Judas paying Pontius Pilate 30 pieces of silver, coloured black, yellow, orange and mauve, 9in (23cm) high.
£150-180 *JO*

A tithe pig group, the woman is mocking the law by offering her baby and pig, c1820, 6½in (16cm) high.
£700-900 *JO*

An Obadiah Sherratt baptism group, with triple oak leaf bocage and may flowers, c1825, 8½in (21.5cm) high.
£4,000-4,500 *LR*

A Staffordshire figure of Christ, c1870, 17in (43cm) high. **£120-140** *JO*

A Staffordshire figure of John Wesley, c1855, 11½in (29cm) high.
£150-170 *JO*

A Staffordshire figure of C.H. Spurgeon, coloured red, blue, green, white and black, 12¼in (31cm) high.
£180-200 *JO*

A Staffordshire figure of John Wesley, c1820, 8½in (21cm) high.
£200-220 *JO*

A Staffordshire group of the Order of Temperance, c1870, 11½in (29cm) high. **£160-185** *TER*

A Staffordshire watch holder in the form of the figure of Moses, wearing a blue coat and pink gown, c1860, 12¼in (31cm) high. **£150-170** *JO*

A Staffordshire figure of St. Matthew, wearing a blue gown, c1820, 8½in (21.5cm) high. **£400-500** *JO*

A Staffordshire group of Protestantism and Popery, c1850, 9½in (24cm) high. **£900-1,100** *JO*

A Staffordshire figure group of Vicar and Moses, 19thC. **£220-240** *WIL*

A Staffordshire figure group of a Holy Water Stoup, Christ and Angels, c1860, 11in (28cm) high. **£110-130** *JO*

A Staffordshire figure of St. John, wearing pink shirt, blue trousers, with green bocage, c1820, 9¼in (23cm) high. **£400-550** *JO*

Watch Holders

A Staffordshire pottery watch holder, formed as a tower with figures, 9½in (24cm) high.
£75-80 *GAK*

A Staffordshire watch holder, on ball feet, coloured brown and yellow, c1825, 8⅓in (21cm) high.
£350-400 *DAN*

A Staffordshire watch holder in the shape of a church, with floral decoration, c1850, 15in (38cm) high.
£350-400 *JO*

Stoneware

A Victorian stoneware teapot and cover, with relief decoration, inscribed in black 'What About a Dish of Tea', 7in (17.5cm).
£25-30 *GAK*

A stoneware Musician and Dancer of Cubist influence, modelled and signed by E.J. Bachelet for Grés Mougin, c1920.
£600-700 *POW*

Sylvac

A Sylvac stylised wall pocket with elves, c1934, 7in (17.5cm) high.   **£30-40** *BKK*

Tea & Coffee Sets

A Rosenthal tea set, by Utmar Alt, from a limited edition of 500, c1965, teapot 6¼in (16cm) high, plate 6¼in (15cm) diam.
£800-1,000 *ABS*

A Rosenthal 10-place tea set, in Bavaria pattern.
£500-600 *ARE*

A coffee set, on plated stand for a Bridge party, by J.H. Middleton & Co, c1920.
£175-200 *TER*

A Clarice Cliff Bizarre Gayday pattern 22-piece sandwich and coffee set, one coffee can damaged. **£520-550** *HCH*

A Clarice Cliff Spring Crocus pattern 15-piece coffee set. **£320-350** *HCH*

A Limoges Haviland 27-piece tea set, with floral decoration and blue and gilt border, early 20thC. **£55-65** *PCh*

Toby Jugs

A Wilkinson Bizarre pattern breakfast service, comprising: teapot, sugar basin, milk jug, 2 tea cups and saucers and a plate. **£520-550** *MAW*

> CROSS REFERENCE
> **Clarice Cliff ———▶ p92**

An A. Neale & Co. Toby jug, complete with measure, in overglaze enamels, turquoise coat, blue hose, brown jug and waistcoat, on pebbled base, restoration to hat, c1800, 10in (25cm) high. **£750-900** *HEY*

A creamware Toby jug, on Georgian base, decorated in translucent glazes, green breeches, blue waistcoat and taupe patterned coat, c1790, 10in (25cm) high. **£650-850** *HEY*

> **MAKE THE MOST OF MILLERS**
> Price ranges in this book reflect what you should expect to *pay* for a similar example. When selling, however, you would expect to receive a lower figure. This will fluctuate according to a dealer's stock and saleability at a particular time, etc. It is always advisable, when selling a collectable, to approach a reputable dealer or an auction house which has specialist sales.

Wade

Wade, Heath & Co. (Ltd), were situated at High Street Works from 1927-38, and from 1938 at Royal Victoria Pottery, Burslem. Their products were marked in a variety of ways, all printed or impressed, and included the word Wade.

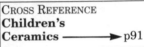

A selection of Wade animal figures.
£1-2.50 each *BAT*

These animals were collected by children from 1950s-70s, some contained in Christmas crackers. Different Series, i.e. Animals (20) and Wildlife (10) are more valuable if in original box, but figures must be perfect.

CROSS REFERENCE
Children's Ceramics ———————➤ p91

CROSS REFERENCE
Children's Ceramics ———————➤ p91

A Wade Heath Walt Disney teapot, 6in (15cm) high.
£275-300 *ARE*

FURTHER READING
The World of Wade Collectible Pottery & Porcelain, Ian Warner and Mike Posgay, 1991

Wall Pockets

Wedgwood

A Wedgwood black basalt tankard, relief, rim with silver mount, Chester 1903.
£185-200 *WIL*

A Wedgwood porcelain figure of a ballet dancer, by Kathleen Goodwin, Portland Vase mark and artist's facsimile signature, 7½in (19cm) high.
£200-220 *P*

A Wedgwood plaque, depicting Study, impressed upper case mark, c1800, 3⅜in (9cm) wide.
£350-375 *CSK*

A wall pocket, shaped as a clown's head, painted black on the reverse Jerome Massier Fils, Vallauris. AM., 10in (25cm) wide. **£225-250** *WW*

A porcelain wall basket, white with coloured violets and leaves and a Minton blue bow, c1880, 7in (17.5cm) high.
£140-160 *SER*

Worcester

A Royal Worcester comport, coloured ivory, green and peach and gilt glazed, impressed Hadley, shape 1232, c1895.
£380-400 *GAK*

A Royal Worcester child figure, Augus, No. 3441, 4⅓in (11cm) high.
£75-80 *AG*

A Flight, Barr & Barr Worcester porcelain night light, badly cracked, base impressed with a crown and FBB, c1830, 6½in (17cm) high.
£600-640 *WIL*

A Grainger's Worcester pierced menu holder, c1880, 4in (10cm) high.
£200-220 *AMH*

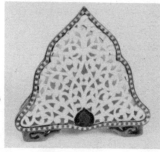

A Worcester ceramic cookie jar, in the form of a loaf of bread, with silver rim, 1900.
£400-500 *DMT*

This jar is available in 3 sizes.

A Chamberlain's Worcester miniature pot, c1820, 2¾in (7cm) high.
£250-275 *AMH*

COMMEMORATIVE WARE
Boer War

A Portobello plate, showing Dr. Jameson of The Jameson Raid, instigator of the Boer War, 9½in (24cm) diam. **£180-200** *OO*

CROSS REFERENCE
Militaria ⟶ p308

A bronze, by Cecil Brown, depicting a colonial soldier from the Boer War, 10½in (26cm) wide.
£1,400-1,500 *OO*

A soap in the shape of Lord Kitchener's bust, 5in (12.5cm) high.
£40-45 *OO*

A silver topped glass jar, 'Gentleman in Kharki', Birmingham 1900, 3½in (9cm) high. **£80-90** *OO*

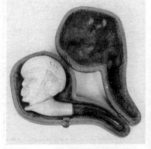

A City of London Imperial Volunteers meerschaum pipe, in case, 4in (10cm) long.
£100-130 *OO*

A jug, commemorating the New Zealand contingent in South Africa, handle modelled as a cannon, 8½in (21cm) high.
£450-500 *OO*

A brass trivot, 'Gentleman in Kharki', to commemorate the Boer War. **£40-50** *OO*

A set of silver spoons, commemorating the Boer War and showing heads of Baden Powell, General White, General Buller, Lord Roberts, Lord Kitchener and General French, marked Chester 1899.
£140-160 *OO*

Political

A two-handled mug, with gilt rim, commemorating Mrs Thatcher becoming Prime Minister, 4in (10cm) high.
£15-20 *BCO*

An R.A.S. China, limited edition commemorative mug, Baroness Thatcher introduction to House of Lords, 1992, 4in (10cm) high. **£10-15** *BCO*

Royalty

A Carlton Ware commemorative mug, to celebrate the engagement and publication of Charles' Charming Challenges on the Pathway to the Throne, by Clive James, illustrated by MARC, and published by Jonathan Cape, 3½in (9cm) high.
£25-30 *FMN*

A Coronet pottery mug, commemorating the Great Fire of Windsor Castle, 3¾in (9.5cm) high.
£15-25 *BCO*

A terracotta plaque of Queen Victoria by F. & R. Pratt & Co, 8½ by 11⅛in (21 by 29cm).
£400-450 *ACA*

An enamelled commemorative beaker of the Coronation of Nicholas II, 1896, 4in (10cm) high.   **£60-75** *TER*

These beakers were given away, which poor people struggled to get in order to sell, however, many people were killed in the crush.

An Edward VIII dish, by J. & G. Meakin 6½in (16cm) wide.
£25-35 *OCA*

A divorce mug, Princess Anne and Mark Phillips, 1992, by Mayfair, 3½in (9cm) high.
£20-25 *BCO*

A coffee tray, commemorating the wedding of H.R.H. Princess Anne and Lieutenant Mark Phillips, 1973, 13in (33cm) wide.   **£3-5** *OCA*

A Bakelite case, containing toothbrush and toothpaste, c1953, 3¼in (8cm) long.
£18-22 *AA*

DOLLS

There has been keen interest during the past few years in celluloid and plastic vinyl dolls. This interest probably originated in America with Barbie and Sindy dolls, G.I. Joe and Action Man. This issue of *Miller's Collectables* concentrates on the year's most sought after dolls.

The condition of celluloid dolls, especially the upper price range Sindy and Action Man dolls, is paramount as is the original box which must reflect the condition of its contents. Keep an eye open for Sindy/Barbie, G.I. Joe/Action Man accessories, they may have been lost or misplaced and will soon command comparatively high prices.

The remainder of the Dolls section has been categorised by the medium of the head. Bisque headed dolls continue to reflect a steady price increase. As predicted in previous editions there now seems little price differential between top quality German manufacturers and the best French makers. Dolls clothes, of course, are still highly sought after.

Look in the Colour Section for further dolls and accessories and refer to *Miller's Antiques Checklist Dolls and Teddy Bears*, for a comprehensive listing of makers and markings.

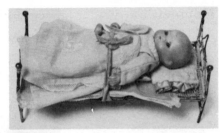

A baby doll, in an iron bed, German, c1915, 8in (10cm). **£120-140** *ChL*

A German bath doll, c1870, 7in (17.5cm). **£60-70** *ChL*

A Queen Mary sailor doll, c1960. **£8-10** *COB*

Charlie McCarthy's ventriloquist dummy, head and hands of carved wood by artist Robert Wallace, glass eyes, movable mouth, hair and monocle, 41in (104cm) high. **£3,800-4,300** *CNY*

l. A papier mâché headed ventriloquist's dummy, modelled as a man with movable mouth, papier mâché hands and legs, eyes need resetting. **£125-150**
r. A similar dummy, dressed in brown check suit, 35in (89cm) high. **£185-200** *CSK*

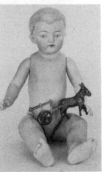

An all-bisque doll, modelled as a boy, with painted blonde hair and features, jointed at shoulders and hips, German, probably by William Goebel, 15in (38cm) high. **£460-480** *CSK*

A jester doll, German, c1870, 9in (23cm). **£350-400** *ChL*

French Bisque Headed Dolls

- Bisque is porcelain at the unglazed stage of manufacture.
- China and porcelain headed dolls are easily recognised as the heads appear shiny.
- Remember heads and bodies can come from different manufacturers.
- Check carefully for damage and repair as this can drastically affect the value.
- Original hair and clothes are important plus points.

A bisque swivel-headed Parisienne, with fixed wrists, jointed wooden body, closed mouth, fixed blue eyes, some overpainting on leg, new hair wig, 18in (46cm).
£2,000-2,250 *CSK*

A pressed bisque headed bébé doll, with closed mouth, blue yeux fibres, pierced ears, brown mohair wig, jointed wood and papier mâché body with fixed wrists, impressed Steiner Fre A 17, 24in (61cm) high.
£3,750-4,000 *CSK*

l. A Schmitt et Fils pressed bisque doll, with closed mouth, fixed brown glass eyes, pierced ears, brown real hair wig and jointed wood and papier mâché body, red firing line down right side of nose, c1880, 15in (41cm) high.
£1,900-2,100 *S*

r. A brown pressed bisque head painted with shellac, probably Jumeau, on Bru body, closed mouth and nostrils fired pink, fixed glass eyes, pierced ears, black mohair and kid wig over cork pate, with kid covered torso and wooden lower limbs, the bisque shoulderplate incised BRU Jne on one shoulder, 5 on the other, in the original skirt, c1880, 16½in (42cm) high.
£5,000-5,250 *S*

A swivel-headed pressed bisque doll, probably by François Gaultier, with closed mouth, fixed blue glass eyes, blonde wig over cork pate and kid body, china forearms, impressed 3 on the head, wearing the original silk dress, 15¾in (40cm) high.
£1,800-2,000 *S*

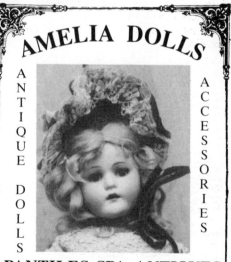

A DEP bisque headed walking doll, French body with German head, open mouth and moulded upper teeth, weighted blue glass flirty eyes, pierced ears, red-brown mohair wig and composition body with jointed arms and keywound walking legs, in original dress, no key, stringing perished, one shoe and sock missing, impressed DEP 19½ and red Geschutz circular stamp, c1900, 22½in (57cm) high. **£625-650** *S*

A Bru Jeune swivel headed shoulder bisque bébé doll, with fixed paperweight eyes, closed mouth, pierced ears, cork pate, replacement real hair wig, kid body with bisque lower arms, shoulderplate incised Bru Jeune No 3, slightly grainy bisque, body worn, one earring missing, c1890, 13½in (34cm) high. **£7,800-8,300** *CSK*

A Radiguet Et Cordonnier swivel head pressed bisque doll, with pale face and slightly smiling closed mouth, fixed spiral glass eyes, finely painted lashes and brows, pierced ears, fair mohair plait over cork pate, the head swivelling on a bisque shoulderplate, on kid body and bisque lower arms, unmarked, 2 discolouration spots below left eye, 1880, 19in (48cm) high. **£30,000-32,000** *S*

Many dolls by this maker had bisque lower legs with a hole in each sole of the foot for the Cordonnier stand. They were ususally incised 'Déposé R.C.' on the shoulderplate.

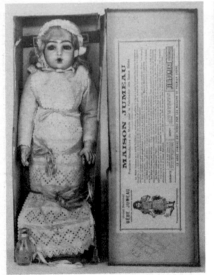

A Tête Jumeau moulded bisque doll, with open mouth and moulded upper teeth, fixed brown glass paperweight eyes, blonde real long hair wig over cork pate and jointed wood and papier mâché body, paint scuffed, with blue stamp on back BÉBÉ JUMEAU Diplôme d'Honneur, stamped in red TÊTE JUMEAU and impressed X 13., 29in (74cm) high. **£1,700-1,900** *S*

A Bébé Teteur, bisque headed doll, with pierced ears, blonde mohair wig, cork pate, jointed wood and papier mâché body with drinking mechanism patented in 1879, dressed in original cotton piqué layette, with drinking bottle, impressed Bru. Jne. 8, in Bébé Jumeau box, c1900. **£3,250-3,500** *CSK*

An early swivel china headed baby doll, with flange neck joint, painted features, skin wig, kid body with china arms, in original whitework gown and underwear, marked on body with Mme Rohmer Breveté SGDG Paris stamp, seam split, c1860, 21in (53cm) high. **£2,700-2,900** *CSK*

German Bisque Headed Dolls

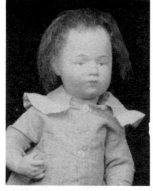

A Simon & Halbig 'Santa' bisque head doll, with weighted blue glass eyes, well painted open mouth with upper teeth, pierced ears, incised S & H 1249 Dep Santa 14 1/2, c1914, 33in (84cm) high.
£950-1,050 *S(NY)*

A bisque headed character doll, glazed inside head, with closed mouth, pale blue painted eyes, pierced ears, composition baby body and boys clothes, by Cuno & Otto Dressel, indecipherable impression, head has been sprayed to cover imperfections in the bisque, 11in (28cm) high.
£1,100-1,200 *CSK*

A J.D. Kestner bisque Oriental doll, impressed F.10.243, with open mouth and 2 upper teeth, fixed brown glass eyes, black mohair wig and curved limb composition body, wearing original silk kimono and hat, hairline crack at side of left eye to ear, c1914, 13in (33cm) high.
£1,250-1,350 *S*

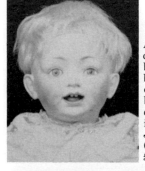

A bisque headed character doll, with blue sleeping eyes, blonde mohair wig over plaster pate, bent-limbed composition body, impressed M 16 J.D.K.226, 20in (51cm) high.
£1,100-1,200 *CSK*

A bisque head 'bride' doll, flaxen wig, sleeping glass eyes, open mouth, jointed composition limbs, impressed K H Walkuro, Germany, original clothing, 24in (61cm) high, in a wicker cradle.
£300-330 *WL*

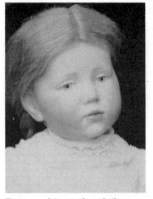

A Kämmer and Reinhardt/ Simon and Halbig bisque doll, with open mouth and upper teeth, weighted blue glass eyes, auburn mohair wig and jointed wood and composition body, impressed 19, in original dress, c1895, 7½in (19cm) high, together with a slatted black trunk containing clothes and accessories, 8¾in (22cm) wide.
£625-650 *S*

A bisque headed child doll, with brown sleeping eyes, moulded brows, pierced ears, fair curly mohair wig, jointed wood and composition body and original Highland outfit, impressed Simon & Halbig, K * R 66, 25in (64cm) high.
£825-850 *CSK*

Peggy, a bisque headed character doll, with closed mouth, painted blue eyes, blonde mohair wig, jointed wood and composition toddler body, contemporary dress, impressed K * R 101 46, Marie, 17in (43cm) high.
£4,000-4,250 *CSK*

FURTHER READING
Delightful Dolls, Thelma Bateman, Washington 1966
The American Doll Artist, Helen Bullard, Boston 1965
Dolls: Makers and Marks, Elizabeth A. Coleman, Washington 1963
The Collector's Encyclopedia of Dolls, Dorothy S., Elizabeth A. and Evelyn J. Coleman, New York 1968
Dolls, Lady Antonia Fraser, London 1963
Wonderful Dolls of Wax, Jo Elizabeth Gerken, Lincoln (Nebraska) 1964
Directories of British, French and German Dolls, Luella Hart, Oaklands (Calif) 1964-65
Dolls and Dollmakers, Mary Hillier, London 1968
Dressing Dolls, A Johnson, London 1969
Dolls & Dolls Houses, Constance King, London 1977
Dolls, J. Noble, London 1968
Dolls of the World, G. White, London 1962
European and American Dolls, G. White, London 1966
Miller's Antiques Checklist, Dolls and Teddy Bears, Mitchell Beazley International Ltd., 1992

A Kämmer and Reinhardt/ Simon and Halbig bisque character doll, with open mouth and upper teeth, weighted flirty brown glass eyes, blonde wig and 5-piece chunky composition body, one glass eye broken, impressed 117 x 34, c1911, 11¾in (30cm) high.
£500-550 *S*

A Kämmer and Reinhardt/ Simon Halbig bisque character doll, with closed mouth, weighted blue glass eyes, fair mohair wig and ball jointed wood and composition body, slight flaking on face, missing toes on one foot, impressed K * R 117/A Simon & Halbig 46, c1911, 18in (46cm) high.
£1,150-1,350 *S*

A Hertel, Schwab for Kley and Hahn bisque character boy doll, with open mouth, trembling tongue and 2 upper teeth, weighted blue glass eyes, brush-stroked moulded hair and 5-piece composition body, unclothed, impressed 154 6, c1912, 14in (36cm) high.
£900-1,000 *S*

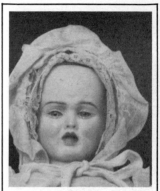

A J.D. Kestner bisque doll, with open/closed mouth with white between the lips, fixed dark brown eyes, pierced ears, the flattened domed head with blonde curly mohair wig and jointed wood and composition body, very slight damage, impressed 137 17, 1889, 28in (71cm) high.
£1,800-1,900 *S*

A bisque turned shoulder headed doll, with closed mouth, blue sleeping eyes, feathered brows, fair mohair wig with plaster pate, stuffed body with kid arms, dressed, probably by Kestner, 18½in (47cm) high.
£2,250-2,500 *CSK*

A three-faced bisque headed doll, probably by Carl Bergner, with smiling, sleeping and crying faces turning in a cardboard cowl by means of a brass ring on the crown, cloth covered torso with pull string Mama-Papa voice box, jointed wood and composition arms and lower legs, in original dress and bonnet, pull strings missing, c1895, 13½in (34cm) high.
£2,500-2,700 *S*

A Kling and Company shoulder bisque doll, with open mouth and upper teeth, weighted brown glass eyes, fair mohair wig and cloth body with bisque lower limbs, in original dress, 2 fingers missing, impressed 124 8 with K in a bell, c1880, 19¾in (50cm high. **£450-475** *S*

An Armand Marseille bisque character doll, with closed mouth, weighted blue glass eyes, blonde mohair wig and curved limb composition body, impressed 550 A.O.M., in knitted suit, c1926, 9in (23cm) high.
£1,500-1,600 *S*

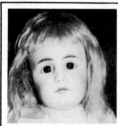

Celluloid, Plastic & Vinyl Dolls

Amanda Jane

Two Amanda Jane black baby dolls.
£8-10 each   *EGR*
These dolls are still produced.

Two Amanda Jane baby and girl dolls, wearing Liberty print clothes, c1980, 6 and 7in (15 and 17.5cm) high.
£30-35 each   *EGR*
These dolls are difficult to find.

Two Amanda Jane black girl dolls, 1970s, 7in (17.5cm) high.
£10-15 each   *EGR*
These dolls are now hard to find.

Two Amanda Jane dolls, with vinyl heads and sleeping eyes, late 1960s, 7½in (19cm) high, with wardrobe of clothes.
£10-15 each   *EGR*

Two 'Miss' Amanda Jane dolls, with painted eyes, c1979, 7½in (19cm) high, with separate wardrobe of clothes.
£20-25 each   *EGR*

Airfix Dolls

- 1939-late 1980s - Airfix Industries produced rubber toys, plastic rattles, small dolls, kits and novelty toys.
- 1950s - Fairies were made.
- 1970s - Vinyl market flourished.
- 1962 - Airfix took over Semco.
- 1967 - Doll division closed.

An Airfix Farrah doll, mid- 1970s, 13in (33cm) high.
£10-12   *EGR*

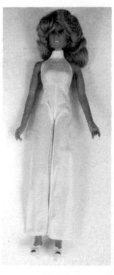

A group of Airfix hard plastic fairy dolls, with painted eyes and swinging arms, 1950s, 4½in (11cm) high.
£5-6 each   *EGR*

A Nanking Cargo blue and white plate, Peony and Pomegranate pattern, c1750, 9in (23cm) diam.
£300-380 *RBA*

A Nanking Cargo tea bowl and saucer, Pagoda Riverscape pattern, c1750, saucer 4⅜in (11.5cm) diam.
£200-250 *RBA*

A Nanking Cargo provincial blue and white plate, covered in barnacles, 7½in (19cm) diam.
£100-120 *RBA*

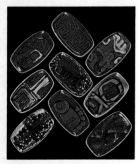

A selection of Poole Studio Pottery bonbon dishes, shape No. 361, c1960, 7in (17.5cm) long.
£20-75 each *NCA*

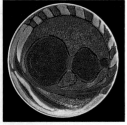

A Poole Studio Pottery plate, studio stamp, c1960, 8in (20cm) diam.
£280-300 *NCA*

Three Poole Studio Pottery Atlantis pots:
l. **£180-200**
c. **£100-120**
r. **£90-100** *NCA*

Three Poole Studio Pottery footed bowls, c1960, 7 to 10½in (18 to 26cm) diam.
£180-200 each *NCA*

A Poole Studio Pottery Atlantis pot, with cadmium glaze, by Guy Sydenham, c1960.
£280-300 *NCA*

A selection of Poole Studio Pottery plates, by unknown artists, marked Studio, 8in (20cm) diam.
£180-200 each *NCA*

A Poole Studio Pottery plate, by Carolyn Wills, marked Aegean, 14in (36cm) diam.
£180-200 *NCA*

A Poole Studio Pottery plate, shape No.3, artist unknown, 8in (20cm) diam.
£180-200 *NCA*

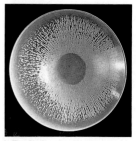

A Poole Studio Pottery bowl, probably by Jefferson & Elsden, c1960.
£180-200 *NCA*

A Poole Studio Pottery plate, c1960, 10in (25.5cm) diam.
£280-300 *NCA*

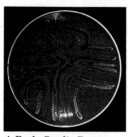

A Poole Studio Pottery plate, c1960, 14in (36cm) diam.
£225-250 *NCA*

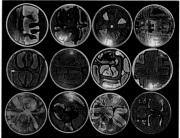

A selection of Poole Studio Pottery dishes, shape No. 49, 2 with Harrod's labels, c1960, 5in (12.5cm) diam.
£20-60 each *NCA*

A Shelley ginger jar, with cover, c1918, 7in (18cm) high.
£160-200 *AJ*

A pair of Shelley and Foley wall plaques, c1912-14, 12in (30.5cm) diam.
These were made at the time the Company name was changed.

A Shelley lustre bowl, unsigned, c1918-21, 12¼in (31cm) diam.
£350-450 *AJ*

A Ridgway hand painted comport, c1845-51, 10in (25cm) diam.
£550-600 *AMH*

A Shelley vase, Moresque pattern No. 8718, c1930.
£50-60 *AJ*

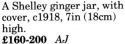

A Shelley Moonlight Series cachepot, c1918, 6in (15cm) high.
£130-150 *AJ*

A pair of Ruskin lamp stands, low fired, marked, 8in (20cm) high.
£60-75 *OCA*

A Shelley lustre clock, c1918-21, 9in (23cm) high.
£250-300 *AJ*

l. A Ridgway hand painted sucrier, c1840, 7in (18cm) diam.
£250-300 *AMH*

A Shelley lustre vase, White Fish Series, unsigned, c1918-21, 10in (25cm).
£175-225 *AJ*

A Spode Imari pattern tea cup and saucer, Etruscan shape, No. 2214, c1825, saucer 5½in (14cm) diam.
£100-125 *CA*

A pair of Prattware blue and white chambersticks, c1850, 5in (12.5cm) high.
£150-180 *CAI*

A Spode sauce tureen, from a 15-piece dessert service, c1830, 6in (15cm) high.
£1,200-1,500 *CAI*

A Spode dessert dish, printed in blue, overpainted in red and gilded, restored, impressed mark, c1820, 11¼in (28.5cm) wide.
£50-65 *CA*

A Spode inkwell, early mark, c1810, 2½in (7cm) diam.
£140-150 *CA*

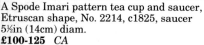

A Spode stoneware plate, marked 48, c1814-33, 9⅝in (24.5cm) diam.
£40-50 *CA*

Part of the Spode 15-piece dessert service, c1830, *featured above far left.*

A William Ridgway blue and white baby's feeding bottle, Humphrey's Clock series, Little Nell by the River, c1835-40, 7in (18cm) long.
£250-300 *CA*

A blue and white saucer, transfer printed with sheep, unmarked, c1815-20, 4¾in (12cm) diam.
£35-45 *CA*

Three blue and white advertisement saucers, makers unknown, 2¼in to 4¼in (6 to 11cm) diam.
£15-25 each *CA*

A Spode plate, Indian Sporting Series, Death of the Bear pattern, heavily restored, c1810.
£30-40 *CA*

A Spode Camilla pattern saucer, marked Printed in England, made in pottery and porcelain from 1891.
£20-25 *CA*

A blue and white transfer ware plate, The Drama, by John Rogers & Son, c1820.
£110-140 *CA*

A blue and white transfer pattern plate, The Hop Pickers, c1820-30, 10in (25cm) diam.
£175-180 *CA*

A Spode saucer/dish, unmarked, 7½in (19cm) diam.
£50-60 *CA*

l. A blue and white tea strainer, unattributed, c1800, 3½in (9cm) diam.
£75-95 *CA*

A Spode stone china coffee can, c1815-20, 2½in (6cm).
£65-85 *CA*

A Spode blue and white transfer ware coffee pot, Two Figures pattern, c1790, 10½in (26cm) high.
£150-175 *CA*

A Chetham & Robinson transfer ware 'Victoria' jug, 6¾in (17cm) high.
£175-200 *CA*

l. A Spode dish, Boy on the Buffalo pattern, c1820, 11in (28cm) wide.
£80-100 *CA*

A blue and white transfer pattern dish, Grazing Rabbits pattern, unattributed, c1820, 8¾in (22cm) wide.
£125-150 *CA*

A pair of Staffordshire figures of a boy and a girl, decorated in the style of Lloyd Shelton, 7in (17.5cm) high.
£300-400 *ANX*

A Staffordshire figure, First Ride, c1850-60, 12½in (32cm) high.
£300-350 *ANX*

A Staffordshire figure of David Garrick as Richard III, c1850.
£250-275 *TER*

A pair of Staffordshire figures of the Prince of Wales and Prince Alfred, c1858, 10½in (26cm) high.
£600-650 *ANX*

A Staffordshire figure of Band of Hope, c1847, 10in (25.5cm) high.
£250-300 *ANX*

A Staffordshire figure group of Royal children and Guardian Angel, c1844, 8½in (21cm).
£165-175 *ANX*

A Staffordshire equestrian figure of Victoria, c1840, 10in (25cm) high.
£300-350 *ANX*

A Staffordshire boat with horse's head, Astley piece from water pageant, 10½in (26cm).
£200-250 *ANX*

A Staffordshire figure group, France, England and Turkey, c1854, 11¼in (29cm) high.
£350-400 *ANX*

A set of 7 Scottish pottery carpet bowls, late
19thC, 2¼ to 3½in (6 to 9cm) diam.
£220-280 *DAN*

A Staffordshire
figure of an organ
grinder, 12in (32cm).
£175-225 *ANX*

A Staffordshire group of
Abraham and Isaac,
c1810, 11½in (29cm) high.
£1,000-1,200 *JO*

A miniature hand
painted ewer, c1830,
4in (10cm) high.
£150-180 *AMH*

A Spode blue and
white double egg
hoop, c1820, 1½in
(4cm) high.
£20-25 *CA*

A Victorian pastille
burner, in the form of a
cottage, 6in (15cm) high.
£150-175 *OCA*

A Victorian
Staffordshire cat,
c1850, 5½in (14cm).
£550-650 *DAN*

A Victorian transfer and hand
coloured tile, English, unmarked,
6in (16cm) square.
£10-12 *TER*

A Spode small pot,
Jumping Boy pattern,
c1820, 3½in (9cm) diam.
£40-50 *CA*

A Dixon & Co pink lustre
Masonic jug, with transfer of
The Agamemnon in a Storm,
c1840, 6½in (16.5cm) high.
£200-250 *IS*

A Coalbrookdale style floral
encrusted pot pourri vase,
c1830, 10¾in (27cm).
£1,150-1,250 *AMH*

A pair of Austrian amphora vases, with enamelled decoration, applied gilded handles, impressed mark, 12in (31cm) high.
£220-240 *ELR*

A Flight & Barr Worcester egg cup, c1815, 2¼in (6cm) high.
£150-180 *AMH*

A Royal Worcester cream jug and sugar basin.
£100-110 *HCH*

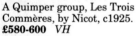

A Quimper group, Les Trois Commères, by Nicot, c1925.
£580-600 *VH*

A Royal Worcester muffin dish and lid, pattern No. 2010, c1870, 8¼in (21cm) diam.
£115-125 *PCh*

A pair of Wedgwood vases, printed and impressed mark, 19thC, 14⅝in (37cm) high.
£650-680 *ELR*

A set of 6 German hand painted Fairytale plates, c1970, 8in (20.5cm) wide.
£80-100 *BIB*

A French figure of a lady, 11⅝in (29.5cm) high.
£450-500 *BIB*

A Royal Worcester figure, The Bridesmaid, by F. G. Doughty, date code for 1949.
£190-210 *AAV*

A Worcester bamboo style vase, 19thC, 8¼in (21cm) wide.
£100-120 *PCh*

Blue Bell Dolls

A Blue Bell black doll, c1970, 21in (53cm) high.
£30-35 *EGR*

A Blue Bell talking doll, 20in (51cm) high.
£20-30 *EGR*

Fewer black dolls were made, therefore they are more difficult to find now.

A Blue Bell 'Miss Heartbeat' doll, 20½in (52cm) high.
£25-30 *EGR*

The heart beats when the button in the tummy is depressed.

Blossom

A Blossom Toys 'My Play Friend' vinyl doll, child size, c1976, 32in (81cm) high.
£30-35 *EGR*

This doll would have cost £10 when new.

A Blossom Toys vinyl walking/talking doll, c1975, 25in (63.5cm) high.
£18-20 *EGR*

A Blue Bell vinyl doll, c1970, 21in (53cm) high.
£25-30 *EGR*

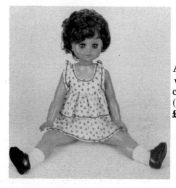

A Blossom Toys vinyl doll, c1975, 25in (63.5cm) high.
£10-15 *EGR*

BND

A BND baby composition doll, with painted eyes and moulded hair, c1938, 12½in (32cm) high.
£30-35 *EGR*

A BND doll, with vinyl head and hard plastic body, c1958, 13in (33cm) high.
£30-35 *EGR*

This was one of the last dolls made by BND.

A BND baby doll, hard plastic, c1952, 9in (23cm) high.
£20-25 *EGR*

These dolls were sold in Marks & Spencers.

CROSS REFERENCE
Colour Section ⟶ p222

Burbank

A Burbank Victorian Series doll, with vinyl head and hands, stuffed body, c1976, 23in (59cm) high.
£20-25 *EGR*

The Victorian Series comprised: Alexandra Rose - Brunette. Victoria Rose - Platinum blonde. Charlotte Rose - Chestnut. Margaret Rose - Blonde. All these dolls had different outfits.

Chilton

A Chilton vinyl baby boy doll, 1960s, 13in (33cm) high.
£10-12 *EGR*

A Chilton 'Babykins' vinyl doll, with baby hair, can suck its thumb, 21in (53cm) high.
£25-30 *EGR*

A Burbank vinyl girl doll, c1975, 16in ((41cm) high.
£10-15 *EGR*

A Chilton vinyl doll, as illustrated in Woman's Weekly throughout the 1960s, 16in (41cm) high.
£10-15 *EGR*

Two Chilton hard plastic dolls, c1950, 7½in (19cm) high.
£10-12 each *EGR*

Hundreds of these dolls were made between early 50s and late 60s and very few have survived intact. They were illustrated in Woman's Weekly with knitting patterns for their clothes.

Crolly

A Crolly doll, dressed in Irish Arran pullover and Donegal Tweed skirt, c1970, 24in (61cm) high.
£20-30 *EGR*

This company made costume dolls such as small Irish Leprechauns, dancers and girls from Connemara.

Faerie Glen

Two Faerie Glen vinyl teenage dolls:
l. Tina, 11in (28cm) high. **£3-5**
r. Gigi, in box, c1970, 12in (30.5cm) high.
£6-8 *EGR*

These dolls were available with various hair shades. Similar to Sindy but not so sought after.

Denys Fisher

Denys Fisher Big Baby and Little Sweet April vinyl dolls.
Large. **£10-12**
Small. **£8-10** *EGR*

Separate outfits were available for both sizes.

A Faerie Glen vinyl teenage doll, with underwear, jewellery and heeled sandals.
£5-15 *EGR*

A Denys Fisher 'Dusty The Golf Champion' vinyl doll, from the Sporting Series, with painted eyes, c1975, 12in (31cm) high.
£18-20 *EGR*

Tonie and Sally, Faerie Glen hard plastic twin dolls, 7in (17.5cm) high.
£25-30 each *EGR*

Faerie Glen started in 1960s making dolls clothes, then made Tonie with long hair and Sally with short hair, outfits could be purchased separately, dolls were unmarked.

Frido

A Frido doll, c1960, 15in (38cm) high.
£10-15 *EGR*

Frido/Trendon/Sasha 1960-80. This company produced rubber balls before making vinyl dolls.

Kleeware

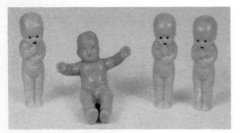

A vinyl rubber doll, c1960, 4in
(10cm) high, hard plastic
'thumbsuck' dolls, c1950, 3in
(8cm) high.
£2-3 each *EGR*

*Kleeware made plastic novelties,
small toys and rattles, also
plastic dolls house furniture.*

A 'Bubble Cut' Barbie, wearing
'Fraternity Dance' dress, c1962,
11in (28cm) high.
£80-100 *EGR*

Mattel

- **Barbie dolls produced c1959-present day.**
- **The first 5 dolls issued were pony tail dolls, numbered 1-5.**
- **A mint condition pony tail doll could fetch in excess of £200.**

Tammy and her sister, Pepper,
c1962-3, 9in (23cm) high, with
original box.
£18-20 *EGR*

*These dolls were made by Ideal
in the U.S.A. Sindy was based
on Tammy.*

Barbie, with silky sheen pony
tail, 'Red Flare', wearing red
velvet coat, hat, bag and gloves,
c1964, 11in (28cm) high.
£80-100 *EGR*

Barbie, a pony tail doll, No. 5,
wearing a sheath dress, with
gold buttons, c1962. **£80-100**
A Midge doll, wearing 'After
Five' outfit, c1963.
£50-80 *EGR*

A Living Barbie, wearing
culottes outfit, named
'Firelights', c1971, 11in
(28cm) high.
£50-60 *EGR*

*All Barbie's outfits had
names.*

Skipper, Barbie's little
sister, wearing a tutu,
c1964, 9in (23cm)
high.
£30-50 *EGR*

Ken, Barbie's boyfriend, wearing 'Campus Corduroys', c1964.
£80-100 *EGR*

A Fashion Queen Barbie, wearing 'Suburban Shopper' dress, c1963, 11in (28cm) high.
£80-100 *EGR*

Model Toys

A Daisy Long Legs model toy doll, in original box, c1973-80, 15in (38cm) high. **£15-20** Amy. **£10-12** *EGR*
Free outfits for Daisy or a free friend, Amy, were available by collecting the 'flower' from the boxes. Very difficult to find Amy because she was not for sale but a gift with 'flowers'.

Morris Mitchell

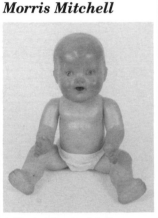

A Marie-Mia vinyl doll, c1945, 11in (28cm) high.
£30-35 *EGR*
Also available in the series were: Marie-José, 9in (23cm) high, Marie-Valerie, 13in (33cm) high, Marie-Lou, 15in (38cm) and Marie-Ann, 24in (61cm) high.

Nisbet

A Happy Dolls Welsh girl, 8in (20cm) high.
£10-15 *EGR*
This series also included Scottish, Irish and English schoolgirl dolls.

Two ballerinas, wood, hard plastic and composition, c1968.
£20-25 each *EGR*
Peggy Nisbet made a figure of The Queen in Coronation Robes in 1953.

Palitoy

An Action Man Red Devil doll, c1978, 12in (30.5cm) high.
£50-100 *EGR*

Outfit only £25-50.

A Palitoy hard plastic doll, with sleeping eyes, c1950, 7½in (19cm) high.
£8-10 *EGR*

Also produced as fairies and costume dolls.

A 'Treasure Babe' baby doll, drink-and-wet, with sleeping eyes, c1958, 16in (40.5cm) high, in original box.
£50-60 *EGR*

A 'Patsy' drink-and-wet rubbery vinyl doll, with fixed glass eyes, c1940, 15in (38cm) high.
£35-40 *EGR*

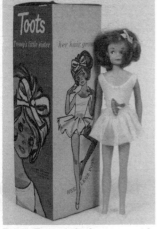

Toots, Tressy's little sister, with key for 'growing' hair, c1965, 9in (23cm) high, in original box.
£10-15 *EGR*

A 'Tippy Tumbles' battery-operated mechanical doll, does somersaults, c1969, 16in (41cm) high. **£30-35** *EGR*

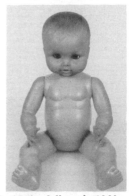

A naked baby doll, early 1960s, 21in (53cm) high.
£30-40 *EGR*

This size made for just one year, others 12in (30.5cm) high.

A Tiny Tears doll, in mint condition, wearing original romper suit and bib, with dummy, c1965, 15in (38cm) high.
£20-30 *EGR*

A Palitoy Action Man sailor, c1967, 12in (30.5cm) high.
£80-100 *EGR*

With original box this doll would be worth £100-150.

CROSS REFERENCE
Colour Section ⟶ p220

A Palitoy vinyl 'Superstar' series doll, late 1970s.
£25-30 *EGR*

A Tressy doll, c1979, in original box.
£10-15 *EGR*

An Action Man Bullet Man, c1976, 12in (30.5cm) high, the face on this doll is different to previous models.
£80-100 *EGR*

A Palitoy Action Girl doll, arm on ratchet so she dances and kicks, c1978, 12in (30.5cm) high, in original box.
£30-50 *EGR*

A Palitoy composition doll, with painted features, wearing a knitted outfit, c1926, 17in (43cm) high.
£35-40 *EGR*

Palitoy/Cascelloid, 1918-1984, made household items, novelties, celluloid novelties.
They were also the early pioneers of vinyl and composition in 1920s.

A Tressy doll, wearing original gold lamé dress, c1970, 12in (30.5cm) high.
£10-15 *EGR*

These dolls were available with a range of outfits and 3 different hair colours.

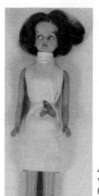

A Palitoy Action pilot, c1967, 12in (30.5cm) high.
£80-100 *EGR*

With original box this doll would be worth £100-150.

A Tressy teen doll, with key to wind out long hair, c1964, 12in (30.5cm) high.
£15-20 *EGR*

Outfits for this doll were available in pale pink, turquoise and lemon. Haircare sets could also be purchased separately.

A teenage doll, complete with earrings, c1961, 23in (58.5cm) high.
£20-23 *EGR*

A Palitoy girl doll, c1965.
£10-15 *EGR*

Series included: Angela, Sarah, Heidi, Fiona, Lucy and Wendy all with different hair styles and dresses, 16 and 18in high.

Pedigree

Two Pedigree black dolls, girl and baby, c1951, 14 and 16in (36 and 41cm) high.
£80-100 each
EGR

Rogark

Three Rogark National Costume dolls, c1955, 6in (15cm) high
£2-3 each *EGR*

These dolls were made in Wales.

A Rogark Irish girl doll, c1950-60, 6in (15cm) high.
£2-3 *EGR*

A Pedigree 'Delite' doll, naked and unmarked, c1947, 6in (15cm) high, with box.
£25-30 *EGR*

Without the original box these dolls are very difficult to identify.

A Pedigree 'Delite' doll, naked, with sleeping eyes, and straight legs, c1950, 6in (15cm) high.
£25-30 EGR

A Pedigree 'Delite' doll, with clothes, c1950, 6in (15cm) high.
£25-30 EGR

A Pedigree composition doll, c1938, 17in (43cm) high.
£50-60 EGR

Pedigree produced dolls from 1921-86. The composition dolls were made from wood shavings left over from wooden toy production.

A Pedigree family of dolls, parents walking and talking, baby just says 'Mama', c1950-53, 17in (43cm) high. **£80-100 EGR**

A Pedigree doll, 'Elizabeth', c1953, 19in (48.5cm) high, with patterns to make Hartnell type dresses. **£80-90 EGR**

A Pedigree doll, 'Baby Posy', c1965, 18in (46cm) high.
£18-20 EGR

Produced in blonde and brunette versions.

A Pedigree vinyl baby doll, c1963, 23in (59cm) high, wearing hand knitted outfit.
£25-30 EGR

A Pedigree black doll, produced from white doll mould, c1953.
£80-90 EGR

A Pedigree black doll,
c1960, 13in (33cm) high.
£18-25 *EGR*

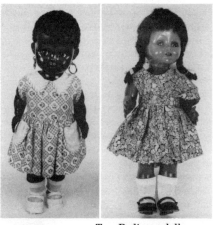

Two Pedigree dolls:
l. An African doll.
r. An Asian doll, c1958,
16in (41cm) high.
£60-80 *EGR*

A Pedigree Sindy doll,
wearing 'Skating Girl' outfit,
c1968, 12in (30.5cm) high.
£15-20 *EGR*

A Pedigree Tommy
Gunn, c1966, 11in
(28cm) high.
£80-100 *EGR*

*This doll was Pedigree
version of Action Man,
produced for just
2 years.*

A Pedigree 'Bonnie Charlie',
c1955, 14in (36cm) high.
£40-50 *EGR*

FURTHER READING
*Action Man The Gold Medal
Doll For Boys,* by New
Cavendish Books, 1993

A Pedigree 'Beauty Skin' doll,
disintegrated limbs, c1950,
13½in (34cm) high.
£30-35 *EGR*

A Pedigree doll, 'Little Miss
Vogue', with twist waist.
£18-25 *EGR*

*This doll preceded Sindy. Sets
of clothes available to purchase
separately.*

A Patch doll, Sindy's little
sister, wearing original
'Dungarees' outfit, c1965, 9in
(23cm) high.
£12-15 *EGR*

A Pedigree Paul doll, with
rooted hair and wearing
original 'Casuals' outfit, c1967,
12in (30.5cm) high.
£20-25 *EGR*

*These dolls with rooted hair
were produced for just one year.*

A Pedigree Sindy doll,
wearing 'Emergency
Ward' nurses
uniform, 1965.
£15-20 *EGR*

A Patch doll, wearing
'Schooldays' outfit,
c1970, 9in (23cm) high.
£12-15 *EGR*

A Pedigree doll, 'First Love',
with twist waist, c1965, 17in
(43cm) high. **£18-20** *EGR*

*This doll was the Pedigree
version of 'Tiny Tears'.*

A Pedigree teenage vinyl
doll, c1960-63.
£20-25 *EGR*

A Poppet doll, Patch's friend,
wearing original tartan outfit,
9in (23cm) high.
£25-30 *EGR*

A Pedigree Sindy doll, wearing
original 'Weekenders' outfit,
c1965, 12in (30.5cm) high.
£12-15 *EGR*

A Pedigree doll, 'The Pin Up',
c1953, 19in (48cm) high.
£80-90 *EGR*

A Pedigree Sindy doll, wearing
original 'Weekenders' outfit,
1963, 12in (30.5cm) high.
£15-20 *EGR*

A Pedigree jointed
doll, 'Pretty Peepers',
in mint condition,
c1958, 22in (56cm)
high.
£80-100 *EGR*

*With a box this doll
would be worth £200.*

A Betsy doll, Patch's American
friend, wearing original clothes,
6in (15cm) high.
£25-30 *EGR*

Very rare.

A Pedigree Paul doll, from the
Sindy set, with moulded head,
wearing original 'Casuals'
outfit, c1965, 12in (30.5cm)
.high. **£15-20** *EGR*

Rosebud

A Rosebud hard plastic doll, c1950, 11in (28cm) high, in box. **£30-40** *EGR*

Hard plastic Rosebud dolls were made in heights of 11, 13, 15 and 17in.

A selection of Rosebud twin dolls, 1960s, 6in (15cm) high. Black doll. **£20-25** Others. **£8-10** *EGR*

Knitting patterns for outfits for Rosebud dolls appeared in Woman's Weekly.

Three Miss Rosebud hard plastic dolls, c1953, 7½in (19cm) high. **£20-25 each** *EGR*

A Rosebud hard plastic black doll, c1950, 11in (28cm) high. **£25-30** *EGR*

Also produced in flesh colour and with jointed knees.

A Rosebud hard plastic black baby doll, c1950, 13½in (34cm) high. **£25-30** *EGR*

Also produced in flesh colour.

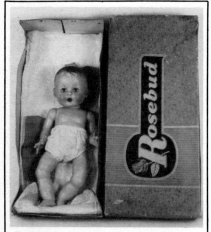

A Rosebud hard plastic baby doll, wearing a nappy, c1955, 16in (41cm) high, in original box. **£50-60** *EGR*

A Rosebud composition doll, c1947. **£60-80** *PC*

A 'Miss Rosebud' vinyl teenage doll, c1962, 14in (36cm) high. **£10-15** *EGR*

A selection of Rosebud baby
dolls, c1955, 6in (15cm) high.
With wigs. **£15-20 each**
With moulded hair.
£8-10 each *EGR*

Rosebud vinyl twins, c1960,
11in (28cm) high.
£10-15 each *EGR*

A Rosebud vinyl
doll, c1961,
27in (69cm) high.
£40-50 *EGR*

*This doll was too
large and heavy
to be popular
with young
children.*

A Rosebud hard plastic doll,
with jointed knees, c1955, 16½in
(42cm) high.
£50-60 *EGR*

Also produced in black.

A Rosebud hard plastic doll,
c1950, 13in (33cm) high.
£25-30 *EGR*

Also produced in black.

Roddy

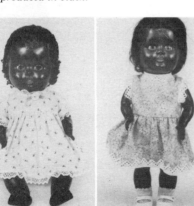

Two Roddy hard plastic dolls,
with tin eyes, c1950, 6in
(15cm) high.
£18-20 each *EGR*

*D.G. Todd & Co, produced
composition dolls between
1930-74, they also made dolls
to Mabel Lucie Attwell
designs. They were unmarked
and are, therefore, difficult
to recognise.*

A Roddy hard plastic
hand assisted walker
doll, 1950s, 12in
(30.5cm) high.
£20-25 *EGR*

*Also produced with
moulded hair.*

Two Rosebud black dolls, a girl
and a baby, c1950, 11in (28cm)
high.
£25-30 each *EGR*

Also produced in flesh colour.

A Roddy hard plastic doll, with tin sleeping eyes, c1950, 10in (25cm) high.
£25-30 *EGR*

The eyes rusted and dropped out easily. Earlier moulds marked Rodnoid.

A Roddy hard plastic teenage walker doll, c1958, 10½in (25.5cm) high.
£12-15 *EGR*

Roddy twin dolls, with sleeping eyes, open mouths and teeth, 1950s, 11in (28cm) high.
£15-20 each *EGR*

A Roddy hard plastic black doll, with top knot, c1955, 9in (23cm) high.
£35-40 *EGR*

Also produced in 15in size.

A Roddy hard plastic baby 'Mama' doll, grey-blue sleeping eyes, c1955, 20in (51cm) high.
£50-55 *EGR*

The face of this doll also made as 21in walkie-talkie doll.

Three Roddy hard plastic dolls: *c.* Walker with plastic dress, c1930s, 6in (15cm) high. **£25-30** *l. & r.* With painted sleeping eyes, 3½in (9cm) high.
£12-15 *EGR*

Also produced in black.

A Roddy hard plastic black walkie-talkie doll, with amber eyes, 1955, 21in (53cm) high.
£70-80 *EGR*

Also produced in flesh colour and with moulded hair.

A Roddy doll, with sleeping eyes, c1958, 15in (38cm) high.
£15-20 *EGR*

A Roddy black doll, c1955, 12in (30.5cm) high.
£25-30 *EGR*

Also produced in flesh colour.

Sarold Dolls

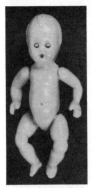

A Sarold hard plastic baby doll, marked, c1950-59, 3in (7.5cm). **£10-15** *EGR*

Two Sarold little girl dolls, c1950. **£10-12 each** *EGR*

Also produced 7in Costume Dolls.

Two Sarold hard plastic girl dolls, with different faces, c1950, 10in (25cm) high. **£15-20 each** *EGR*

Tudor Rose

A selection of Tudor Rose hard plastic dolls, with straight and jointed legs, a plastic rattle lying in front, all c1955. Dolls. **£8-10 each** Black doll. **£10-12** *EGR*

Tudor Rose made plastic novelties and rattles c1950s-60s, painted eyes - 1950, glassene eyes - 1960.

A Tudor Rose hard plastic black doll, c1955, 8in (20cm) high. **£10-12** *EGR*

Also produced in flesh colour.

Semco

A Semco Pollyanna doll, marked Semco, early 1960s, 30in (76cm) high. **£30-35** *EGR*

A Semco doll, with pink hair, c1964, 30in (76cm) high. **£30-35** *EGR*

Vogue

'Ginny' a Vogue doll, in original box, by Matchbox, 8in (20cm) high. **£8-10** *EGR*

Vogue Dolls were American. Matchbox also made 'Moppits' with soft bodies and Disco Girl teenage dolls.

CROSS REFERENCE
Airfix Dolls ⟶ p144

William & Steer

Two William & Steer hard plastic dolls, with sleeping eyes, 12in (30.5cm) high.
£10-15 each *EGR*

William & Steer, 1947-1950s, originally made parts for other companies.
These models are the only ones known to have been marketed under their name.

Wax Headed Dolls

A poured wax headed doll, with blue sleeping eyes, pierced ears, inset light brown hair, stuffed body with wax limbs, wearing contemporary dress, restored, c1878, 18in (46cm) high.
£450-475 *CSK*

A poured shoulder wax doll, with moulded face, with fixed blue glass eyes, red-blonde real hair and cloth body, with poured wax lower limbs, some damage, wearing original silk dress and a selection of other clothes, in a box, 19¼in (49cm) high.
£1,100-1,300 *S*

Cloth-Headed Dolls

Traumerchen, a rare painted cloth-headed sleeping baby doll, with sand-filled stockinette body, by Käthe Kruse, some damage, c1925, 20in (51cm) high.
£1,200-1,300 *CSK*

These dolls were originally produced as teaching aids for baby care.

A Lenci doll, c1930, 16in (41cm) high.
£250-260 *ChL*

l. An unusual cloth doll, modelled as 'George', the cartoon character, by Tom Webster, from the Daily Mail, the felt face with red nose and cheeks, moustache and googlie inset eyes, stuffed body and original outfit of felt jacket, trousers, hat and shoes, wing collar and tie, Chad Valley label on foot and Tom Webster's 'George' label on jacket, c1926, 11in (28cm) high. **£300-350**
r. A Lenci painted felt-faced adult doll, modelled as a sad pierrot, with cotton body and 4-piece torso, carrying painted wooden mandolin, c1920, 21in (53cm) high.
£425-450 *CSK*

A Lenci cloth doll, with painted features, brown eyes, fair mohair wig and felt body with swivel joints at neck, shoulders and hips, c1930, 16½in (42cm) high, in original box.
£1,050-1,250 *S*

Papier Mâché Headed Dolls

A shoulder papier mâché head, with open mouth and 4 bamboo teeth, fixed black glass eyes, domed head with black painted curls, nose repaired, slight cracking, French c1840, 9in (23cm) high.
£420-450 *S*

Pincushion Dolls

A German half doll, c1920, 5in (13cm) high.
£60-80 *BAT*

Dolls Clothes

A yellow and blue silk doll's dress, trimmed with bows and pleated frills, c1874, 19in (48cm) long, and a silk fashionable doll's dress, trimmed with black beads and lace, 15in (38cm) long.
£600-650 *CSK*

A French bébé's pink satin and lace frock, possibly Jumeau, c1880, 13½in (34cm) long, a red silk dress, printed with horseshoes, 11in (28cm) long, and a baby doll's robe and petticoat, 15in (38cm) long, together with other clothes.
£1,100-1,300 *CSK*

Dolls' Clothes Patterns

Dolls' knitting patterns, printed in womens' magazines throughout the 1950s and 1960s. **£1-2 each** *EGR*

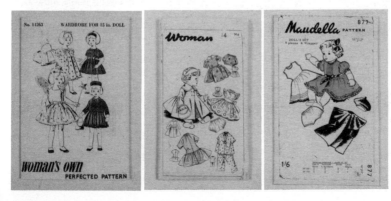

Dolls' sewing patterns available through womens' magazines throughout the 1950s and 1960s, designed to reflect the fashions of the day.
£1-2 each *EGR*

Dolls' knitting patterns, printed in womens' magazines throughout the 1950s and 1960s.
£1-2 each *EGR*

Dolls' knitting patterns showing designs for hard plastic dolls which were available throughout the 1950s and 1960s.
£1-2 each *EGR*

A painted wooden dolls' house with original floor and wallpapers, interior doors, some fireplaces and a fitted bath, c1890, 28in (71cm) high.
£3,000-3,500 *CSK*

Dolls' Houses

A wooden dolls' house on arcaded stand, by Evans & Cartwright, window frames repainted, re-papered and painted inside, mid-19thC, 52in (132cm) high.
£5,000-5,500 *CSK*

A card dolls' house on wooden frame, with opening windows, American, probably by Built-Rite of Warren, Ohio, c1940, 35in (89cm) wide.
£200-250 *CSK*

A Lines Bros. painted wooden dolls' house, with printed paper on roof, sides and back, original floor and wallpapers, c1924, 32½in (82cm) wide.
£300-325 *CSK*

A painted wooden dolls' house, modelled on Princess Elizabeth's Welsh Cottage, given to the Princess on her 6th birthday in April 1932, by the people of Wales, with original floor and wallpapers, post WWII, with Triang label, 30in (76cm) wide.
£360-400 *CSK*

A Palladian style wooden dolls' house, damaged and partly overpainted, c1860, 36½in (93cm) high.
£3,000-3,250 *CSK*

This dolls' house was modelled on Sherborne House, Newlands Sherborne, Dorset, built for Henry Seymour Portman Esq, and designed by an architect named Bastard of Sherborne.

A wooden box back dolls' house, with balcony rail, 35in (89cm) high.
£480-520 *CSK*

A carpenter made dolls' town house, later wired for electric light, fair condition, probably English, early 20thC, 22½in (57cm) high.
£270-300 *S(NY)*

A painted wooden dolls' house, marked in pencil H 138/6 by Christian Hacker, overpainted, new roof, 39in (99cm) high.
£720-780 *CSK*

A wrought iron balcony, with iron garden furniture and hanging baskets, 16in (41cm) long.
£225-250 *CD*

A large wooden Spanish style dolls' house, painted to simulate brickwork with plain wood sides, late 19thC, 53in (135cm) wide.
£9,500-10,000 *CSK*

A model of a butcher's shop, English, early 19thC with 20thC additions, 24in (61cm) wide.
£10,000-11,000 *S*

Dolls' House Dolls   Dolls' House & Dolls' Accessories

A pair of silver doll's spectacles.
£22-25 *ChL*

A pair of silver scissors.
£8-30 *ChL*

A dolls' house doll, c1900,
4½in (11cm) high.
£75-85 *ChL*

A dolls' house doll, c1900,
4½in (11cm) high.
£75-80 *ChL*

A doll's watch
pendant.
£30-35 *ChL*

A toy watch, c1940.
£18-20 *ChL*

Two pairs of dolls'
silver miniature
scissors.
£5-25 each
ChL

A silver
chatelaine
for dolls.
£35-40
ChL

Two pairs of dolls'
silver lorgnettes.
£22-25 each
ChL

Silver 'Stork' miniature scissors.
£28-30
ChL

A George III silver dolls' tea set, comprising teapot and 3 cups, maker's mark struck twice D.B., late 18thC, 1½in (4cm) high. **£550-575** *L*

Dolls' House Furniture

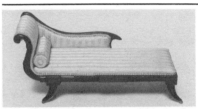

A Regency chaise longues, with carved wood by D. Booth, 6in (15cm) long.
£80-100 *CD*

A set of silver-gilt and enamel dolls house furniture, comprising: a sofa, coffee table and 4 chairs, French, late 19thC, sofa 3in (7.5cm) wide. **£600-650** *L*

A William and Mary inlaid walnut table, with dovetail joints, 3in (8cm) wide.
£350-370 *CD*

A suite of enamelled miniature brass furniture, Austrian, late 19thC, firescreen 4⅛in (11cm) high. **£900-950** *S*

A Continental dolls' table, possibly Dutch, mid-19thC, 4in (10cm) wide. **£275-300** *L*

A set of Victorian silver dolls' chairs and table, comprising 6 chairs and one table, by David Bridge, 1891, table 21in (5cm) wide. **£225-250** *L*

A set of silver dolls house furniture, comprising: a settee and 5 chairs, 2 legs on settee broken, possibly French, late 19thC, settee 1¾in (4.5cm) wide.
£125-150 *L*

DRINKING

A Bavarian tankard, with lithophane of scenic picture in base, 9in (23cm) high.
£50-60 *EB*

A pair of Victorian wine flasks, with Sheffield plate tops, 7½in (44cm) high.
£100-145 *ACA*

A Swedish peg tankard, 18thC, 8in (20cm) high.
£700-800 *JAC*

A German stoneware stein, with raised verse and scenes of wine drinkers and musicians, c1800. **£185-195** *CS*

A Ridgway pottery jug, with Sheffield plate hinged lid and raised Robert Burns scenes, dated 1835.
£150-185 *CS*

A copper ale muller, early 18thC, 12in (30.5cm) long.
£70-75 *SAD*

A German stoneware lidded wine flagon, c1860. **£200-275** *CS*

A French café soda syphon, with painted base.
£80-125 *REL*

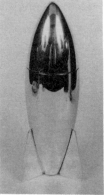

An electroplated rocket-shaped cocktail shaker, by Garrard & Co, 10in (25cm) high.
£200-300 *KAC*

A Victorian wine flask, with Sheffield plate top, 8in (20cm) high.
£65-85 *ACA*

CROSS REFERENCE
Bottles ———————➤ p29

Barrel Taps

Two brass barrel taps, c1880,
10in (25cm) long.
£40-50 each *MofC*

A brass barrel tap, mounted on
wood, c1880, 7 by 15in (17.5 by
38cm). **£80-95** *MofC*

Two brass barrel taps, c1880,
7in (17.5cm) long.
£40-50 each *MofC*

Bottle Openers

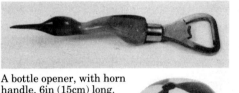

A bottle opener, with horn
handle, 6in (15cm) long.
£15-18 *AA*

A spelter ware jockey
cap bottle opener,
c1930, 3½in (9cm)
wide. **£25-35** *KOH*

Two wooden barrel taps, 1880,
11in (28cm) long.
£15-25 each *MofC*

Champagne

A collection of 5
various types of
leather cased
champagne
taps, with
instructions for
use.
£25-45 each
CS

Bottle Tops

A Groucho Marx papier
mâché bottle top, with
revolving eye,
c1930, 4in (10cm) high.
£16-18 *TER*

A bottle top, shaped
as a lady's head,
c1930, 3in (7.5cm)
high. **£6-8** *TER*

A pair of brass mounted mahogany champagne
coolers, with central brass carrying handles
and folding lids, each with 2 brass bands, 13in
(33cm) wide. **£3,100-3,400** *B*

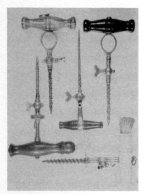

A collection of champagne taps, with wood and bone handles.
£30-65 each *CS*

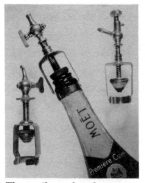

Three silver plated champagne stoppers, with dispensing taps.
£30-60 *CS*

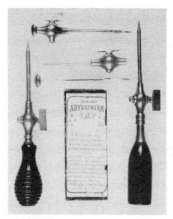

A selection of champagne and soda water taps.
top: **£10-15 each**
left: **£20-30**
right: **£30-50** *CS*

Cork Drawers

A cast iron bar cork drawer, 'Safety', c1900.
£80-120 *CS*

A brass pub bar cork drawer, 'The Don', late 19thC.
£70-120 *CS*

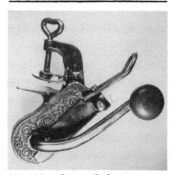

A cast iron bar cork drawer, 'Hektor', with clamp type fitting, c1890.
£120-200 *CS*

Corkscrews

A folding bow pocket corkscrew, with button hook, leather punch for boot lace holes and a hoof pick, c1870.
£40-80 *CS*

A miniature corkscrew, with cut and faceted steel stem, fluted helix and turned bone handle, c1820.
£60-100 *CS*

These miniatures were used for medicine and perfume bottle corks.

A silver sheath pocket corkscrew, by Samuel Pemberton of Birmingham, c1790.
£120-180 *CS*

A Continental all steel side wind corkscrew, c1890.
£30-45 *CS*

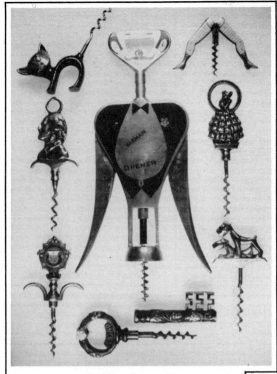

A collection of figural type corkscrews. **£5-45 each** German lady's legs. **£70-120** *CS*

A selection of corkscrews: 'The Bottle Boy', stirrup folding bow, a brass figural ship and a pocket sheath advertising whisky. **£5-10 each** *CS*

A multi-tool, with 11 tools, hinged including a fluted worm corkscrew, stamped Barrett, Strand, London, c1830. **£160-240** *CS*

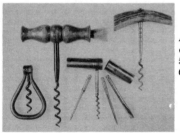

A selection of corkscrews. **£5-15 each** *CS*

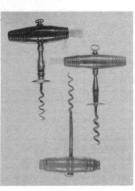

Three corkscrews, c1840-1850. **£15-60 each** *CS*

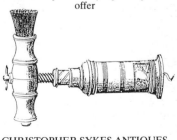

Funnels

A Sheffield plate wine funnel, the tab enables the top to be used as a strainer when hooked over the edge of a punch bowl, c1820.
£80-100 *CS*

l. A wine funnel, with beaded decoration and applied with engraved oval cartouche, made by John Deacon, London 1781, 4⅓in (11cm) high, 2oz.
£325-350
r. A wine funnel, with detachable reeded strainer, engraved with crest, London 1801, 6in (15cm) high, 4oz 10dwt.
£250-275 *WIL*

A silver wine straining funnel, with raised grape decoration, by Rebecca Eames and Edward Barnard, London, c1810.
£300-350 *CS*

CROSS REFERENCE
Ceramics
  Carltonware ⟶ p90

Labels

A set of 4 Victorian silver plate wine bottle labels, Marsala, Hock, Madeira and Moselle, 1850.
£70-100 *CS*

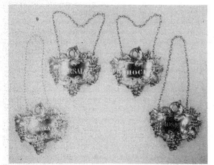

A collection of 15 silver wine decanter or bottle labels, showing a variety of designs.
£25-80 each
Enamel Mountain label.
£1,200-1,500 *CS*

Guinness

A Guinness rubber advertising figure.
£40-45 *COB*

Tasting Bowls

Four French silver tastevins, 19thC.
£70-250 *CS*

A silver tastevin wine sampler, with typical indentations, c1900.
£60-80 *CS*

Whisky

A bottle of Duncan MacAlpine Finest Scotch Whisky, bottled and blended by Forth Blending Co, Glasgow, label slightly torn, stopper cork, lead capsule, fine wire mesh covering bottle, 5cm level from base of capsule, 70°, blended.
£290-310   *C(S)*

A bottle of Royal Strathythan Old Scotch Whisky, bottled by Chivas Brothers, Aberdeen, Purveyors by Special Appointment to His Majesty King George V and Her Majesty Queen Alexandra, driven cork, embossed lead capsule, top shoulder level, c1910
£1,000-1,100   *C(S)*

l. A Certificate of Analysis dated 1894 by Stevenson Macadam incorporated into front label. Certificate of Analysis dated 1894 by Granville H. Sharpe incorporated into rear label.

A bottle of Ronald Gordon Fine Malt Choice Highland Whisky, bottled and guaranteed by Ronald Gordon, Leith, 'From the Heath Covered Mountains of Scotia I Come', driven cork, paper seal over lead capsule, 5.5cm level from base of capsule, late 19thC.
£775-800   *C(S)*

A half bottle of Glen Boyne Finely Matured Old Scotch Whisky, G.G. McRobie, Portsoy, Scotland, established 1846, label depicts Glen Boyne Castle, driven cork, lacking capsule, mid-shoulder level, 30° under proof.   **£170-190**   *C(S)*

A bottle of Drum Major, not less than 42% proof spirit, stopper cork, lead capsule, 2cm level from base of capsule, produced by N.W. Spratt (Liqueurs) Ltd, London W1.   **£125-145**   *C(S)*

Irish Whiskey

A bottle of John Jamieson & Son Pure Old Pot Still Dublin Whiskey, distilled by John Jamieson & Son, Bow Street Distillery, bottled by Fred Hirst, Wine Merchant, Strand, Todmorden, driven corks, lacking capsules.
£190-210   *C(S)*

Welsh Whiskey

A bottle of Welsh Whiskey, bottled and guaranteed by P. Baker & Co., Llangullen, 3-piece moulded glass bottle, branded, driven cork, lacking capsule, label torn but legible, mid-shoulder level, late 19thC.
£280-300   *C(S)*

EGG CUPS

A Mason's egg cup, c1910.
£18-20 *ACA*

A floral printed egg cup, with printed inside edge.
£10-15 *ACA*

A Hammersley egg cup, with Violets pattern.
£10-14 *ACA*

A double egg cup, with transfer print. **£10-15** *ACA*

A Victorian egg cup set, restored, 5in (12.5cm) diam. **£25-35** *AA*

Two Copeland Spode Italian pattern blue and white pattern egg cups. **£15-20** *ACA*

A Bridgwood Indian Tree pattern egg cup.
£10-13 *ACA*

A Copeland Spode Italian pattern blue and white pattern egg cup.
£18-22 *ACA*

A Crown Staffordshire egg cup, c1930.
£8-10 *ACA*

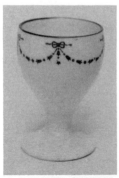

A Collingwood egg cup.
£10-12 *ACA*

l. A Grosvenor egg cup. **£8-10**
r. A Grimwade egg cup, c1906.
£8-10 *ACA*

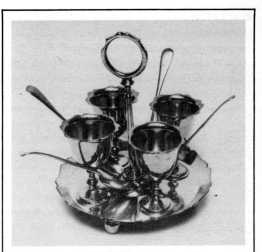

A set of 4 EPNS egg cups, with spoons, early 20thC.
£65-70 *ACA*

A blue and white Royal Doulton 'Norfolk' egg cup, c1910, 1¾in (4cm) high.
£12-14 *AA*

A Shelley egg cup, c1930.
£20-25 *ACA*

A floral printed egg cup, with scalloped edge and gold rim.
£12-16 *ACA*

A floral printed egg cup.
£15-20 *ACA*

An egg cup with floral decoration, 1920s, 2¼in (6cm). **£7-8** *AA*

CROSS REFERENCE
Ceramics ➔ p98

Two egg cups, depicting Red Riding Hood and Old Mother Hubbard, c1930, 2⅜in (6cm) high.
£6-8 each *AA*

EPHEMERA

An Edwardian Notice, found by a pond in Hampshire. **£30-50** *COB*

An imitation One Million pound bank note, reputedly used in the film 'The Million Pound Note', 1954, given to a previous owner by Gregory Peck. **£110-120** *VS*

It is believed there were 8 similar copies of the note produced for the film, though others were destroyed during filming.

A passport, c1846, 3¾ by 6in (9 by 15cm). **£45-85** *WAB*

A British passport, issued 1918. **£10-15** *COB*

WWI German Proclamations in Belgium and France, complete, by Dobson Molle & Co, VG. **£42-45** *VS*

Autographs

Eva Braun, a black and white photograph taken as a child in a garden, signed by her in later life, surmounted by a gold swastika, engraved E.B. **£2,600-2,700** *BIR*

Sir Robert Baden Powell, a menu for the 7th Annual Balaclava Dinner (13th Hussars Old Comrades Association), 25th October 1924, signed in pencil, G. **£55-60** *VS*

Naomi Campbell, a colour photograph, signed with first name only, 8 by 10in (20 by 25cm), EX. **£44-48** *VS*

BEWARE OF SIGNATURES!
- **Autographs dedicated to a particular person are more likely to be genuine.**
- **Many famous people, especially Marilyn Monroe and John F. Kennedy, had staff sign on their behalf, so ensure that the signature is authentic.**
- **Beware of printed signatures - that is pictures which were reproduced after the negative or original photograph was signed.**
- **Look closely to make sure that the signature was not produced with a rubber stamp.**
- **Autographs on an appropriate item, e.g. a theatre programme, menu or music score, are highly prized and command a premium.**

Astronauts

Jim Henson, surrounded by the Muppets, a signed colour photograph, 8 by 10in (20 by 25cm), EX. **£80-85** *VS*

Florence Nightingale, a piece signed in ink, FR. **£62-65** *VS*

Neil Armstrong, a half length signed photograph showing him seated during a mission review meeting at Merritt Island Launch Area, 8 by 10in (20 by 25cm), G. **£85-90** *VS*

Valentina Tereshkova, a signed photograph, 7 by 4¼in (17.5 by 10cm), VG. **£90-95** *VS*

Cheques

A cheque signed by Groucho Marx, made payable to Theta Cable California for $8, dated 17th May 1971, VG.
£110-120 *VS*

A cheque signed by J. Paul Getty, made payable to Evans & Reeves Nurseries for $641.47, dated 11th February 1948, G.
£85-90 *VS*

A cheque signed by Lou Costello, made payable to cash for $25, dated 31st May 1945, G. **£120-130** *VS*

Literary

Robert Browning, a signed envelope, addressed in his hand to the Secretary of the Athenaeum Club, 3rd March 1884, mounted with a reproduction photograph, VG.
£95-100 *VS*

Thomas Hardy, one page of a signed letter to the editor of the Thrush, 31st January 1901, VG.
£200-220 *VS*

Rudyard Kipling, a signed quotation, 'And there is no discharge in this war', VG.
£65-70 *VS*

H. G. Wells, a signed piece with several additional words in his hand, VG.
£35-40 *VS*

P. G. Wodehouse, a signed piece cut from the end of a letter, G.
£50-55 *VS*

John Steinbeck, an album page signed and inscribed, mounted beneath a reproduction photo, 6 by 5in (15 by 12.5cm) G.
£100-110 *VS*

Musical

Arturo Toscanini, a postcard signed and inscribed, Buenos Aires, 5th July 1940, VG.
£115-125 *VS*

LOUIE ARMSTRONG.

Louis Armstrong, a signed photograph, 5 by 7in (12.5 by 17.5cm), and an unsigned programme for his British tour, 1956, G.
£110-120 *VS*

Richard Rodgers, a photograph, signed and inscribed, 8 by 10in (20 by 25cm), VG.
£55-60 *VS*

One page signed by Glenn Miller, to Mr. A. R. Maydwell, regretting to inform him that the United States Army does not permit the distribution of photographs of its officers, mounted with a reproduction photograph, 7 by 9in (17.5 by 23cm), VG.
£330-350 *VS*

Sam Cooke, a signed piece of feint ruled paper, October 1962, mounted with 2 reproduction photographs, G.
£110-120 *VS*

Gene Vincent, a signed newspaper photograph, FR.
£50-55 *VS*

MT	Mint
EX	Excellent
VG	Very Good
FR	Fair
G	Good
P	Poor
VR	Varying Condition

The Beatles, a collection of album pages, individually signed by each, apparently obtained in person on the set of 'Help!', G-VG.
£350-375 *VS*

MICHAEL JACKSON

A white paper napkin, autographed in blue ink by James Dean.
£540-560 *CNY*

Michael Jackson, a signed and inscribed photograph, 8 by 10in (20 by 25cm), EX.
£95-100 *VS*

Political

Joachim von Ribbentrop, A signed document, 25th November 1944, FR to G.
£100-110 *VS*

Sir Winston S. Churchill, a fully signed piece, G.
£325-350 *VS*

A signed souvenir programme for The Blue Ball at The Hurlingham Club, 29th June 1983, signed by Margaret Thatcher and also signed by Jeffrey Archer, Cecil Parkinson, Leon Brittan, and with a piece signed by Michael Heseltine, VG. **£85-90** *VS*

Jacqueline Kennedy, a photograph with full signature Jacqueline Kennedy Onassis, 8 by 10in (20 by 25cm), G.
£160-170 *VS*

Chiang Kai-Shek, a signed and inscribed made-up colour photograph, 8 by 10in (20 by 25cm), G.
£100-110 *VS*

Royalty

King George III, a signed piece, G.
£35-40 *VS*

Queen Mary, a signed postcard,photograph by Hay Wrightson of London, 1930, VG.
£60-65 *VS*

CROSS REFERENCE
Commemorative Ware ──────▶ p136

Emperor Maximilian of Mexico, a signed one page document,16th July 1865, G. **£200-225** *VS*

Queen Elizabeth II and Prince Philip, a signed photograph, 1956, 11¼ by 8¼in (28.5 by 21cm), VG.
£425-450 *VS*

Queen Victoria, a signed photogravure, 20 by 26in (51 by 66cm), VG.
£425-450 *VS*

An autographed note on the reverse by Adolph Tuck of Raphael Tuck & Sons read: 'This Photogravure proof was forwarded by me on Friday, January 8th, 1897, with a letter addressed to Sir Arthur John Bigge for the purpose of being signed by the Queen, for facsimiling on the publication by my firm Raphael Tuck & Sons Limited and returned to Coleman Street this day Monday 11th January by special messenger from Buckingham Palace with Her Majesty's autograph signature and date 1987 attached'; the Queen evidently signed in blue indelible pencil as a second choice, a first attempt ('Vict') in ink to the border has blotted.

Queen Elizabeth I, a signed document, creating a bond for over £16,500 lent to the States of Holland, one page, 1578, P.
£400-420 *VS*

The document is countersigned by the Earl of Leicester, Lord Burghley, Sir Christopher Hatton and others. Though a rare and historically interesting document, it is in extremely poor condition being extensively dismembered due to being slashed upon repayment of the loan, heavily creased, scuffed and, while the text is on the whole legible, the signatures are extremely faded and virtually untraceable.

Sport

A colour photograph, signed by Mike Tyson, 8 by 10in (20 by 25cm), EX.
£70-75 *VS*

Babe Ruth, a small signed piece cut from the end of a letter, 1956, G.
£180-200 *VS*

CROSS REFERENCE
Sport ⟶ p399

Theatre

Brigitte Bardot, a signed colour photograph, 8 by 10in (20 by 25cm), EX.
£32-38 *VS*

Ingrid Bergman, a signed postcard, Picturegoer, EX.
£55-60 *VS*

Dan Blocker, a signed and inscribed photograph, 8 by 10in (20 by 25cm), VG.
£110-120 *VS*

Noël Coward, a signed sepia postcard from 'In Which We Serve', 1943, G.
£85-90 *VS*

Charlie Chaplin, a black and white signed photograph, 'Faithfully, Chas Chaplin', 7 by 5in (18 by 12.5cm).
£600-625 *CNY*

Josephine Baker, an autographed photograph, inscribed on right hand corner 'To "charming" Mr & Mrs Curtis, with my greatest "admiration", Sincerely Josephine Baker June 20/27 Paris'.
£1,300-1,500 *CNY*

W. C. Fields, an autographed black and white glossy photograph, from 'Follow The Boys', 1944, inscribed in green ink 'To Mr Cary from W. C. Fields', 8 by 10in (20 by 25cm).
£425-450 *CNY*

Walt Disney, a signed card, VG.
£330-350 *VS*

Joan Crawford, a signed photograph, 9½ by 7½in (23.5 by 19cm), VG.
£48-52 *VS*

Glennis Lorimer, 'The Gainsborough Lady of Gainsborough Pictures', being the young woman featured at the beginning of the 1940s Gainsborough Films, signed, 5⅛ by 3¾in (13.5 by 9cm), G.
£25-30 *VS*

Errol Flynn, a signed album page, VG.
£100-110 *VS*

A black marker sketch of Alfred Hitchcock's profile, by himself, signed 'Alfred Hitchcock', 10 by 8in (25 by 20cm).
£1,500-1,600 *CNY*

Laurel & Hardy, signed postcard, 1934, VG.
£380-400 *VS*

Marilyn Monroe, autographed photograph, signed in green ink 'To Gregory "My Ardent Fan" Love & Luck Marilyn Monroe', 10 by 8in (25 by 20cm).
£1,200-1,400 *CNY*

Grace Kelly, signed photograph, 8 by 10in (20 by 25cm), VG.
£160-170 *VS*

Carole Lombard, signed sepia postcard, VG.
£230-250 *VS*

Groucho Marx, album page signed with first name only, mounted beneath a photograph, 16½ by 20½in (42 by 52cm) overall, G.
£55-60 *VS*

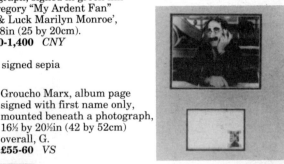

James Stewart, signed original pen and ink sketch of 'Harvey', VG.
£75-80 *VS*

Laurence Olivier, sepia photograph with full signature, 6½ by 8½in (16 by 21cm), VG.
£90-100 *VS*

Basil Rathbone, signed sepia postcard, EX.
£85-90 *VS*

Audrey Hepburn, in costume from 'My Fair Lady', signed and inscribed photograph, 8 by 10in (20 by 25cm), VG.
£75-80 *VS*

Peter Sellers, in costume as Inspector Clouseau, signed and inscribed, 8 by 10in (20 by 25cm), VG.
£110-120 *VS*

Rudolph Valentino, sepia toned photograph, signed 'Sincerely Rudolph Valentino', further inscribed 'To Johnny Johnson In memory of my Brother Rudolph with deep appreciation Alberto Valentino - Sept. 1962', 8 by 10in (20 by 25cm).
£380-400 *CNY*

Autographed Programmes

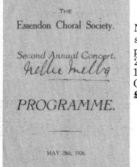

Nellie Melba, signed concert programme, 28th May, 1926, G-VG.
£22-28 *VS*

Bela Lugosi, postcard signed in red ink, VG.
£225-250 *VS*

Bela Lugosi often signed autographs in blood red ink, especially on photographic cards featuring him in his role as Count Dracula.

Judy Garland, autographed black and white glossy photograph, inscribed 'To George: Many More Rainbows! Judy Garland.'
£600-625 *CNY*

Josephine Baker, signed programme for the Palladium Variety Show, 1974, VG.
£85-90 *VS*

My Fair Lady, a first night programme for The Theatre Royal, Drury Lane, 30th April, 1958, signed to the front cover by various attending celebrities, including Ingrid Bergman, Kay Kendall, Dirk Bogarde, Cecil Beaton (costume designer for the show), Alan Jay Lerner (lyricist of the show) Zachary Scott, Ruth Ford, Hanya Holm (who choreographed the show), also signed to inside photo pages by the 5 main stars, Rex Harrison, Julie Andrews, Stanley Holloway, Zena Dare and Robert Coote, VG.
£140-150 *VS*

A programme for the European Gala Premiere of Not as a Stranger, Leicester Square Theatre, London, signed to front cover by Robert Mitchum, Gloria Grahame, Olivia de Havilland and Broderick Crawford, VG.
£35-40 *VS*

Paul McCartney, signed concert programme for Wings UK tour, 1979, FR. **£45-50** *VS*

Andrew Lloyd Webber, a card signed and inscribed, also by Tim Rice, with attached handbill for Jesus Christ Superstar at the Palace Theatre, 9½ by 12in (23.5 by 31cm) overall, VG.
£80-85 *VS*

Vivien Leigh and Laurence Olivier, signed theatre programme for Caesar and Cleopatra at the St James's Theatre, 10th May 1951, G.
£100-110 *VS*

Frank Sinatra, signed theatre programme, London Palladium, 1950s, VG.
£85-90 *VS*

Arthur Miller, signed theatre programme for Death of a Salesman, G.
£52-58 *VS*

Vivien Leigh, signed theatre programme for A Streetcar Named Desire, Aldwych Theatre, London, VG.
£120-130 *VS*

Cole Porter, a signed and inscribed programme for Leave It to Me, Imperial Theatre, 15th May 1939, VG.
£185-195 *VS*

Blotters

A blotter, c1900, 8¾ by 6in (22 by 15cm). **£4-5** *COL*

A diary and blotter, 1939, 10½ by 8½in ((26.5 by 21cm).
£3-4 *COL*

Calendars

A selection of pin-up calendars, 1930s and 1940s.
£6-7 each *COB*

A collection of 5 chromolithographic calendars, one in the form of a fan, dated 1898, 4 dated 1902.
£370-390 *CSK*

Cartoons & Illustrations

William Heath Robinson, The New Pussyfoot Test, pen, ink and watercolour, signed, 1920, 14 by 10in (35.5 by 25.5cm).
£2,250-2,500 *Bon*

Henry Mayo Bateman, The Snooker Player, pen and black ink, unframed, 13 by 9in (33 by 23cm).
£840-880 *Bon*

Carl Giles, 'Don't panic, dear - the ambulance is on the way', cartoon from the Daily Express of the Giles family enjoying the pleasures of the Spacehopper, signed, 18¼ by 10½in (46 by 26.5cm), framed and glazed.
£270-290 *CSK*

Charles Schulz, Peanuts Daily Strip, August 26th, 1983, United Features Syndicate, pen and ink on paper, inscribed 'Best wishes - Charles Schulz', matted, 6½ by 22½in (16.5 by 57cm).
£625-650 *S(NY)*

CROSS REFERENCE
Autographs ———▶p182

Tom Browne, an original pen and ink sketch, signed by Browne, rubber stamp to reverse, Tom Browne Wollaton, Hardy Road, Blackheath, 7 by 10½in (17.5 by 26.5cm), G.
£100-110 *VS*

Henry Mayo Bateman, The Barber, pen and black ink, signed and inscribed with a poem, stamped verso by A. E. Johnson, unframed, 16 by 11¼in (40.5 by 28.5cm).
£425-450 *Bon*

Charles Schulz, Peanuts Sunday page, December 19th, 1954, United Features Syndicate, pen and ink on paper, signed by the artist, 16½ by 23½in (42 by 59.5cm).
£4,800-5,000 *S(NY)*

Carl Giles, Magic Chemical Set, 2 illustrations in one frame, watercolour and bodycolour, signed, 10 by 12½in (25.5 by 32cm) each.
£2,700-2,900 *Bon*

Cigarette Cards

- Collectors prefer cards to be in mint condition.
- Cards stuck down in albums are seriously devalued.

Morris's, Actresses, black and white, set of 30, c1898. **£50-60** *MUR*

Carreras Ltd, Kings and Queens, set of 50, 1935. **£55-60** *MUR*

Co-operative Wholesale Society, musical instruments, set of 48, EX. **£95-100** *VS*

W. D. & H. O. Wills, Arms of Public Schools, set of 25, 1933. **£30-35** *MUR*

W. D. & H. O. Wills, Time and Money, a set of 50, c1908. **£45-50** *MUR*

Cope Bros. & Co. Ltd, Dickens Gallery, set of 50, c1900. **£380-400** *MUR*

R. J. Lea Ltd, Famous Views, set of 48, issued 1936.
£10-12 *MUR*

John Player & Sons, Cats, set of 24, 1936.
£140-145 the set *MUR*

Lambert & Butler, Motor Cycles, set of 50, 1923.
£140-150 *MUR*

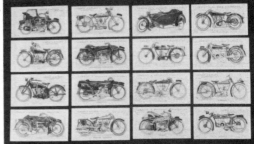

J. A. Pattreiouex Ltd, Dirt Track Riders, set of 50, G-VG.
£170-190 *VS*

Ogden's, Yachts and Motor boats, set of 50, VG.
£50-55 *VS*

Taddy & Co, British Prominent Footballers, 600 cards issued.
£6-8 each *MUR*

FURTHER READING
The Guide to Cigarette Card Collecting, Current Values, Albert's (19th Edition), 1994. *The Catalogue of British and Foreign Cards; Cigarette Card News and Trade Card Chronicle; Catalogue of Trade Card Issues,* The London Cigarette Card Co. Ltd., Somerton, Somerset
Cigarette Card Values, Murray Cards (International) Ltd., 51 Watford Way, Hendon, NW4. 1994

Gabriel, Cricketers Series, set of 20, c1902. **£280-300 each** *MUR*

W. D. & H. O. Wills, Vanity Fair, set of 50, 1902. **£190-200** *MUR*

John Player & Sons, Horses, set of 25, 1939. **£65-70** *MUR*

John Player & Sons, Motor Cars set of 50, first issue 1936. **£50-55** *MUR*

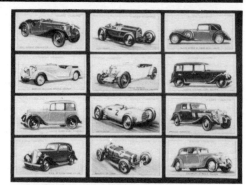

Ogden's, British Costumes, set of 50, c1905. **£265-275** *MUR*

Trade Cards

Fry's Nursery Rhyme cards, set
of 50, 1917.
£100-110 *MUR*

Pacific Trading Co, Land of Oz,
songs and quiz questions on
reverse, set of 110, 1990.
£10-12 *MUR*

Brooke Bond Tea, Disney Cards, set of 25, 1989.
£3-4 *MUR*

Joseph Lingford, British War
Leaders, set of 36, c1949.
£32-36 *MUR*

Comics

A collection of 28 Conan The
Barbarian Comic Books from
the White Mountain Collection,
October 1970-April 1973,
Marvel Comics Group.
£1,400-1,500 *S(NY)*

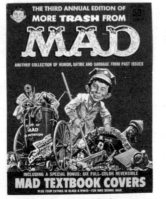

A collection of 37 Mad
magazine, annuals with interior
premiums. **£2,000-2,500** *S(NY)*

*Some of the most widely read of
all annuals, these magazines
are always found in very good
condition, and almost never
found with premiums intact.*

CROSS REFERENCE
Colour Section ⟶ p217

A collection of Science Fiction
Comic Books, including
Amazing Adventures, Nos. 1-6,
Amazing Adult Fantasy, Nos. 8-
14, World of Fantasy, Nos. 16-
19, Strange Worlds, Nos 1-5,
and In Your Hands.
£800-1,000 *S(NY)*

Whiz Comics, Nos. 3-6, April-
July 1940, Fawcett Publication.
£1,100-1,300 *S(NY)*

The Gaines File Copies of Crypt
of Terror, Nos. 17, 18, and 19,
Tales From the Crypt, Nos. 20-
46, Crime Patrol, Nos. 15 and
16, 1950-55, E. C. Comics.
£16,000-17,000 *S(NY)*

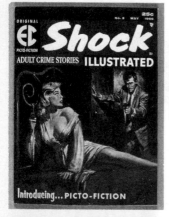

The Gaines File Copies of Crime
Illustrated, Nos. 1 and 2, Shock
Illustrated, Nos. 1-3, Terror
Illustrated, Nos. 1 and 2,
Confessions Illustrated, Nos. 1
and 2, 1955-56, E. C. Comics.
£2,000-2,500 *S(NY)*

A collecton of Modern Love
Comic Books, Nos. 1-8,
June/July 1949-August/
September 1950, E. C. Comics.
£500-600 *S(NY)*

*The Modern Love run is the
rarest of all the E. C. 'Pre-Trend'
titles.*

A collection of 67 Gene Autry's
Comic Books, 1948-1954, Dell
Comics.
£400-450 *S(NY)*

A collection of 97 The Avengers
Comic Books, Nos. 1, 2, 4-40,
43-100, 1963-1972, Marvel
Comics.
£2,500-3,000 *S(NY)*

A collection of 22 Pep Comics
and Laugh Comics from The
Mile High Collection.
£2,000-2,500 *S(NY)*

A collection of Gunfighter Comic Books, Nos. 5-14, Summer 1948-March/April 1950, E. C. Comics. **£500-600** *S(NY)*

Comic Artwork

Cover artwork of Detective Comics, No. 59, January 1942, D. C. Comics, pen and ink on illustration board.
£9,000-10,000 *S(NY)*

Cover artwork by Johnny Craig, of The Vault of Horror, No. 28, 1952, E. C. Comics, pen and ink on paper, 19 by 13½in (48.5 by 34.5cm).
£1,900-2,100 *S(NY)*

Fifty-two copies of The Amazing Spider-Man from the White Mountain Collection, June 1964-August 1973.
£4,000-5,000 *S(NY)*

Cover artwork by Michael Thibodeaux of The Last of the Viking Heroes, No. 5, 1988, Genesis West Comics, 15 by 10in (38 by 25.5cm).
£1,100-1,200 *S(NY)*

Cover Re-Creation by Jack Kirby and Martin Lasick of Amazing Fantasy, No. 15, pen and ink on paper with paper stat logo paste-over, c1970s, 10½ by 20in (26.5 by 51cm).
£3,700-3,900 *S(NY)*

A collection of Detective Comics, including Real Fact Comics, No. 5, D. C. Publication, Detective Comics, Nos. 104, 204, 205, 213, 220, 228, 230, 236, and 259.
£1,700-1,900 *S(NY)*

Cover for Mad magazine, by Jack Rickard, No.186, October 1976.
£3,900-4,000 *CNY*

Cut-Outs

Three cut-outs, Macks, Toytown, Nos. 96, 97, and 99, Captain Hook, The Crocodile, G. **£38-42** *VS*

Three cut-outs, Macks, Toytown, Nos. 12, 33, 95, including The Model Wheelbarrow and Wendy from Peter Pan, G. **£40-45** *VS*

Guides

A museum guide, 1945, 8½ by 5in (21 by 13cm). **£1-2** *COL*

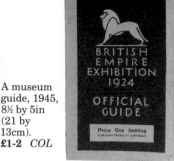

An official guide for the British Empire Exhibition, 1924, 8½ by 5½in (21 by 14cm). **£4-5** *COL*

Menu Cards

Three Moët et Chandon table menus, by Alphonse Mucha, 6 by 8¾in (15 by 22cm), VG. **£45-50 each** *VS*

Postcards

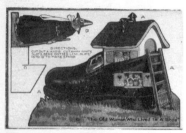

A collection of 34 Holiday Camps postcards, including Butlins and Pontins, 1939, VR. **£38-42** *VS*

Four Boer War postcards, including Théâtre de la Guerre, John Bull, and British Telegrams, G. **£33-35** *VS*

Two Gospel Wagons postcards, one of a motor van, the other a horsedrawn vehicle, FR-G. **£50-55** *VS*

Six Comedy postcards, by G. M. Payne, including Aids to Scouting, published by Gale & Polden, Nos. 1416-21, G-VG. **£25-28** *VS*

Eight chromo vignettes of authors and their homes, with advertisements to reverse for Byon & Badot Chocolat, G-VG. **£42-45** *VS*

A colour postcard of R.M.S. Titanic, No. 1829, G. **£33-35** *VS*

A sepia postcard of a Yorkshire motor bus and crew, 'Nameplate to Portsmouth', G. **£38-42** *VS*

Four comedy adverts, with overprint adverts, for Hannick of Brussels, G. **£22-25** *VS*

A motor bus, North Finchley, London, G. **£22-25** *VS*

Seven WWII French Patriotic cards, showing fighting ships and the people they were named after, by Paul Igert, 1942, G. **£25-28** *VS*

Four cards by Beatrice Mallet, advertisements for St Michel Cigarettes, including Footballer and Builder, G. **£40-45** *VS*

"GENTLEMEN PREFER SITTING OUT!"

Twenty Bonzo postcards, Valentines, 1127-1290, G. **£50-55** *VS*

I DID BUT SEE HER PASSING BY!

Fifteen Bonzo postcards, Valentines, 912-991, G. **£45-50** *VS*

London Life, Rotary, Boulter's Lock, VG. **£72-75** *VS*

Three postcards of Tosca, by L. Metlicovitz, published by Ricordi, G-VG. **£42-45** *VS*

Six cards by Raoul Frank, showing German battleships, published by Seegers, VG. **£42-45** *VS*

Six embossed comedy postcards, published by H.W.B., G. **£18-30** *VS*

Six postcards by Louis Wain, Tucks, Lucky Cats!, Series 3266 complete, as issued 4+2, VG-EX. **£160-180** *VS*

Eleven Bonzo postcards, published by R.P.S., Nos. 1015-21, 1023-26, VG. **£32-35** *VS*

Silks

A piece of woven silks, with alpha, crests and flags, and 'With love to my Sweetheart', G. **£28-30** *VS*

A black and white woven silk panel, by Dumini, published by Neyret, 7¼ by 10in (18 by 25cm), G. **£33-38** *VS*

A woven silk advertising card for Thomas Stevens, 'Specialists silk woven ribbons for hats and caps', G. **£250-275** *VS*

A black and white woven silk panel, showing a man carrying 2 girls across a stream, 7 by 13in (17.5 by 33cm), G. **£45-50** *VS*

FAIRGROUNDS

A wood carousel figure of Mickey Mouse holding a camera, 1930s, 38in (97cm) high. **£1,800-1,900** *S*

FANS

A painted leaf fan, the ivory sticks painted with flowers, North European, possibly Swedish, c1750, 10in (25cm). **£120-140** *CSK*

For a further selection of Fairgrounds, please refer to *Miller's Collectables Price Guide,* **Volume V, pp204-207.**

Battaglia del Re Tessi e del re
Tinta, 1619, an engraving after
Jacques Callot, of a mock battle
between the companies of
weavers and dyers on the Arno,
17thC, 9 by 11½in (23 by 29cm).
£1,100-1,200 *CSK*

A printed fan, the paper leaf
applied with 3 hand coloured
engravings, trimmed with
sequins, with bone sticks,
German, old repairs, c1790,
10⅛in (26cm).
£330-360 *CSK*

A printed fan, with hand
coloured etched leaf, wooden
sticks, French, c1790, 9½in
(24cm). **£150-170** *CSK*

A pierced ivory brisé fan,
engraving printed in colour on
silk and painted, slight damage,
c1790, 11in (28cm), in 18thC
box.
£1,100-1,300 *CSK*

A painted leaf fan, wooden
sticks, late 18thC, 10in (25cm).
£600-625 *CSK*

A printed Revolutionary fan,
hand coloured leaf and wooden
sticks, French, c1793, 10½in
(26cm).
£300-330 *CSK*

A printed fan, with bone sticks,
the guardsticks pierced and
silvered, French, c1785, 10½in
(26cm).
£160-180 *CSK*

A painted leaf fan, with ivory
sticks, the guardsticks pierced,
c1770, 11in (28cm), in 18thC
fan box.
£160-180 *CSK*

A lithographic racing
fan, Ch. Seitz,
Manneheim, printed
on mauve satin, with
wooden sticks, one
guardstick repaired,
c1890, 12in (30.5cm).
£900-950 *CSK*

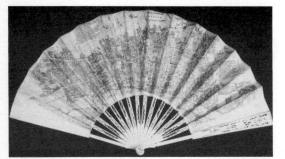

A printed telescopic map fan, a 'New & Correct Plan of London, including all ye New Buildings', the leaf engraved by R. Bennett, the reserves with Hackney Coach prices, the plain reverse stamped Clarke & Co. No.26, Strand, the ivory sticks with over guardsticks of carved and pierced bone, English, c1760, 10½in (26cm).
£2,800-3,000 *CSK*

A Japanese wooden brisé fan, lacquered in gold, the guardsticks decorated with shibayama work, with cord tassels, late 19thC, 9in (23cm).
£2,800-3,000 *CSK*

A horn brisé fan, c1825, 6in (15cm).
£225-250 *CSK*

A painted leaf fan, the ivory sticks also painted, mother-of-pearl guardsticks, 5 pieces mother-of-pearl missing, English or North European, c1750, 10in (25cm).
£300-325 *CSK*

A printed fan, 'Les Horoscopes ou le Devin Moderne Dedies au Beau Sexe', with wooden sticks, slight tears, French, c1800, 9½in (24cm). **£300-330** *CSK*

A fan, with embroidered silk leaf, the wooden sticks with bone filets, leaf stained and split, c1780, 11in (28cm).
£110-130 *CSK*

A fan, the leaf painted with figures in a landscape, collector's stamp SPBPT imperial eagle below and date 1768, ivory sticks carved, pierced and painted, c1768, 10in (25cm). **£550-600** *CSK*
The mark is probably that of an Institution in St Petersburg founded by the Empress Catherine the Great, possibly the public theatre, which was founded for public education.

A chicken skin leaf fan, with ivory sticks, carved and pierced with figures, Italian, c1780, 11in (28cm).
£1,250-1,500 *CSK*

FISHING

- The most collectable reels and tackle were made by Hardy Bros of Alnwick. Other makers to look for include Farlow, Illingworth Malloch, Allcock and Ogden Smith.
- A reel is more valuable if it is marked with the maker's name.
- Avoid reels that are cracked, bent or damaged - an original finish and good condition will fetch a much higher price.

A carved wooden salmon, c1930, 53 by 20in (134.5 by 51cm).
£750-800 *WAB*

A brass salmon-shaped corkscrew and bottle opener.
£30-35 *GHA*

CROSS REFERENCE
Corkscrews ⟶ p176

Two Hardy brass rod spikes.
£15-20 each *GHA*

A pair of embossed fish prints, in original frames, c1890, 20 by 16in (51 by 41cm).
£100-145 *TER*

Two gut cast boxes, with casts, 3¼ and 4¼in (8 and 10.5cm) diam.
£8-15 each *WAB*

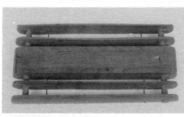

A fishing cast holder, with centre box, 19thC, 7 by 3½in (17.5 by 9cm).
£10-25 *WAB*

A Farlow line drier, 'The Sextile'.
£60-80 *JMG*

These were made of brass before 1912 and are very collectable pieces.

A bream, mounted in a bowfronted, gilt lined case, 24 by 14in (61 by 36cm).
£425-450 *GHA*

A Hardy C.C. de France, 2-piece split cane rod, 108in (274cm).
£350-450 *GHA*

A hinged brass clearing ring,
with locking latch, 2¼in (6cm).
£120-150 *GHA*

A New Hall porcelain plate,
with fishing scene, early 19thC.
£250-300 *GHA*

A turned wooden
priest, 19thC,
9in (23cm) long.
£60-80 *GHA*

Creels

A wicker creel.
£60-65 *GHA*

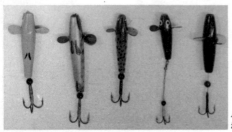

A French wicker and leather
creel, probably American,
c1920.
£45-65 *WAB*

Flies

A black japanned cast and fly
box.
£50-55 *GHA*

A black japanned cast
and fly box.
£60-65 *GHA*

Two Hardy fly fishing boxes,
3½ by 2½in (9 by 6cm) and 6 by
3½in (15 by 9cm).
£25-35 *WAB*

Lures

A selection of fishing lures.
£4-8 each *GHA*

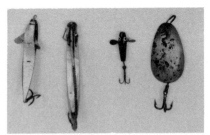

A selection of lures and spoons.
£4-10 each *GHA*

Nets

A gillie's ash framed landing net, from the Royal Dee, 19thC, 96in (243.5cm) long.
£130-150 *GHA*

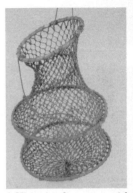

A Victorian keep net, with bamboo rings, 16in (41cm) high.
£10-20 *WAB*

An ash framed landing net, 19thC, 54in (137cm) long.
£80-120 *GHA*

A bamboo handled landing net and tip tube, 60in (152cm) long.
£15-25 *WAB*

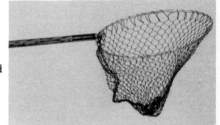

Reels

A 4in brass winch reel, with curved crank and turned ivory handle, 19thC.
£125-185 *GHA*

A 6in wooden sea reel, made by Peetz, Victoria BC, Canada, brass back on spool.
£30-40 *JMG*

A 4¼in plate wind reel, by J. Bernard & Son, London.
£100-200 *GHA*

A brass 1in clamp foot winch, 19thC.
£200-250 *GHA*

A 7in Nottingham centre pin, brass star back reel.
£65-70 *GHA*

A brass clamp foot winch, with bone handle, 19thC.
£150-180 *GHA*

A 4¼in Alex Martin of Scotland reel, 'The Thistle', very like a Hardy Perfect.
£50-65 *JMG*

A 2in brass Malloch side caster, with Gibbs patent lever.
£70-90 *GHA*

A large wood and brass Scarborough reel.
£60-65 *GHA*

Two Victorian brass anti-foul salmon reels, 4 and 3¾in (10 and 9.5cm) diam.
£45-75 each *WAB*

A 4¼in Marston Crosslé reel, with twin bone handles, ebonite on back.
£50-65 *JMG*
This is a very rare reel.

A 4in Wilkes Osprey reel, made in England, pre-WWII.
£40-50 *JMG*

A 4½in Allcock Aerial reel, c1925.
£60-80 *JMG*

A 4½in Westley Richards reel, 'The Rolo', patented 1911, by Walter Dingley, D inside.
£55-70 *JMG*

A 5½in Horwood of Killin reel, special narrow drum reel for trolling in Loch Tay, very rare.
£80-100 *JMG*

A 3½in brass sea reel, by Ogden Smith, London.
£40-45 *GHA*

A 2⅝in Malloch, 'The Sidecaster', smallest model, probably 1920s.
£50-65 *JMG*

A 4in Ogden Smith of London, wide drum reel, with white handle, c1917.
£40-50 *JMG*

A spinning reel, made in Brevete, France, marked 'Les Graduations Indiquent La Limite du Depart Dunylon'.
£30-40 *JMG*

A 2in brass plate wind reel, by C. Farlow & Co. Ltd, London, in a leather case.
£60-80 *GHA*

A 2in brass plate reel, by Anderson of Edinburgh, in a leather case.
£60-80 *GHA*

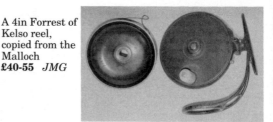

A 4in Forrest of Kelso reel, copied from the Malloch
£40-55 *JMG*

Two wooden coarse fishing reels, one with a brass face Slater catch mechanism, the other with Bickerdyke line guard, c1930, 4½ and 4in (11 and 10cm) diam.
£20-35 each *WAB*

A 4in Allcock 'The Brighton' reel, Bickerdyke lineguard, c1939.
£60-80 *JMG*

A 4in Malloch of Perth reel, 'The Sun & Planet', extremely rare reel, ebonite on the back.
£80-100 *JMG*

Hardy

A 2⅝in 'Uniqua' fly reel.
£75-85 *GHA*

A 4⅜in Perfect brass faced reel, c1903.
£200-250 *JMG*

This large size reel is very rare.

A 2¾in Perfect all brass reel, 1896 check. **£600-800** *GHA*

A 4¼in Perfect brass faced reel, nickel silver lineguard, ivorine handle, c1910.
£120-150 *JMG*

A 4in Silex Major 'Spitfire' model reel, by Jimmy Smith, c1940s.
£60-70 *JMG*

A 4¼in 'St George' reel, wide drum, made only c1920-25.
£300-400 *JMG*

A 3⅝in 'Uniqua', in good condition, c1920.
£50-65 *JMG*

A 4⅜in 'Hydra' reel, post-war model.
£20-30 *JMG*

A 3½in fly reel, 'The Davy', only about 80 of these reels made, 1930s.
£80-100 *JMG*

A 4in 'Uniqua' reel, 1910.
£30-40 *JMG*

This reel was made by Walter Dingley who left the Company that year.

A Jock-Scott bait-cast reel.
£60-80 *JMG*

A 3in 'The Bouglé' reel, c1910.
£200-250 *JMG*

'The Altex' reel, second early model, curved at bottom of the body.
£100-140 *JMG*

A 4in Silex Major reel.
£100-120 *GHA*

A 3⅛in Perfect reel, with agate lineguard, c1920, in Hardy leather case. **£80-120** *JMG*

A 4¼in Super Silex reel, with brass foot and ivorine rim check lever, in leather case.
£200-220 *GHA*

A 4¼in St. George reel, only made 1920-25.
£400-500 *JMG*

A 2⅝in 'Uniqua' with ivorine handle, horseshoe latch, c1920s.
£75-100 *JMG*

A 4in Perfect, with wide drum, no ball bearings, c1917.
£120-150 *JMG*

A 4⅛in Hardy Perfect, 'Eunoch' model, with extra Hardy metal piece opposite the handle, c1917.
£100-125 *JMG*

A 3⅝in Perfect 'Silent Check' reel, with agate line guide, smooth brass foot, heavily perforated inside casing behind the handle plate.
£950-1,000 *ND*

This model was known as 'The Eunoch', as it was constructed without ball bearings.

> **FURTHER READING**
> *Fishing Tackle, A Collectors Guide,* Graham Turner, Ward Lock, 1989.

FOSSILS, GEOLOGY & PREHISTORY

Fossils

Fossil collecting during Victorian times was very popular and exquisitely boxed collections were formed. But like so many older collecting areas, such as postage stamps, cigarette cards and coins, fossil collecting has been quiet over the past few years. Suddenly, due to the film Jurassic Park, interest has dramatically increased. As a result, we have included in this year's edition a selection of fossils as well as geological and mineral samples. Only time will tell if the resurgence of interest in fossils will be sustained, but one thing we can be sure of, there are very few collectables older than these.

A collection of professionally mounted fossil samples, with 4 lift-out trays, 200+ samples, 18¼in (46cm) wide.
£650-700 *CSK*

Devonian trilobite, Flexicalymene Ouzregi, Erfoud, Morocco, 3½in (9cm) long.
£8-10 *GBL*

A large trilobite, from Erfoud, Morocco, 5½in (14cm) long.
£100-120 *GBL*

Lower Cretaceous/Upper Jurassic water nymphs, Shandong Province, China, 2½in (6cm) square.
£50-60 *GBL*

A fine fossil fish, belonging to the Dapedwin orbis Agassiz, Jurassic period, 180-135 million years B.C., mounted and cased, 18⅛in (47cm).
£750-775 *Bon*

A letter accompanying this fossil from the Natural History Museum states that all the similar specimens in the museum come from the lower Liaie clay pits around Barrow-on-Soar, Leicestershire.

Ordovician trilobite, tracks of Flexicalymene species, from Ohio, USA, 4 by 4in (10 by 10cm).
£20-25 *GBL*

A mid-Jurassic pine cone, Araucaria Mirabilis, Patagonia, Argentina, 2⅓in (6cm) wide.
£225-250 *GBL*

A Cretaceous shark's tooth Lamna species, Morocco, 3in (7.5cm) wide.
£10-12 *GBL*

Devonian trilobite, greenops species, Issoumour, Morocco, approx. 380 million years old.
£20-25 *GBL*

A fossil rhino skull, Hydracodon nebrascensis, Oligocene, Badlands, South Dakota, USA, 18½ by 8in (47 by 20cm).
£1,500-1,600 *Bon*

A Placoderm fossil fish, Bothryolepis canadensis, Upper Devonian, Miguaska, Gaspesie, Canada, 12¼ by 7½in (31 by 19cm). **£2,000-2,100** *Bon*

A large three-toed dinosaur foot imprint, size of foot 12in (30.5cm).
£650-675 *Bon*

Quarried near Swanage, Dorset.

Plesiosaur vertebra, Jurassic Era, Oxfordshire, 2 by 3½in (5 by 9cm).
£20-25 *GBL*

A section through a mid-Jurassic pine cone, Araucaria Mirabilis, Pategonia, Argentina, 3¼in (8cm) long.
£150-175 *GBL*

A collection of Dominican Republic fossilised amber, the vast majority with insect inclusions.
£2,700-2,800 *Bon*

A fossil Pachypleurosaur, Permian, from Switzerland, 13 by 9in (33 by 23cm).
£2,400-2,500 *Bon*

A fossilized turtle, Stylemys nebrascensis, Oligocene, South Dakota, USA, 16½in (42cm).
£1,100-1,200 *Bon*

A dinosaur bone, Utah, USA, 3 by 1½in (8 by 4cm).
£8-9 *GBL*

Oligocene Oredon skull, predecessor of camel, Merycoidodon species, Sioux County, Nebraska, USA, 6in (15cm) wide.
£125-150 *GBL*

Dinosaur Eggs

With interest in fossil collecting once again on the increase, prices too are going up. This year at Bonhams in London a nest of dinosaur eggs, laid between 70 and 100 million years ago, sold for over £50,000. Similarly, the dinosaur eggs featured here also attained a high price, as did the 23 pieces of fossilized dinosaur droppings which sold for £3,000. This could prove to be the investment of the decade - there is no telling what they will be worth in another million years.

Upper Cretaceous tooth of Mosasaurus species reptile, Morocco, 4in (10cm) long.
£20-22 *GBL*

A large Sauropod egg, 7 by 6½in (17.5 by 15cm).
£4,800-5,000 *Bon*

A rare nest of 10 Sauropod eggs, embedded, size of eggs 5½in (14cm) diam, average nest size, 18in (46cm).
£48,000-54,000 *Bon*

A rare nest of 5 Sauropod eggs, embedded, 15 by 8½in (38 by 21.5cm).
£13,000-13,500 *Bon*

Twenty-three pieces of fossil dinosaur droppings, agatized, cut and polished, Hanksville, Utah, USA.
£3,100-3,300 *Bon*

Geology

A collection of geological samples, some professionally mounted, in 7 cardboard boxes.
£330-350 *CSK*

Rose quartz, from Madagascar, 7in (17.5cm) wide.
£15-20 *GBL*

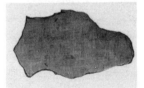

Cut and polished section of the Gibeon iron meteorite, Great Namaqualand, Nambia, 6½in (16cm) wide.
£300-350 *GBL*

First found in 1836, Gibeon is an unusual meteorite, found in a desolate area in the Nambian desert where the strewn field is over 275kms long. Recovered specimens often show evidence of flight markings.

Stibnite with barite, Baia Mare, Rumania, 2in (5cm) wide. **£20-22** *GBL*

Smokey quartz group, from Urals, Russia, 21 by 14in (53 by 36cm).
£600-650 *GBL*

Cotham marble, Bristol, 6¼in (15.5cm) wide.
£12-15 *GBL*

A green fluorite, Rogerley Mine, Frosterley, Co. Durham, 5½in (14cm) wide.
£20-25 *GBL*

Spodumene var kunzite, from Nuristan, Afghanistan, 2½in (6cm) wide.
£50-70 *GBL*

Almadine garnet, from Fort Wrangell, Alaska, 2¼in (5.5cm) wide.
£3-4 *GBL*

Topaz crystal in matrix, Himalayan Mountains, North Pakistan, 4 by 3½in (10 by 9cm).
£675-725 *GBL*

Iron meteorite, from Sikhote-Alin, Russia, 107gr, 2½in (6cm).
£325-350 *GBL*

The Sikhote-Alin iron meteorite fall was the largest in recorded history.
An estimated 23 tons of crystallised iron/nickel fell out of a clear blue sky at 10.30am on February 12, 1947, in thick forest in the Sikhote-Alin mountains, 25 miles from Novopoltavka Maritime Province.
The balide or fireball lasted about 5 seconds. The main crater was 26 metres across and 6 metres deep.

Implements

Native sulphur with aragonite, from Sicily, 3in (8cm) wide.
£20-25 *GBL*

Four thin-butted flint trapezoid outline axes, Danish Neolithic, circa 2,500-2,000 B.C., 9in (23cm).
£560-570 *Bon*

A group of finely flaked Egyptian prehistoric flint implements, including notched sickle blades, points, knives and nose scraper, 5th millennium B.C. **£340-380** *Bon*

A selection of thirteen Egyptian Acheulian flint implements, including ovate hand axes, points, and a 'spoke-shave', circa 200,000 B.C.
£1,500-1,600 *Bon*

Three thin-butted flint axes, of trapezoid outline, one honey coloured, Danish Neolithic, 9½in (24cm).
£340-360 *Bon*

A group of Danish Neolithic flint implements, including trapezoid flint axes, one a hafted dagger and polished chisels, circa 2,500-2,000 B.C.
£400-425 *Bon*

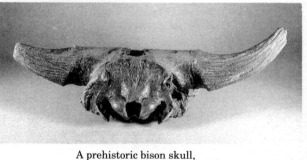

A prehistoric bison skull, Pricus, Germany, 29½ by 12in (75 by 30.5cm).
£550-575 *Bon*

Batman, No. 1, Spring 1940, the origin of Batman is retold by Bob Kane in this first issue which also features the first appearance of Joker and the Catwoman. **£13,000-14,000** *S(NY)*

The Amazing Spider-Man, No. 1, March 1963, Marvel Comics Group. **£6,750-7,200** *S(NY)*

Whiz Comics, No. 1, February 1940, Fawcett Publications, restored. **£3,500-4,000** *S(NY)*

Classic Comics, No. 1, 1st Edition, The Three Musketeers, in very good condition. **£750-850** *S(NY)*

The Fantastic Four, No. 1, Comic Book, from the White Mountain Collection, November 1961, Marvel Comics Group. **£18,700-19,200** *S(NY)*

Sensation Comics, No. 1, January 1942, National Periodicals Publications. **£1,500-2,000** *S(NY)*

Marvel Comics, No. 1, November 1939, Timely Publications, restored. **£10,500-11,000** *S(NY)*

Military Comics, No. 1, August 1941, Quality Comics Group, in good condition. **£520-550** *S(NY)*

Captain America Comics, No. 1, March 1941, autographed by Jack Kirby, some restoration. **£3,000-3,500** *S(NY)*

Flash, No. 105, Comic Book, good condition. **£1,200-1,500** *S(NY)*

The Incredible Hulk Comic Books,
Nos. 1-6, 1962-63, very good
condition.
£4,000-4,500 *S(NY)*

Archie Comics, Nos. 1-7 and 9-10,
1942-44, MLJ Magazine, very
good condition.
£4,200-4,800 *S(NY)*

The Incredible Hulk
Comics, Nos. 1-6 and 102,
1962-1968, Marvel
Comics.
£400-500 *S(NY)*

Detective Comics,
No. 28, June 1939,
D.C. Comics.
£1,500-2,000 *S(NY)*

Boy Commandos, Nos.
2,3,7,8,10 & 12, 1942,
National Periodical
Publications.
£2,500-3,500 *S(NY)*

The Human Torch
Comics, Nos. 1-10, & 13,
1940-43, Timely Comics,
very good condition.
£2,500-3,000 *S(NY)*

Tales of Suspense,
Nos. 39, 41, 43-99,
1962-67, Marvel
Comics, very good
condition.
£1,500-2,000 *S(NY)*

A collection of Superman's
Pal Jimmy Olsen, and
Superman's Girlfriend
Lois Lane comic books
and annuals, 1950s-60s.
£1,500-2,000 *S(NY)*

A Tarzan
Sunday page,
March 19,
1950, signed
Burne
Hogarth,
United
Features
Syndicate.
£10-12,000
S(NY)

A Frank Frazetta
hand painted and
signed print of cover
art for Thunda King
of the Congo, 1952 .
£1,200-1,500 *S(NY)*

The Gaines File Copies
of Crime SuspenStories,
Nos. 1-27, 1950-55,
E.C. Comics.
£6,200-6,500 *S(NY)*

All Star Comics, No. 3,
Winter 1940-41, D.C.
Publication, restoration
by Susan Cicconi.
£2,000-2,500 *S(NY)*

Detective Comics, No. 8,
1937, D.C. Comics.
£3,000-3,500 *S(NY)*

An Action man dressed as a footballer, 1970, sold either complete in box or separately. Action Man. **£20-50** Sealed box. **£80-100** *EGR*

An Action Man Talking Commander, pull cord mechanism, c1970, 12in (30.5cm). **£50-100** *EGR*

An Action Man Talking Commander, 8 random commands, c1968, 12in (30.5cm) high. **£80-100** *EGR*

An Action Girl, with fully jointed elbows, knees and ankles, c1974, 12in (30.5cm). **£20-30** *EGR*

An Action Man Grenadier Guard, c1973, 12in (30.5cm) high. **£100-150** Outfit only. **£30-50** *EGR*

An Action Man Royal Hussars uniform, from series of famous British uniforms, c1973. **£30-50** *EGR*

An Action Man Olympic Champion, with shiny track suit and accessories, c1968, 12in (30.5cm) high. **£80-100** *EGR* Action man was produced for 18 years.

A G.I. Joe, Hasbro, USA, c1964, 12in (30.5cm) high. Mint, no box. **£80-100** Boxed. **£100-200** *EGR*

An Action Man Action Soldier, c1967, 12in (30.5cm) high, with original box. **£100-150** *EGR*

An Action Girl, with fully jointed elbows, knees and ankles, c1974, 12in (30.5cm) high. **£20-30** *EGR*

A Denys Fisher
'Dusty' British
Airways girl, in
original box.
£18-20 *EGR*

A BND walkie talkie
doll, 1950s, 21in
(53.5cm) high.
£45-55 *EGR*

A Burbank vinyl doll,
wearing Brownie uniform,
c1970-77, 13in (33cm) high.
£8-10 *EGR*

A Denys Fisher 'Jennie'
schoolgirl, with Brownie camping
outfit, c1975, 7½in (19cm) high.
£10-15 *EGR*

'Francie',
Barbie's friend,
c1966, 11in
(28cm) high.
£40-50 *EGR*

A Burbank Goldilocks doll,
with vinyl head and hands,
body stuffed with beans, 10in
(25cm) high.
£5-6 *EGR*

An Almar costume
hard plastic doll, made
in London, c1964-78,
8in (20cm).
£2-3 *EGR*

A Rexard Mary Queen of
Scots historical costume doll,
hard plastic, various
costumes available, c1960,
8in (20cm) high. **£10-15** *EGR*

Two Amanda Jane girl dolls,
with painted eyes, c1970, 7in
(17.5cm) high.
£15-20 each *EGR*

Two Amanda Jane vinyl baby dolls, with
painted eyes, c1970, 6in (15cm) high.
£10-15 each *EGR*
These dolls are still produced.

A Barbie Fashion Queen
doll, with red hair,
wearing Friday Night
Date dress, c1963.
£80-100 *EGR*

Dolls knitting patterns, showing designs for hard plastic dolls, available throughout the 1950s and 1960s.
£1-2 each *EGR*

Silky, Tressy's sister, updated version of Toots, in original box, c1970, 9in (23cm) high.
£10-15 *EGR*

A Palitoy walkie talkie hard plastic doll, with sleeping eyes, c1953, 20in (50.5cm) high. **£80-100** *EGR*

A Frido doll, 1960s, 11in (28cm) high.
£10-15 *EGR*

A Palitoy 'Blythe' doll, pull cord changes eye colours, c1972, 9in(22.5cm) high.
£25-30 *EGR*

A Palitoy Mandy Lou, with side-glancing eyes, 1960s, 14in (35.5cm) high.
£8-10 *EGR*

A Girl Dress Me doll, promoted in Girl comic, dressed in clothes with Girl logo, c1955, 14½in (37cm) high. **£65-75** *EGR*

A Palitoy doll, with hard plastic head, 'beauty skin' body, wearing original clothes, c1952, 17½in (44cm) high. **£80-100** *EGR*

Rosebud twin dolls, who appeared in Woman's Weekly with all their outfits to knit, 1950s, 6in (15cm) high. **£8-10 each**

Three Sasha vinyl dolls, with painted eyes, c1980, 12 to 16in (30.5 to 41cm) high.

A Morris Mitchell
Prince Charming doll,
with sleeping eyes,
c1947, 13in (33cm) high.
£30-35 *EGR*

A Crolly walking talking
vinyl doll, with nylon hair,
c1930-70, 26in (66cm) high.
£40-50 *EGR*

A BND composition
doll, with sleeping
eyes, marked on back,
c1930-60, 16in (41cm)
high. **£40-45** *EGR*

A Chilton teenage
doll, with
underclothes, c1961,
15in (38cm) high.
£15-20 *EGR*

Two Denys Fisher Bionic
Woman dolls, c1970-80, with
original box.
Large. **£20-25**
Small. **£15-20** *EGR*

A Rexard Scottish
costume doll, c1970,
8in (20cm) high.
£2-3 *EGR*

A Lesney doll, Handy
Mandy, with soft body
and gripping hands,
c1978, 16in (40.5cm) high.
£8-10 *EGR*

A Palitoy doll,
Patti Pitta Pat,
1960s, 21in (53cm)
high.
£20-25 *EGR*

Two Amanda Jane vinyl girl dolls,
with painted eyes, one with a pottery
dog, c1980. **£10-15 each** *EGR*

BND twins, 'Toddlers', each
with sleeping eyes and voice
box, c1955, 13in (33cm) high.
£30-40 *EGR*

A Morris Mitchell, Marie
Valerie, with fixed glassine
eyes, 13in (33cm) high.
£30-35 *EGR*

A bisque headed child doll, with blue sleeping eyes, jointed wood and composition body. **£950-1,100** *CSK*

A bisque headed character doll, by Kestner, Roullet & Decamps, impressed 7, 13in (33cm) high. **£1,100-1,250** *CSK*

A French bisque headed bébé, incised Bru Ne 7, c1870, 20in (51cm) high. **£10,500-11,000** *CNY*

A Hertel, Schwab and Co. bisque character doll, impressed 141 3, 11in (28cm) high. **£1,000-1,100** *S*

A Bähr and Pröschild bisque character doll, for Kley and Hahn, impressed 536 4, c1912, 16in (41cm) high. **£950-1,100** *S*

A bisque headed character doll, with brown sleeping eyes, jointed wood and composition toddler body, impressed K*R Simon & Halbig 117 55, 20½in (52cm) high. **£5,000-5,250** *CSK*

A bisque headed bébé, with jointed wood and papier mâché body, impressed 8 with Schmitt shield, 17in (43cm). **£2,800-3,000** *CSK*

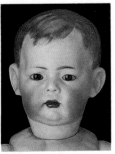

A bisque headed googlie eyed doll, impressed Heubach Koppelsdorf 319.5/o A.H. Schalkau D.R.G.M. **£3,150-3,300** *CSK*

A Kammer & Reinhardt/Simon & Halbig bisque character doll, c1911. **£4,250-4,500** *S*

A J. D. Kestner bisque Oriental doll, impressed K 14 243, c1914, 17in (43cm) high. **£4,350-4,600** *S*

l. A French pressed bisque doll, with brown glass eyes, kid body, impressed circle and dot Bru Jne 5, c1875, 17in (43cm) high. **£7,250-7,500** *S*

Moon Over Miami, 20th
Century Fox, 1941, one-sheet,
41 by 27in (104 by 68.5cm).
£4,500-5,000 *CNY*

The Wizard of Oz, MGM,
1939, one-sheet, linen backed,
41 by 27in (104 by 68.5cm).
£3,200-3,800 *CNY*

The Roaring Twenties, Warner
Brothers, 1939, one-sheet, paper
backed, 41 by 27in (104 by
68.5cm).
£2,800-3,500 *CNY*

Miracle on 34th Street,
20th Century Fox, 1947,
81in (205.5cm) square.
£1,250-1,750 *CNY*

A Night To Remember, Rank,
1958, original English six-sheet,
linen backed, 81in (205.5cm)
square. **£700-900** *CNY*

The Maltese Falcon, Warner
Brothers, 1941, one-sheet, linen
backed, 41 by 27in (104 by
68.5cm). **£2,500-3,000** *CNY*

Devil Dogs Of The Air, Warner Bros,
1935, three-sheet, 81 by 41in (205.5
by 104cm). **£3,500-4,000** *CNY*

l. Blonde Venus, Paramount, 1932,
13 by 9in (33 by 22.5cm).
£2,500-3,000 *CNY*

Winds Of The Wasteland, Republic, 1936.
£4,000-4,500 *CNY*

Stowaway, 20th Century Fox, 1936, three-sheet.
£2,500-3,000 *CNY*

Hell's Angels, United Artists, 1937, re-issue, one-sheet, linen backed.
£1,750-2,500 *CNY*

Flash Gordon's Trip to Mars, Universal, 1938, one-sheet, linen backed, 41 by 27in (104 by 68.5cm).
£5,500-6,000 *CNY*

Some Like It Hot, United Artists, 1959, three-sheet.
£1,000-1,500 *CNY*

The Ghost Of Frankenstein, Universal, 1942, three-sheet.
£4,000-5,000 *CNY*

Singin' In The Rain, MGM, 1952, three-sheet, linen backed.
£700-900 *CNY*

Creature From The Black Lagoon, Universal, 1954, three-sheet, linen backed, 81 by 41in (205.5 by 104cm).
£6,000-7,000 *CNY*

The Iron Mask, United Artists, 1929, one-sheet, linen backed.
£2,500-3,000 *CNY*

l. Son of Frankenstein, Universal, 1939, one sheet, linen backed, 41 by 27in (104 by 68.5cm).
£13,500-15,000 *CNY*
This poster was photographed prior to linen backing.

Yunge, Shell For Anti-Knock, colour lithograph, 1930, 30 by 45½in (76 by 115cm). **£1,500-1,700** *P*

Edward McKnight Kauffer, Actors Prefer Shell, colour lithograph, printed by Waterlow and Sons, 1935, 30 by 45in (76 by 114cm). **£2,250-2,500** *P*

Edward McKnight Kauffer, Aeroshell Lubricating Oil, colour lithograph, 1932, 30 by 44in (76 by 113cm) **£2,250-2,500** *P*

Tristram Hillier, Tourists Prefer Shell, colour lithograph, signed in pen and ink, printed by Baynard Press, 1936, 30 by 45in (76 by 114cm). **£1,850-2,000** *P*

l. Abram Games, Shell Lubricating Oil, Stays On The Job, colour lithograph, 1939, 30 by 45in (76 by 114cm). **£950-1,000** *P*

Edward McKnight Kauffer, New Shell Lubricating Oils, colour lithograph, printed by Waterlow & Sons, 1937, 30 by 45in (76 by 114cm). **£900-950** *P*

V. L. Danvers, The Quick Starting Pair - Oil and Petrol, colour lithograph, printed by Waterlow & Sons, 1926, 30 by 45in (76 by 114cm). **£300-325** *P*

Edward McKnight Kauffer, To Visit Britain's Landmarks, colour lithograph, 1936, 30 by 45in (76 by 114cm). **£750-800** *P*

l. J. S. Anderson, Motorists Prefer Shell, colour lithograph, printed by Waterlow & Sons, 1935, 30 by 45in (76 by 114cm). **£1,700-1,900** *P*

Two Art Nouveau style menus, c1924.
£5-6 each *COB*

A selection of I-Spy books.
£1-3 each *COB*

l. A selection of 6 luggage labels, 1930s.
£8-10 each *COB*

IL ÉTAIT UNE BERGÈRE

Four watercolour and ink paintings, c1930.
£30-40 each *COB*

A French Line restaurant menu.
£5-6 *COB*

A British Grand Prix official programme, Silverstone, 14th May, 1949.
£30-35 *COB*

Sheet music from Walt Disney's film Snow White and the Seven Dwarfs, 1930s.
£6-7 *COB*

A Harrods Store brochure, 1963.
£10-12 *COB*

A French fan, with painted leaf, the mother-of-pearl sticks pierced and gilt, some damage, c1750, 10½in (26cm), in red morocco fan box. **£5,750-6,250** *CSK*

A fan, with leaf painted to show an orchestra, the verso with a lady and Cupid playing music, the ivory sticks carved and pierced with chinoiserie, repairs, c1730, 11½in (29cm). **£625-650** *C*

A North European fan, with painted leaf, the ivory sticks pierced and painted with chinoiserie, c1775, 8in (20cm). **£740-780** *CSK*

A French fan, with satin leaf painted with ballooning scenes, carved and pierced ivory sticks, 1783. **£4,750-5,000** *C*

A horn brisé fan, painted, slightly warped, c1830, 7in (17.5cm). **£150-160** *CSK*

A fan with painted leaf, with pierced mother-of-pearl sticks, slight damage, c1815, 6in (15cm). **£1,000-1,100** *CSK*

A fan, with painted leaf, the tortoiseshell sticks carved, pierced and gilt, c1750, 9in (23cm). **£2,100-2,300** *C*

A fan, the mother-of-pearl sticks carved, pierced and gilt, repaired, c1730, 11in (28cm). **£1,100-1,200** *C*

l. A printed fan, the leaf a hand coloured stipple engraving, with wooden sticks, German or French, c1795, 9½in (24cm). **£225-250** *CSK*

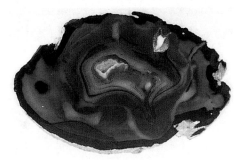

Agate, from Brazil, 8in (20cm) wide.
£15-18 *GBL*

Eocene, Green river shales, Mioplosus species, Wyoming, USA, 12 by 10in (30.5 by 25cm). **£180-210** *GBL*

Cretaceous fossil wood, Brazil, 12in (30.5cm) wide.
£80-90 *GBL*

Cobaltian calcite, from Mashamba West Copper Mine, Shaba Province, Zaire, 2in (5cm) wide.
£30-35 *GBL*

Ammonite, Eparietites species, Lower Jurassic Age, Scunthorpe.
£100-120 *GBL*

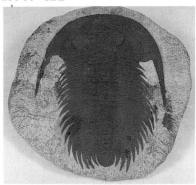

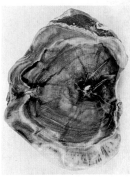

Devonian trilobite, Paradoxides species. Morocco, 350 million years old. **£200-235** *GBL*

Ammonite, Fordingham ironstone, Aegasteroceras species, Jurassic, Scunthorpe, 6½in (16cm) wide. **£200-250** *GBL*

Opalised fossil wood, Springsure, Queensland, Australia, 5½in (14cm) wide.
£60-75 *GBL*

l. Turritella terebralis fossil shells, Lower Miocene Age, Bordeaux, France. **£20-25** *GBL*

r. Lower inferior oolite ammonite, Ludwigia Murchisonae, Dorset, 7in (17.5cm) wide.
£100-130 *GBL*

Agate, from Brazil,
9in (22.5cm) wide.
£20-25 *GBL*

Pyrite, fools gold,
Navajum, La Rioja,
Spain, uncut, 4in
(10cm) high.
£60-75 *GBL*

Quartz crystal, from Arkansas,
USA, 10in (25cm) wide.
£375-425 *GBL*

Crocoite, Tasmania,
4⅓in (11cm) wide.
£10-15 *GBL*

Amethyst, from Southern Brazil,
10in (25cm) wide.
£125-150 *GBL*

Malachite, from Zaire,
8in (20cm) wide.
£300-350 *GBL*

Barite, from Pohla,
Saxony, 4in (10cm) wide.
£60-70 *GBL*

Ruin marble, Paesina, Florence, Italy,
used for furniture, 18in (45.5cm) wide.
£20-25 *GBL*

Aquamarine crystals on
matrix, Gilgit, Himalaya
Mountains, 7in (17.5cm)
wide. **£3,000-3,200** *GBL*

Specular hematite with
quartz, from Beckermet
Mine, Egremont,
Cumbria, 4⅜in (12cm)
high. **£30-40** *GBL*

Polished serpentine, from The
Lizard, Cornwall, 10¼in (26cm) high.
£18-22 *GBL*

Pyrite, fools gold, from Peru,
8in (20cm) wide.
£60-80 *GBL*

A Maltese glass vase, predominantly green, signed, 20thC, 6in (15cm) high.
£35-40 *SER*

A Bohemian etched glass goblet, 4½in (11cm) high.
£75-85 *FMN*

Two mercury glass mugs, c1860, with inscriptions, 3½in (9cm) high.
£125-145 each *MJW*

A Bohemian etched glass vase, 7½in (19cm) high.
£80-90 *FMN*

A Nailsea glass pipe, c1860, 21½in (54cm) long.
£400-450 *MJW*

A mercury glass double walled vase, marked Varnish & Co, c1880, 9in (23cm) high.
£500-620 *ARE*

Three mercury glass goblets, c1850:
l. Varnish & Co, 9¼in (23cm) high. **£200-220**
c. Hale Thompson, 5in (13cm) high. **£150-175**
r. Varnish & Co, 8in (20cm) high.
£175-200 *ARE*

A satin glass egg paperweight, c1815, 4in (10cm) high.
£30-40 *SER*

A pair of German glass rummers, made for the Islamic market, c1860, 5½in (14cm) high.
£250-285 *MJW*

Webb's Queen's Burmese glass, c1890-1900:
l. Acid stamped night light, 4in (10cm) high.
£100-135 *c.* Vase, 6¼in (16cm) high. **£325-365**
r. A pair of vases, 3¼in (8cm) high. **£650-680** *MJW*

A blue glass double
overlay vase, 10in
(25cm) high.
£70-80 *MJW*

An Arts & Crafts claret
jug, by James Powell,
c1900, 11¼in (29cm) high.
£350-385 *MJW*

A pair of glass paperweights, filled with sea
shells, on marble mounts, c1860, 2⅜in (6cm)
square. **£325-350** *MJW*

A set of 4 Italian handmade glass fish, c1955,
9in (22.5cm) high.
£90-100 *OCA*

A glass pen stand, with hounds, c1880,
5⅞in (15cm) high. **£300-350** *MJW*
*Usually called 'Nailsea' but normally
made around Stourbridge.*

A French hyacinth
vase, c1870, 8in
(20cm) high.
£125-150 *MJW*
l. A faux cameo glass
plate, Val St. Lamert,
Belgium, c1890, 6in
(15cm) diam.
£200-245 *MJW*

A pair of mercury glass
salts, by Vanish & Co,
c1845, 3in (7.5cm) high.
£150-180 *MJW*

An 'End of Day' candle-
stick, with colours
overlaid on white glass,
c1845, 9¼in (23cm) high.
£30-40 *SER*

GLASS

- **Early lead glass has a greenish tinge, while later techniques produced progressively more transparent glass.**
- **Lead glass should emit a clear ring when tapped with a fingernail - BE CAREFUL!**
- **It was not until c1850, when coloured glass was first used for bottles, decanters and tumblers, that it became popular.**
- **Look for the pontil mark on the base of glass - it could have been polished off, but the mark will still be visible.**
- **The presence of a pontil mark alone is no guarantee of age.**

A spirit dispenser, c1880, 20in (51cm) high. **£400-500** *ARE*

A Victorian Nailsea style jug, 3½in (9cm) high. **£30-40** *AA*

A set of 4 Italian handmade glass fish, c1950-60, 11 to 14in (28 to 36cm) wide. **£80-100** *OCA*

A ship in a bottle, 11½in (29cm) long. **£85-95** *BWA*

CROSS REFERENCE
Shipping ⟶ p387
Models ⟶ p389

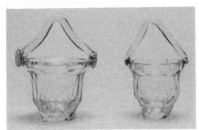

Two glass baskets from a hanging stand for sweetmeats, c1750, 4 and 3½in (10 and 8.5cm) high. **£220-245** *MJW*

An English crystal ball, c1910, 4½in (11.5cm) high. **£40-45** *TER*

A glass bottle, c1790, 8in (20cm) high. **£100-150** *MJW*
Possibly used for emergencies at dinner parties!

A glass chamber pot, with fold-over rim and simple scrolled handle, 18thC, 8in (20cm) diam. **£380-400** *MCA*
Believed, by family tradition, to have been used by one of Queen Anne's ladies-in-waiting.

A 'Nailsea' snuff jar, with olive green crown, and turned-over rim, c1820, 11in (28cm) high. **£130-145** *Som*

Bird Feeders

A selection of glass bird feeders, 3 with blue stoppers, c1800, 5¼ to 6½in (13 to 16.5cm) high.
£125-245 each *MJW*

Biscuit Barrels

A pale green cased glass biscuit barrel, with silver plate cover, English, 1890, 8½in (21.5cm) high.
£150-165
ARE

A biscuit barrel, with silver lid, decorated with ferns, c1880, 6½in (16.5cm) high.
£150-180 *MJW*

Bottles

Three glass bottles, French:
l. c1760, 6in (15cm).
£100-125
c. c1760, 7in (17.5cm).
£150-180
r. c1740, 6½in (16.5cm).
£125-150 *MJW*

l. & r. A pair of green wrythen moulded spirit bottles, c1830, 11½in (29.5cm) high.
£650-700
c. An amethyst spirit bottle, with plain body, c1830, 12½in (32cm) high.
£440-480 *Som*

A bottle, engraved 'Brandy', c1850, 4in (10cm) high.
£60-70 *MJW*

Carnival Glass

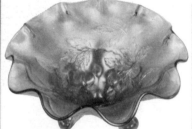

A carnival glass three-legged bowl, c1910, 8in (20cm) diam.
£20-30 *TER*

MAKE THE MOST OF MILLERS

Condition is absolutely vital when assessing the value of any item. Damaged pieces appreciate much less than perfect examples. However, a rare, desirable piece may command a high price even when damaged.

Claret Jugs

A decanter/claret jug, by Hukin & Heath, designed by Christopher Dresser.
£460-480 *Sim*

CROSS REFERENCE
Art Nouveau ⟶ p22
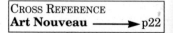

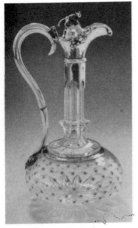

A claret jug, with etched band of diamonds, notched cut neck, applied handle, and notched spire stopper, c1880, 10in (24.5cm) high.
£170-190
Som

A mid-Victorian silver mounted shaft and globe claret jug, by Creswick & Co, Sheffield 1861, 10½in (26cm) high overall.
£1,800-1,900 *HSS*

A claret jug, by William Comyns & Sons, London 1898, 10¾in (27.5cm) high.
£800-825 *WIL*

Cruet Bottles

A pair of blue cruet bottles, with gilt wine label cartouches, 'Soy' and 'Kyan', gilt facet cut ball stoppers, c1790, 4in (10cm) high. **£600-650** *Som*

Cranberry Glass

A table centre, on mirrored base, 6in (15cm) high.
£130-150 *TER*

A Victorian glass decanter, 11in (28cm) high.
£120-150 *FMN*

A jug, with twisted handle, c1890, 7½in (19cm) high.
£250-290 *ARE*

A Nailsea bowl, c1860, 5½in (14cm).
£120-130 *AMH*

An Irish cruet bottle, c1780, 6in (15cm) high.
£90-110 *MJW*

Two cruet bottles, with stoppers, c1780, 6½ and 7in (15 and 17.5cm) high.
£80-100 each *MJW*

Custard Cups

An engraved custard cup, c1790, 2½in (6.5cm) high.
£125-145 *MJW*

Decanters

A tantalus containing two decanters, on a stand, c1880, 13in (33cm) high.
£150-200 *CAI*

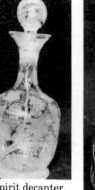

A spirit decanter, with foot ring, finely engraved with hops and barley, engraved ball stopper, c1860, 8in (19.5cm) high.
£180-200 *Som*

A cut glass swirl decanter, c1890, 11½in (29cm) high.
£90-110 *DUN*

A decorated glass spirit barrel, c1880, 10½in (26.5cm) high.
£120-140 *DUN*

A pair of cut glass Greek key pattern decanters, c1870, 12½in (31.5cm) high.
£250-300 *DUN*

Three decanters, with diamond, strawberry diamond, fluted and prism cutting, mushroom stoppers, c1825, largest 8½in (21.5cm) high.
£220-240 each *Som*

A pair of spirit decanters, with cut mushroom stoppers, c1825, 7½in (19cm) high.
£800-850 *Som*

A decanter and stopper, c1850, 12in (31cm).
£200-225 *MJW*

A decanter, c1840, 13in (33cm) high.
£125-170 *MJW*

A cut glass duck decanter, c1920, 7in (17.5cm) high.
£200-250 *DUN*

A Newcastle decanter, c1840, 13in (33cm) high.
£100-150 *MJW*

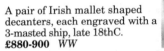

A silver mounted cut glass decanter, c1884, 8in (20cm) high.
£180-200 *DUN*

A pair of Irish mallet shaped decanters, each engraved with a 3-masted ship, late 18thC.
£880-900 *WW*

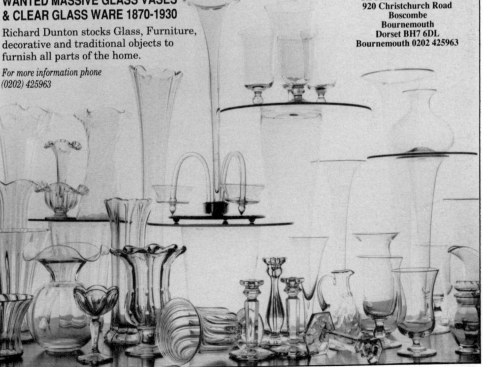

Drinking Glasses

A mixed twist flute, with trumpet shaped bowl and air twist threads, c1760, 7½in (19cm) high.
£920-940 *Som*

Two balustroid wine glasses, with ogee bowls on stems with central ball knops, c1750:
l. Plain conical foot, 5in (13.5cm).
£280-290
r. Folded conical foot, 5½in (14cm) high.
£210-220 *Som*

An ale glass, with waisted trumpet bowl engraved with hops and barley, multiple spiral air twist stem, c1750, 8in (20.5cm) high.
£700-750 *Som*

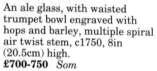

A green wine glass, with cup shaped bowl, coarse incised twist, swelling knop, on a plain conical foot, c1760.
£900-950 *Som*

Four coloured wine glasses: c1880, 5in (12.5cm) high.
l. Amethyst. **£80-90**
c. Green and red. **£20-30 each**
r. Blue. **£60-70** *MJW*

l. A set of 6 wine glasses, with cup bowls and plain stems, c1860, 5¼in (13.2cm) high.
£250-260
r. A set of 8 wine glasses, the ovoid bowls with drawn flute cut stems, c1850, 5in (12.5cm) high.
£380-400 *Som*

Three ale glasses, with funnel bowls, double series opaque white twists, on plain conical feet, c1760, largest 8in (20cm) high. **£300-320** *Som*

A light green double bowl wine glass, with short stem, the bowls with moulded strawberry prunts, c1780, 5¾in (14.5cm) high.
£880-900 *Som*

l. A wine glass, with bell bowl, multiple spiral air twist, on plain conical foot, c1745, 6¾in (17cm) high.
£460-480
r. A wine glass, with round funnel bowl, on a stem with a single spiralling cable air twist, on folded conical foot, c1745, 7in (17.5cm) high. **£400-420** *Som*

An amber glass goblet, c1810, 9½in (23.5cm) high.
£120-170 DUN

A set of 6 Victorian panel cut champagne flutes, c1840, 8in (20cm) high.
£300-360 DUN

A set of 6 cut glass goblets, c1890, 5½in (13.5cm) high.
£90-120 DUN

A pair of cut glass and engraved goblets, c1900, 6in (15cm) high.
£40-50 DUN

A set of 6 Victorian panel cut goblets, c1880.
£140-160 DUN

A clear glass champagne flute, c1900, 6in (15cm) high.
£40-60 DUN

A pair of cut glasses, engraved with fighting cocks, c1900, 5in (12.5cm) high.
£30-40 DUN

A Victorian green glass panel cut goblet, c1850, 5in (12.5cm) high.
£45-50 DUN

A green wine glass, early 19thC, 5in (12.5cm) high.
£30-40 DUN

A set of 6 Victorian panel cut champagne flutes, c1860, 7in (17.5cm) high.
£200-250 DUN

A set of 6 Victorian panel cut open bowl goblets, c1880, 5in (12.5cm) high.
£90-120 DUN

A set of 6 cut and etched hock glasses, with amber stems, c1900, 7in (17.5cm) high.
£180-220 DUN

l. A wine glass, with trumpet bowl, drawn stem with multiple spiral air twist, on plain conical foot, c1750, 6½in (16cm) high.
£360-380

r. A wine glass, with round funnel bowl, on a stem with a single series corkscrew 'mercury' twist, on plain conical foot, c1750, 6½in (16cm) high.
£460-480 *Som*

An 'export' type wine glass, the cup bowl on a hollow knopped stem, plain domed foot, c1760, 6¼in (15.5cm) high.
£520-550 *Som*

Two wine glasses, with ogee bowls, double series opaque twists, on plain conical feet, c1760, largest 6in (15cm) high.
£240-280 each *Som*

Dumps

A Victorian green glass dump, 5in (12.5cm) high.
£75-100 *ACA*

A Victorian green glass dump, 7in (17.5cm) high.
£100-120 *ACA*

These large glass dumps were generally used as doorstops.

A Victorian green glass dump, 3½in (8cm) high.
£75-100 *ACA*

A Victorian green glass dump, 6in (15cm) high.
£100-125 *ACA*

Finger Bowls

Three green finger bowls, c1830: 2½ to 3¾in (6 to 9cm) high.
£65-80 each *Som*

A blue finger bowl, with leaf band and looped gilt decoration, c1810, 3¾in (9cm).
£600-625 *Som*

l. A blue cylindrical finger bowl, c1820, 3in (7.9cm) high.
£400-425

r. A light green wrythen finger bowl, 3½in (8.5cm).
£120-130 *Som*

Flasks

A pair of Irish cut glass water flasks, c1780, 5½in (13.5cm) high.
£250-300 *MJW*

Goblets

A glass flask and tumbler, engraved with vines, c1830, tumbler 2¾in (7cm), and flask 6¼in (15.5cm) high.
£250-285 *MJW*

A Bohemian glass 2-handled goblet, engraved with vines, c1760, 5¼in (13cm) high.
£125-170 *MJW*

A goblet, with round funnel bowl, solid base section and air tear, folded conical foot, c1700, 6½in (16cm) high.
£1,600-1,650 *Som*

A goblet, with bucket bowl, on a multiple spiral air twist stem, plain conical foot, c1750, 7in (17.5cm) high.
£480-500 *Som*

A goblet, with flared rim and annulated band round the body, knopped stem and loop handle, c1820, 5½in (14cm).
£210-220 *Som*

A goblet, with round funnel bowl, on a stem with base knops and air tear, folded conical foot, c1710, 8in (20cm) high.
£2,000-2,100 *Som*

Jelly Glasses

Two jelly glasses:
l. With a double ogee rib moulded bowl, collar and mould ribbed domed folded foot, c1760, 4¼in (10.5cm) high.
£80-90
r. With hexagon bowl, air beaded plain domed foot, c1760, 4in (10cm) high.
£150-160 *Som*

A set of 8 jelly glasses, with wide fluted trumpet bowls, plain conical feet, c1840, 4⅓in (11cm) high.
£160-170 *Som*

MAKE THE MOST OF MILLERS

Price ranges in this book reflect what you should expect to *pay* for a similar example. When selling, however, you would expect to receive a lower figure. This will fluctuate according to a dealer's stock and saleability at a particular time, etc. It is always advisable, when selling a collectable, to approach a reputable dealer or an auction house which has specialist sales.

Lacemakers' Lamps

A lacemaker's lamp, c1760, 3in (8cm) high.
£250-300 *MJW*

CROSS REFERENCE	
Sewing ⟶	p385
Lighting ⟶	p292

A lacemaker's lamp, c1780, 8in (20cm) high.
£250-300 *MJW*

Lustres

A pair of Victorian cranberry lustre vases, decorated in gilt and enamel colours, with concentric rings of lustre drops, 15in (38cm) high.
£450-470 *Mit*

A pair of Victorian blue glass lustres, in original condition, 13in (33cm) high.
£450-500 *BRK*

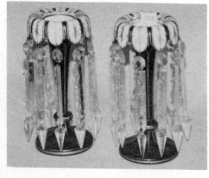

A pair of green glass lustres, with opaque white turned over tops, gilt leaf vines, feather gilt work, mid-19thC, 10in (25cm) high.
£400-420 *GAK*

MAKE THE MOST OF MILLERS

Condition is absolutely vital when assessing the value of any item. Damaged pieces appreciate much less than perfect examples. However, a rare, desirable piece may command a high price even when damaged.

Lalique

A Lalique opalescent bowl, Roscoff pattern, signed R. Lalique, France, 16in (41cm) diam.
£500-525 *MCA*

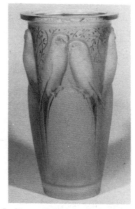

A Lalique Ceylan vase, with flared rim, signed R. Lalique, France, 9½in (23.5cm) high.
£1,500-1,600 *AH*

Monart

A Monart glass bowl, signed, 9¼in (23cm) diam.
£45-50 *BWA*

Monart and Vasart glass have been regular features in previous editions of *Miller's Collectables Price Guides*, available from Millers Publications.

Paperweights

A St. Louis crown paperweight, mid-19thC, 7.2cm wide.
£1,200-1,400 *CSK*

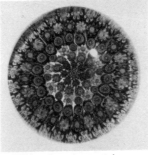

A Clichy close concentric millefiori pedestal paperweight, on a clear circular foot, mid-19thC, 7.2cm diam.
£2,300-2,500 *CSK*

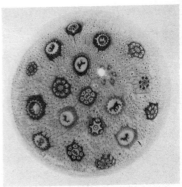

A Baccarat pink and white carpet-ground scattered millefiori paperweight, mid-19thC, 7.8cm diam.
£3,500-3,700 *CSK*

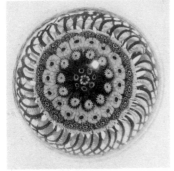

A St. Louis concentric millefiori mushroom paperweight, on a star cut base, mid-19thC, 7.5cm diam. **£1,600-1,800** *CSK*

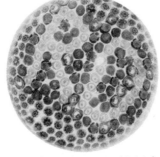

A Clichy carpet-ground initial paperweight, with the letters R D, mid-19thC, 8.3cm diam.
£1,600-1,800 *CSK*

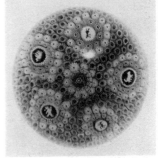

A St. Louis green carpet-ground concentric millefiori paperweight, mid-19thC, 6.5cm diam.
£4,800-5,000 *CSK*

Patch Stands

Two patch stands:
l. c1740, 3⅜in (8.5cm) high.
£250-295
r. c1750, 3in (7.5cm) high.
£300-345
MJW

A selection of patch stands, 3¼ to 5in (8 to 12.5cm) diam. **£300-480 each** *MJW*

Patch stands were used by ladies to keep their patches or beauty spots.

CROSS REFERENCE
Kitchenalia ⟶ p285

Patty Pans

Six glass patty pans, with folded rims, c1780, from 4in to 4¾in (10 to 12cm).
£330-340 *Som*

Three glass patty pans, c1745-1770, 1¼in to 3in (3cm to 7.5cm) high. **£50-100 each** *MJW*

Romano-Syrian Glass

A glass bottle, 1st-2nd Century AD, 4¾in (12cm).
£450-485 *MJW*

Many Roman glass items were found in garrison towns and spas, and possibly contained bath oils and perfumes, usually found in sandy places in the Middle East.

Three bottles, 2nd-3rd Century AD, 5 to 7in (12.5 to 17.5cm) high.
£400-500 each *MJW*

A Roman cosmetic pot, 1st-2nd Century AD, 2⅜in (6cm) high.
£200-265 *MJW*

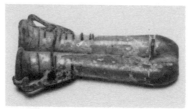

A double flask, 1st-3rd Century AD, 5in (12.5cm) long.
£400-450 *MJW*

A bottle, 2nd-3rd Century AD, 6¼in (15.5cm) high.
£300-350 *MJW*

A flask, 2nd-3rd Century AD, 13in (33cm) long.
£250-285 *MJW*

Two miniature bottles, 2nd-3rd Century AD, 2½ to 3in (6 to 7.5cm) high.
£150-300 each *MJW*

A Roman bottle, 1st-2nd Century AD, 5¾in (14cm) high.
£150-185 *MJW*

A bottle, 1st-2nd Century AD, 5⅓in (14cm) high.
£450-480 *MJW*

Two flasks, 2nd-3rd Century AD, 4 to 4⅓in (10 to 11cm) long.
£165-180 *MJW*

A flask, 2nd-3rd Century AD,
5in (12.5cm) high.
£200-225 *MJW*

Scent Bottles

A red double-ended scent bottle,
with silver gilt tops, 4in (10cm)
long.
£125-150 *BWA*

Tazzas

A Bohemian tazza,
engraved with
leaves and flowers,
c1740,
5in (12.5cm) high.
£300-345 *MJW*

A North German green perfume
bottle, c1700, 9½in (23.5cm)
long.
£90-115 *MJW*

> **Miller's is a price
> GUIDE not a price
> LIST**

Vases

Three hyacinth vases:
l. Amethyst, c1860, 5⅜in (14cm).
£60-70
c. Vaseline, c1870, 7¼in (18cm).
£100-145
r. Amber, 5¾in (14.5cm).
£45-55 *MJW*

A pair of green and multi-
coloured glass vases, with brass
tops, 6in (15cm) high.
£50-60 *ROW*

A Bohemian
Jugendstil glass
vase, c1880,
10¼in (26cm).
£100-135 *MJW*

An Art glass
vase, 1950s,
8in (20cm)
high.
£18-25 *AA*

A Moser and Shone amethyst
glass vase, 10in (25cm) high.
£300-400 *ZEI*

Three celery vases:
l. Engraved with ferns, c1870,
9¼in (23cm) high.
£100-135
c. Cut glass, c1830, 10in (25cm)
high.
£200-240
r. Moulded blown, c1840, 9in
(22.5cm).
£100-135 *MJW*

GRAMOPHONES

An HMV Model 460 table gramophone, with Lumière pleated diaphragm and quarter veneered oak case, some damage, c1924-5, 22in (55.5cm) deep. **£650-750** *CSK*

A Figuraphone children's tinplate clockwork gramophone, with 3 records. **£220-250** *MAW*

An HMV Model 25 gramophone, with No. 2 soundbox with clip, gooseneck tone arm and black Morning Glory horn, in oak case, c1926. **£900-1,000** *CSK*

A Gramophone Company Senior Monarch gramophone, with triple spring motor, Exhibition soundbox, oak horn and case, trade plaque J. B. Galbraith & Sons, Glasgow, c1910. **£1,600-1,700** *CSK*

A Primaphone compact portable gramophone, with Thorens Imperial soundbox, tone arm and wood horn mounted in lid, in polished wood case, c1929, 9¾in (24.5cm) wide. **£270-300** *CSK*

An HMV Monarch gramophone, with double spring motor, 10in (25cm) turntable, Exhibition soundbox, oak case and red Morning Glory horn, c1910. **£1,000-1,200** *CSK*

A gramophone, in the form of a miniature grand piano, in a walnut case, 39in (99cm) high. **£800-1,000** *CSK*

An HMV Model XIII mahogany cabinet grand gramophone, with Gramophone Co HMV Exhibition soundbox 5175, c1910, 49in (124cm) high. **£450-650** *CSK*

A 'Hero' horn gramophone, with Reform type soundbox, quick release needle clip, shaded blue/green flower horn and oak case, c1910. **£450-550** *CSK*

A French Menstrel phonograph, c1900.
£500-600 *TTM*

An HMV portable gramophone, 1930s, 11in (28cm) wide.
£60-70 *TTM*

A brass horn gramophone, Gramophone Co, style No.6, c1903. **£800-900** *TTM*

An HMV wind-up gramophone, with record storage in lid, 1930s, in Rexine covered plywood case, 6½ by 11⅓in (16 by 29cm).
£45-100 *RMV*

A Bing Pygmy Phone, 1940s.
£80-100 *TTM*

> **For a further selection of gramophones and gramophone needle tins, see *Miller's Collectables Price Guide, Vol V*, pp245-246.**

HATPINS

A collection of hat flash pins, Bakelite set with diamanté and silver dots, 1920s, 2 to 3in (5 to 8cm) long.
£20-30 each
BAT

A Peter Pan gramophone, probably Swiss, mid-1920s.
£100-150 *TTM*

A selection of hat flash pins, Bakelite set with diamanté and silver, c1920, 3 to 4in (8 to 10cm) long.
£10-30 each *BAT*

> CROSS REFERENCE
> **Art Deco ⟶ p23**

HORSEBRASSES & HARNESS

A mounted brass horse's browband with rosettes and ribbons, 18in (46cm) long.
£30-35 *SAD*

A facepiece, inscribed 'Mason, Saddlers, Perth', on leather with crescent brass, c1925.
£50-55 *SAD*

Heavy horse harness with crupper, 19thC.
£90-95 *SAD*

Two early cast horse brasses.
£25-30 each *SAD*

A decorated loin strap for a heavy horse, c1895, 20in (51cm) long.
£50-60 *SAD*

l. An early cast horse brass.
£25-30
r. A Queen Victoria Golden Jubilee horse brass, 1887.
£70-75 *SAD*

A decorated hame plate, Queen Victoria's Jubilee, 1887, 7 by 4in (17.5 by 10cm).
£75-80 *SAD*

l. A heavy cast horse brass, 4½ by 3¼in (11 by 8cm).
£25-30
r. A Queen Victoria's Jubilee horse brass.
£30-35 *SAD*

An anchor horse brass, on leather with red plush backing.
£40-48 *SAD*

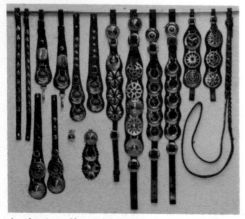

A selection of horse brasses, on original leather martingales, with lead rein and brass hanging rail, 19thC.
£675-700 *GH*

HORTICULTURAL & FARM EQUIPMENT

An iron planter, painted green, 33in (84cm) high.
£70-80 *AL*

A wheel-on-stand for straw rope making, c1880.
£100-120 *AL*

A fox trap, 19thC.
£40-50 *PC*

JEWELLERY

An EPNS belt.
£45-50 *SBA*

A Bakelite and chrome bracelet
and necklace, c1920.
£40-60 *BAT*

A Continental chevron link
bracelet, with sprung bar clasp.
£600-625 *CSK*

A pair of Continental cuff links,
by Piaget, applied with the crest
of The Sultan of Oman, in
maker's fitted case.
£320-340 *CSK*

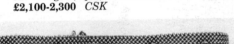

An 18ct gold, opal, diamond and ruby bracelet.
£2,100-2,300 *CSK*

A diamond and ruby
10 stone mesh link
bracelet.
£325-350 *CSK*

An Edwardian floral garland
openwork pendant, set with
central pearl and half pearls,
suspended from a neck chain.
£550-575 *CSK*

CROSS REFERENCE
Art Deco ⟶ p23

An 18ct gold, cabochon aquamarine and
sapphire ring, applied with maker's plaque
'Antonini', with a pair of matching 18ct
gold clip earrings.
£680-720 *CSK*

Arts & Crafts

A Liberty & Co. silver and
enamel openwork cloak clasp,
designed by Jessie M. King,
stamped marks L & Co with
Birmingham hallmarks for 1905.
£640-680 *C*

A ring, by Arthur & George
Gaskin, with opal cabochon
within golden wire ropework
mount.
£750-775 *P*

A W.H. Haseler silver and enamel
waist clasp, designed by Jessie M.
King, for Liberty, with
polychrome enamel decoration,
with maker's marks W.H.H. and
Birmingham hallmarks for 1906.
£2,200-2,400 *C*

A set of 6 Guild of Handicraft white metal buttons, in original fitted case.
£350-450 *C*

A necklace, with a plaque of mother-of-pearl and 2 green stained chalcedony cabochons.
£140-160 *P*

CROSS REFERENCE
Buttons ⟶ p42

A brooch, set with 6 cabochons of Mexican fire opals, marked ZW & Co, Made in England, 1¾in (4.5cm) wide.
£160-180 *P*

A brooch, attributed to Sibyl Dunlop, set with citrine, pastes and chrysolite, 1in (2.5cm) diam and another brooch, also attributed to Dunlop, set with fire opals, chrysoberyls and moonstones, 1½in (4cm) wide.
£300-325 *P*

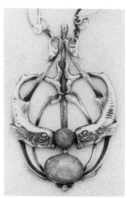

A white metal pendant, set with opals, by Edgar Simpson, stamped ES.
£1,800-1,900 *C*

Black Glass Jewellery

A black glass brooch.
£12-20 *HAY*

Do not confuse black glass jewellery with jet jewellery, although black glass used to be known as French jet.

A black glass necklace with tassel.
£30-45 *HAY*

Bog Oak Jewellery

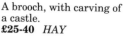

A brooch, with carving of a castle.
£25-40 *HAY*

A brooch, with circular carving.
£20-30 *HAY*

Bog oak jewellery is made from bog oak trees recovered from the peat bogs in Ireland. In many cases the actual material can date from the Ice Age.

A brooch, carved with shamrocks.
£25-35 *HAY*

A brooch, with gilt and bead decoration.
£25-40 *HAY*

An expanding bracelet.
£35-45 *HAY*

A brooch, inset with beads.
£30-40 *HAY*

Bois Durci

A brooch, with crystals and gilt.
£25-35 *HAY*

A brooch, with cut-out carving of a castle.
£35-45 *HAY*

A Bois Durci bracelet.
£30-40 *HAY*

- **Bois Durci is a cellulose based material which was moulded into shapes.**
- **Patented by Lepage in Paris in 1855.**
- **Only made commercially between 1860-75, hence scarce today.**
- **Sometimes moulded into plaques and used to adorn furniture, especially pianos.**

Brooches

A carved opal head and diamond brooch.
£360-380 *CSK*

A marcasite seal brooch, 20thC, 1in (2.5cm) wide.
£15-20 *JO*

A marcasite and agate spider brooch, 1½in (4cm) high.
£15-20 *JO*

Two silver golfing brooches, 1¾ and 1½in (5 and 4cm) high.
£25-30 each *JO*

CROSS REFERENCE	
Sport ⟶	p399
Golf ⟶	p405

A brooch with rose diamond, lasque diamond and gem cluster, early 20thC.
£250-275 *CSK*

l. A marcasite crab brooch, 1½in (4cm) wide.
£15-20
r. A sea horse brooch, 1¼in (3cm) high.
£20-25 *JO*

A marcasite duck brooch, 1in (2.5cm) wide.
£10-12 *JO*

A marcasite and amethyst treble clef brooch, 20thC, 2¼in (6cm) high.
£25-30 *JO*

A marcasite and agate butterfly brooch, 20thC, 1¾in (5cm) wide.
£25-30 *JO*

A marcasite fish brooch, with amethyst, 20thC, 1¾in (5cm) wide.
£35-40 *JO*

A marcasite elephant brooch, 20thC, 2in (5cm) wide.
£15-20 *JO*

A silver dragon brooch, 20thC, 2in (5.5cm) wide.
£20-25 *JO*

A silver elephant, 20thC, 2¼in (6cm) high.
£20-25 *JO*

A silver and marcasite teddy bear brooch, 1in (2.5cm) high.
£15-20 *JO*

A gold dragonfly brooch, set with 53 diamonds, 15 opals and 2 rubies. **£2,600-2,800** *AH*

Two marcasite cat brooches, 20thC, 1in (2.5cm) high and 2in (5.5cm) wide.
£15-20 *JO*

Horn Jewellery

- **Horn, from cows, oxen and buffalo can be split and flattened when heated.**
- **Horn can also be ground up and heated under pressure to a dough-like substance.**
- **Can be pressed into moulds or even turned on a lathe when hardened.**

A brooch, in the form of a hand holding a floral arrangement.
£25-35 *HAY*

A brooch, with carved hand.
£25-30 *HAY*

An intricately carved horn brooch.
£15-20 *HAY*

A brooch, with mother-of-pearl insert.
£25-30 *HAY*

A horn bracelet.
£20-30 *HAY*

An expanding bracelet.
£20-30 *HAY*

A carved brooch.
£25-35 *HAY*

A brooch, intricately carved as a cross.
£40-45 *HAY*

A brooch, with floral carving.
£20-30 *HAY*

A brooch, a hand holding a posy.
£25-35 *HAY*

Himalayan Jewellery

A brass spoon, worn on a belt, c1800, 3in (7.5cm) long.
£45-65 *RAM*

A small standing shrine, Nepal, early 19thC, 1½in (4cm).
£140-195 *RAM*

A silver holy water pot, used for pouring on effigies, set with coral and turquoise, 19thC, 2½in (6cm).
£125-175 *RAM*

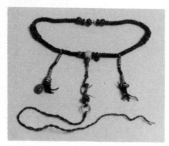

A mala or rosary of 108 horn and cornelian beads with amber central bead, c1900, 16in (41cm).
£150-225 *RAM*

A carved jade butterfly set in brass, 18thC, 2 by 1½in (5 by 4cm).
£125-175 *RAM*

Belts

A silver belt, engraved with dragons and silver and cloth hanging piece to attach purse or flint purse, 18thC, 36 by 2½in (92 by 6cm).
£350-450 *RAM*

A cloth and silver belt, the repoussé work with a central bird, mid-19thC, 24 by 3¼in (61 by 8cm).
£150-200 *RAM*

Bracelets

A silver bracelet, set with turquoise, mid-19thC, 1in (2.5cm) wide.
£180-250 *RAM*

A silver bracelet set with coral and turquoise, mid-19thC, ½in (2cm) wide.
£250-350 *RAM*

Earrings

A pair of silver earrings, with turquoise and coral, mid-19thC, 5in (13cm) long.
£150-250 *RAM*

A pair of silver and coral earrings, probably to wear on headdress, Western Tibet, mid-19thC, 3in (7.5cm) long.
£120-150 *RAM*

A pair of silver and turquoise earrings from Lhasa, often worn as part of headdress, 18thC, 2½in (6cm) long.
£450-600 *RAM*

A pair of silver earrings, with turquoise and coral, attachment tops for headdress, early 19thC, 4in (10cm) long.
£150-250 *RAM*

> **MAKE THE MOST OF MILLERS**
> Condition is absolutely vital when assessing the value of any item. Damaged pieces appreciate much less than perfect examples. However, a rare, desirable piece may command a high price even when damaged.

Headpieces

A silver hairpiece, with coral and turquoise, mid-19thC, 4 by 3in (10 by 8cm).
£450-600 *RAM*

A silver headpiece, set with turquoise and coral, worn on forehead, late 19thC, 2in (5cm) diam. **£65-95** *RAM*

Flint Purses

A brass hairpiece, set with coral and turquoise, in double thunderbolt motif, 18thC, 1¾in (4.5cm) diam.
£275-325 *RAM*

A silver flint purse, in leather and iron, with traces of enamel, Mongolia, early 19thC, 2½ by 2in (6 by 5cm).
£150-200 *RAM*

A gilded brass, turquoise and coral hairpiece, worn by a high ranking male official in centre of headdress, early 19thC, 3½in (9cm) high.
£300-600 *RAM*

A silver repoussé work hairpiece, with coral and turquoise, 19thC.
£500-750 *RAM*

A flint purse, with brass, leather and iron, decorated with 3 dragons, mid-19thC, 4 by 3in (10 by 7.5cm).
£125-175 *RAM*

A Ladakh cornelian and blue glass hairpiece, set in silver with copper back, often sewn on headdress, 1in (2.5cm) wide.
£75-115 *RAM*

A silver headpiece, set with glass and leather disc behind, worn on forehead, 1½in (4cm) diam.
£80-95 *RAM*

A copper and mosaic turquoise headpiece, 17thC, 2in (5cm) diam.
£250-350 *RAM*

Necklaces

A round cornelian bead necklace, re-strung, 16in (41cm) long.
£65-120 *RAM*

Two blood red coral necklaces, re-strung.
£2,000-3,000 *RAM*

This colour is the most highly valued by Tibetans, and believed very lucky.

A cornelian barrel necklace, re-strung, 16in (41cm) long.
£65-130 *RAM*

A cornelian melon necklace, re-strung, 25in (63.5cm) long.
£200-300 *RAM*

Two turquoise necklaces, beads between 200 and 500 years old, re-strung, 14in (35.5cm) long.
£150-180 each *RAM*

A silver hairpiece from headdress, set with glass, coral, turquoise and malachite, 19thC, 2 by 1½in (5 by 4cm).
£195-250 *RAM*

Prayer Boxes

A silver prayer box, or ghau, with central gilded section and turquoise centre, early 18thC, 2¾ by 3in (7 by 7.5cm).
£150-200 *RAM*

A round silver prayer box, set with coral and turquoise, portrait of important lama often shows through central hole, early 19thC, 3in (7.5cm) diam.
£195-295 *RAM*

A brass prayer box, or ghau, inlaid with turquoise, the back opening to put prayers and relics inside, 18thC, 2½in (6cm) wide.
£175-250 *RAM*

A round prayer box, or ghau, with eight-armed deity, mid-19thC, 1in (2.5cm) diam.
£125-175 *RAM*

A silver filigree prayer box, set with coral and turquoise and stylised tree motif, Ladakh, 19thC, 3in (7.5cm) wide.
£150-225 *RAM*

A silver repoussé prayer box, or ghau, with elephant, monkey, hare and bird and central endless knot motif, 3½in (9cm) diam.
£150-250 *RAM*

A 22ct gold prayer box ,or ghau, set with turquoise and glass, 18thC, 3½in (8.5cm) square.
£1,500-2,000 *RAM*

A 22ct gold prayer box, or ghau, with fine filigree work and set with turquoise, 18thC, 3in (7.5cm) wide.
£1,500-2,000 *RAM*

A silver prayer box, or ghau, set with turquoise, early 19thC, 4 by 3in (10 by 7.5cm).
£150-250 *RAM*

A silver prayer box, set with coral and turquoise, 19thC, 3 by 3½in (7.5 by 8.5cm).
£225-295 *RAM*

A silver prayer box, or ghau, with turquoise and gilding, mid-19thC, 1¾ by 1½in (5 by 4cm).
£100-150 *RAM*

Rings

A silver ring, set with coral and turquoise, from Ladakh, 1in (2.5cm) wide.
£65-85 *RAM*

A silver and coral ring, possibly worn in the hair, 19thC, 1in (2.5cm) high.
£85-125 *RAM*

Two rings:
l. Silver and coral, 19thC.
£50-75
r. Silver and turquoise, 19thC. **£45-65** *RAM*

A Nava Ratna gold ring, set with central white sapphire, surrounded by sapphire, topaz, pearl, cat's-eye, ruby, turquoise, coral and diamond, from Newar, Nepal, 19thC.
£350-650 *RAM*

Nava Ratna means nine precious stones and would be presented to a wife on her wedding day, to be worn only at festivals and weddings, not as a symbol of marriage.

A brass, turquoise and glass ring, made from a single earring, c1900.
£50-80 *RAM*

A silver ring, set with coral and turquoise, early 19thC, 1in (2.5cm) wide.
£225-250 *RAM*

A large ring, set with coral and turquoise, early 19thC.
£175-225 *RAM*

A silver and turquoise ring, mid-19thC.
£65-120 *RAM*

Three silver rings, with central settings of turquoise, coral and cornelian, 19thC.
£45-65 each *RAM*

A selection of silver and coral rings and hair rings, 19thC, ½in to 2in (1.5 to 5cm).
£55-150 each *RAM*

Seals

A silver and iron wax seal, with flower motif, 18thC, 2in (5cm) high.
£130-160 *RAM*

A selection of brass, iron and chased iron seals, 17th-18thC, 1 to 2in (2.5 to 5cm).
£50-150 each *RAM*

Whitby Jet Jewellery

A padlock, with a metal clasp.
£20-30 *HAY*

A portrait miniature.
£60-90 *HAY*

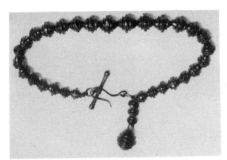

An ornately carved watch chain.
£35-50 *HAY*

Bracelets

An expanding bracelet.
£30-40 *HAY*

An expanding bracelet.
£35-50 *HAY*

An expanding bracelet.
£40-55 *HAY*

An expanding bracelet.
£60-75 *HAY*

A bracelet, with an engraving of a bird.
£35-45 *HAY*

A bracelet with a large carved central segment.
£45-60 *HAY*

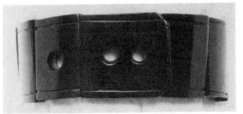

A bracelet.
£30-40 *HAY*

A buckle effect bracelet.
£25-35 *HAY*

MAKE THE MOST OF MILLERS

Price ranges in this book reflect what you should expect to *pay* for a similar example. When selling, however, you would expect to receive a lower figure. This will fluctuate according to a dealer's stock and saleability at a particular time, etc. It is always advisable, when selling a collectable, to approach a reputable dealer or an auction house which has specialist sales.

A heavily carved bracelet.
£45-60 *HAY*

A Whitby jet bracelet, with character pigment indented.
£30-40 *HAY*

Brooches

A leaf brooch.
£60-85 *HAY*

A brooch, with unusual carving.
£55-70 *HAY*

A horseshoe brooch, showing the underside of a hoof.
£40-60 *HAY*

A brooch, with acorn carving.
£70-90 *HAY*

Two brooches, with floral and fruit carving.
£65-85 each *HAY*

A brooch, carved as a cameo.
£80-100 *HAY*

Beware as jet cameos are being faked.

A brooch, with crystal star design.   **£25-35** *HAY*

A brooch, in the form of a star.
£40-50 *HAY*

Two miniature brooches.   **£15-20 each** *HAY*

A collection of name brooches.   **£25-30** *HAY*

An initial brooch, with a metal pin.
£15-25 *HAY*

A collection of ornately carved brooches. **£15-25 each** *HAY*

A compass brooch, with a gilt bow. **£20-30** *HAY*

A collection of brooches, carved in various designs. **£15-25 each** *HAY*

A brooch, depicting a horseshoe and horses' hooves. **£25-35** *HAY*

Two brooches, one with a carving of a church. **£25-35 each** *HAY*

A brooch, with floral carving. **£40-50** *HAY*

An inlaid bar brooch. **£15-25** *HAY*

A brooch, with the name 'Ada Jane'. **£25-30** *HAY*

Earrings

A pair of earrings, carved
as horseshoes.
£25-30 *HAY*

A pair of drop earrings,
with gold wires.
£60-80 *HAY*

A pair of earrings, with
floral carvings.
£40-60 *HAY*

Necklaces

A necklace with carved pendant.
£100-150 *HAY*

A necklace, with large links
and drop beads.
£50-80 *HAY*

A necklace.
£60-90 *HAY*

A necklace with three drop beads.
£65-100 *HAY*

A necklace, with carved and
plain beads.
£60-85 *HAY*

Pendants

A Maltese cross pendant.
£40-50 *HAY*

A pendant, with carved
diamond design.
£60-80 *HAY*

Three carved pendants.
£65-90 each *HAY*

A miniature pendant.
£50-70 *HAY*

An anchor-shaped pendant.
£15-20 *HAY*

A pendant, initialled in silver.
£80-90 *HAY*

Pins

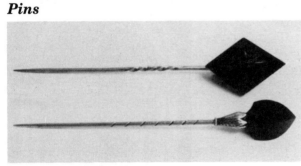

Two hat pins, with silver pins.
£15-25 each *HAY*

A hat pin, with carving.
£15-25 *HAY*

A hat pin.
£20-30 *HAY*

Vulcanite

- Black jewellery was popular during Queen Victoria's period of mourning for Prince Albert from 1861 until her death.
- Pressed horn vulcanite and celluloid provided affordable alternatives to the much more expensive jet.
- Vulcanite is the end result of vulcanised rubber.

A linked necklace, with a cross.
£24-40 *HAY*

A cameo brooch.
£25-35 *HAY*

A carved necklace, with carved drops.
£50-70 *HAY*

A heavily carved pendant.
£35-45 *HAY*

A bracelet, with decorative carving.
£20-30 *HAY*

A pair of drop earrings, with gold wires.
£30-35 *HAY*

Two floral design bar brooches.
£8-12 each
HAY

Two intricately carved bar brooches.
£8-12 each *HAY*

JUKEBOXES

A Wurlitzer Model 1015 jukebox, with 24 song selections, 25, 10 and 5 cent coin slots, unrestored, cylinder cracked, c1940, 58in (147cm) high.
£4,800-5,000 *S(NY)*

For a further selection of Jukeboxes, please refer to *Miller's Collectables Price Guide, Volume V,* pp262-264.

A Tibetan coral necklace, some damage, restrung, 200-300 years old, 14in (36cm) long. **£1,250-1,850** *RAM*

Two Tibetan coral necklaces, showing imperfections in coral growth, restrung. **£650-1,500 each** *RAM*

A Tibetan turquoise and coral necklace, 200-500 years old, 25in (63.5cm) long. **£650-850** *RAM*

A Tibetan silver pendant, set with coral and turquoise, mid-19thC, 4in (10cm) long. **£195-275** *RAM*

A Tibetan silver prayer box or ghau, with filigree work, set with turquoise, back opens. **£125-225** *RAM*

A Tibetan turquoise necklace, high quality stones, 200-500 years old, 18in (46cm) long. **£400-450** *RAM*

A pair of Tibetan gold earrings, set with turquoise, late 18thC, 4in (10cm) long. **£1,350-1,950** *RAM*

A Tibetan brass and turquoise prayer box, 18thC, 3in (8cm) long. **£450-650** *RAM*

A Tibetan amber necklace, set with turquoise, restrung, over 200 years old. **£950-1,500** *RAM*

A pair of Tibetan coral earrings, set with etched gzi beads, 1,000-2,000 years old, 3in (7.5in) long. **£550-650** *RAM*

A Tibetan silver pendant, with repoussé work and coral centre, 3½in (9cm) square. **£125-165** *RAM*

A pair of repoussé gold on silver earrings, as worn by Sherpa women, mid-19thC.
£200-300 *RAM*

A silver necklace, Nepal, late 19thC, bottom centre piece 3in (7.5cm) diam.
£200-250 *RAM*

A Tibetan silver, gilt, and turquoise chatelaine, early 19thC.
£250-450 *RAM*

A silver and coral amulet, sealed with prayer inside, Nepal, c1900, 3in (7.5cm) square.
£90-120 *RAM*

A Tibetan silver, gilt, and coral chatelaine, early 19thC.
£250-450 *RAM*

A Tibetan silver headpiece, set with turquoise and coral, early 19thC, 4in (10cm) diam.
£300-650 *RAM*

A bronze Jambhala, Tibet, 15thC, 2in (5cm) high.
£450-550 *RAM*

A Tibetan 22 carat gold prayer box filled with pitch, early 19thC, 1⅝in (4cm) wide.
£150-200 *RAM*

An articulated silver fish, head opens to store kohl, Nepal, late 19thC, 5in (12.5cm) long.
£110-150 *RAM*

A spoon, to wear on a belt, mid-19thC, 4in (10cm) long. **£50-75** *RAM*

A gilded copper repoussé centrepiece, Sino-Tibetan, 4in (10cm) wide.
£800-1,200 *RAM*

A Tibetan leather, silver and gilded brass pouch, worn on a belt, with 2 fish motifs, early 19thC, 5in (12.5cm) wide.
£200-300 *RAM*

A Tibetan gilded bronze dorje, 2½in (6.5cm) long.
£40-50 *RAM*

A Tibetan silver bracelet, set with coral and turquoise, mid-19thC, 1in (2.5cm) wide.
£500-600 *RAM*

A Tibetan silver ghau, the central gilded brass section set with coral and turquoise, 2¼in (6cm) long. **£200-300** *RAM*

A Tibetan silver ghau, with gilded brass and coral centre, c1800, 4in (10cm) long.
£150-250 *RAM*

A Tibetan silver prayer box, set with coral and turquoise, red amber centre, early 19thC, 4in (10cm) diam.
£200-300 *RAM*

A Tibetan brass repoussé sheath and knife, with dragon, flaming pearl and protective deity's head, c1800, 15in (38cm) long.
£200-300 *RAM*

A pair of Tibetan silver and turquoise earrings, mid-19thC, 1½in (4cm) diam.
£125-175 *RAM*

A Tibetan silver hairpiece, 'Tsi-Yu', with turquoise centre and surround, worn plaited in hair or sewn on headdress, mid-19thC, 4in (10cm) long.
£120-220 *RAM*

A Bakelite and chrome necklace and bracelet, c1920. **£40-60** *BAT*

A glass bead necklace, c1930. **£10-20** *BAT*

A necklace and bracelet, with plastic oranges and glass leaves, c1920. **£20-30** *BAT*

A selection of costume jewellery, brooches with glass stones and a bracelet, c1950, 2½ to 3in (6 to 7.5cm) wide. **£20-50 each** *BAT*

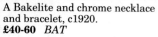

An Art Deco silver and black enamel cigarette case, the cover of abalone and mother-of-pearl, 3in (7.5cm) wide, 3oz 10dwt. **£380-400** *MSW*

A Victorian gold brooch, with centre star set with half pearls. **£120-150** *MSW*

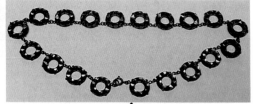

An amethyst, glass and metal necklace, c1920. **£20-30** *BAT*

l. A glass necklace, c1930. **£10-20** *BAT*

An Art Deco frosted glass brooch, set with diamonds in platinum and 18ct gold. **£550-650** *MSW*

A Winnie the Pooh lunch box and Thermos, both in mint condition, 1967.
£225-250 *CNY*

A green plastic lunch box in the shape of a pickle with a handle, in mint condition, 1972.
£120-150 *CNY*

A Street Hawk lunch box and Thermos, with action shots from the show, both in mint condition, 1984.
£200-250 *CNY*

A Mickey Mouse and Donald Duck lunch box, in good condition, 1954.
£275-300 *CNY*

A Batman prototype kit lunch box and Thermos, in mint condition, with original artwork, 1985.
£600-650 *CNY*

A Black Hole lunch box and Thermos, both in mint condition, 1979.
£100-125 *CNY*

A Bobby Orr, The Six Million Dollar Man, lunch box and Thermos, 1974.
£150-175 *CNY*

The reverse of the Bobby Orr, The Six Million Dollar Man, lunchbox and Thermos, featured *left*.

A James Bond black lunch box and Thermos, in very good condition, 1966.
£475-500 *CNY*

A Disneyland lunch box and Thermos, with official entry blank for Donald Duck's free trip to Disneyland contest and the McCall's use-tested seal on the handle, in mint condition, 1960.
£650-675 *CNY*

A UFO Sky 1 space vehicle lunch box and blue Thermos, 1973.
£120-160 *CNY*

l. A Zorro lunch box and Thermos, in very good condition, 1966.
£220-250 *CNY*

A Beatles lunch box and Thermos, showing a picture of each member of the band, in very good condition, 1966.
£400-450 *CNY*

A pair of French opera glasses, with mother-of-pearl eyepieces and tubes, late 19thC. **£300-350** *S*

A 1¼in English spyglass, early 19thC, 4in (10cm) long. **£175-200** *S*

A pair of French enamel and mother-of-pearl opera glasses, by A. R. Glass, c1880. **£500-620** *ARE*

A pair of French opera glasses-on-handle, with mother-of-pearl eyepieces, late 19thC. **£450-480** *S*

r. A 1¼in spyglass, with 6 gilt brass draws, the tube with guilloche decoration, early 19thC, 4in (10cm) long extended. **£150-175** *S*

A 1¼in spyglass, with 4 gilt brass draws and turned ivory tube binding, by Worthington & Allan, c1830, in a leather case, with telescopic handle and ivory grip. **£650-700** *S*

A French 1¼in brass spyglass, c1800, 4in (10cm) long extended. **£330-380** *S*

A pair of Art Nouveau opera glasses, with enamelled decoration on dark blue ground. **£350-380** *AAV*

r. Two pairs of French opera glasses, with telescopic handles, one enamelled in pale yellow, the other with mother-of-pearl binding to tube handle, late 19thC. **£300-350** *S*

A half glazed pot, Liao Dynasty, 4½in (11.5cm) high. **£250-300** *ORI*

A bowl, with incised decorated interior, Song Dynasty, 7¼in (18cm) diam. **£250-285** *ORI*

A pair of terracotta figures, Tang Dynasty, 9 to 10in (22.5 to 25cm) high. **£200-225** *ORI*

A tomb figure, early Ming Dynasty. **£450-550** *ORI*

A terracotta camel, Tang Dynasty, 12in (31cm) high. **£850-1,250** *ORI*

A moulded vase, embossed with flower decoration, Song Dynasty, 8in (20cm) high. **£250-285** *ORI*

A glazed koro, Ming Dynasty, 3in (7.5cm) high. **£55-60** *ORI*

A cast iron Buddha, Ming Dynasty, 10¾in (27cm) high. **£700-750** *ORI*

A terracotta ram, Tang Dynasty, 5in (13cm) long. **£80-100** *ORI*

A tea cup, Ming Dynasty, 3½in (9cm) high. **£70-90** *ORI*

A pair of panels, hand painted in gold leaf on lacquer, 19thC, 26in (66.5cm) long. **£700-1,000** *ORI*

A celadon bowl, with mask feet, incised design on exterior, Ming Dynasty, 4½in (12cm) high. **£500-600** *ORI*

A dish, embossed with traditional Chinese fish, Song Dynasty, 6in (15cm) diam. **£150-180** *ORI*

A wine jar, Song Dynasty, 7in (17.5cm) high. **£280-325** *ORI*

A Japanese goten or temple, used in the Hina Dolls Festival, c1950.
£200-250 *ORI*

A Japanese boy's Day Festival doll, 10in (25cm) high.
£150-170 *ORI*

A Kutani porcelain elephant koro, c1860, 6in (15cm) high.
£250-300 *ORI*

A Japanese Ichimatsu triple jointed play doll, c1930, 14½in (37cm) high.
£200-225 *ORI*

A pair of Japanese Hina dolls, depicting Emperor and Empress, c1780, Emperor 14½in (37cm), Empress 12½in (32cm) high. **£3,000-3,500** *ORI*

A Chinese embroidered wall hanging, early 19thC, 54in (137cm) wide.
£1,300-1,500 *ORI*

A Satsuma dragon vase, late 19thC, 5½in (14cm) high.
£75-85 *ORI*

A Japanese boy's Day Festival Samurai doll, c1890, 10in (25cm) high.
£100-120 *ORI*

A silhouette, by E. Foster of Derby, painted on paper, c1840.
£200-225 *TER*

Lady Caroline Price, by Andrew Plimer, gilt metal frame, 2⅛in (5.5cm) high.
£1,500-1,600 *C*

A Gentleman, by Andrew Plimer, signed and dated 1786, gilt metal frame, 1¾in (5cm) high.
£1,000-1,200 *C*

A Lady, by William Grimaldi, signed and dated 1801, gold frame, 3in (7.5cm) high.
£1,800-1,900 *C*

Caroline Mathilde, Queen of Denmark, by Francis Sykes, gilt metal mount, 2in (5cm) high.
£575-650 *C*

An Officer, by circle of Jean-Baptiste Isabey, 2¼in (5.8cm) high.
£700-800 *C*

A cut paper silhouette of a boy holding a whip, by William James Hubard, c1830, 10½in (26.5cm) high.
£150-200 *TER*

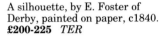

Louis XVIII of France, whilst exiled in Bath, painted on glass by Charles Rosenberg.
£1,000-1,200 *TER*

A Gentleman, by Edward Miles, gold frame, 2¾in (7cm) high.
£800-1,000 *C*

A double cut paper silhouette, by William James Hubard, in original frame, 14in (36cm) wide. **£300-400** *TER*

A Gentleman, by William Singleton, gold frame with seed pearl and stud border, 2in (5cm) high. **£700-800** *C*

A Lady, by Charles Robertson, gold frame, 3in (7.5cm) high.
£1,800-1,900 *C*

A Southern Railway Merchant Navy Class
locomotive nameplate.
£11,000-12,000 *SRA*

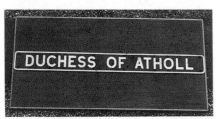

An LMS Princess Coronation Class
nameplate.
£14,000-15,000 *SRA*

An exhibition standard gauge O two rail electric model of the
LNER Class J39 0-6-0 locomotive and tender, No 1448, built
by J.S. Beeson, 15in (38cm) long, with showtrack and glazed
case. **£1,600-1,800** *CSK*

An L&NWR/White Star
Line joint poster.
£300-400 *SRA*

A GWR Bulldog Class nameplate, 'Inchcape'.
£3,000-3,500 *SRA*

A platform sign, c1950, 54in (137cm) long.
£50-60 *COB*

A 3½in gauge model of a GWR King class
steam locomotive, King John.
£4,000-5,000 *SRA*

A GWR Castle Class locomotive
nameplate, 'Hampden'.
£7,500-8,000 *SRA*

A 5in gauge model of an L&NWR steam
locomotive railway tank engine.
£5,000-7,000 *SRA*

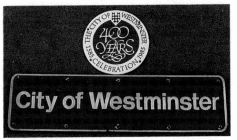

A British Railways High Speed Train nameplate and badge.
£800-1,000 *SRA*

A L&NW Railway nameplate.
£20,000-22,000 *SRA*

A GWR nameplate, the first of the Duke Class.
£7,000-8,000 *SRA*

An LNER Football Class nameplate.
£10,000-10,400 *SRA*

A Great Northern Railway brass number plate.
£2,500-3,000 *SRA*

A Royal Marine Presentation Certificate, 1898.
£15-20 *COB*

An LNER poster.
£150-200 *SRA*

Three pieces of original artwork for Union Castle Line menus and brochures, all pre-war.
£10-30 each *COB*

A Stella Polaris cruise brochure, 1927.
£10-15 *COB*

A Canadian Pacific travel brochure, 1930s.
£10-12 *COB*

A Great Central Railway timetable poster.
£100-150 *SRA*

A Union Castle Line sweet tin.
£10-15 *COB*

Sheer underwear, worn by Madonna on the Who's That Girl? tour, 1987, with 'KISS' in felt and rhinestones. **£1,500-1,700** *S(NY)*

A set of The Beatles character dolls, housed in a toy theatre, 1964. **£4,000-4,500** *CSK*

A stage suit, worn by James Brown, at the Apollo Theatre, New York, 1964. **£6,000-6,500** *CSK*

James Brown Sings Out Of Sight, Smash Records, 1968, together with a jacket and photograph. **£6,000-6,500** *CSK*

An Elvis Presley jumpsuit, cape and belt, c1972. **£12,000-12,500** *S(NY)*

A 1942 Martin D 18 acoustic guitar, bought by Elvis Presley in early 1950s, together with various documents of provenance. **£100,000-110,000** *CSK*

A velvet coat worn by James Brown on stage, 1967, together with an album of The James Brown Show. **£2,800-3,000** *CSK*

A leather jacket, worn by Michael Jackson in 'Beat It', with Marc Laurent Paris label inside. **£5,250-5,500** *S(NY)*

A pair of shoes, worn by Prince on 'Purple Rain' tour, with an autograph and a photograph. **£2,500-3,000** *S(NY)*

A pair of pants, worn in concert by Jimi Hendrix, c1968. **£11,000-12,000** *S(NY)*

A Cloud custom-made solid body guitar, used by Prince.
£11,500-11,750 *CSK*

A Gibson ES335 guitar, No. A 35714, with 22-fret fingerboard, 1960.
£4,500-4,750 *CSK*

An Alembic bass guitar, used by John Entwistle of The Who, c1975.
£4,750-5,000 *CSK*

A Peter Cook bass guitar, 'The Axe', used by John Entwistle.
£4,250-4,750 *CSK*

A trumpet, made by King Musical Instruments, played by Dizzy Gillespie.
£35,000-40,000 *S(NY)*

A Piphone Model B Double Bass, played by Bill Haley, c1950.
£3,250-3,500 *S(NY)*

A command module from Star Trek, 1966-69, and a reproduction of Captain Kirk's chair. **£10,000-10,500** *CNY*

A Starship Enterprise tunic, worn by Leonard Nimoy as Mr Spock, by Western Costume Company.
£3,600-4,000 *CNY*

A Rowan & Martin's Laugh-In award, c1970.
£2,000-2,500 *CNY*

A jacket, made by the Western Costume Co, worn by Dick Van Dyke in Mary Poppins, Disney, 1964. **£3,000-3,500** *CNY*

r. A jacket, dress shirt and bow tie, designed by Acuna, worn by Liberace.
£700-750 *CNY*

Who Framed Roger Rabbit?
gouache on celluloid,
Touchstone Pictures, 1988,
8¾ by 11¾in (22 by 30cm).
£3,500-4,000 *S(NY)*

Peter Pan, gouache on trimmed
celluloid, Walt Disney Studios,
1953, 11¼ by 15in (29 by 38cm).
£11,000-11,500 *S(NY)*

Fantasia, gouache on laminated
celluloid, Walt Disney Studios,
1940, 11¼ by 14in (29 by 36cm).
£3,500-4,000 *CNY*

Mickey Mouse, gouache on
celluloid, Walt Disney Studios,
6¾ by 10in (17 by 25cm).
£2,800-3,000 *CNY*

Snow White and the Seven
Dwarfs, gouache on celluloid,
Walt Disney Studio, 1937,
8¾ by 10in (17 by 25cm).
£6,500-7,000 *S(NY)*

Pinocchio, gouache on
celluloid, Walt Disney Studios,
1940, 8 by 10½in (20 by 26.5cm).
£8,000-8,500 *S(NY)*

The Aristocats, gouache on multi-
cel set-up, Walt Disney Studios,
1970, 11 by 13¼in (28 by 34cm).
£1,000-1,500 *CNY*

Mr Mouse Takes a Trip, gouache on
celluloid, Walt Disney Studios, 1940,
10 by 16in (25 by 40.5cm).
£8,000-8,500 *S(NY)*

Charlie Brown's All-Stars,
Bill Melendez Studio, 1966,
10½ by 38¾in (26 by 98.5cm).
£1,600-1,800 *S(NY)*

Snow White and the Seven
Dwarfs, gouache on celluloid,
Walt Disney Studios, 1937,
8 by 11½in (20 by 29cm).
£10,000-10,500 *S(NY)*

Lady and the Tramp, watercolour
on board, Walt Disney Studios,
c1970, 16 by 26in (41 by 66cm).
£1,000-1,100 *CSK*

An English gilt and brass pocket barometer, c1880, in fitted case, 3¼in (8cm) diam.
£175-200 *TER*

A daguerreotype sensitising chamber, mahogany box, c1845, 10in (25cm) high.
£1,800-1,900 *S*

A French book-form camera obscura, with leather covered case, late 18thC.
£13,500-14,000 *S*

A French 8 x 11cm sliding box camera, the mahogany body with brass bound Chevalier lens with rack-and-pinion focusing, mid-19thC.
£850-895 *S*

An S.O.L. 9 x 12cm Sigriste Jumelle camera, with E. Krauss Planar Zeiss f3.8 160mm lens, No. 40528, French, c1900, in maker's leather case. **£5,500-6,000** *S*

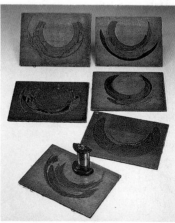

A Gaumont Demeny 35mm chronophotographe cinematographic camera, French, c1899.
£8,000-8,500 *S*

A 4 x 4¾in reflex camera obscura, the walnut body with silver plated lens, mid-19thC, 7in (17.5cm) long. **£1,300-1,400** *S*

A French 20½ x 12cm sliding box stereoscopic camera, mahogany box, with a pair of Derogy brass bound lenses, mid-19thC. **£3,600-3,800** *S*

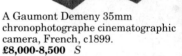

A French 9 x 11cm sliding box camera, Lerebours & Secretan lens, mid-19thC.
£1,800-1,900 *S*

l. A Goldschmidt's binocular camera, with brass viewing lens, Swiss, c1890.
£10,000-11,000 *S*

A set of 6 hand coloured anamorphic prints, with silvered mirror in mahogany stand, in shaped metal box. **£3,000-3,500** *S*

A tinplate 'Lanterna De Orient' magic lantern, German, c1890, with a set of 12 hand painted lantern slides. **£6,000-6,500** *S*

A mahogany and brass triunial lantern, with 3 sets of lime and gas illuminants, and 3 cases of accessories, English, c1880. **£23,000-25,000** *S*

A Culpeper-type compound microscope, stamped E. Nairne, London, c1760, 17½in (45cm) high, with accessories and mahogany case. **£8,500-9,500** *CSK*

An R & J Beck brass monocular microscope, in mahogany case. **£680-720** *RID*

l. A lacquered brass binocular microscope, signed Smith & Beck, 1856. **£11,000-13,000**
r. A laquered brass compound monocular microscope, signed Powell & Lealand, 1860. **£8,000-9,000** *CSK*

A floor standing peep box, possibly German, early 19thC, 56in (142cm) high, with 4 printed views. **£3,750-4,000** *S*

l. A clockwork double stereoscopic viewer, in walnut veneered case, probably French, c1880, 24in (61cm) long, in original painted pine carrying case. **£2,500-2,800** *S*

A panoramic peep box, probably Italian, late 17thC, with hand painted cloth backed European views, 22in (56cm) high. **£3,800-4,200** *S*

A Carlo Ponti megalethoscope, Italian, c1860, 33in (84cm) long, with 20 day-night albumen prints. **£12,000-13,000** *S*

KITCHENALIA

A gas stove lighter, c1930,
6½in (16.5cm) long.
£2-4 *AL*

A Thermos flask, with Bakelite
cup/top, c1925, 8in (20cm) high.
£10-12 *AL*

A wooden butter dish with glass
liner, c1900, 6in (15cm) diam.
£18-20
A butter knife, 7½in (18.5cm)
long.
£10-12 *AL*

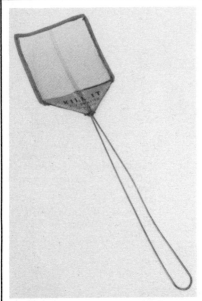

A 'Kill-It' fly swat, c1920.
£6-8 *AL*

A tin cake stand and icing set,
c1930, stand 8in (20cm) diam.
£6-8
Icing set.
£8-10 *AL*

An aluminium hot
water bottle,
c1930, 9in (22.5cm)
high.
£10-12 *AL*

Three Georgian silver plated
skewers, 10 to 12in (25 to 31cm)
long.
£7-10 each *AL*

A set of 14 cast silver menu
holders, each in the form of a
London street trader, maker's
mark TCJ, London 1972, largest
2¾in (7cm) high.
£1,100-1,300 *P(S)*

Three Horlicks mixers, one with
original box, c1920-30, 6 to 8in
(15 to 20cm) high.
£10-15 each *AL*

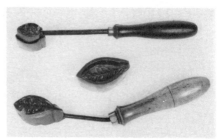

A selection of velvet leaf irons,
c1890, largest 8¾in (22cm) long.
£30-35 each *AL*

Two Guernsey milk/cream cans:
l. Copper, with Guernsey crest,
6½in (16.5cm) high.
£15-20
r. Brass, half pint, marked
Marlins, Guernsey, 5in (12.5cm).
£14-18 *AL*

A Homepride flour man, the hat
was a sieve, the face a mixing
bowl, with pastry cutters inside.
£10-20 *WAB*

CROSS REFERENCE
**Collectables of
the Future** ——→ p432

A Patent apple corer, c1920,
6in (15cm) high.
£14-15 *AL*

A selection of bread tins,
c1930-50, largest 10½in
(26.5cm) long.
£5-10 each *AL*

A tin flour or sugar sifter,
c1930, 3½in (9cm) high.
£8-10 *AL*

A wire pot lifter, c1930,
7½in (19cm) diam.
£6-8 *AL*

A velvet pattern
iron, c1890,
3¾in (9cm) high.
£10-12 *AL*

Bowls & Dishes

A potato masher, c1900, 9½in (24cm) long.
£6-7 *AL*

A metal pastry cutter, c1900, 4in (10cm) wide.
£5-8 *AL*

A mixing bowl, with pale blue interior, c1900, 10in (25cm) diam.
£10-12 *AL*

An advertising pie dish, by T.G. Green, 6in (15cm) wide.
£8-10 *AL*

A mixing bowl, with dark blue interior, c1900, 10⅝in (diam).
£14-16 *AL*

A mixing bowl, c1900, 16in (41cm) diam.
£14-16 *AL*

A shallow pottery pie dish, c1900, 11½in (29.5cm) wide.
£8-10 *AL*

Bread Knives

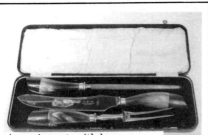

Two Victorian bread knives:
Top: Bakelite handle, 12in (31cm) long. **£8-10**
Bottom: Bone handle, 11½in (29.5cm) long.
£18-22 *AL*

A bread knife, with a wooden handle, c1920, 15in (38cm) long.
£18-20 *AL*

A carving set, with horn handles, c1890, 14½in (37cm) wide, in original box.
£35-40 *AL*

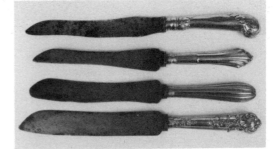

A selection of wedding cake knives, c1880, largest 13in (33cm) long.
£12-22 each *AL*

Two bread knives:
Top: Metal handled, 11¾in (30cm) long.
£10-20
Bottom: Ivory handle, 13½in (34cm) long.
£25-28 *AL*

Cake Decorations

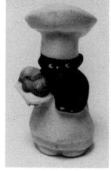

A black baker, c1930,
3in (7.5cm) high.
£20-30 *BAT*

A boy on skis, c1930,
3in (7.5cm) wide.
£45-50 *BAT*

A boy on a sledge, 1930s,
2½in (6.5cm) high.
£35-45 *BAT*

A '21' key cake decoration,
c1930, 2in (5cm) long.
£15-25 *BAT*

CROSS REFERENCE
Colour Section ⟶ p71

A Santa Christmas cake
decoration, c1930, 2in
(5cm) high.
£20-30 *BAT*

Two birds, c1930,
2in (5cm) wide.
£15-25 *BAT*

*Cake decorations are
sometimes mistaken
for Victorian, but
they were made up
until the 1930s.*

A boy in a bunny
suit, c1930,
3in (7.5cm) high.
£15-20 *BAT*

A cherub wedding cake
decoration, c1930, 6in
(15cm) high.
£80-120 *BAT*

A cherub, c1930, 2in (5cm) high.
£20-30 *BAT*

A pair of shoes, c1930.
£15-25 *BAT*

Cake Stands

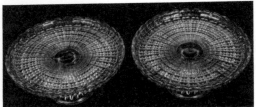

A pair of pressed glass cake stands, c1900, 7¾in (19cm) diam. **£10-12 each** *AL*

A pressed glass cake stand, c1890, 9in (22.5cm) diam. **£15-18** *AL*

A pressed glass cake stand, c1890, 8½in (21.5cm) diam. **£15-18** *AL*

A pressed glass cake stand, c1890, 9in (22.5cm) diam. **£15-18** *AL*

<table>
<tr><td>Cross Reference
Glass ──────▶ p233</td></tr>
</table>

CROSS REFERENCE
Glass ──────▶ p233

Cornish Kitchen Ware

Thomas Goodwin Green started to make pottery in 1864, but it was not until the turn of the century that he found fame and fortune with his range of white earthenware products with their distinctive blue bands. The items chosen here display a range of marks which enable easy identification and dating.

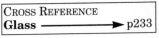

A blue and white teapot, by Green & Co. Ltd, c1970, 5½in (14cm) high. **£25-30** *AL*

A pair of blue and white salt and pepper pots, by Green & Co. Ltd, c1970, 5in (12.5cm). **£14-16 each** *AL*

A blue and white cheese dish, by Green & Co. Ltd, c1930, 8½in (21.5cm) diam. **£15-20** *AL*

A blue and white butter dish, by Green & Co. Ltd, c1930, 6¾in (17cm) diam. **£12-15** *AL*

MAKE THE MOST OF MILLERS

Condition is absolutely vital when assessing the value of any item. Damaged pieces appreciate much less than perfect examples. However, a rare, desirable piece may command a high price even when damaged.

Enamel Ware

A blue and white coffee jar, by Green & Co. Ltd, c1950, 6½in (16.5cm) high.
£20-25 *AL*

A half pint measure, possibly for shellfish, 4in (10cm) high.
£14-18 *AL*

Three jugs, with blue rims and handles, c1900-30, 5 to 12in (12.5 to 30.5cm) high.
£8-10 each *AL*

A flour bin, c1930, 9in (22.5cm) high.
£8-10 *AL*

A blue flour bin, with windmill, c1900, 7⅓in (18.5cm) high.
£10-12 *AL*

A flour bin with dark blue lettering, c1900-30, 12½in (31.5cm) high.
£15-18 *AL*

A flour bin, c1900-30, 12in (30.5cm) high.
£15-18 *AL*

A bread bin, with blue windmill picture and lettering, c1900-30.
£18-20 *AL*

A bread bin, c1900-30, 9½in (23.5cm) high.
£15-18 *AL*

A bread bin, c1900, 13in (33cm) high.
£5-7 *AL*

A flour bin, c1900-30, 8⅓in (21cm) high.
£8-10 *AL*

A green flour bin, c1930, 9¾in
by 7in (24 by 17.5cm) high.
£10-12 *AL*

A Cow & Gate milk food
measure, c1920, 5in (12.5cm)
high.
£8-10 *AL*

Three jugs, c1900-30,
10½ to 13in (26.5 to 33cm) high.
£8-15 *AL*

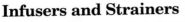

Infusers and Strainers

Four tea infusers, c1930, 5 to
6in (12.5 to 15cm) long.
£2-3 each *AL*

A commemorative
tea strainer,
6in (15cm) long.
£8-10 *AL*

A silver metal coffee
strainer, c1960,
6in (15cm) long.
£3-4 *AL*

> **CROSS REFERENCE**
> **Metalware**
>   **Silver** ────▶ p306

Two tea strainers, 4 to 6in
(10 to 15cm) long.
£3-4 each *AL*

A coffee strainer,
engraved Hotel
de Flandre,
Bruges,
3½in (9cm) diam.
£5-6 *AL*

A tea infuser, in the shape of a teapot on a
tray, c1960, 2¼in (5.5cm) diam.
£7-8 *AL*

Jars and Pots

Two potted meat pots, c1910,
1½ and 2½in (3.5 and 6cm) high.
£4-5 each *AL*

Two James Keiller Dundee
marmalade jars, c1910.
£4-5 each *AL*

Two Maling Ware Frank
Cooper's Oxford marmalade
jars, c1910, 4¼ and 3¾in
(10.5 and 9cm) high.
£6-8 *AL*

Knife Trays

A pine knife tray, c1890,
14in (35.5cm) long.
£25-30 *AL*

A pine knife tray, c1890,
15¾in (39.5cm) long.
£20-25 *AL*

A tin knife tray, c1850,
14in (36cm) long.
£15-20 *AL*

A beech knife tray, c1900,
12in (30.5cm) long.
£15-20 *AL*

Moulds

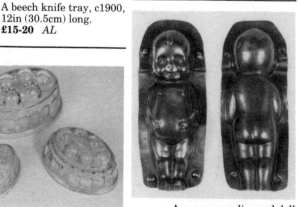

A pottery jelly mould, c1870,
8in (20cm) wide.
£18-22 *AL*

A selection of glass jelly
moulds, c1930.
£4-5 each *AL*

A copper googlie-eyed doll
chocolate mould, c1910,
8in (20cm) high.
£75-85 *TER*

A glass jelly mould, c1930, 7in (17.5cm) wide.
£5-7 *AL*

A glass rabbit jelly mould, c1930, 8in (20cm) wide.
£8-10 *AL*

Two pattie tins, c1920.
£4-5 each *AL*

Nutcrackers

Pie Funnels

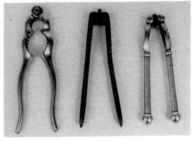

Three pairs of nutcrackers, c1920-30, 5 to 5½in (12.5 to 14cm) long.
£4-5 each *AL*

A selection of glass jelly moulds, c1930.
£5-10 each *AL*

A Denby pie funnel, c1960, 2½in (6cm) high.
£5-6 *AL*

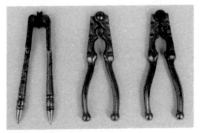

Three pairs of nutcrackers, 1920-30, 5in (12.5cm) long.
£4-5 each *AL*

A selection of pie funnels, 2½ to 3½in (6 to 8.5cm) high.
£2-4 each *AL*

Rolling Pins

A pair of nutcrackers, with blue handles, c1930, 6in (15cm) long.
£8-10 *AL*

Two pottery rolling pins, c1900-20, 17 and 20in (43 and 51cm) long.
£15-20 each *AL*

CROSS REFERENCE
Iron ⟶ p299

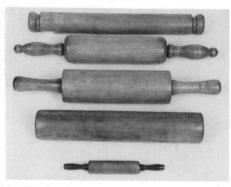

A selection of wooden rolling pins, c1920s, 7¼in to 17in (18 to 43cm) long.
£6-7 each *AL*

A glass rolling pin, c1900, 14in (35.5cm) long.
£14-16 *AL*

A 'Roll-Rite' glass rolling pin, to be filled with water, c1930, 13¾in (34.5cm) long.
£8-12 *AL*

A pottery rolling pin, with metal handles, 17in (43cm) long. **£14-16** *AL*

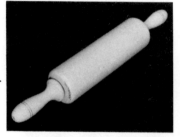

A pottery 'Nut Brown' rolling pin, British, c1930, 16½in (42cm) long.
£14-16 *AL*

Scoops & Spoons

Three bone spoons, c1890-1900, 4½ to 4¾in (11 to 12cm) long.
£3-5 each *AL*

Three horn scoops, c1900, 3½in to 5in (8.5 to 12.5cm) long.
£4-12 each *AL*

A horn scoop, c1860, 7in (17.5cm) long.
£18-20 *AL*

Three horn spoons, c1880-1900, 5 to 7½in (12.5 to 18.5cm) long.
£4-12 each *AL*

Three horn scoops, c1890-1900, 4½ to 6in (11 to 15cm) long.
£7-8 each *AL*

CROSS REFERENCE
Metalware
 Spoons ⟶ p304

Three caddy spoons:
l. From Bude, c1960,
3in (7.5cm) long. **£1-2**
c. A silver metal spoon,
3½in (8.5cm) long. **£6-8**
r. A brass spoon, 2¾in
(7cm) long.
£6-8 *AL*

Two metal baby milk measuring
spoons, advertising Trufood and
Maypole, c1930, 3in (7.5cm)
long. **£3-4 each** *AL*

Steels

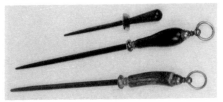

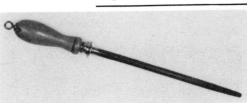

Three horn handled steels,
c1890, 10½ to 21in (26 to 53cm)
long. **£6-15 each** *AL*

A butcher's steel, c1920, 17½in (44cm) long.
£6-8 *AL*

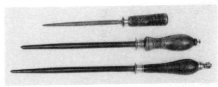

A stag horn handled steel, with
silver top, c1900, 12½in (31.5cm)
long. **£10-12** *AL*

A selection of steels, c1840-96,
11 to 16½in (28 to 41.5cm) long.
£5-7 each *AL*

Tins & Containers

A steel with silver mount,
c1904, 11½in (29cm) long.
£8-10 *AL*

A spice tin, c1870,
6½in (16.5cm) diam.
£30-35 *AL*

A kitchen tin with
egg timer, c1920,
5¼in (13cm) high.
£15-18 *AL*

Two kitchen tins,
c1920-30,
8in (20cm) high.
£10-12 each *AL*

A Camp coffee string tin,
7in (17.5cm) high.
£12-15
Two Camp coffee bottles, 6½ and
8½in (16 and 21cm) high.
£2-4 each *AL*

LIGHTING

A pair of brass railway lamps, c1840.
£180-200 *CAI*

A rush light holder, 16thC,
7in (18cm) high.
£150-200 *SAD*

CROSS REFERENCE
Railways ⟶ p360

A brass blackamoor taper
holder, c1735.
£100-150 *SAD*

A lighthouse night light,
c1930, 6in (15cm) high.
£35-40 *TER*

An early brass oil lamp.
£85-100 *CAI*

A Victorian oil lamp,
in the form of a snowy
owl, slight damage,
29in (74cm) high.
£290-320 *LT*

An Edwardian brass oil
lamp, with original
shade, 17in (43cm) high.
£70-80 *JMC*

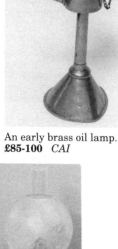

A ceramic oil lamp,
with brass base,
etched globular shade,
converted to electricity.
£275-300 *GAK*

A pair of gilt brass and
mahogany adjustable
standard lamp/tables,
each with reeded S-
shaped arm, oval
piecrust table top on
turned column
supports and acanthus
carved tripod base,
claw-and-ball feet,
67in (170cm) high.
£1,600-1,800 *P(O)*

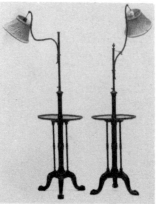

A Victorian brass oil lamp, with
reeded and embossed reservoir
and etched glass shade, c1890,
21in (53cm) high.
£325-350 *S(S)*

Two bicycle oil lamps:
l. c1900, 5in (12.5cm) high.
£30-35
r. A back lamp, c1900,
4in (10cm) high.
£28-32 *SAD*

A Victorian hall lantern, with
cut decoration to the glass
panels and scrolled bronze
frame.
£240-280 *LRG*

**For a further selection of
bicycle lamps, see *Miller's
Collectables Price Guide*,
Volume IV, pp 48-52.**

A Victorian brass oil lamp, with
gadrooned vase-shaped
reservoir supporting etched
shade, c1890, 17in (43cm) high.
£240-280 *S(S)*

A Victorian oil lamp,
with brass base and
etched shade in fuschia
design, circular wick,
25in (64cm) high.
£100-120 *JMC*

A Victorian brass Corinthian
column oil lamp, with chimney,
etched shade and moulded
yellow glass reservoir, c1880,
34in (86cm) high.
£375-600 *S(S)*

A Victorian brass oil lamp, with
chinoiserie painted reservoir,
glass chimney and shade,
c1870, 26in (66cm) high.
£325-375 *S(S)*

An original Famos nickel
plated oil lamp, with
fluted shade, c1920, 26in
(66cm) high.
£70-80 *JMC*

A Victorian brass and glass oil
lamp, with shade and chimney,
the green glass reservoir
painted with flowers, c1890,
27in (68cm) high.
£450-500 *S(S)*

An ormolu mounted opaque
glass oil lamp, with embossed
band and 2 lions mask ring
handles, 19thC, 27in (68.5cm)
high.
£220-260 *PCh*

A blackout
emergency lamp.
£6-10 *COB*

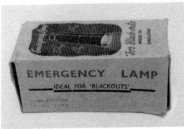

LEATHER & LUGGAGE

A metal hat box, 10½in (26.5cm) diam.
£15-25 *WAB*

A crocodile and silk lined fitted case, 18in (33cm) long.
£150-250 *WAB*

A leather musical instrument case, c1920, 29in (74cm) long.
£30-40 *AHL*

A leather hat box, with original fittings, 12in (30.5cm) wide.
£55-85 *WAB*

A leather briefcase, c1950, 16½in (41.5cm) long.
£18-22 *AHL*

A vellum steamer trunk, well travelled, c1930, 40½in (102cm) wide.
£240-260 *AHL*

A leather travelling case, 10in (25cm) high.
£20-35 *WAB*

A green canvas travelling case, with green leather trim, c1930, 18in (46cm) wide.
£50-60 *AHL*

Two leather suitcases:
large, 24 by 13in (61 by 33cm).
£40-45
small, 20 by 12½in (51 by 32cm).
£12-18 *WAB*

A leather case, 10in (25cm) wide.
£30-40 *AHL*

A leather hat case, 15in (38cm) wide.
£35-55 *WAB*

A leather hat box, c1920, 10in (25cm) high.
£60-80 *AHL*

A leather Gladstone bag, c1920, 27in (68.5cm) wide.
£60-70 *AHL*

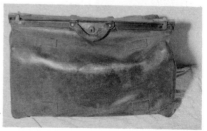

METALWARE
Brass

A wire basket,
7in (17.5cm) square.
£35-45 *MofC*

A brass frog, 1⅜in (3.5cm)
long. **£5-15** *DAN*

A pair of Georgian brass candle
snuffers and tray, c1760.
£100-110 *SAD*

A brass bed warmer,
9in (22.5cm) diam.
£30-40 *NM*

A decorative brass plaque,
15½in (39cm) diam.
£12-15 *NM*

A door stop, General Gordon,
11½in (29cm) high.
£130-150 *DAN*

A Georgian brass and steel
footman, 12in (30.5cm) high.
£250-300 *JAC*

A brass door stop, Warwick
coat-of-arms, c1850, 13¾in
(35cm) high.
£350-400 *DAN*

A brass skillet, 17thC.
£150-200 *JAC*

A pair of trays, with fleur-de-lys
decoration, 11in (28cm) diam.
£25-30 *NM*

An elephant, 2⅜in (6cm) high.
£5-15 *DAN*

A brass tray with a stags head,
9in (22.5cm) diam.
£10-15 *NM*

A selection of 4 brass animals,
1¾ to 3¼in (4.5 to 8cm) high.
£5-15 each *DAN*

A brass hot water bed warmer,
12in (30.5cm) wide.
£35-40 *NM*

A brass bowl,
15in (38cm)
diam.
£25-30 *NM*

Bronze

A bronze cauldron, 16thC,
4in (10cm) high.
£55-60 *SAD*

A lion paperweight, on pewter
base, 4in (10cm) high.
£120-150 *DAN*

CROSS REFERENCE
Oriental ──────➤ p330

A stand, early 19thC, 5in
(13cm) high.
£50-60 *SAD*

Two Viennese gilt bronze cats
sitting on a bench, 1¾in (4.5cm)
high.
£150-165 *TER*

A bronze figure of Fortuna,
after J. De Bologne, 25in
(63.5cm) high.
£450-500 *HSS*

A bronze diver,
c1909, 5in ,
(12.5cm) high.
£30-35 *COB*

A pair of Oriental
vases, polished
with chased details
of entwined
serpents, 16½in
(42cm) high.
£110-130 *GAK*

A bronze figure, with polished silvered patina, 'Graceful Movement', by Alexander Archipenko, 25¾in (66cm) high.
£825-875 *ALL*

A cast bronze of a young girl with kitten, by Juan Clara, 14in (36cm) high.
£380-420 *AAR*

Chimney Ornaments

A pair of brass greyhounds, 7½in (19cm) long.
£130-150 *DAN*

A bell metal figure of 'Napoleon', mid-19thC, 5¾in (14.5cm) high.
£70-75 *DAN*

A brass elephant, 4⅓in (11cm) long.
£80-120 *DAN*

A pair of cast iron sheep, 9in (22.5cm) long.
£100-140 *DAN*

A pair of St. Bernard dogs, with barrels, 8½in (21cm) long.
£140-180 *DAN*

A brass horse, 4in (10cm) long.
£45-55 *DAN*

Copper

A portable picnic heater, c1880, 6½in (16cm) long.
£50-60 *SAD*

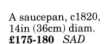

A saucepan, c1820, 14in (36cm) diam.
£175-180 *SAD*

A set of saucepans with lids, c1820, 7 to 12in (17.5 to 30.5cm) diam.
£400-450 *SAD*

A set of 4 roasting trays, 14 to 18in (36 to 46cm) square.
£60-75 *GRF*

A pair of brass horses, 9½in (24cm) long.
£120-150 *DAN*

A chafing dish, with detachable
handle, c1910, 10in (25cm) diam.
£60-70 *TER*

An urn, c1880, 12in
(31cm) high.
£100-120 *AL*

A Victorian frying pan,
made by Benham & Son,
London, 9½in
(24cm) diam.
£40-50 *NM*

Fenders

A brass and filigree cut steel
fender, on 3 brass ball feet,
19thC, 45in (114cm) long.
£300-325 *PAR*

A Victorian brass fender,
45in (114cm) long.
£200-220 *PAR*

A Victorian iron fender, c1890,
36in (91.5cm) long.
£40-50 *SAD*

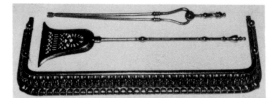

A fender, 36in (91.5cm) long, and a pair of Georgian
steel fire irons. **£90-95 each** *PAR*

Fireside Implements

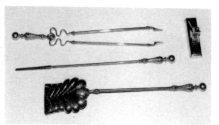

A set of cast steel fire
implements, 19thC,
28in (71cm) long.
£90-95 *PAR*

A Regency bronze coal
pick, used for a stove.
£80-90 *WW*

A wrought iron hearth shovel, 17thC, 24in
(61cm) long. **£35-38** *SAD*

A cast iron fireback, c1810.
19in (48cm) wide.
£120-130 *SAD*

A brass coal
box, 11½in
(29cm) high.
£50-70 *GRF*

A pair of iron log tongs, c1690.
£40-45 *SAD*

A wrought iron poker,
7½in (19cm) long.
£15-20 *SAD*

An iron pot hook, c1640.
£80-90 *SAD*

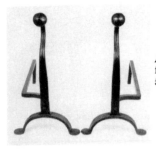

A pair of wrought iron
fire dogs, c1850.
£150-160 *SAD*

A pair of wrought iron spit dogs,
c1595, 23in (59cm) high.
£250-260 *SAD*

Iron

CROSS REFERENCE
Kitchenalia ⟶ p281

A pair of iron nut crackers,
in the form of a dog, 9in
(22.5cm) long.
£20-30 *DAN*

A cast iron trivet, 9⅛in
(23.5cm) high.
£30-40 *GRF*

A pair of cast iron garden urns,
each with moulded rim and
mask decorated loop handles,
on square bases, 19thC, 30½in
(77.5cm) high.
£900-950 *AH*

CROSS REFERENCE
Metalware
Trivets ⟶ p307

A cast iron footman,
9in (22.5cm) high.
£30-50 *GRF*

A cast iron urn and trivet,
urn 16in (40.5cm) high.
£120-150 *GRF*

A Holbey painted cast iron dog,
American, late 19thC.
£150-250 *DMT*

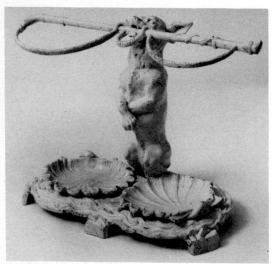

A wrought iron wafering iron, c1695, 30in (76cm) long. **£80-90** *SAD*

A cast iron Medici lion, early 19thC. **£120-200** *DMT*

A Victorian cast iron whip stand, depicting a begging dog holding his master's hunting whip, registration mark for 1880, No. 45, 25in (63.5cm) high. **£800-850** *WW*

Pewter

A pair of marriage plates, by A. Carter, c1760. **£95-100** *SAD*

Pewter has been a regular feature in previous editions of *Miller's Collectables Price Guides,* available from Millers Publications.

Lead

A filigree picture frame, with a signed engraving, 7¾ by 6in (19 by 15cm). **£40-45** *ROW*

Silver

A seal, by Hester Bateman, c1790, 1¼in (3cm) wide. **£175-200** *AMH*

A silver vinaigrette, in the form of an apple, Birmingham c1875, ¾in (2cm) wide. **£100-130** *CA*

A lead horse and jockey, with screw holes at the base, possibly made for advertising purposes, 8in (20cm) long. **£150-200** *PC*

CROSS REFERENCE
Sewing ──────➤ p385

A silver filigree bodkin holder, English, early 19thC, 3¾in (9cm) long. **£50-85** *CA*

HALLMARKS
- **There are usually 4 hallmarks - sometimes 5.**
- **The specific hallmark designates the town in which the piece was assayed.**
- **The standard mark shows the required quality of silver which has been attained. The British mark is a lion walking to the left.**
- **The annual mark is a letter which denotes the year of manufacture - 'J' is not usually used.**
- **The maker's mark is usually shown as initials.**
- **Between 1784 and 1890 the head of the sovereign was marked on all silver and gold proving the levy had been paid.**

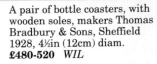

A pair of bottle coasters, with wooden soles, makers Thomas Bradbury & Sons, Sheffield 1928, 4½in (12cm) diam.
£480-520 *WIL*

A silver table lighter, London 1888, 4½in (11.5cm) high.
£250-275 *AMH*

A mustard pot, by Roberts & Hall, Sheffield 1849, 3½in (9cm) high.
£350-400 *AMH*

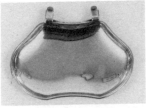

A lemon tea saucer, Birmingham 1905, 3½in (9cm) wide.
£45-50 *AMH*

l. A lancet case, by Hilliard & Thomason, Birmingham 1876, 3in (7.5cm) high.
£100-120
r. A vesta case, by S. Mordan, Birmingham 1889, 1½in (4cm) high. **£70-80** *AMH*

A George III salver, with bright cut oval cartouche, on 4 feet, by John Crouch and Thomas Hannam, London 1791, 12½oz.
£425-450 *GAK*

Two pin trays, London c1890, largest 6¾in (17cm) long.
£85-110 each *AMH*

A tobacco box, by R. Cox, London 1751, 5¼in (13cm) wide.
£600-650 *AMH*

CROSS REFERENCE
Smoking ⟶ p393

A silver faced timepiece, depicting a policeman holding an enamel clock dial, marked M & CL, Birmingham c1907, 6in (15cm) high.
£750-865 *ARE*

A jug, by Mappin & Webb, London 1892, 3in (7.5cm) high.
£100-110 *AMH*

A silver vesta case, showing a tennis player, Birmingham c1885, 1¼in (3cm) high.
£150-200 *CA*

A rocker blotter, Birmingham 1890, 5in (12.5cm) high.
£150-200 *AMH*

For more information on hallmarks, see *Miller's Silver & Sheffield Plate Marks*, available from Millers Publications.

CROSS REFERENCE
Sport ⟶ p399

A silver cream jug, by Nathaniel Smith, Sheffield 1797, double duty mark, 6in (15cm) high.
£575-625 *AMH*

Three bookmarks, c1900, 3 to 3¾in (7.5 to 9cm) long.
£30-70 each *HOW*

A potato ring, decorated with cows, swans, foliage and scrolls, Dublin 1913, 18in (46cm) diam.
£750-775 *SWO*

A folding mirror, by Hilliard & Thomason, Birmingham 1856, 3¾in (9cm) diam.
£375-400 *AMH*

A pap boat, London 1798, 4⅓in (11cm) wide.
£325-350 *AMH*

Pap boats were for pulping babies' food.

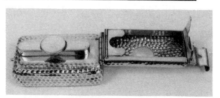

A curling tong heater, London 1898, 4in (10cm) long closed.
£150-175 *AMH*

A tobacco rasp, London c1689, 3in (7.5cm) long.
£650-750 *AMH*

A pair of silver dishes, Birmingham 1894, 5½in (14cm) wide.
£175-200 *AMH*

l. & r. A pair of candlesticks, with fluted Doric columns, detachable beaded sconces, Birmingham 1963, 12in (31cm) high.
£580-600
c. A large trumpet-shaped flower vase, by the Gold & Silversmiths Co, London 1910, 11½in (29.5cm) high.
£210-225 *GAK*

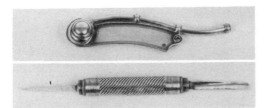

A folding apple corer and fruit knife, by J. Willmore, Birmingham 1831, 7in (17.5cm) long.
£575-625 *AMH*

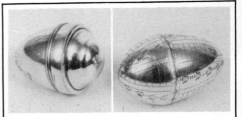

Two nutmet graters, by Samuel Pemberton:
l. Birmingham 1802.
£250-300
r. Birmingham 1796.
£375-400 *AMH*

A silver gilt campaign stove, by Frd. Purnell, London 1888, 5½in (14cm) high.
£575-625 *AMH*

A claret jug, by Edward Hutton, London 1882, 13in (33cm) high.
£1,250-1,450 *TVA*

> **DID YOU KNOW**
> Hallmarks from lesser items can be cut-out and transposed to larger more important pieces. This can be detected by breathing on the hallmark. If it has been transposed a fine line will be visable.

Children's Silverware

A christening mug, with simulated crocodile finish, London 1899, 2½in (6cm) high.   **£90-100** *TRU*

A child's rattle, London c1765, 5½in (14cm) long.
£650-700 *AMH*

A christening tankard, embossed with scrolls and floral sprays, initialled 'WRS', gilded interior, maker Thomas Whipham, London 1748, 4in (10cm) high, 7oz.
£180-200 *WIL*

Salts

A pair of George III boat-shaped pedestal salts, with gilt interiors, by Peter, Anne and William Bateman, London 1805.
£220-240 *GAK*

A set of 4 cauldron salts, with gilt interiors and rims, by Philip Rundell, London 1821, 1611gr.
£2,800-3,000 *HSS*

A child's rattle, by M. Cripps, London 1786, 5½in (14cm) long.
£600-700 *AMH*

Sugar Sifters

A Sterling silver and cut glass sugar sifter, 6½in (16.5cm) high.
£60-70 *DEL*

A sugar sifter, Birmingham 1900.
£285-300 *DEL*

A sugar sifter, London 1938, 6¾in (17cm) high.
£130-150 *DEL*

A George II silver caster, probably by George Hunter, London 1749, 6in (15cm) high.
£300-325 *SWO*

A sugar sifter, Birmingham 1931, 7in (17.5cm) high.
£150-170 *DEL*

A sugar sifter, Chester 1901, 10¼in (26cm) high.
£200-240 *DEL*

Spoons & Scoops

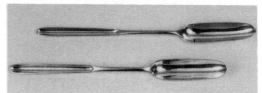

A pair of marrow scoops, by J. Duke, Chester 1778, 9in (23cm) long.
£450-550 *AMH*

Two caddy spoons:
l. By Matthew Linwood, Birmingham 1813, 3¼in (8cm) long.
£240-260
r. By George Unite, Birmingham 1847, 3½in (9cm) long.
£240-260 *AMH*

A selection of four caddy spoons, various makers, 19thC.:
£150-220 each *AMH*

A pair of caddy spoons, by Stokes & Ireland, Birmingham 1893, 4¼in (11cm) long.
£220-240 *AMH*

Two caddy spoons:
Above. By J. Taylor, Birmingham c1813, 3¼in (8cm) long. **£200-220**
Below. By Hester Bateman, London 1787, 3¼in (8cm) long.
£250-270 *AMH*

A caddy spoon, in the form of a hand, by Jos. Snatt, London 1809, 3in (7.5cm) long.
£500-550 *AMH*

A selection of caddy spoons, various makers, 19thC:
£200-350 each *AMH*

Two caddy spoons:
l. Sheffield 1791, 4in (10cm) long.
£230-250
r. London 1796, 3¼in (8cm) long.
£240-260 *AMH*

A caddy spoon, London 1892, 5½in (14cm) long.
£120-130 *AMH*

A rat tail basting spoon, by Wm. Scarlett, London 1715, 13in (33cm) long.
£650-700 *AMH*

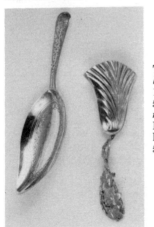

Two caddy spoons:
l. By J. Wren, London 1806, 4in (10cm) long.
£275-300
r. By J. Newton Mappin, Birmingham 1885, 3in (8cm) long.
£220-240 *AMH*

Above. A sucket spoon, c1675, 6½in (16.5cm) long.
£225-250
Below. A mashing spoon, by Thomas Borthwick, Inverness, marked 1784, 6½in (16.5cm) long. **£350-400** *AMH*

Teapots & Services

A Continental silver teapot, with squirrel finial, 19thC.
£260-280 *LRG*

Above. A trefid spoon, by John Cory, London 1706, 8in (20cm) long. **£375-400**
Below. A seal top spoon, by E. Hole, London 1626, 7½in (19cm) long. **£600-650** *AMH*

A French silver tea service, with plated tray, by Odiot, 19thC, 146oz.
£4,200-4,400 *HCH*

A George IV silver teapot, with reeded body band and shell mounted handle, London 1829, 19oz. **£225-250** *GAK*

A four-piece tea and coffee service, with octagonal pear-shaped bodies, swan neck spouts and scroll handles, London 1911, 67.5oz. **£880-940** *WW*

Tea Strainers

A tea strainer, London 1950, 5¼in (13cm) wide. **£80-100** *DEL*

A three-piece tea set, the teapot with hinged cover and ebonised handle, two-handled sugar bowl and milk jug, Sheffield 1916, 35oz 10dwt. **£330-350** *WIL*

A Sterling silver tea strainer, with handle, 6in (15cm) long. **£80-90** *DEL*

A tea strainer-on-stand, Birmingham 1931, 4¼in (11cm) wide. **£100-115** *DEL*

Silver Plate

A pair of grape scissors, English, c1900, 6¾in (17cm) long. **£55-65** *TER*

SHEFFIELD PLATE

- **Sheffield Plate is a thin layer of silver fused to a copper base.**
- **Later pieces, especially if stamped 'Sheffield Plated', are electroplated and not genuine Sheffield Plate.**

A toast rack, designed with tennis racquets, c1920, 6½in (16.5cm) long. **£125-150** *ARE*

A pair of owl pepperettes, 5½in (14cm) high. **£400-600** *ARE*

CROSS REFERENCE
Sport ─────────➤ p399

A pair of Sheffield plate and cut glass salts, c1790, 5in (12.5cm) high. **£600-800** *CB*

A pair of Old Sheffield plate snuffers on a tray, by G. Gibbs, c1810, 11in (28cm) long.
£225-250 *AMH*

A large cannon, c1930.
£25-30 *COB*

Tin

Toasting Forks

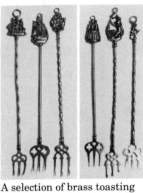

A selection of brass toasting forks, largest 20in (51cm) long.
£5-8 each *NM*

A brass 'Bonzo' toasting fork, 19½in (49cm) long.
£8-10 *NM*

An extending brass toasting fork, with the head of Kia Ora.
£10-15 *NM*

CROSS REFERENCE
Toys ➔ p444

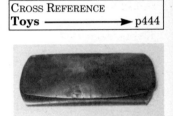

A spectacle case.
£2-3 *PAR*

A silver telescopic toasting fork, London 1898, 17in (43cm) long.
£250-275 *AMH*

A Victorian brass trivet, 10½in (26.5cm) high.
£60-70 *NM*

Trivets

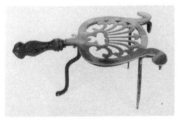

A brass trivet, 18thC, 11½in (29.5cm) long.
£45-50 *SAD*

A brass trivet, 9in (22.5cm) long.
£15-20 *NM*

An iron trivet, 10in (25cm) high.
£15-20 *SAD*

Two Victorian brass trivets, 7 and 8in (17.5 and 20cm) long.
£15-20 each *NM*

MILITARIA

An Erskine cartridge loader,
15in (38in) long.
£75-125 *WAB*

A copper and brass army
bugle, c1915, 10½in
(26.5cm) high.
£70-75 *SAD*

A basket for shell cases, c1915,
20in (50.5cm) high.
£90-95 *MofC*

A Bakelite sign,
c1940.
£5-6 *COB*

A miniature portrait on ivory,
depicting a WWI officer of the
Durham Light Infantry, in a
bronze frame and leather
covered case, with officer's
bronze collar badge.
£220-240 *WAL*

For a further selection of
**Trench Art, please refer
to *Miller's Collectables
Price Guide, Vol V,
pp322*, available from
Millers Publications.**

Badges

A wooden powder keg , with
original chain, initialled,
9in (22.5cm) diam.
£60-75 *PSC*

A brass Trench Art aircraft,
made from parts of bullets
and shell cases, c1918.
£30-40 *COB*

An album of regimental,
shop and hotel crests,
c1895.
£50-60 *COB*

An officer's cap badge of the
Armoured Car Company,
Shanghai Volunteer Corps and
a pair of matching collars.
£170-190 *WAL*

An officer's silver glengarry badge of the Cameronians, hallmarked Birmingham 1900.
£150-160 *WAL*

A Victorian other ranks' white metal glengarry of the 4th Volunteers Battallion, the East Surrey Regiment.
£45-50 *WAL*

A cap badge of the Connaught Rangers, 1800.
£40-45 *SAD*

An officer's gilt and silver plated cap badge of the Royal Dublin Fusiliers.
£120-140 *WAL*

An officer's gilt and silver plated forage cap badge, of the Leinster Regiment.
£125-140 *WAL*

A pair of Motor Machine Gun titles, red on khaki cloth, and a pair of brass two-part Motor Machine Gun titles.
£170-190 *WAL*

A Victorian officer's brass and white metal martingale badge of the Royal Horse Guards.
£40-45 *WAL*

A yellow on blue flash of the 3rd Indian Division, The Chindits, and a few personal effects of Lt. D. C. M. Collins.
£375-395 *WAL*

A silver badge of the Rhodesian African Rifles, hallmarked Birmingham 1965, and a companion collar badge, marked 'silver'.
£45-50 *WAL*

CROSS REFERENCE
Horse Brasses ⟶ p247

A badge of the Coldstream Guards, 19thC, 3¼ by 2¾in (8 by 7cm).
£30-36 *SAD*

A Victorian other ranks' white metal glengarry badge of the 1st Volunteer Battalion, the West Yorkshire Regiment.
£70-80 *WAL*

An officer's cast puggaree badge, 2nd Bengal Light Infantry, not hallmarked.
£155-175 *WAL*

A glengarry badge of the 88th Connaught Rangers Regiment.
£110-120 *WAL*

A Sudanese provincial police officer's silver and enamel cap badge of Darfur province, hallmarked Birmingham 1928.
£110-120 *WAL*

An other ranks' white metal cap badge of the 5th West Middlesex Rifle Volunteers.
£75-80 *WAL*

A glengarry badge of the 34th Cumberland Regiment.
£200-210 *WAL*

A Victorian officer's brass bit boss badge of the 2nd Life Guards.
£45-50 *WAL*

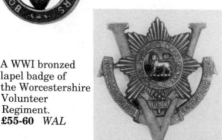

A WWI bronzed lapel badge of the Worcestershire Volunteer Regiment.
£55-60 *WAL*

An other ranks' blackened glengarry badge of the Border Rifle Volunteers, post-1902.
£65-75 *WAL*

A Victorian brass martingale badge of the 15th King's Hussars.
£85-90 *WAL*

A WWI bronzed cap badge of the United Arts Volunteer Rifles. **£70-75** *WAL*

A badge of the Canadian 2nd Armoured Car Regiment and a pair of Armoured Cars shoulder titles. **£70-80** *WAL*

A Victorian other ranks' white metal glengarry of the Ist Volunteer Battallion, the Shropshire Light Infantry. **£75-85** *WAL*

A WWI Free French officer's bronze cap badge, of the Ist Battalion F. M. Commando. **£210-230** *WAL*

Helmet Plates

A Victorian officer's silver puggaree badge of the Rifle Brigade, hallmarked Birmingham 1886. **£85-90** *WAL*

An officer's gilt French pattern shako plate, of the Ist West India Regiment, 1855. **£180-190** *WAL*

A Victorian other ranks' Maltese cross helmet plate of the Border Rifle Volunteers, in darkened brass. **£85-90** *WAL*

An other ranks' white metal and brass helmet plate of the 2nd Dragoon Guards. **£50-60** *WAL*

A Victorian officer's silver plated helmet plate of the Newcastle Engineer Volunteers. **£160-180** *WAL*

A Russian other ranks' Crimean War brass helmet plate of the 31st Regiment, with contemporary engraving on the back 'The Battle of the Alma. 20th Sept 1984. Given to Mrs. Stepney Powell by Sergeant Russell, Coldstream Guards, August 1855'. **£340-360** *WAL*

Belts & Belt Plates

A pre-1857 officer's gilt and silver plated waist belt plate of the 30th Bengal Native Infantry.
£330-350 *WAL*

The 30th Bengal Native Infantry mutineered in 1857.

An officer's bi-metal waist belt plate of the Scinde Irregular Horse.
£100-110 *WAL*

An officer's gilt thistle lace waist belt of the King's Own Scottish Borderers.
£180-190 *WAL*

An Edward VII officer's silver mounted shoulder belt and pouch of the 14th King's Hussars, hallmarked Birmingham 1906.
£650-675 *WAL*

An officer's gilt and silver waist belt plate of the 20th Deccan Horse, hallmarked Birmingham 1907.
£280-290 *WAL*

An officer's waist belt plate of the 29th Lancers Deccan Horse, with silver plated badge on burnished plate.
£240-250 *WAL*

Edged Weapons

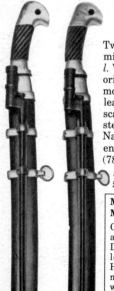

Two Russian 1881 pattern military shasquas:
l. With plain curved blade, original polish, plated steel mounted hilt, wood grips, leather covered wooden scabbard with silver plated steel mounts and Moisin Nagent socket bayonet, engraved 'K.16.R', 31in (78.5cm) long. **£145-165**
r. With brass mounted hilt. **£185-195** *WAL*

MAKE THE MOST OF MILLERS

Condition is absolutely vital when assessing the value of any item. Damaged pieces appreciate much less than perfect examples. However, a rare, desirable piece may command a high price even when damaged.

A Japanese shinto wakisashi, with braid bound rayskin covered tsuka, round iron tsuba, in a black lacquered saya, reasonable condition, blade 18in (46cm) long. **£270-290** *ASB*

A silver mounted Arabian 'Mecca' jambiya, recently manufactured, in traditional style.
£400-420 *ASB*

Daggers

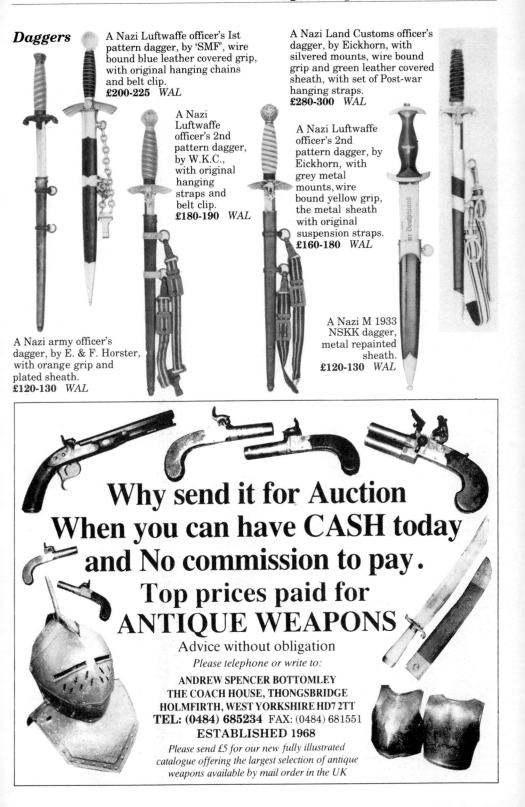

A Nazi Luftwaffe officer's Ist pattern dagger, by 'SMF', wire bound blue leather covered grip, with original hanging chains and belt clip.
£200-225 *WAL*

A Nazi Luftwaffe officer's 2nd pattern dagger, by W.K.C., with original hanging straps and belt clip.
£180-190 *WAL*

A Nazi army officer's dagger, by E. & F. Horster, with orange grip and plated sheath.
£120-130 *WAL*

A Nazi Land Customs officer's dagger, by Eickhorn, with silvered mounts, wire bound grip and green leather covered sheath, with set of Post-war hanging straps.
£280-300 *WAL*

A Nazi Luftwaffe officer's 2nd pattern dagger, by Eickhorn, with grey metal mounts, wire bound yellow grip, the metal sheath with original suspension straps.
£160-180 *WAL*

A Nazi M 1933 NSKK dagger, metal repainted sheath.
£120-130 *WAL*

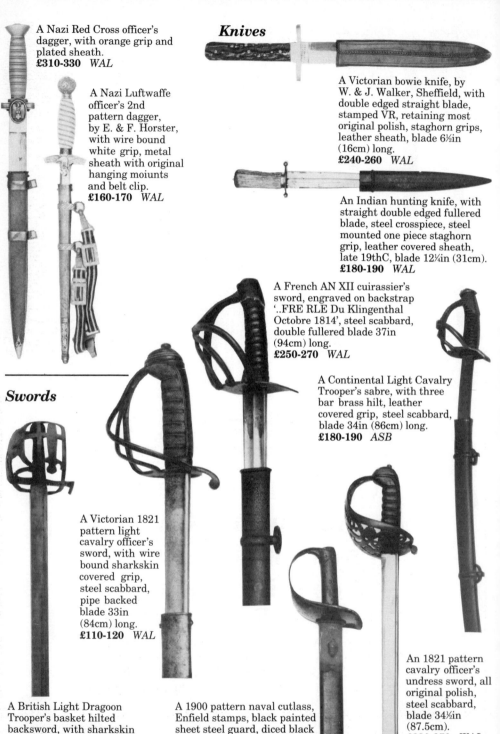

A Nazi Red Cross officer's dagger, with orange grip and plated sheath.
£310-330 *WAL*

A Nazi Luftwaffe officer's 2nd pattern dagger, by E. & F. Horster, with wire bound white grip, metal sheath with original hanging moiunts and belt clip.
£160-170 *WAL*

Knives

A Victorian bowie knife, by W. & J. Walker, Sheffield, with double edged straight blade, stamped VR, retaining most original polish, staghorn grips, leather sheath, blade 6½in (16cm) long.
£240-260 *WAL*

An Indian hunting knife, with straight double edged fullered blade, steel crosspiece, steel mounted one piece staghorn grip, leather covered sheath, late 19thC, blade 12¼in (31cm).
£180-190 *WAL*

A French AN XII cuirassier's sword, engraved on backstrap '..FRE RLE Du Klingenthal Octobre 1814', steel scabbard, double fullered blade 37in (94cm) long.
£250-270 *WAL*

A Continental Light Cavalry Trooper's sabre, with three bar brass hilt, leather covered grip, steel scabbard, blade 34in (86cm) long.
£180-190 *ASB*

Swords

A Victorian 1821 pattern light cavalry officer's sword, with wire bound sharkskin covered grip, steel scabbard, pipe backed blade 33in (84cm) long.
£110-120 *WAL*

An 1821 pattern cavalry officer's undress sword, all original polish, steel scabbard, blade 34½in (87.5cm).
£230-250 *WAL*

A British Light Dragoon Trooper's basket hilted backsword, with sharkskin covered grip, straight single edged blade, good condition, mid-18thC, blade 33in (84cm).
£660-680 *ASB*

A 1900 pattern naval cutlass, Enfield stamps, black painted sheet steel guard, diced black leather grips, steel mounted leather scabbard, blade 27in (69cm) long.
£100-110 *WAL*

A Victorian 1827 Rifle Volunteer officer's sword, etched with crown, VR, '5th Essex Rifle Volunteers', with steel hilt, wire bound fishskin covered grip, steel scabbard, blade 31in (79cm).
£200-220 *WAL*

A Scottish officer's basket hilted broadsword, by Wilkinson, No. 54146, fullered double edged blade, etched with crowned 'GVR' cypher amidst thistles, wire bound fishskin grip, red felt covered buckskin liner, crimson tassels, brown leather Field Service scabbard, and a plated steel dress scabbard with oilskin bag, manufactured 1917, 33in (84cm) long.
£300-325 *WAL*

A Georgian naval cutlass, ribbed Iron Dundas pattern grip, plain sheet iron bowl guard, plain curved blade 29in (74cm) long.
£160-180 *WAL*

A Scottish basket hilted backsword, with 2 full length fullers, mid-18thC, blade 31in (79cm) long.
£625-650 *ASB*

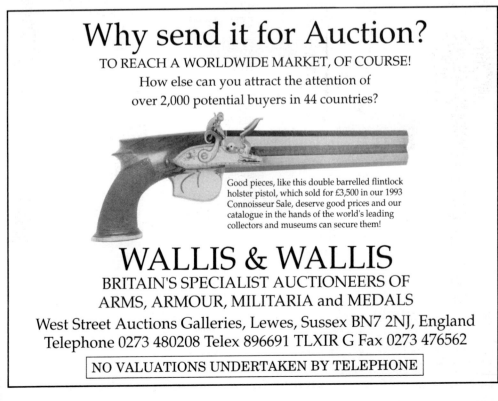

A Victorian Scottish Field Officer's sword of the Royal Scots Fusiliers, by Henry Wilkinson, with straight double edged blade, steel scabbard, blade 32in (81cm) long.
£500-525 *WAL*

A Victorian 1889 pattern staff sergeant's sword, by Mole, with original polish, wire bound fishskin covered grip, steel hilt, issue marks for 1892 and 1902, plain blade 31in (79cm) long. **£55-65** *WAL*

An officer's blue torrin cap of the 5th Royal Irish Lancers, with scarlet top, gilt piping and embroidered badge.
£200-225 *WAL*

Gorgets

A Georgian officer's copper gilt gorget.
£140-150 *WIL*

A Georgian officer's copper gilt universal pattern gorget, with original chamois liner.
£260-280 *WAL*

Headdress

A Victorian other ranks' lance cap of the 12th Lancers, with green and yellow boss, cap lines and plume missing.
£185-200 *S(S)*

An officer's blue peaked cap of the 35th Sikhs, with scarlet piping, black lace headband, plain leather pouch and chinstrap with regimental buttons, silver plated badge.
£210-230 *WAL*

A Hussar other ranks' busby, the crimson bag with yellow facings, red horsehair plume, fawn cap lines, 9th Lancers badge attached.
£90-100 *S(S)*

A Victorian officer's Albert pattern helmet of the Princess Charlotte of Wales's Dragoon Guards, red leather and silk lining, dented, plume missing.
£825-850 *S(S)*

Medals

A South Africa 1877-79 and a Cape of Good Hope medal.
£260-280 *WAL*

An Arctic 1875-76 medal, awarded to N. C. Petersen, Danish Interpreter and Dog Driver to the 1875-76 Expedition, H. M. S. Alert. **£2,000-2,250** *SPI*

A Field Officer's small gold medal for 'Vittoria' and Waterloo medal, with original steel clip, awarded to Major R. M. Cairnes, Royal Artillery. **£6,400-6,800** *SPI*

A Gulf medal, 1990-91, with bar 16th January to 28th February 1991, in its original box, together with 3 sew-on rosettes. **£160-170** *WAL*

A 1914-15 star, a British War medal, and a Victory medal, (2202 Gnr/A Cpl J. B. Orchard, R.A.). **£75-80** *WAL*

A Zulu War medal for the Victoria Cross Action at Hlobane Mountain, in silver mounted frame with silver scroll label inscribed 'Ronald George Elidor Campbell', 'Lieut. and Captain, Coldstream Guards', 'Zulu War 1879'. **£4,300-4,600** *SPI*

A Naval General Service 1793-1840 medal, 6 clasps, awarded to Richard Levertine A.B. **£7,800-8,200** *SPI*

FURTHER READING
Battle Honours of the British Army (1911), C.B. Norman, David & Charles, Newton Abbot, Reprint 1971.
Collecting Medals and Decorations, Alec A. Purves, Seaby, London, Third Edition 1978.
Spink's Catalogue of British Orders, Decorations and Medals, E.C. Joslin, Webb & Bower, 1983.

The Dickin Medal or 'Animal V.C.', posthumously awarded to Simon, ship's cat, H. M. S. Amethyst, during the Yangtse Incident, bronze, 45mm diam.
£24,000-25,000 *SPI*

The Dickin Medal, named after the founder of the People's Dispensary for Sick Animals, Maria Elizabeth Dickin C.B.E., has been awarded 53 times. Simon was the only cat to receive the award.
The Recommendation states: "SIMON, Neuter Cat, (Died before award) Served on H.M.S. Amethyst during the Yangtse Incident, disposing of many rats though wounded by shell blast. Throughout the incident his behaviour was of the highest order although the blast was capable of making a hole over a foot in diameter in a steel plate."

A Queen's South Africa medal, one bar Defence of Kimberley, King's South Africa, both date bars, and a British War medal, and a Mayor of Kimberley Siege Star 1900.
£210-230 *WAL*

A British North Borneo Company 1899-1900 medal, one clasp, Tambunan, awarded to Francis George Atkinson, in glazed frame with silver name plate.
£1,650-1,850 *SPI*

Pistols

A 16 bore Spanish miquelet flintlock belt pistol, good condition, c1790, barrels 5in (12.5cm) long.
£725-750 *ASB*

A 15 bore Spanish Ripoll style miquelet flintlock pistol, with steel barrel, walnut stock, lightly pitted overall, c1770, barrel 7in (17.5cm). **£825-850** *ASB*

A 26 bore British pattern 1796 Sea Service flintlock pistol, with steel belt hook and brass furniture, storekeepers' mark for 1806, barrel 12in (30.5cm).
£875-900 *ASB*

A 16mm French Gendarmerie percussion pistol, with round barrel, back action lock marked 'Mre Rie de St Etienne', ramrod replaced, barrel 5in (12.5cm).
£450-470 *ASB*

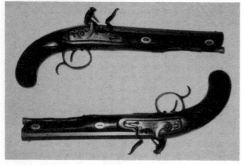

FURTHER READING
Badges of the British Army 1820-1960,
F. Wilkinson, Arms & Armour Press, 1992.
*Campaign Medals of the British Army 1815-
1972,* R.W. Gould, Arms & Armour Press, 1994
Sword, Lance & Bayonet, Charles Ffoulkes &
E. C. Hopkinson, Arco Publishing Co., 1967.
Military Fashion, John Mollo Barry & Jenkins.
Collecting Metal Shoulder Titles, R. A. Westlake,
Frederick Warne, 1980.
Weapons of the British Soldier,
Col. H. C. B. Rogers, Sphere Books Ltd., 1972.
Swords of the British Army, Brian Robson,
Arms & Armour Press, 1983.

A pair of flintlock travelling
pistols, by Manton.
£1,350-1,450 *MR*

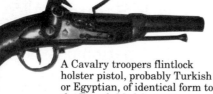

A Cavalry troopers flintlock
holster pistol, probably Turkish
or Egyptian, of identical form to
the French Modele 1822.
£550-580 *ASB*

A pair of English 18 bore full stocked
percussion officer's or duelling pistols,
signed Lacy & Co, London, (J. G. Lacy &
D. W. Witton, Hardwaremen, City of
London, 1815-32), in a mahogany case
with brass corners, lined interior, c1820.
£1,800-1,900 *ASB*

A Tower Land Service
flintlock pistol.
£325-350 *MR*

A 5 shot .31 Colt model 1849
pocket percussion revolver,
barrel 6in (16.5cm) long, 10½in
(26.5cm) overall.
£120-140 *WAL*

A 6 shot .31 Allen & Thurber
self cocking percussion
pepperbox revolver, slightly
fluted cylinder 3⅓in (8.5cm),
7in (17.5cm) long.
£350-370 *WAL*

A 5 shot bore Beaumont Adams
double action percussion
revolver, London proved, barrel
5¾in (14cm) long, in green felt
lined mahogany case.
£480-500 *WAL*

A 6 shot .44 Rogers and Spencer
single action army percussion
revolver, underlever ramrod,
barrel 7¼in (18.5cm) long, 13in
(33cm) overall.
£775-800 *WAL*

A Belgian Herman 4 barrelled
80 bore ring trigger percussion
pepperbox revolver, turn off
damascus barrels, 2¾in (7cm),
7½in (19cm) long.
£250-260 *WAL*

A .31 Colt 1849 pocket model revolver, refinished, action defective, barrel 5in (12.5cm) long.
£325-350 *ASB*

A .320RF Moore's Patent 'Belt Model' 7 shot revolver, octagonal barrel with ejector rod, scroll engraved bronze frame and plain walnut grips, barrel 5in (12.5cm) long. **£475-500** *ASB*

A 5 shot .36 Manhattan Firearms Co. Navy single action percussion revolver, barrel 6in (15cm), 11in (28cm) overall.
£275-300 *WAL*

Powder Flasks

A .41 RF Remington double barrelled derringer, with chequered hard rubber grips, c1888.
£465-475 *ASB*

A 6 shot .455/.476 Webley Mark III double action service revolver, barrel 4in (10cm) long, with leather holster. **£230-250** *WAL*

A 9mm 'Export' Mauser model 1896 self loading pistol, with ribbed walnut grips, barrel 4in (10cm) long.
£325-350 *WAL*

A pressed lanthorn powder flask, with adjustable sprung brass charger, 7½in (18.5cm) long. **£85-90** *WAL*

MINIATURES

An ivory single comb, a double comb, and penknife, 1in (2.5cm).
£15-30 each *TER*

A pair of powder flasks, original colour and strings, 10¾ by 4⅓in (27 by 11cm).
£350-375 *PSC*

A German butcher's shop, late 19thC, 6½in (16cm) high.
£250-300 *HAL*

CROSS REFERENCE
Dolls House Furniture ⟶ p173

MIRRORS

An Edwardian silver framed
dressing table mirror, by
William Comyns, London 1904,
12 by 15in (30.5 by 38cm).
£430-450 *GAK*

Barbola Mirrors

A mirror, c1930, 9in (22.5cm) high.
£50-60 *MW*

A three-piece mirror.
£160-180 *MW*

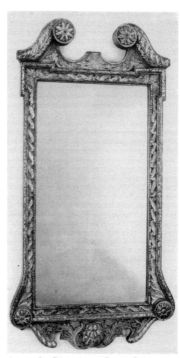

An early Georgian giltwood
looking glass.
£850-900 *LRG*

A mirror, 1920-30,
9in(22.5cm) high.
£30-40 *BAT*

A mirror, c1930,
12½in (31.5cm)
wide.
£35-45 *FMN*

A Bavarian mirror, with fine
hand carved wooden frame.
£225-250 *PAR*

An Art Nouveau copper
and silver plated table
mirror, with female
figure, signed 'R. Aurill',
33in (83.5cm) high.
£480-500 *GAK*

A mirror, c1930, 9in (22.5cm)
high. **£50-60** *MW*

A mirror, c1930, 11in (28cm) high.
£100-120 *MW*

A swing mirror, c1930,
13in (33cm) high.
£135-145 *MW*

A swing mirror, c1930,
18in (46cm) high.
£140-150 *MW*

MONEY BOXES

A painted cast iron hoop-la
bank, by John Harper & Co.
Ltd, c1900, 8½in (21.5cm) high.
£300-325 *CSK*

A cast iron Darktown battery
mechanical bank, by J. & E.
Stevens, c1888, 9¾in
(24cm) wide.
£3,000-3,200 *S(NY)*

A cast iron Punch and Judy
mechanical bank, c1884.
£3,500-3,600 *S(NY)*

A mahogany, walnut,
ebony and sycamore
money box, c1790.
£800-1,000 WA

A cast iron eagle
and eaglets
mechanical bank,
by J. & E.
Stevens, 6¾in
(17cm) long.
£600-800 *S(NY)*

A speaking dog cast iron mechanical bank, by J. & E. Stevens, 7¼in (18cm) high.
£2,000-2,200 *CNY*

A cast iron cat and mouse mechanical bank, by J. & E. Stevens, 11½in (29cm) high.
£1,250-1,450 *S(NY)*

A New Creedmore cast iron mechanical bank, by J. & E. Stevens, 10in (25cm) long.
£1,200-1,300 *CNY*

A money box with movable head, 5¼in (13cm) high.
£15-25 *WAB*

A Mickey Mouse china money box, c1960.
£18-24 *COB*

A Victorian pig money box, with registration number, 6in (15cm) long.
£90-100 *KOH*

CROSS REFERENCE
Toys ⟶ p444

A George V Royal Bank money box, 1910, 5¼in (13cm) high.
£40-50 *NM*

An Edwardian inlaid double money box, with key, 6in (15cm) wide. **£25-30** *HAY*

A brass bear money box.
£10-15 *COB*

A handmade wood and brass money box, 6in (15cm) high.
£100-120 *TER*

A steel money box casket, probably German, late 17thC, 8¼in (21cm) wide.
£440-460 *MofC*

Three Wade National Westminster Bank money boxes, c1970.
£10-18 each *BAT*

These boxes were given away free to children

Two tin bank money boxes, unbranded, 4 and 1¼in (10 and 3cm) high.
£25-45 each *WAB*

CROSS REFERENCE
Tins, Signs & Advertising ⟶ p440

CROSS REFERENCE
Collectables of the Future ⟶ p432

An 'Artillery' cast iron mechanical bank, by J. & E. Stevens, red coat version, 6in (15cm) high.
£1,400-1.600 *CNY*

A cast iron monkey and coconut mechanical bank, by J. & E. Stevens, c1886, 8½in (21.5cm) high.
£1,500-1,600 *S(NY)*

A cast iron humpty dumpty mechanical bank, by Shepard Hardware Co, 7½in (19cm) high.
£3,000-3,200 *S(NY)*

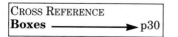

An Edwardian double money box, with transfer view of a castle, 6in (15cm) wide.
£18-20 *HAY*

CROSS REFERENCE
Boxes ⟶ p30

Cash Tills

A silvered brass cash till, inscribed 'The National', late 19thC, 17in (43cm) high.
£150-170 *S(S)*

A National till, 17in (43cm) high.
£150-200 *GRF*

MONKEYS

Collectables need not be centered on a particular medium but can instead be based on a theme. This intriguing collection of monkeys, shown below, is a good example of a thematic approach to forming an individual collection.

A pair of Chinese bronze vases with monkeys, 2½in (6cm) high.
£200-300 *DMT*

Two German ceramic caricature bedroom candlesticks, 19thC, 6½in (16cm) high.
£250-350 *DMT*

A French bronze figure of a monkey, signed by Gilbert, 12in (30.5cm) high.
£800-900 *DMT*

A pair of French brass monkey candlesticks, 7in (17.5cm) high.
£480-600 *DMT*

CROSS REFERENCE
Candlesticks ———→ p64
Lighting ———→ p292

A pair of French terracotta baboons, c1870, 15in (38cm) high.
£3,000-4,000 *DMT*

An English brass cigarette holder, c1910, 4⅓in (11cm) high.
£250-300 *DMT*

An English rustic carved wood monkey, 19thC, 4in (35.5cm) high.
£150-250 *DMT*

A Spanish painted spelter tobacco jar, c1880, 8½in (21cm) high.
£450-600 *DMT*

A French terracotta figure of an Arabic girl with a monkey, c1880, 16in (40.5cm) high. **£600-700** *DMT*

A set of 22 framed black and white prints, by W. Lawton, 11 by 7in (28 by 17.5cm).
£180-220 each *DMT*

MOTHER-OF-PEARL

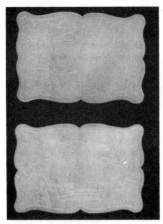

Two armorial engraved counters, c1810, 1½in (3.5cm) wide.
£12-15 each *TER*

An Edison 'suitcase' home phonograph, model A, No. H32954, in oak case with transfer on lid.
£750-775 *CSK*

A mahogany musical nécessaire, in the form of a grand piano.
£750-775 *CSK*

MUSICAL

A Swiss singing bird in a cage, late 20thC, 11¾in (30cm) high.
£280-300 *Bon*

A white metal singing bird box, opening to form cigarette boxes, 4¾in (12cm) wide.
£1,800-1,900 *CSK*

CROSS REFERENCE
Smoking
Cigarette Boxes → p33

Instruments

A violin labelled François Nicholas, Paris, 1810, 14in (36.5cm) long, with a carrying case and a bow.
£800-825 *CSK*

A brass kettle drum, 25in (64cm) diam.
£125-150 *REL*

A Bébe Jumeau Lioret phonograph doll, with 'Le Merveilleaux' movement, 3 cylinders, a bisque head, composition arms and legs and original clothes, 24in (61cm) high.
£2,500-2,700 *CSK*

CROSS REFERENCE
Dolls ————→ p138

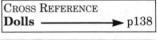

A silver model of the His Master's Voice trademark, with Jubilee hallmark for 1935, made by Mappin and Webb, on a wood plinth, 3½in (8.5cm) wide.
£750-775 *CSK*

A guitar, labelled M. G. Contreras, Madrid, with rosewood back and ribs, cedar front, c1970, length of back 19in (48cm), in a case.
£680-700 *CSK*

A German viola, labelled John Scheerer 1904, length of back 15½in (39cm).
£1,400-1,500 *CSK*

A German guitar, labelled Jul. Heinr. Zimmermann, London, in a case.
£225-250 *CSK*

A metal bodied Dobro guitar,1937, length of back 18¾in (47.3cm).
£900-950 *CSK*

| CROSS REFERENCE |
| **Rock & Pop** ⟶ p366 |

A boxwood and ivory single flageolet, branded Clementi & Compy, London, 13½in (34.5cm) long.
£150-170 *CSK*

A Spanish guitar, labelled Antonio Carlos Garcia, Madrid, length of back 16¾in (42cm), in a carrying case.
£425-450 *CSK*

A Boehm system rosewood flute, with silver plate keys, 23¾in (60cm) long, in a fitted case.
£200-220 *CSK*

A double-action pedal harp, by Sebastian Erard, with 7 pedals.
£1,500-1,700 *CSK*

A German mandolin, by Marcelli, c1890.
£120-130 *SAD*

A five-keyed boxwood and ivory flute, branded Astor, London No. 79, with silver keys and pewter plugs, 22in (56cm) long.
£185-210 *CSK*

A double-action pedal harp, by Sebastian Erard, with 43 strings and 8 pedals, 68in (172.5cm) high.
£3,250-3,500 *CSK*

A 28 button Anglo system concertina, labelled G.F. Payne, London, with bone buttons and fretted rosewood end plates, 6¼in (15.5cm) diam, in a hexagonal box,.
£225-250 *CSK*

Musical Boxes

A musical box, by Bremond, playing 12 airs, accompanied by drum, castanet and 6 bells with automaton mandarin strikers, in burr walnut case, 25½in (65cm) wide.
£3,500-3,750 *CSK*

An interchangeable 2 cylinder musical box, playing 6 airs each, 31in (79cm) wide.
£1,250-1,500 *CSK*

An interchangeable cylinder musical box, with three eight-air cylinders, tune indicator, zither attachment, 29in (73.5cm) wide.
£1,700-1,800 *CSK*

A key-wind musical box, playing 8 airs, 16in (40.5cm) wide.
£1,500-1,700 *CSK*

A twenty-four-air musical box, by P.V.F., 21in (53.5cm) wide.
£1,200-1,400 *CSK*

A Kallope disc music box, c1880, 11½in (29cm) wide.
£300-400 *TTM*

A six-air cylinder musical box, the lever wound movement, with 33cm cylinder, Swiss, late 19thC, 20½in (52cm) wide.
£500-550 *Bon*

CROSS REFERENCE
Gramophones ⟶ p246

A 'Flutina' orchestral musical box, c1862, 30½in (77.5cm) wide.
£4,800-5,200 *CSK*

ORIENTAL

A Chinese robe rack, mid-19thC, 63 by 49in (160 by 124.5cm).
£450-500 *ORI*

A Japanese white glazed pottery model of a seated cat, 9½in (24cm) high.
£525-550 *CSK*

A Chinese archaic-style bronze two-handled censer, 10½in (26.5cm) high.
£425-450 *CSK*

A Chinese dark green jade cong, 7in (17.5cm) wide.
£720-740 *CSK*

A Japanese hibachi, keyaki wood, used for tea ceremony, c1880, 14in (35.5cm) high.
£900-1,050 *ORI*

A Chinese rootwood carving of a standing figure of Guanyin, holding 2 lotus sprays, 60½in (153cm) high.
£3,500-3,750 *CSK*

A late Arita style model of a dog seated on its haunches, wearing a bell collar, 10in (25cm) high.
£240-260 *CSK*

A pair of Japanese cloisonné enamel panels.
£350-375 *P(S)*

A Ming blue and white globular jar, early 17thC, 7½in (18.5cm) high. **£330-360** *CSK*

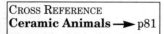

CROSS REFERENCE
Ceramic Animals ➔ p81

CROSS REFERENCE
Ceramics ➔ p117

A Japanese fruitwood carving of a standing caparisoned elephant, with ivory tusks, 4¼in (10.5cm) long.
£275-300 *CSK*

A funerary urn, Song Dynasty, 22in (56cm) high.
£200-250 *ORI*

Bowls

A Chinese red lacquer bowl, 10¼in (25.5cm) diam.
£575-600
CSK

A Chinese jade bowl, carved in the Mughal style, cover missing, 5¼in (13cm) diam.
£110-130 *CSK*

A Peking yellow glass bowl, 4¼in (10.5cm) diam.
£160-180
CSK

Baskets

A Chinese foot storage basket, 18in (46cm) high.
£30-50 *ORI*

A bamboo ikebana basket, 14½in (36.5cm) high. **£100-150** *ORI*

An ikebana bamboo basket, 26in (66cm) long.
£30-50 *ORI*

A ikebana bamboo basket, 15in (38cm) high.
£100-150 *ORI*

Boxes

A Chinese guri-lacquer box,
3in (7.5cm) diam.
£100-120 *CSK*

A chinese silver box, 2¾in (7cm)
diam. **£350-370** *CSK*

A kai-oke, in black lacquer box,
decorated with engraved copper
work, mid-19thC, 17in (43cm)
high. **£1,000-1,200** *ORI*

Inros

A gold lacquer four-case
inro, 3¼in (8cm) long,
with attached ivory
netsuke modeled as a
rat, 3in (7.5cm) long.
£230-260 *CSK*

A Japanese gold lacquer four-
case inro, decorated in iroe
hiramakie and takamakie with
a battle scene, with glass ojime,
2⅜in (6cm) high.
£380-400 *CSK*

Jade

A Chinese pale celadon
jade carving of a boy
holding a jar,
2¼in (5.5cm) high.
£220-240 *CSK*

A Chinese pale celadon jade
vase, with pierced handles and
a hardstone turquoise and coral
tree, 18thC, 6½in (16.5cm) high.
£425-450 *CSK*

Snuff Bottles

A flattened moss agate table
snuff bottle, with mask ring
handles and stopper, 4in (10cm)
high, and a lobed wood table
snuff bottle, 4in (10cm) high.
£200-250 *CSK*

Tsuba

An oval iron
tsuba, decorated
in gilt hirazogan
and takazogan,
3½in (9cm) high.
£260-280
CSK

A mokkogata iron
tsuba, decorated
in hirazogan and
takazogan, 3¼in
(8cm) high.
£200-225 *CSK*

A circular iron tsuba, gilt
to each side, 3¼in (8cm)
diam, and an iron
snowflake tsuba, 3in
(7.5cm) diam.
£280-300 *CSK*

OSBORNE PLAQUES

Osborne plaques were produced between 1899 and 1965 in Faversham, Kent by Arthur Osborne. The finish applied to these three-dimensional wax images was trade named Ivorex, and every piece was hand produced. By 1939 there were 440 different designs, usually buildings, historic events and personalities, and up to 45,000 items were produced annually.

Windsor Castle, c1934, 3 by 4in (7.5 by 10cm).
£18-25 *JMC*

The Tower of London, c1930, 4 by 3in (10 by 7.5cm).
£18-25 *JMC*

Charles Dickens in his study at Gadshill, c1914, 6 by 8in (15 by 20cm).
£40-50 *JMC*

St. Paul's Cathedral, c1916, 4 by 3in (10 by 7.5cm).
£18-25 *JMC*

An Irish spinning wheel, c1933, 5 by 4 in (12.5 by 10cm).
£20-25 *JMC*

Burn's Cottage, Alloway, Ayr, c1915, 3 by 4in (7.5 by 10cm).
£18-25 *JMC*

Prior's Gateway, Canterbury Cathedral, c1910, 7 by 6in (17.5 by 15cm).
£40-45 *JMC*

A Cornish fishwife, 8 by 6in (20 by 15cm).
£35-40 *JMC*

Llyn Llydaw and Snowdon, c1923, 4 by 6in (10 by 15cm).
£15-20 *JMC*

Wells Cathedral from Tor Hill,
c1924, 3 by 4in (7.5 by 12.5cm).
£18-25 *JMC*

St. Ives, Cornwall, c1951,
4 by 5in (10 by 12.5cm).
£18-25 *JMC*

Lincoln Cathedral, 6 by 8in
(15 by 20cm).
£20-25 *JMC*

The Houses of Parliament,
c1921, 3 by 4in (7.5 by 10cm).
£18-25 *JMC*

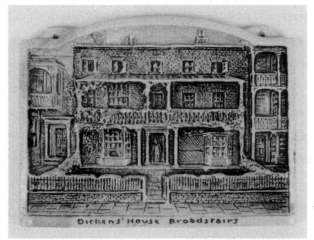

The Guildhall, Faversham,
7 by 9in (17.5 by 22.5cm).
£40-45 *JMC*

Charles Dickens' house,
Broadstairs, 3 by 4in
(7.5 by 10cm).
£20-25 *JMC*

PAPERWEIGHTS

A black slate inlaid micro-
mosaic paperweight, inlaid with
medallions depicting classical
architecture, 19thC.
£525-550 *BWe*

A pair of glass paperweights,
cased in blue, lined in silver,
c1850.
£350-395 *ARE*

MAKE THE MOST OF MILLERS

Price ranges in this book reflect what you should
expect to *pay* for a similar example. When selling,
however, you would expect to receive a lower figure.
This will fluctuate according to a dealer's stock and
saleability at a particular time, etc. It is always
advisable, when selling a collectable, to approach a
reputable dealer or an auction house which has
specialist sales.

PAPER MONEY

Paper bank notes are increasing in popularity as collectors items. In particular 'error' bank notes, which have been included at the end of this section, are realising very high prices. 'Error' notes are interesting in that they are often discovered quite by accident by observant bank clerks and shop keepers.

Adding to the excitement of note collecting this year is the special issue of £50 notes to commemorate the 300th anniversary of the Bank of England. The notes display a portrait of Sir John Houblon, first Governor of the Bank. The Bank of Scotland celebrates its 300th anniversary in 1995.

An emergency WWII issue ten shilling note.
£18-20 *BAN*

The emergency WWII issue saw the introduction of the silver security thread for the first time, and resulted in a change of colour from brown to purple between 1940-48 before reverting to its pre-war colour. The design itself was introduced in 1928.

English Bank Notes

Ten Shillings Notes

A Bank of England ten shilling note, 1960-1970.
£8-10 *BAN*

A third design type issued and signed by Bradbury in a short period, 1914-19.
£130-140 *BAN*

One Pound Notes

A Bank of England one pound note, introduced 1960.
£12-15 *BAN*

Introduced in 1960 and known as the 'Queen's Portrait' design type. The example illustrated bears a serial letter M which signifies that it is a replacement note used to replace rejected misprinted notes of the same denomination.

One of the famous 'Bradbury' issues which took their name from the Secretary to the Treasury who signed them. The first design type of the one pound and ten shilling notes were actually printed on ungummed paper earmarked for postage stamps.

A one pound note, brown and white, serial no. 6877, Southampton Bank, 1 January 1821.
£260-280 *SPI*

An emergency WWII issue one pound note.
£5-6 *BAN*

The last one pound note issued by the British Linen Bank in July 1970.
£10-12 *BAN*

A one pound note, serial No. 2, black and white, hand numbered, hand dated 2nd March 1797 and the name of Abraham Newland entered in ink at centre, signed by Thomas Triquet.
£55,000-58,000 *SPI*

Sold with a letter from Horace Bowen, Chief Cashier of the Bank of England (1893-1902), dated 27 Jan 1894, "Note No. 2 is undoubtedly genuine and is undoubtedly the second one pound note issued". Thomas Triquet, a clearer at the Bank, was authorised to sign notes up to £5.

Five Pounds Notes

A Bank of England trial black and white five pound note, London, 23 June 1842.
£400-500 *SPI*

A Bank of England five pound note, signed by B. G. Catterns (1929-1934), 21 February 1934, Leeds.
£260-280 *SPI*

A Bank of England black and white 'Fiver', 20th July 1939.
£42-45 *BAN*

The classical item in the Bank of England series, the world famous black and white 'fiver'. Simplicity itself reflecting the Bank of England's view of technical excellence over artistic elaboration as the most effective way of beating the forger. This principal reached as far as the type and character of the paper and its watermark.

A Bank of England five pound note, featuring the 'helmeted head' of Britannia design type, which succeeded the black and white 'fiver'.
£15-18 *BAN*

A Bank of England five pound note, signed by B. G. Catterns (1929-1934), 1st July 1932, London.
£70-80 *SPI*

A Bank of England five pound note, which succeeded the 'helmeted head' of Britannia, and printed in blue.
£10-12 *BAN*

A Bank of England Wellington five pound note.
£8-10 *BAN*

Known as the 'Wellington fiver', the portrait of the first Duke of Wellington on the reverse together with a vignette of a 19th century engraving of the Battle of Fuentes de Onoro in 1811.

A British Linen Bank five pound note, 3 February 1961.
£40-42 *BAN*

One of the most elusive modern Scottish notes for the collector to obtain. An interim issue by Thomas de la Rue following the purchase of the banknote and stamp printing business of Waterlow & Sons Limited in 1961. Only 4 dates of issue, all in the same year, with a total print figure of 1 million notes. The survival rate for collectors is of course only a fraction of this very small amount.

A Bank of England five pound note, signed by C. P. Mahon (1925-1929), 5 October 1926.
£220-240 *SPI*

A British Linen Bank five pound note, March 1968. **£12-14** *BAN*

Scottish Bank Notes

Scottish bank notes were the most colourful and varied bank notes of all the United Kingdom notes issued during the post-WWII period. In 1950, when the first of the modern amalgamations took place there were eight Scottish banks in existence. The last amalgamation took place in 1970 when the British Linen Bank was absorbed by the Bank of Scotland. With each amalgamation the bank issued a new note.

A Clydesdale and North of Scotland Bank twenty pound note, May 1951. **£60-65** *BAN*

The first design type issued by the first of the modern Scottish amalgamations in 1950 between The Clydesdale Bank Ltd and the North of Scotland Bank Ltd.

A Bank of Scotland one pound note, August 1988. **£5-8** *BAN*

The very last note issued in this denomination by this Bank in August 1988. The design type commenced in August 1970 following merger with The British Linen Bank.

A North of Scotland Bank Limited one pound note, March 1928. **£30-35** *BAN*

The National Bank of Scotland five pound note, July 1955. **£40-45** *BAN*

The Clydesdale Bank Limited one pound note, April 1935, **£18-20** *BAN*

The only Glasgow based note issuer remaining today. The other present day note issuers are both Edinburgh based banks and historically much older. The Clydesdale Banking Company were founded in 1838, the Royal Bank of Scotland in 1727 and the Bank of Scotland in 1695.

The Clydesdale Bank Limited five pound note, March 1948. **£220-240** *BAN*

One of the rarest of all the Scottish post-WWII issues.

A Bank of Scotland five pound note used since 1931. **£50-52** *BAN*

The high denomination issues of the Bank of Scotland and the Royal Bank of Scotland were the largest issues produced in the United Kingdom including 'black and white' issues of the Bank of England. They survived in this size until 1969 in the case of the £20 note and are known with great affection as 'horse blankets' in collecting circles.

A Clydesdale Bank PLC one pound note, November 1988.
£6-8 *BAN*

This was the very last one pound note issued by the Clydesdale Bank in this denomination in November 1988.

The Union Bank of Scotland Ltd one pound note, October 1927.
£30-35 *BAN*

First introduced by the Union Bank of Scotland Ltd in 1924. The first bank to abandon the much larger square notes of the Scottish issuers.

The National Bank of Scotland one pound note, 1915.
£120-125 *BAN*

The most spectacular of all the famous Scottish 'squares' as they are known, because of their shape and size which was standard with all Scottish note issuers until 1928 when the Bank of Scotland reduced their one pound note. The first reduction took place in 1924. In the day of the 'squares' one pound was a lot of money which would go a long way and the one pound note looked like real money of significant stature, with colour printing. Introduced in 1893.

The Union Bank of Scotland Limited five pound note, May 1949.
£40-45 *BAN*

The Royal Bank of Scotland one pound note, March 1943.
£12-15 *BAN*

A design type which existed from 1927 until 1967. It finally achieved fame in 1989 when an engravers apprentice walked into the Head Office of The Royal Bank of Scotland in Edinburgh and 'confessed' to a youthful indiscretion in 1956. He had engraved his signature on the plate. It remained undiscovered for 33 years until his confession in 1989. His signature will be found on the reverse side of the note.

The National Bank of Scotland one pound note, November 1927.
£28-30 *BAN*

The first note for this bank when it reduced the size of the one pound note in 1927 along with other Scottish note issuers in the 1920s.

A Royal Bank of Scotland one pound note, March 1987.
£2-3 *BAN*

The present day surviver of the Scottish one pound note. Introduced in October 1987.

The North of Scotland Bank Limited twenty pound note, March 1930.
£55-60 *BAN*

Irish Bank Notes

The Bank of Ireland one pound note, May 1936.
£15-18 *BAN*

The Central Bank of Ireland ten pound note, with a portrait of Lady Hazel Lavery, resting on a traditional Irish harp, December 1976.
£22-25 *BAN*

A Provincial Bank of Ireland Limited five pound note, January 1972.   **£18-20** *BAN*

A Northern Bank Limited one pound note, January 1940.   **£12-15** *BAN*

Isle of Man Bank Notes

An Isle of Man ten shilling note.   **£8-10** *BAN*

An Isle of Man Bank Limited one pound note January 1956.
£28-30 *BAN*

Error Notes

Error notes are an extremely popular collecting field commanding high prices for printing errors which should not have escaped the many inspection processes. Broadly speaking, the bigger the mistake, the higher the price they will command, particularly if the error note is still in good condition.

The type of mistake is also very broad, including missing serial numbers, serial numbers which vary on the same note, missing design elements and missing colours.

A Bank of England one pound note, J. S. Fforde (1966-1970), 1967 green and white, no serial numbers printed although N47J8 is visible printed on reverse.   **£150-180** *SPI*

A Bank of England twenty
pound note.
£48-50 *BAN*

*The Queen's portrait is
obviously missing with some of
the wording on the note,
including, on this item 'I
Promise to Pay the Bearer on
Demand' and others.*

*Extra paper, which
on rarer occasions
can include a
substantial part of
the next note on
the sheet, as much
as 30 to 40% more
in the case of very
recent new issues.*

A Bank of England ten
pound note.
£90-95 *BAN*

A Bank of England ten pound
note.   **£78-80** *BAN*

PHOTOGRAPH
FRAMES

*Extra paper but a different
shape. 'Shark's fin', 'rudder',
'slip'n stick' are all part of the
error note collectors vocabularly.*

A silver frame, 1922, 10 by 7in
(25 by 17.5cm).
£140-160 *DEL*

A silver frame, Birmingham
1912, 7 by 5in (17.5 by 12.5cm).
£120-130 *DEL*

A silver frame, Chester 1911,
4 by 3in (10 by 7.5cm).
£60-70 *DEL*

A silver frame, London 1902,
8½ by 6in (21 by 15cm).
£180-200 *DEL*

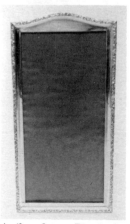

A silver frame, Birmingham
1910, 9 by 5in (22.5 by 12.5cm).
£135-150 *DEL*

A silver photograph frame,
Birmingham 1914, 4in
(10cm) diam.
£75-85 *DEL*

CROSS REFERENCE
Metalware
Silver ———→ p117

A Victorian copper frame, 2 by 1¾in (5 by 4.5cm). **£18-25** *NM*

A silver frame, Birmingham 1912, 7 by 5in (17.5 by 12.5cm). **£120-140** *DEL*

Three micro-mosaic frames, mid-19thC. **£170-190** *WIL*

PINCUSHION DOLLS

A French pincushion doll, c1920, 4in (10cm) high. **£40-60** *BAT*

A pinhead swansdown powder puff doll, c1920, 5in (12.5cm) diam. **£40-60** *BAT*

CROSS REFERENCE
Dolls ⟶ p138

A silver frame, Chester 1918, 6½ by 5in (16 by 12.5cm). **£110-125** *DEL*

PLAYING CARDS

A silver frame, Birmingham 1920, 9 by 6¼in (22.5 by 15.5cm). **£120-135** *DEL*

A transformation deck of 52 engraved cards, printed by E. Olivatte, 6 Leigh St., Burton Creeson, January 1st 1828, entitled 'Kaloprosopion', in original box. **£220-240** *CSK*

Two decks of 52 engraved Swiss cantons cards, the reverse printed in dots forming hexagonal shapes, c1870. **£460-480** *CSK*

POLICE

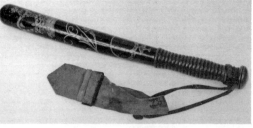

A Westminster truncheon, with armband, 16⅓in (42cm) long.
£150-200 *RdeR*

A William IV Special Constable's truncheon, 20in (50.5cm) long.
£150-200 *RdeR*

A police rattle, c1847, 10in (25cm) long.
£50-55 *SAD*

A pressed cardboard policeman sweet container, 1950s, 13in (33cm).
£10-20 *BAT*

PORTRAIT MINIATURES

A 15ct yellow gold locket, with portrait painted on ivory, set with seed pearls, 1½in (3.5cm) high, with fitted case.
£200-250 *BWA*

A watercolour on paper, by Herve, Strand, London, 2¾in (7cm) high.
£85-110 *PSC*

A watercolour on ivory, c1860, 1¾in (5cm) high.
£70-80 *PSC*

A watercolour on ivory, 4in (10cm) high.
£200-285 *PSC*

A watercolour on ivory of an English officer, 4¾in (12cm) high.
£250-275 *PSC*

A watercolour on ivory, 4in (10cm) high. **£125-150** *PSC*

A watercolour on ivory of
Captain George Davison, 5½in
(14cm) high.
£370-390 *PSC*

A watercolour on ivory portrait
of Mr. Lucas, 5in (12.5cm) high.
£140-165 *PSC*

CROSS REFERENCE
Silhouettes ——————→ p391

A watercolour on ivory, the
reverse containing a lock of
hair, 2½in (6 5cm) high.
£290-320 *PSC*

A young nobleman, in double
collared brown tunic with
yellow sleeves, by Horace Hone,
enamel signed and dated
London 1806, 4½in (11cm) high.
£640-680 *CSK*

A watercolour on paper portrait
of a girl, 6¼in (16cm) high.
£125-140 *PSC*

A watercolour on ivory, 18thC,
5in (12.5cm) high.
£295-325 *PSC*

A watercolour gouache on ivory,
of Doctor Wharton, by Feular,
1829, 3in (7.5cm) high.
£250-275 *PSC*

A watercolour on ivory
portrait of a vicar, 18thC,
2¾in (7cm) high.
£200-225 *PSC*

A blue crystal glass cigar
holder, c1920, 4in (10cm) long.
£40-50 *DP*

A pipe-shaped cigarette holder, c1920,
4½in (11cm) long. **£30-40** *DP*

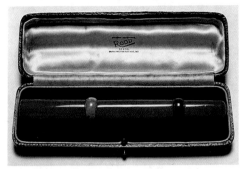

An amber and gold cigar holder, in a silver
case, c1906, 3in (7.5cm) long. **£60-70** *DP*

An amber, blue and green cigarette
holder, 6¼in (15.5cm) long.
£140-150 *DP*

A glass cigar holder, named and dated
'J. Greenfield 1895', 4in (10cm) long.
£130-150 *DP*

A Dunhill silver cigarette holder, with
interchangeable coloured mouthpieces,
c1952, 5in (12.5cm) long. **£150-160** *DP*

A twisted Meerschaum and amber cigar
holder, c1910, 5in (12.5cm) long. **£40-50** *DP*

A yellow glass cigarette holder,
c1900, 3½in (8.5cm) long.
£15-20 *DP*

A Meerschaum cigar holder, the amber
end carved with a coat-of-arms, c1880.
£100-120 *DP*

A plastic cigarette holder, c1920, 3in (7.5cm) long.
£10-15 *DP*

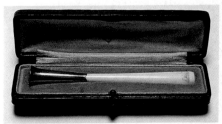

A gold and ivory cigarette holder, c1915.
£50-60 *DP*

Mickey Mantle's last All-Star bat, game used, 1967, with letter of authenticity.
£10,000-11,000 *S(NY)*

A Quaker Oats Babe Ruth cardboard advertising sign, 1930s, 16 by 20in (41 by 51cm).
£6,500-7,000 *S(NY)*

A set of 48 Goudey Sport Kings Gum cards, all in excellent condition, 1933.
£11,000-12,000 *S(NY)*

A set of 24 Delong Gum cards, including Lou Gehrig, very good condition, 1933.
£9,000-10,000 *S(NY)*

A set of 96 Goudey Gum baseball cards, including 19 Hall of Famers, 1934.
£15,000-16,000 *S(NY)*

A T213 Type 2 Coupon Cigarettes card of Ty Cobb, in very good condition, 1914.
£2,000-2,500 *S(NY)*

A 1888 Goodwin Champions baseball 10 page album, with front and back covers.
£4,000-5,000 *S(NY)*

A Goudey Gum card of Babe Ruth, No. 181, very good condition, 1933.
£4,000-5,000 *S(NY)*

l. Ninety-three World Series baseball programmes, from 1936 to 1992.
£7,000-8,000 *S(NY)*

Mickey Mantle's Yankee jacket, by McGregor, size 46, together with 2 letters of authenticity, 1960s.
£8,000-9,000 *S(NY)*

r. A T3 Turkey Red Cigarettes card of Ty Cobb, in good condition, 1911, 8 by 5¾in (20 by 15cm).
£4,000-4,500 *S(NY)*

Then and Now, 600 Golf Courses on the LNER, including St. Andrews, by A. R. Thompson, chromolithographic poster, framed, 40 by 25½in (102 by 65cm). **£1,600-1,700** *S*

l. A long nosed putter, by Hugh Philp, St. Andrews, with thorn head, replacement hickory shaft, c1855. **£1,250-1,500** *S*

An L. Johnson patent conical wooden headed putter, with stamping to head and hickory shaft, c1890. **£3,250-3,750** *S*

A long nosed driver, by Tom Morris, St. Andrews, with beech head and greenheart shaft, c1870, 46⅛in (117cm) long. **£10,000-11,000** *S*

A Simplex type patent No. 5 iron, with aluminium head, stamped A. W. Powell, shaft shortened, c1905. **£1,600-1,800** *S*

A Brown's patent perforated niblick, by Winton & Co., Montrose, c1906. **£2,500-2,750** *S*

A long nosed grassed driver, by Hugh Philp, St. Andrews, c1830, 42in (107cm) long. **£6,750-7,250** *S*

A long nosed long spoon, by Hugh Philp, St. Andrews, c1850. **£6,000-6,500** *S*

A Lennox mug, sold by Tiffany's of New York, c1900, 5½in (14cm) high. **£1,000-1,100** *S*

A Doulton Series Ware jug, 6in (15cm) high. **£350-450** *S*

A small headed rut iron, with 5in hosel and lancewood shaft, c1850. **£5,250-5,750** *S*

Crans sur Sierre, after Peikert, lithographic golf poster, 39½ by 24⅛in (100 by 62cm), framed and glazed. **£1,250-1,500** *S*

A Victorian Stanhope, in the form of a gentleman's tie pin, with risqué picture, 3¼in (8cm) long, in original case.
£60-70 *PC*

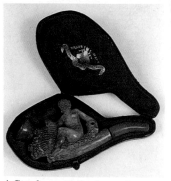

A Stanhope telescope, with views of Forth Bridge, 2½in (6cm) high.
£40-50 *PC*

A Stanhope, in the form of a Cornish shoe, c1930, 4in (10cm) long.
£5-10 *PC*

A Stanhope scent bottle, with 6 views, 2½in (6cm) long.
£45-55 *PC*

A Stanhope, in the form of a Meerschaum pipe, with a military commemorative picture, 4½in (11cm) long, with case.
£55-75 *PC*

An Alpine house kaleidescope, press chimney to see pictures, c1970, 3in (8cm) wide.
£5-6 *PC*

A Stanhope Cutie Doll, with pictures of Penmaenmawk and Llanfairfeichan, 1in (2.5cm) high.
£20-30 *PC*

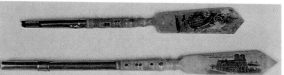

Two Stanhopes in the form of ivory paper knives/pen holders.
£15-20 each *PC*

A Stanhope magnifying glass, with ivory handle, with views of Nailsworth.
£40-50 *PC*

A Stanhope propelling pencil, commemorating the 1937 Coronation of H M George VI and Queen Elizabeth, 4¼in (11cm) long.
£30-40 *PC*

r. A Stanhope pin, made for Grand Flying Exhibition 1912, 2¼in (5cm).
£65-75 *PC*

l. Three Stanhope tape measures: *l.* and *c* bone, *r.* wood, with views of Wimereaux.
£30-40 *PC*

A Stanhope perfume bottle, with views of Crystal Palace, 2in (5cm) high.
£50-60 *PC*

A beadwork purse.
£30-60 *LB*

A Victorian
beadwork purse.
£30-50 *LB*

A Victorian beadwork
purse.
£30-60 *LB*

A beaded bag, on silk velvet
with silk interior, hallmarked
silver clasp, 11½in (29cm) long.
£250-285 *KOH*

A beadwork purse,
4in (10cm) high.
£65-85 *LB*

A metal and beadwork bag.
£40-60 *LB*

An American
beadwork purse.
£20-60 *PC*

A Victorian beadwork
bag.
£40-60 *LB*

A Victorian beadwork
purse.
£30-40 *LB*

A Victorian beadwork
lampshade.
£70-100 *LB*

A tapestry and beadwork
handbag, with silver top,
18thC. **£100-200** *LB*

A Victorian beadwork
bag.
£40-60 *LB*

A Victorian gentleman's waistcoat.
£100-150 *LB*

A gentleman's waistcoat, 18thC.
£300-400 *LB*

A child's silk dress, 1930.
£15-25 *LB*

A floral print lined jersey dress, stole gloves and belt.
£100-150 *CNY*

A Frank Usher ivory duchesse satin evening gown, c1960.
£50-55 *S(S)*

A Gina Fratini blue silk organza evening dress, printed with geometric designs, c1970.
£30-40 *S(S)*

A set of 4 marabou feather boas, black, white, pink with gold and cream, and black and white.
£500-550 *CNY*

A Bill Gibb silk chiffon dress, decorated with glass bugle beads, c1970.
£125-150 *S(S)*

A Bill Gibb cream crêpe dress, with feather and leather thonged waistcoat, c1970.
£250-275 *S(S)*

An Emilio Puci silk jersey cocktail dress, c1965.
£20-30 *S(S)*

An Edwardian velvet, silk and satin gown.
£160-180 *LB*

GRAYS
ANTIQVE MARKETS

A reversible basket quilt, by
Elizabeth Sanderson, 1870.
£600-800 *PC*

A pieced, appliqué and
reverse appliqué cotton
quilt, probably
Baltimore, mid-19thC.
£3,000-4,000 *S(NY)*

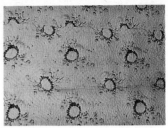

A Durham quilt, c1920, 68 by 75in
(172.5 by 190.5cm).
£120-180 *LB*

A sailor's woolwork picture of a man o'
war, 19thC, 9½ by 12⅛in (24 by 32cm).
£340-380 *CAG*

A needlework, Berlin work
and beadwork picture, mid-
19thC, 22 by 20in (56 by
51cm).- **£450-650** *DMT*

A Victorian silk patchwork quilt,
90 by 86in (228.5 by 218.5cm).
£200-300 *LB*

A needlework sampler,
by Mary Clothilda Dare,
1837, in original frame.
£15,000-16,000 *S(NY)*

A pair of stitched felt pictures, in
moulded frames, c1790, each 15½ by
17⅛in (39 by 44cm).
£3,750-4,000 *C*

An Amish pieced cotton
quilt, probably Lancaster
County, Pennsylvania,
c1930, 80 by 82in (203 by
208cm), in a Plexiglass box.
£5,000-6,000 *S(NY)*

A Durham rose quilt,
1890, 96 by 82in (243.5
by 208cm).
£200-250 *LB*

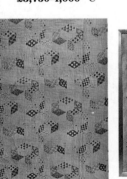

A machine made quilt,
1920, 56 by 68in (142 by
172.5cm).
£80-100 *LB*

A Berlin work picture
of a parrot in garden,
c1850.
£300-400 *DMT*

A silk embroidered
needlework panel, early
19thC.
£100-120 *LB*

POSTERS

These Men Use Shell - Guardsmen, colour lithograph by Ben Nicholson, printed by Waterlow and Sons, 1938, 30 by 45in (76 by 114cm).
£640-660 *P*

For High Performance, Vickers Wellesleys, colour lithograph by James Gardner, printed by Waterlow and Sons, 1939, 30 by 45½in (76 by 115cm).
£720-740 *P*

Smokers Prefer Shell, colour lithograph, printed by Baynard Press, 1936, 30 by 45in (76 by 114.5cm).
£1,400-1,500 *P*

The Quick Starting Pair, colour lithograph by Septimus Edwin Scott, printed by Waterlow & Sons, 1926, 30 by 45in (76 by 114cm). **£200-225** *P*

Grand Prix de France, Saint Gaudens 1952, by J. des F.?, lithograph in colour, printed by Schuser, Paris, 24 by 15in (61 by 38cm).
£260-280 *CSK*

All the Honours in 1929, colour lithograph, with an extensive tear and one area missing, 1929, 30 by 48in (76 by 112cm).
£160-180 *P*

The North Wales Coast from the Great Orme, lithograph in colours by Norman Wilkinson, c1930, printed by S. C. Allen & Company, 40 by 50in (101 by 127cm).
£300-325 *CSK*

Wales, GWR, LMS, a lithograph in colours by Leonard Richmond, c1940, 38½in by 50in (98 by 127cm).
£190-200 *CSK*

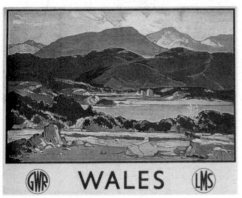

Eté, a lithograph in colour by Alphonse Mucha, printed by F. Champenois, 1896, diagonal tear, otherwise good condition, 41 by 22in (104 by 56cm).
£2,400-2,600 *CSK*

Fraserburgh Glorious Sands, Bathing, Golf, Tennis, by H. G. Gawthorn.
£460-480 *ONS*

A 1940s war poster, reproduced from the original 1920s poster, 517 Corps Field Survey Squadron, Royal Engineers, 12½ by 9in (31.5 by 22.5cm).
£3-4 *COL*

A South Bank Exhibition, Festival of Britain, poster, 1951.
£4-5 *COL*

Montreux-Oberland-Bernois, Chemin de Fer Suisse, lithograph in colours by Eric Hermes, printed by Sauberlin & Pfeiffer S. A. Vevey, 1929, 40 by 25in (102 by 63cm).
£525-550 *CSK*

Knockholt Beeches, London General Transport, lithograph in colours by Harold Sandys Williamson, printed by The Dangerfield Printing Co Ltd, London, 1929, 40 by 25in (101 by 63cm), and 6 other posters.
£420-440 *CSK*

Blood Donors, lithograph in colours by Abram Games, printed by Field Sons & Co Ltd, 1943, 14½ by 9½in (37 by 24cm).
£285-310 *CSK*

Chamonix, SNCF, lithograph in colours by J. Fillacier, printed by Gaston Gorde, Paris, c1940, 38 by 23in (97 by 58cm).
£400-420 *CSK*

Royal London, Buckingham Palace, London Underground, lithograph in colours by John Bainbridge, printed by The Baynard Press, 1953, 39½ by 24⅛in (100 by 62cm).
£225-250 *CSK*

The Poster, lithograph in colour by Sidney Ransom, printed by David Allen & Sons, 1898, 30 by 19½in (76 by 50cm).
£240-260 *CSK*

FURTHER READING
Historic Televisions and Video Recorders, by Michael Bennett-Levy, published by MBL Publications.

RADIOS & TELEVISIONS

Radios

The earliest primitive radio equipment was usually homemade and is not really desired by collectors. The 'classic' radios were made from about 1922-1928 and were often battery powered. In modern times these batteries proved difficult to find, so to overcome this dilemma many of the radios were converted to work on mains electricity. The conversion itself however proved to be very expensive.

The most popular area for collectors at present are 'mass market' models produced between about 1926 - 1946. These are often collected for their cabinets as well as for their works.

The post-war produced radios are now becoming collectable and this is the area where bargains can still be found. The early sixties solid state sets are also being collected but largely by specialists to date. This is certainly an area to watch for the future.

A St. Dunstan's one valve 'radio for the blind', in mahogany case, with battery/accumulator operated headphone listening, 1930s, 7¼ by 13½in (18 by 34cm). **£30-60** *RMV*

A Delores De-Luxe 6-valve receiver, in plate glass case, with visible valves and 3 condensers and coils, on Bakelite base, by Fred W. Geordes Co., Newark, N. J., 29½in (75cm) high. **£575-600** *CSK*

A GECoPhone 2-valve receiver, type BC 2001, in a mahogany 'smoker's cabinet' case, with instruction card in doors and BBC transfer, c1923, 16½in (41.5cm) high. **£850-875** *CSK*

A boxed set of electric cable samples, early 20thC, 19¾in (50cm) wide. **£15-25** *WAB*

A Telsen MacNamara Golden Voice radio, c1932, 19½in (49cm) high. **£50-60** *HEG*

A Marconi radio, model No. 238, c1937, 17½in (44cm) wide. **£80-100** *HEG*

A Ferranti 145E radio, with Bakelite case, c1945, 18in (46cm) high. **£120-140** *HEG*

An Ekco AC85 radio, with Bakelite case, c1934, 21in (53cm) wide. **£200-220** *HEG*

A Bush DAC 90 radio, late 1940s. **£30-40** *TTM*

An Ekco SH25 radio,with Bakelite case, c1931, 18in (45.5cm) high. **£350-400** *HEG*

An Ekco AC86 radio, Bakelite case, c1935, 21½in (54.5cm) wide. **£200-250** *HEG*

A Vinco crystal set, c1920, 5⅓in (13.5cm) high. **£50-95** Headphones in working order. **£15-20** *RMV*

A Pilot 'Little Maestro' AC/DC radio, with veneered wood case, c1939, 8 by 12in (20 by 30.5cm). **£20-55** *RMV*

A Murphy SAD 94L electric radio, with Bakelite case, c1945, 13⅓in (34cm) high. **£180-200** *HEG*

A Peter Pan AC mains valve radio, with Bakelite case, made in Royal Leamington Spa, late 1940s, 12in (30.5cm) wide. **£25-50** *RMV*

An Emerson battery portable radio, American, c1948, 9in (22.5cm) wide. **£30-40** *HEG*

A Decca Prestomatic electric radio, c1936, 20in (51cm) high. **£150-175** *HEG*

A Philco radio, 'The People's Set', model No. 333, c1930, 16in (40.5cm) high. **£150-350** *RMV*

A Pilot B2 radio, with Bakelite case, American, made for the South African market, c1942-45, 15in (38in) wide. **£80-100** *HEG*

CROSS REFERENCE
Colour Section ➔ p426

A Marconi TI5DA radio, c1948, 9in (22.5cm) wide.
£50-60 *HEG*

A Ferguson 203 electric radio, c1949, 11in (28cm) wide.
£80-100 *HEG*

A Marconi portable battery valve P17B radio, with chrome faced plastic case, c1948-49, 9½in (24cm) wide.
£20-40 *RMV*

A Bush DAC 10 radio, with Bakelite case, c1950, 12½in (31.5cm) wide.
£50-60 *HEG*

A GEC BC 4940 radio, with Bakelite case, c1950, 16in (41cm) wide.
£60-80 *HEG*

A crystal set radio, with white Bakelite case, 1950s, 4½in (11cm) wide.   **£15-25** *RMV*

EARLY WIRELESS & TELEVISION SETS WANTED
SOME EXAMPLES OF TYPES AND PRICES PAID

MARCONI MULTIPLE TUNER
£2,000

W.W.I. TRENCH RECEIVER
£700

GEC° PHONE 2 VALVE

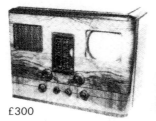

£400

HMV MARCONI TELEVISION

BAIRD TELEVISOR
£1,500

ERICSSON 4 VALVE
£800

£300

ALL OTHER EARLY WIRELESS/TELEVISION SETS WANTED.
ALSO HORN GRAMOPHONES, PHONOGRAPHS, TELEPHONES ETC.
MR. YATES, THE HEWARTHS, SANDIACRE, NOTTM. NG10 5NQ 0602 393139

A Portadyne Princess portable radio, with blue painted Bakelite case, c1948, 11in (28cm) wide. **£50-60** *HEG*

A Champion AC/DC mains valve radio, wood case, MW/LW bands, late 1950s, 12½in (31.5cm) wide. **£15-25** *RMV*

A Ferguson portable radio, c1954, 11½in (28.5cm) wide. **£25-30** *HEG*

A G. Marconi T37DA AC/DC valve radio, with Bakelite case, c1950, 13in (33cm) wide. **£20-30** *RMV*

A Roberts RT7 push button transistor radio, with wooden case and turntable base, 1962, 13in (33cm) wide. **£25-35** *RMV*

A Pye P29 UBQ mains/battery radio, with black Bakelite case and chrome fittings, c1952, 13½in (34cm) wide. **£60-80** *HEG*

A Marconi P20B battery/valve portable radio, with Rexine covered metal case and plastic lid, with aerial inside, c1949, 7¼in (18cm) wide. **£30-50** *RMV*

A Champion mains operated valve radio, AM/FM bands, with wooden case, 1960s, 14in (36cm) wide. **£15-30** *RMV*

An HMV 1356 AC/DC mains valve radio, the polished wood case with Bakelite front, c1949, 14⅛in (36.5cm) wide. **£35-55** *RMV*

A Murphy U198H AC/DC valve radio, with Bakelite case, c1953, 10½in (26cm) wide. **£25-45** *RMV*

A Bestone radio, plastic cased, AC only with LW/MW, imported, mid-1950s, 10in (25cm) wide. **£20-30** *RMV*

An EMI Aerialite band BIII converter, in a metal case, channel 6-13 tuning, for 'BBC only' black and white televisions to enable ITV reception, 1955-1960s, 10in (25cm) wide. **£10-12** *RMV*

A wrist radio, 1970s.
£10-15 *COB*

An Isis (Hong Kong) transistor radio, MW only, with plastic and metal case, 1960, 10in (25cm) wide. **£10-35** *RMV*

Two Baird transistor portable radios, in wood and hardboard Rexine covered cases, 1960s, 11in (28cm) wide. **£5-15 each** *RMV*

An Ultra transistor radio, c1956, 12½in (31.5cm) wide. **£50-60** *HEG*

Televisions

A Decca 1000 television receiver and optical unit, housed in a bureau-type cabinet, c1952, 25in (64cm) wide.
£100-150 *RMV*

A Murphy U310 black and white television, the plywood case with Bakelite surround, c1959, 17in (43cm) screen, 19in (48cm) wide.
£45-75 *RMV*

A Ferguson Model 941T black and white television, BBC only, 405 line, 9in (22.5cm) screen, plywood case, 1949.
£50-75 *RMV*

A McMichael television table/trolley, with built-in radio, early 1950s, 21in (53cm) wide.
£15-30 *RMV*

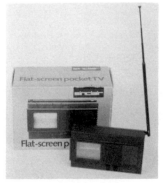

A Clive Sinclair portable television, late 1970s.
£20-45 *RMV*

A GEC Model BT 2147 black and white television, BBC only, 405 line, with Bakelite case, c1950, 9in (22.5cm) screen, 13½in (34cm) wide.
£100-150 *RMV*

RAILWAYS

Railway collectables fall within three categories:

1. **Pre-1921**: The period in which over one hundred railway companies operated within the U.K.

2. **1921-1947**: During this period these companies amalgamated into four regional groupings, London North Eastern Railways (LNER), London Midland Scottish Railways (LMS), Great Western Railways (GWE) and Southern Railways (SR).

3. **1957**: The year in which the four Railway companies were nationalised to form British Railways.

Railway collectables from the first period are keenly sought by collectors, especially timetables and route maps of disused railways. Collectables from the second period are more readily available, with GWR items being the most sought after. Locomotive nameplates are generally regarded as the ultimate prize by enthusiasts and, therefore, attain very high prices whenever they appear on the market. British Railways' memorabilia is more desirable if it relates to any preserved railway.

A brass locomotive steam whistle, mounted on wooden base, 10in (25cm) high.
£75-100 *COB*

A Pullman car brass lamp, c1930, 14in (36cm) high.
£200-250 *SRA*

A GNR dining car cream jug, c1920.
£15-20 *COB*

A GNSR engraved window glass, 49¼in by 30½in (126 by 77cm).
£1,450-1,650 *CSK*

A London, Midland & Scottish Railway post grouping lamp, 9in (22.5cm) high.
£55-60 *SAD*

A Port of London Victoria Docks copper and brass railway oil can. **£50-58** *SAD*

A Pullman silver plated jug, 6in (15cm) high.
£30-40 *COB*

A Hull & Barnsley Railway Company enamel sign.
£200-300 *SRA*

A Victorian hand warmer, 9in (22.5cm) high.
£30-35 *SAD*

A Great Central Railway teapot. **£80-100** *SRA*

A selection of 1930s railway passes.
£2-3 each *COB*

A Scottish Region totem sign, 1950s, 36 by 10in (92 by 25cm).
£100-150 *SRA*

Locomotive Builders' Plates

An LNER locomotive maker's plate, 1945.
£200-250 *SRA*

A Great Central Railway builder's plate, 1911, 9 by 6in (22.5 by 15cm).
£300-400 *SRA*

A locomotive maker's plate, 1895, 32 by 8in (81 by 20cm).
£800-1,000 *SRA*

A Victorian cast iron railway carriage plate, 1899.
£40-50 *COB*

A British Railways works plate, from an experimental diesel locomotive, 1950.
£400-500 *SRA*

A Chapman & Furneaux private builder's plate, 1898.
£1,000-1,500 *SRA*

A cast iron railway carriage plaque, pre-1922, 12in (22.5cm) wide. **£100-120** *COB*

MAKE THE MOST OF MILLERS

Condition is absolutely vital when assessing the value of any item. Damaged pieces appreciate much less than perfect examples. However, a rare, desirable piece may command a high price even when damaged.

A workplate, dated 1875, 12⁵ (30.5cm) wide.
£400-500 *SRA*

Locomotive Headboards

A cast aluminium locomotive headboard, 48in (122cm) wide.
£800-1,000 *SRA*

A headboard, carved in Coronation year.
£300-400 *SRA*

An LNER B17 class nameplate, 48in (122cm).
£2,800-3,200 *SRA*

An LMS locomotive nameplate and badge.
£12,000-14,000 *SRA*

An LMS Royal Scot Class nameplate.
£6,000-6,500 *SRA*

An LMS Jubilee Class nameplate.
£3,000-3,500 *SRA*

Locomotive Nameplates

A Great Western Railway Star Class nameplate.
£4,000-4,500 *SRA*

A Great Western Railway Manor Class nameplate.
£4,500-5,000 *SRA*

An LNER A3 Class nameplate.
£4,500-5,000 *SRA*

An LNER A4 Class nameplate.
£8,000-10,000 *SRA*

An Isle of Wight Railway nameplate.
£2,500-3,000 *SRA*

A Great Western Railway combined nameplate and numberplate.
£4,500-5,000 *SRA*

An industrial locomotive nameplate.
£250-300 *SRA*

A Southern Railway Schools Class 4-4-0 locomotive nameplate, c1930, 32in (81cm) long.
£3,600-3,800 *S*

The Dulwich was built in 1930 and withdrawn from service in 1961 when it had a recorded mileage of 999,665.

A Southern Railway Schools Class 4-4-0 locomotive nameplate, No.30-932, in original wood packing case and a copy of the British Rail original bill of sale, 45¼in (115cm) wide.
£4,800-5,200 *CSK*

An LMS nameplate and badge.
£10,000-12,000 *SRA*

A Southern Railway Battle of Britain Class locomotive nameplate, and badge.
£10,000-12,000 *SRA*

A Great Western Railway Hall Class nameplate.
£2,000-2,500 *SRA*

A London and North Western Railway nameplate, mounted on a wooden plaque, 1899.
£3,000-3,500 *SRA*

A Kent and East Sussex Railway nameplate.
£2,000-2,500 *SRA*

A GWR Castle Class 4-6-0 locomotive nameplate, No. 4094, with hollow cast brass letters on backplate, brass surround, 69in (175cm) wide.
£6,200-6,500 *CSK*

Locomotive Numberplates

A GWR cabside numberplate.
£1,000-1,500 *SRA*

A GWR cabside numberplate.
£1,000-1,500 *SRA*

A GNR brass cabside
numberplate.
£2,800-2,900 *SRA*

A smokebox
numberplate.
£600-700 *SRA*

Models

A 7mm scale model of the LMS Jinty 0-6-0
side tank locomotive, No. 7261, finished
in black, 3½ by 8¾in (8.5 by 22cm).
£150-160 *CSK*

A 3½in gauge gas fired model of
the L&NWR 2-2-2 locomotive
and tender, No. 531, Lady of the
Lake, built by A. Bowling,
finished in LNWR livery and
lining, with carrying boxes, 9½
by 34in (24 by 86cm).
£2,000-2,200 *CSK*

*This model was awarded the
Silver Medal at the Bristol and
South West Model Engineering
and Hobby Exhibition, 1987.*

A 3½in gauge model of
the 0-6-0 side tank
locomotive Rob Roy,
built by H. Hallas,
10¼ by 21¼in
(26 by 54cm).
£500-550 *CSK*

A 7mm two rail electric model of
the Great Western Railway 0-6-0
saddle tank, No. 2048, 8in (20cm)
long, and an 060 saddle tank,
No. 3, Jupiter, 7¾in (19cm) long.
£125-150 each *CSK*

A gauge I live steam spirit fired model of the
GWR King Class 4-6-0 locomotive and
tender, No. 6000 King George V, in original
paintwork.   **£2,250-2,750** *CSK*

This model has not been steamed.

A 3¼in gauge wooden display
model of the NER Worsdall
Class PI 0-6-0 locomotive and
tender, No. 25, built by
N. Downing, 1972, finished in
NER green livery and lining, 10
by 38¼in (25 by 97cm), display
base and Perspex cover.
£125-150 *CSK*

A gauge I live steam spirit fired model of the 0-6-4 side tank, No. 143, finished in red and black, 14in (35.5cm) long.
£190-220 *CSK*

A GWR Saint Class 4-6-0 locomotive and tender, No. 2950, Taplow Court, built by Dyson, 3¾ by 17⅛in (9 by 44.5cm).
£375-400 *CSK*

Railway Ephemera

A selection of various railway guides, 1949.
£5-8 each *COB*

A British Railways poster.
£50-60 *SRA*

A British Railways, Western Region, poster.
£50-60 *SRA*

CROSS REFERENCE
Posters —————▶ p353

Two railway guides, 1939 and 1948.
£10-15 each *COB*

The Model Railway Handbook catalogue, c1947.
£10-15 *COB*

A Description of the Patent Locomotive Steam Engine of Messrs. Robert Stephenson and Co, London, by John Weale, 1838, with 4 folding engraved plates, illustrations and engraved diagrams, 22½ by 34in (56.5 by 86cm).
£225-250 *CSK*

An Autorails PLM lithograph in colours, by Troy, printed by A.G.L. Danel, Paris, backed on linen, 39 by 24in (99 by 61cm).
£275-300 *CSK*

A LNER poster, by Tom Purvis.
£300-400 *SRA*

ROCK, POP & FILM MEMORABILIA
Rock & Pop

The demand for rock and pop items is very high and consequently so are the prices they fetch. This demand is almost entirely directed towards the 'greats' of the rock world, with contemporary, as well as veteran stars, commanding high prices. For example, Madonna, Prince and Michael Jackson are as sought after as Bill Haley, Elvis Presley and the Beatles.

Beatles memorabilia is now in such demand that entire auctions are held solely for their items. The Rolling Stones, Jimi Hendrix, The Who and Cream are also extremely popular with collectors.

The real trick is to spot at the time which artists will become collectable. There are many groups like the Bay City Rollers, Edison Lighthouse and Boney M who, although very popular at the time with a string of hit records, just don't make it in the memorabilia stakes. The golden rule for rock and pop collectors, like so many areas of collectables, is to collect for pleasure rather than investment.

A Statue of Liberty stage costume, used by Elton John, accompanied by a photograph, 1977. **£2,400-2,800** *CSK*

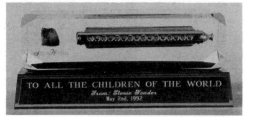

A harmonica, donated by Stevie Wonder, for an auction at Paramount Studios, Hollywood, 1992, 5 by 11in (12.5 by 28cm). **£750-775** *CSK*

Michael Jackson's hat, with 5 postcards. **£1,000-1,100** *S(NY)*

Michael Jackson's leather jacket from the Thriller video, in bright red with black trim, 1983. **£3,500-3,700** *S*

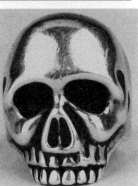

A skull shaped ring, inscribed Take It So Hard, from a limited edition issued to promote Keith Richards' solo album Talk Is Cheap, 1988. **£340-380** *CSK*

MAKE THE MOST OF MILLERS

Condition is absolutely vital when assessing the value of any item. Damaged pieces appreciate much less than perfect examples. However, a rare, desirable piece may command a high price even when damaged.

A mirror ball, accompanied by a letter from Pete Townshend's office stating that this 'is the actual Mirror Ball which was featured in the Tommy film', starring The Who, 39½in (100cm) diam. **£590-620** *CSK*

A handwritten sheet of lyrics by Jimi Hendrix, to the song Suddenly November Morning, c1968.
£2,350-3,000 *S(NY)*

A contract and sheet music, for My Dream, signed in blue ballpoint pen by Bill Haley, June 1st 1958.
£400-500 *S(NY)*

CROSS REFERENCE
Ephemera
Autographs ⟶ p182

A pair of tan boots, with 4¼in (11cm) heels, the right boot signed and inscribed 'Much Love-Stevie Nicks', and a tambourine, both used by Stevie Nicks on her first tour with Fleetwood Mac in 1975. **£650-700** *CSK*

Madonna's black satin bustier, signed Madonna in gold felt pen, together with 4 photographs.
£9,000-9,500 *CSK*

The bustier was given by Madonna to the choreographer of the 1987 World Tour.

A pink leather bracelet, covered in spikes and studs, worn on stage by Madonna.
£950-1,000 *S(NY)*

Various items worn by Kiss in concert, each item with a letter of authenticity, 1970s.
£2,200-2,300 *S(NY)*

Album Covers

A Decca EP cover, The Rolling Stones, signed on the front by all 5 members of the group, 1964, 7in (17.5cm) square.
£375-400 *CSK*

An autographed poem by Marc Bolan, 57 lines on 4 pages, dated June 5th 1968, and the transcript, typed by Marc Bolan's wife, June.
£190-210 *CSK*

An original sleeve proof, Here's the Sex Pistols, 1977, with another sleeve proof entitled God Save Sex Pistols, framed and glazed, 30 by 17¼in (76 by 44cm).
£1,000-1,100 *S*

'God Save Sex Pistols' was one of the suggested titles for the band's first album.

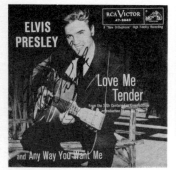

A single sleeve, Love Me Tender, RCA 1960, signed and inscribed 'Best Wishes Elvis Presley,' in black felt pen, c1974.
£800-850 *CSK*

An Atlantic Records Led Zeppelin album cover, signed 'Best Wishes John Bonham, Good Luck Robert Plant, Best Wishes Jimmy Page and John Paul Jones', 1968.
£750-775 *CSK*

A single sleeve, Happenings Ten Years Time Ago, signed by Jeff Beck, Jimmy Page, Keith Relf, Chris Dreja and Jim McCarthy of The Yardbirds.
£525-550 *CSK*

An album cover, Big Brother & The Holding Company, autographed 'Love Janis Joplin', 17 by 25in (43 by 63.5cm).
£2,000-2,300 *S(NY)*

Beatles

A Rolling Stones album cover, Sticky Fingers, signed on the front by Mick Jagger, Keith Richards, Charlie Watts and Bill Wyman in gold felt pen, and by Mick Taylor.
£575-600 *CSK*

An album cover, A Night at the Opera, autographed by all 4 members of Queen, 15in (38cm) square.
£700-750 *S(NY)*

A sheet of printed music for And I Love Her, 1964, signed on the cover by all 4 Beatles, 11 by 8½in (28 by 21cm).
£2,250-2,500 *CSK*

A Capital Records autographed single, I Am The Walrus, by John Lennon, 1967.
£1,300-1,400 *CSK*

A set of Yellow Submarine ceramic Beatle figures, each marked on the foot W. Goebel, W. Germany 1968, 8¾in (22cm) high.
£3,250-3,500 *S*

Sheet music for the single 'Please Please Me', the cover signed by the Beatles, 1963, mounted, framed and glazed, 12 by 15in (30.5 by 38cm).
£1,300-1,400 *S*

An Australian album, Please Please Me, signed on the back by all 4 Beatles, 6¼ by 4¼in (15.5 by 11cm). **£1,300-1,400** *CSK*

A souvenir concert programme for The Beatles Christmas Show, 1963-64, signed on the inside cover, additionally signed by Billy J. Kramer, The Dakotas, Cilla Black, and signed and inscribed, To Sandra with love from Rolf Harris.
£850-875 *CSK*

A TWA red canvas bag, with white lettering and piping, printed 'The Beatles To The USA, August 1965'. **£900-925** *S*

An Apple Records Award, inscribed 'To Commemorate The Beatles 1st Apple Single, Hey Jude, 4th September 1968', 4in (10cm) high.
£2,100-2,200 *S(NY)*

A pair of black leather Chelsea boots, with pointed toes, size 8, worn by John Lennon c1964, accompanied by a letter of authenticity.
£3,200-3,400 *CSK*

A souvenir concert programme for The Beatles/Mary Wells Tour, 1964, signed on the cover in black biro, and additionally signed by other artists in the line-up, including Mary Wells.
£750-775 *CSK*

Guitars

An Alvanez 12 string acoustic guitar, the body signed by Mike Rutherford, Phil Collins and Tony Banks.
£1,150-1,250 *CSK*

The guitar is believed to have been used by Mike Rutherford and was donated by Genesis to Rhino Rock Charity at the Guards Polo Club Autumn Festival in 1991.

A Gibson ES335 guitar, previously owned by Dave Edmunds, c1966.
£1,500-1,600 *S*

A Ned Callan solidbody bass guitar in a sunburst finish, maple neck, 20 fret bound rosewood fingerboard, used by John Entwistle on The Who's 1989 Tour, and accompanied by a letter confirming the provenance. **£2,400-2,600** *CSK*

A Fender Stratocaster electric guitar, autographed by Stevie Ray Vaughan, with a carrying case. **£2,500-2,600** *S(NY)*

A 1989 Fender Stratocaster 12 string solidbody electric guitar, used by Greg Lake on Emerson, Lake and Palmer's 1991 U.S. tour. **£875-925** *CSK*

A 1937 Epiphone Olympic archtop acoustic guitar, with case. **£450-475** *CSK*

A Gibson Les Paul standard guitar, signed by Jimmy Page, in plush lined shaped Gibson case, and a letter of provenance. **£1,850-1,950** *S*

A 1952 Gibson Les Paul solidbody electric guitar, maple top with a gold finish, mahogany body and neck, 22 fret rosewood fingerboard, in brown case. **£1,200-1,300** *CSK*

A 1979 Fender Precision bass electric guitar, owned by Chris Jasper, and played by Marvin Isley of the Isley Brothers, on tour, with a letter of authenticity. **£1,600-1,700** *S(NY)*

A Gibson 335 semi acoustic electric guitar, black finish, used by Roy Orbison, with letter of authenticity, early 1970s. **£4,500-4,700** *CSK*

Posters

The Seekers rock poster, in purple and black, white linen backed, 30 by 40in (76 by 101.5cm).
£470-500 *S(NY)*

Presentation Discs

A Jimi Hendrix framed presentation gold disc, Are You Experienced?, presented to Warner Bros. Records, 20¾ by 16¾in (53 by 43cm).
£1,000-1,200 *CSK*

A Beatles framed presentation gold disc, Sergeant Pepper's Lonely Hearts Club Band, presented to Circus Magazine, with certificate, 20¾ by 16¾in (53 by 43cm).
£1,600-1,700 *CSK*

CROSS REFERENCE
Ephemera ──────▶ p182
Posters ──────▶ p353

A poster for the Rolling Stones' concert at the Bremen Stadthalle, Germany on March 29th, 1967, in red and black on white, 23¼ by 33in (59 by 84cm).
£1,800-1,900 *S*

A John and Yoko framed presentation gold disc, Double Fantasy, 20¾ by 16¾in (53 by 43cm).
£1,100-1,300 *CSK*

An Elvis Presley framed platinum Album Award for Elvis in Concert, 21 by 17in (53.5 by 43.5cm).
£480-500 *S(NY)*

A signed Jimi Hendrix poster, printed in black on white, English, 1967, 20 by 16½in (51 by 42cm).
£1,150-1,350 *S*

A Michael Jackson signed gold 45 Award, for We Are The World, 17 by 13in (43.2 by 33cm).
£1,300-1,400 *S(NY)*

A presentation framed platinum disc, Wings Over America, presented to Denny Laine, 20¾ by 16¾in (53 by 43cm).
£800-850 *CSK*

Film Memorabilia
Animation Art

A production cel on production background, The Snowman, 12 by 16in (30.5 by 40.5cm). **£1,000-1,200** *CAT*

A Walt Disney Studio gouache on celluloid, Peg from Lady and the Tramp, 1955, framed, 10 by 12in (25.4 by 30.5cm). **£1,200-1,400** *S(NY)*

A Warner Bros. Studios gouache on full celluloid, Bugs Bunny with a cake, unframed, 10½ by 12⅜in (26.5 by 31.5cm). **£750-850** *CNY*

A Walt Disney production cel, Who Framed Roger Rabbit, Porky Pig, 1988, 12 by 16in (30.5 by 40.5cm). **£6,000-7,000** *CAT*

A Walt Disney gouache on multi-cel set up, applied to a printed background, Mowgli and Baloo, Jungle Book, 1967, unframed, 8 by 10in (20 by 25cm). **£850-950** *CNY*

A Walt Disney Studio gouache on celluloid, The Academy Awards, Minnie, Donald and Daisy, framed, 1988, 9 by 11½in (22.5 by 30cm). **£1,100-1,200** *S(NY)*

A Warner Bros. Studios gouache on full celluloid, Daffy Duck, with a footprint stamp, unframed, 10½ by 12½in (26.5 by 31.5cm).
£750-850 *CNY*

A Walt Disney watercolour production background, Alice in Wonderland, 1951, 9 by 12in (22.5 by 30.5cm).
£7,000-7,500 *CAT*

A Walt Disney graphite on paper drawing, Pinocchio, Jiminy Cricket, 1940, 12 by 16in (30.5 by 40.5cm).
£600-700 *CAT*

Lobby Cards & Posters

An RKO poster, Follow the Fleet, 1936, linen backed, 41 by 27in (104 by 68.5cm).
£5,100-5,200 *CNY*

A Vitagraph poster, The Man from Monterey, 1933, linen backed, 41 by 27in (104 by 68.5cm).
£2,500-2,600 *CNY*

A Walt Disney Studio production cel, Who Framed Roger Rabbit, Roger Rabbit holding Jessica's hand, 1988, 12 by 16in (30.5 by 40.5cm).
£1,300-1,500 *CAT*

A Columbia poster, Ridin' for Justice, 1931, linen backed, 41 by 27in (104 by 68.5cm).
£2,200-2,300 *CNY*

An MGM poster, The Devil's Brother, 1933, paper backed, 41 by 27in (104 by 68.5cm).
£4,000-4,100 *CNY*

An MGM lobby card, The Wizard of Oz, 1939, 11 by 14in (28 by 35.5cm).
£2,600-2,700 *CNY*

A Universal poster, Smash Up, 1947, linen backed, 81 by 41in (205.5 by 104cm).
£750-850 *CNY*

A Buena Vista poster, One Hundred and One Dalmations,1961, linen backed, 41 by 27in (104 by 68.5cm). **£500-600** *CNY*

A Buena Vista poster, Sleeping Beauty, 1959, linen backed, 41 by 27in (104 by 68.5cm).
£500-600 *CNY*

An RKO poster, My Favourite Wife, 1940, paper backed, 41 by 27in (104 by 68.5cm).
£500-600 *CNY*

Memorabilia

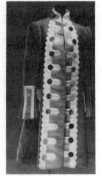

A Wizard of Oz costume, Metro Goldwyn-Mayer, 1938, worn by one of the inhabitants of the Emerald City, 40in (102cm) long.
£3,500-3,600 *S(NY)*

A pair of shoes, worn by Bette Davis in The Virgin Queen, 20th Century Fox, 1955.
£800-900 *S(NY)*

A pair of buckskin trousers, worn by James Stewart in How the West Was Won, 1963.
£1,700-1,800 *CNY*

Originally purchased in the MGM 1970 public auction.

A tunic and belt, worn by Charlton Heston in Ben Hur, 1959, marked on the inside collar 'Property of MGM'.
£3,400-3,500 *CNY*

A pair of Joan Crawford's matching shoes and pink leather handbag, made by Saks Fifth Avenue, shoes size 6B.
£150-200 *CNY*

A 1945 Best Actress Acadamy Award, presented to Joan Crawford, for her performance in Mildred Pierce.
£46,000-47,000 *CNY*

SCALES, WEIGHTS & MEASURES

A set of guinea scales, late 18thC, 4in (10cm) wide.
£70-80 *DHo*

These scales were used by gentlemen to weigh their coins, as gold could be clipped off - a crime punishable by death.

A Victorian silvered nickel alloy ¼ gill measure, 2in (5cm) high.
£10-12 *PSA*

A pair of brass grocery scales, with porcelain pan, by Bartlett & Son, Bristol, 33in (84cm) high. **£180-200** *DHo*

A wood and metal grain measure, c1880, 13½in (34cm) high.
£80-95 *MofC*

A set of bucket weights, engraved Borough of Batley, De Grave & Co Ltd, Makers London, with stamps for George V 1932, in fitted mahogany case, 17¼in (44cm) wide.
£1,300-1,400 *CSK*

A James I lead weight, stamped with a crown over 'I' and a dagger.
£120-140 *CSK*

A part set of bucket measures, the gallon signed Maguire & Gatchell Ltd 470 Dawson St. Dublin, the other measures Imperial half gallon, quart, pint, half pint and gill, dated 1893. **£600-650** *CSK*

A wooden grain measure, 14in (36cm) high.
£35-35 *MofC*

A set of brass bell weights, engraved North Riding Yorkshire, unsigned, dated 1902, in fitted mahogany case, 21in (53cm) wide.
£700-750 *CSK*

SCIENTIFIC INSTRUMENTS

A Raphael's Patent opsiometer, in mahogany case, 12½in (32cm) high. **£600-625** *CSK*

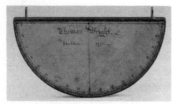

A surveying protractor, signed Thomas Wright Storkton 1795, 6¼in (16cm) wide. **£260-280** *CSK*

A Butterfield-type silver octagonal dial, signed on the horizontal plate Delure Paris, in velvet lined fitted leather case, 18thC, 3⅛in (8cm) wide. **£650-700** *CSK*

An American ballooning barograph, by Negretti & Zambra, London, stamped with patent April 23rd 1878, made in USA, 9½in (24cm) wide. **£250-275** *CSK*

A Crooke's pattern discharge tube, on mahogany base, 15in (38cm) high. **£340-380** *CSK*

A large demonstration burning glass, mounted in an iron frame, c1850, 22in (56cm) high. **£1,000-1,200** *CSK*

A black enamelled Model 50 binocular microscope, signed Beck, London, with a collection of accessories and large part case, 35in (89cm) high. **£1,500-1,600** *CSK*

A silver mounted horn calendar box, probably Dutch, 5¾in (15cm) wide. **£340-380** *CSK*

A bone ivory artillery sector, unsigned, with scales relating to Italian, French, Dutch and English shot and powder, straight edge with a 12in scale, 17thC. **£2,000-2,200** *CSK*

CROSS REFERENCE	
Militaria ⟶	p308

An oxidised and lacquered brass astronomical spectroscope, signed Grubb & Son Dublin, in fitted mahogany case, c1868, 14½in (37cm) wide. **£540-580** *CSK*

The Grubb family were important makers of astronomical instruments in the 19thC. Howard Grubb, later Sir Howard, joined his father Thomas in 1865. In 1868 Thomas took over the firm and it is likely that this instrument dates from this period.

An Abbe's apertometer, by Carl Zeiss Jena, in fitted velvet lined red leather case, and a black enamelled microtome, by Sartorius-Werke Gottingen.
£450-475 *CSK*

A Philips' Planisphere star finding chart, with black leatherette frame, 6¼in (16cm) wide. **£65-85** *CSK*

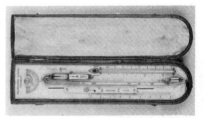

A Cary 1¾in brass refracting telescope, mid-19thC, with mahogany bound tube, 42½in (108cm) extended.
£230-280 *Bon*

A Society of Arts type microscope, signed Davis Leeds, in fitted mahogany case, 9½in (24cm) high.
£425-450 *CSK*

A Wheatstone apparatus, for showing the independence of the plane of oscillation in relation to other motions, in mahogany case with brass carrying handle, late 19thC.
£480-520 *CSK*

An early Improved Pocket Barometer, signed T. Cooke York, with ivorine dial, broken thermometer body tube, in fitted silk lined leather case, 9⅜in (24.5cm) long.
£180-210 *CSK*

Optical Equipment

A pair of cloisonné and brass opera glasses, 19thC.
£125-145 *GAK*

CROSS REFERENCE
Colour Section ➡ p279

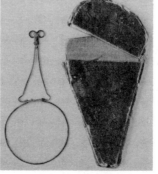

A magnifier, with single copper wire frame, in red leather paper card case, mid-18thC, 3¼in (8cm) high. **£340-380** *CSK*

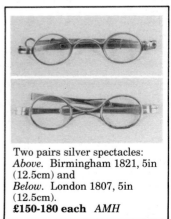

Two pairs silver spectacles:
Above. Birmingham 1821, 5in (12.5cm) and
Below. London 1807, 5in (12.5cm).
£150-180 each *AMH*

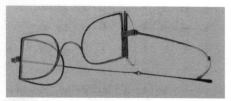

A pair of double D-end
spectacles, in wooden case, late
18thC.
£240-280 *CSK*

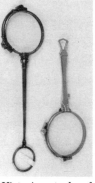

Two Victorian steel and
metal lorgnettes.
£25-35 each *VB*

A pair of Martins
Margins, with round lens
and arched bridge, in
pressed leather covered
case, c1760.
£420-460 *CSK*

A pair of binoculars in leather
case, by Bausch and Lomb
Optical Co, Rochester, New
York, 5½in (14cm) high.
£40-45 *AHL*

A pair of blued steel spectacles,
with round lenses, gilt
embossed label Jones, 62
Charing Cross X.
£875-925 *CSK*

*With manuscript memorandum
in ink 'These spectacles belonged
to the Duke of Wellington. They
were given to me on leaving
Strathfield Saye to return to
India on 31st December 1841. I
bequeath these to my dear Child
Louisa Michal (?), June 14th
1843 Simlah C.H. Churchill'.
Thomas Jones worked from 62
Charing Cross (1816-50).*

A monacle, c1900.
£15-20 *VB*

Two Victorian mother-of-pearl
and tortoiseshell lorgnettes.
£50-90 *VB*

A pair of 'Nuremberg' single
wire round rim nose spectacles,
with leather nose grips, in fitted
pressed leather case, c1700,
1¾in (5cm) wide.
£2,500-2,750 *CSK*

An Edwardian sterling
silver lorgnette, 4¼in
(11cm) long.
£70-80 *AA*

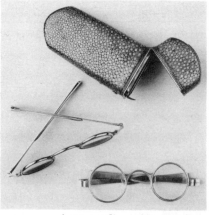

A compendium of 2 pairs of
silver round lens spectacles, in
shagreen case, late 18thC.
£800-850 *CSK*

Medical Instruments

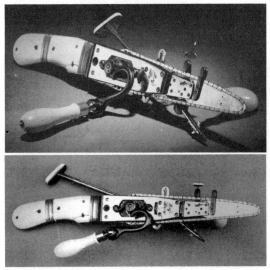

A Japanned ear trumpet, by Dowling, c1880, 6in (15cm) high.
£40-60   *CS*

A tooth key, signed Ferguson, with turned bone handle, 6in (15cm) long.
£300-325   *CSK*

A mechanical steel and ivory chainsaw, signed Heine of Wurzburg, the chain operated by a toothed cog wound by a handle.   **£25,000-26,000**   *CSK*

A few examples were supplied to America for use during the Civil War and last appeared in a medical catalogue there in 1871. The need for speedy amputation was lessened by the use of anaesthetics.

A surgeon's brass blood letting scarificator, by Robert Simpson of 9 Clerkenwell Green, London, 13 blades, c1790.
£25-28   *CS*

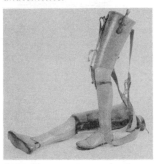

A double amputees pair of jointed wooden artificial legs, with steel frame, 19thC.
£480-520   *CSK*

A mahogany domestic medicine chest, with fitted interior for 13 bottles, glass mortar and pestle, 2 pillboxes, brass scales, glass pallet and other items, mid-19thC, 12¾in (32.5cm) wide.
£1,600-1,700   *CSK*

Three stethoscopes:
l. A 2-part fruitwood monaural, with adjustable earpiece, 19thC, 7⅛in (18cm) high.
£250-270
c. A fruitwood monaural stamped Down Bros. London, late 19thC, 14¾in (38cm) high.
£775-800
r. An ebonised feotal stethoscope with large fluted bell chest piece, in 2 parts, 6¾in (17cm) high.
£220-250   *CSK*

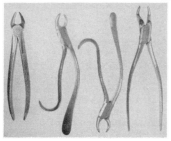

A selection of dental forceps:
l. By J. M. Everard of London, 1840
centre. Right and left handed, by Morson of New York
r. By Diebolt.
£35-50 each   *CS*

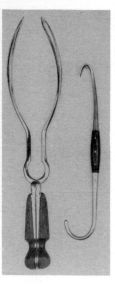

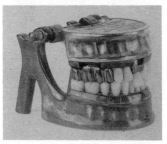

l. A pair of Barnes forceps, with chequer grip ebony handles, signed Eggington Manchester. *r.* A crochet, with ebony handle, hook and crook, signed Ferris & Co. Bristol. **£160-180** *CSK*

A surgical trephine skull saw, with cherrywood handle, brass shank and steel saw, c1820. **£95-100** *CS*

A dental demonstration model, signed Wekabe 2 D.R.P. Ausl.Pat.Angem No.7252, with detachable teeth, on hinged joint, 3¼in (8cm) wide. **£850-900** *CSK*

A Smellie's scissor perforator, iron with shaped blade and guard, unsigned, c1750, 11in (28cm) long. **£850-900** *CSK*

Sextants

A miniature brass sextant, 4in (10cm) wide. **£80-120** *COB*

A lacquered brass box sextant, signed Yeates, 2 Grafton St, Dublin, in fitted velvet lined leather case, 4½in (11cm) wide. **£420-460** *CSK*

A boxed sextant, F Smith & Sons chronometer makers, compass adjusters, 23 Oxford Street, Southampton, c1870, 10¼in (26cm) square. **£400-500** *AHL*

SCRIPOPHILY

Canada

A £100 Debenture for the Levis & Kennebec Railway Co, printed in pale blue, dated 1875. **£145-150** *SCR*

A £100 bond of The Atlantic Quebec & Western Railway Company, formed to build railway of 362 miles, hand signed by the Earl of Ranfurley, dated c1911. **£16-18** *SCR*

A share certificate of the San Antonio Land & Irrigation Company, dated 1913. **£10-12** *SCR*

China

A share certificate of the Pekin Syndicate Ltd, green and black. **£90-95** *SCR*

Formed in 1897 by an Italian, Angelo Luzatti, the company's objective was to secure mining rights in Shansi Province.

A £20 bond for the 1913 Re-organisation Loan, one of the largest Chinese loans organised by the foreign powers, engraved by Waterlow. Brown. **£12-15** Blue. **£30-35** *SCR*

£21 million net was expected to be raised with about £1 million going towards the crowning of Yuan Shik Kai as Emperor. Large parts of the loan proceeds disappeared mysteriously.

A French registered share certificate of the Banque Industrielle de Chine, yellow, black and red. **£35-40** *SCR*

A £20 bond for the Hukuang Railway, French issue, green and black, 1911. **£35-37** *GKR*

The Hukuang loan was raised to finance the construction of various railway lines, including the line from Wuchang connecting with the Canton/Kowloon Railway. Hukuang means 'land of the wide lakes'.

Europe

A 5% Loan certificate of the city of Vienna, mauve and brown, 1921. **£18-20** *GKR*

A Founders share certificate of the Compagnie Maritime de la Seine, light and dark brown, 1899. **£30-32** *GKR*

A 6% cumulative share certificate for £20 of the Ottoman Railway, from Smyrna to Aidin of his Imperial Majesty the Sultan, 1905.
£60-65 *GKR*

The Company was in London in 1862 and ran the first railway line in the Asian part of the Ottoman Empire. In 1935 the Turkish state acquired the railway for £1,825,840.

A share certificate of the Barcelona Traction Light & Power Co Ltd, red and black, engraved by Waterlow.
£18-20
£20 bond, green and black bond, 1911.
£38-40 *SCR*

A share certificate of the 'Colón' Compañia Transaerea Española, green and beige, dated 1928.
£40-45 *SCR*

Great Britain

An early share certificate of the Newry Warrenpoint & Rostrevor Railway Company, printed on vellum with affixed red seal, dated 1846.
£80-85 *SCR*

Incorporated in 1846 to construct a railway of 7 miles from Newry to Rostrevor with a branch line to Warrenpoint.

A 4% Loan certificate of the Schuldverschreibung, issued to purchase street car lines to construct a second aquaduct, pink and white, Austria, 1902.
£20-22 *GKR*

A share certificate of the Duke of Cornwall's Harbour & Launceston & Victoria Railway Company, dated 1836.
£425-450 *SCR*

A one share certificate of the Herne Bay Pier Company, dated 1842.
£190-195 *SCR*

Construction of the pier was commenced in 1831, five eighths of a mile long, and it was rebuilt in 1873 and lengthened in 1898.

A share certificate of The Electric Clock Company Ltd, black on yellow, dated c1868.
£32-35 *SCR*

A £100 Debenture of the Moss Hall Coal Co. Ltd, Lancashire colliery, large red seal, only 1,400 issued, 1898-89.
£8-9 *GKR*

A share certificate of the Liverpool, Manchester & Newcastle-upon-Tyne Junction Railway, incorporated in 1846 at the end of the second railway boom, large red embossed seal, dated 1st August 1846.
£85-90 *GKR*

A share certificate of Dartmoor Consolidated Tin Mines, Sheepstor, 1824.
£220-225 *SCR*

Russia

A £100 share certificate of the Riasan-Koslow Railway Company, Moscow, 1865, text in English, Russian and German, multi-coloured.
£155-158 *GKR*

A 100 share certificate of The Russian Tobacco Company, printed by Waterlow & Sons Ltd, green and black, c1915, 15 by 10½in (38 by 26cm).
£22-25 *GKR*

A £20 Bond of the City of Moscow, orange and brown.
£10-12 *GKR*

U.S.A.

A share certificate of the Wagner Palace Car Company, c1888.
£23-25 *SCR*

A share certificate of the Cleveland & Pittsburgh Railroad Company, green and black, c1950.
£6-8 *SCR*

A $1000 bond of the Pine Creek Railway Company, hand signed by William K. Vanderbilt.
£160-165 *SCR*

A $1000 bond of the Cleveland Cincinnati Chicago & St Louis Railway Co, brown, dated 1893.
£23-25 *SCR*

Confederate States

An 8% Coupon Bond for $1000, Act of Congress, with figure of President Jefferson Davis, 20th February 1863.
£28-30 *GKR*

A $1000 bond of the West Shore Railroad Company, red and black, c1918.
£8-10 *SCR*

A common stock certificate of the Pittsburgh Youngstown & Ashtabula Railroad Company, brown and black, c1892.
£22-25 *SCR*

An 8% Coupon Bond for $50, Act of Congress, February 28th 1861. **£25-28** *GKR*

An unissued 100 share certificate of The Columbus Southern Railway Loco Company, green and black, c1890. **£6-8** *SCR*

A 100 share certificate of the Pittsburg Allegheny & Manchester Traction Company, green and black, c1895.
£12-15 *SCR*

SERVIETTE RINGS

A wooden serviette ring, hand painted with Egyptian scenes, 1920s, 2in (5cm) diam.
£8-10 *ROW*

A $1000 First Mortgage Bond of the Stafford Meadow Coal Iron & City Improvement Co, of Scranton, with coupons, pale pink and black, 1858.
£35-37 *GKR*

A bond of the Beech Creek Railroad Company, brown and black, dated 1892.
£28-30 *SCR*
No more than 1,000 of these bonds were issued.

SEWING

A carved coquilla nut sewing accessories container, 5¾in (15cm) long.
£100-110 *PSC*

A Victorian skirt hem lifter.
£15-20 *VB*

A bird-shaped tape measure, c1920, 2¼in (6cm) wide.
£12-16 *TER*

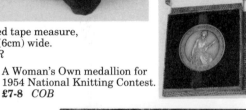

A Woman's Own medallion for 1954 National Knitting Contest.
£7-8 *COB*

A wooden expanding wool winder.
£10-15 *VB*

A selection of Victorian mother-of-pearl cotton winders.
£15-30 each *VB*

l. A gold tape measure, London 1891, 2¾in (7.5cm). **£220-250**
r. A silver tape measure, Birmingham 1887, 2¾in (7.5cm).
£130-140 *AMH*

Two wooden glove darners, 5 and 4in (12.5 and 10cm) long.
£4-7 each *VB*

A selection of tape measures, c1820-1910.
£20-35 each *VB*

Two Victorian thimble holders, a carved wood walnut and a mother-of-pearl boat.
£25-35 each *VB*

Two mother-of-pearl and ivory needle books, c1850.
£20-30 each *VB*

Two Victorian carved spool holders, with mother-of-pearl tops.
£15-19 each *VB*

A Regency red leather sewing box, with brass paw feet and fully fitted interior.
£600-800 *WA*

Three beaded, mother-of-pearl and ivory candle needle holders, c1850.
£25-45 each *VB*

A Tunbridge ware sewing clamp, c1860.
£75-85 *VB*

Pincushions

Three mother-of-pearl sandwich pincushions and one ivory waxer, c1820-80.
£15-25 each *VB*

Two ivory pincushions, c1820.
£20-25 each *VB*

Sewing Machines

A mahogany and velvet pincushion, 20thC, 3in (7.5cm) high. **£10-15** *HAY*

An ebony pin box, with velvet pincushion lid, c1920.
£15-18 *HAY*

A Singer hand-operated sewing machine, and case, c1920.
£35-45 *AHL*

A Singer hand-operated sewing machine, and case, c1930.
£10-20 *WAB*

A Wheeler & Wilson No. 1 hand-operated sewing machine, in walnut case, c1867, 17½in (44cm) wide.
£2,000-2,200 *CSK*

A Shakespear lockstitch sewing machine, by Royal Sewing Machine Co. Ltd, Birmingham, with accessories, instruction leaflet and original wooden box with label in lid.
£250-275 *CSK*

SHIPPING

A souvenir lifeboat ring, from P & O Iberia cruise, 1962, 5in (12.5cm).
£6-10 *BAf*

A brass ships' telegraph, c1920, 18in (46cm) diam.
£340-350 *AHL*

A souvenir lifeboat ring from a P & O liner, RMS Ballaarat, with hand painted ship in centre, c1800, 9in (23cm) wide.
£60-80 *BAf*

A Cunard White Star Line ships' copper cooking pot, c1920.
£50-70 *COB*

A Cunard White Star Line ships' copper cooking pot, c1940.
£50-70 *COB*

A brass ships' telegraph head unit, by A. Robinson Ltd, Liverpool, c1960, 9in (22.5cm) diam.
£170-200 *BAf*

A ships' wheel, 1930s, 20in (51cm) diam.
£120-150 *BAf*

A ships' copper water container, c1880, 12in (30.5cm) square.
£75-95 *MofC*

One of four brass portholes, 10in (25cm) diam.
£140-150 *AHL*

A ships' wheel.
£90-95 *WEL*

An EPNS dish, RMS Mauretania, c1930, 6½in (16cm) diam.
£20-25 *BAf*

A china ashtray, Geest Line, c1970, 6in (15cm) long.
£5-10 *BAf*

A QE2 commemorative ash/pin tray, 1969.
£6-10 *COB*

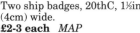

Two ship badges, 20thC, 1½in (4cm) wide.
£2-3 each *MAP*

An early outboard motor, with twin horizontally opposed water cooled cylinders, embossed Fortis, Power Engineering Company Ltd., Manchester No.A63, 44in (112cm) high.
£125-145 *CSK*

A replica medal to commemorate the sinking of The Lusitania, with box, c1918, 2¼in (6cm) diam.
£25-30 *BAf*

Two Cunard badges, 20thC, 1½ and ¾in (4 and 2cm) wide.
£1-2 each *MAP*

A souvenir bell from a P & O liner, 1950s, 4⅓in (11cm) high.
£10-15 *BAf*

A postcard of RMS Olympic Giant, White Star liner, 8in (20cm) long.
£8-12 *COB*

A brass powder compact, RMS Aquitania, c1930, 3in (7.5cm) diam.
£20-25 *BAf*

CROSS REFERENCE
Toiletries ———➤ p442

A napkin ring, Ellerman Lines, 1950s, 2in (5cm) diam.
£10-15 *BAf*

A cruet set carved from the teak of HMS Iron Duke, the flagship of Admiral Jellicoe, Jutland, 1916, 5⅓in (14cm) diam.
£20-25 *BAf*

A soot etched and painted plate, by P.C. Bottriell, RMMV Winchester Castle, c1960, 12in (30.5cm) diam.
£45-50 *BAf*

Menus

A dinner menu from S.S.
Andorinha, June 3, 1925.
£4-5 *COB*

A Cunard White Star Line
menu, 1930s.
£6-8 *COB*

A Canadian Pacific Banff
Springs Hotel menu.
£5-6 *COB*

A luncheon menu for
Fyffes Line, 1960s.
£4-5 *COB*

Model Ships

A wooden model
of Gripsholm,
1956, 6½in
(16.5cm) long.
£20-25 *BAf*

A menu from S.S. Korea sailing
to San Francisco, December
1929. **£5-7** *COB*

A wood and metal electric
powered model of the German
battleship Scharnhorst, 15¾ by
45⅓in (40 by 115cm).
£320-340 *CSK*

A Hornby Minic metal model of
the Queen Mary, c1976, 10in
(25cm) long.
£12-18 *BAf*

A 1:40 scale model of a Thames
penny paddle steamer, c1890,
38in (96.5cm) long.
£650-750 *BAf*

A fibreglass wood and metal display model of the destroyer HMS Amethyst, built by R. Bartlett, 13 by 38¼in (33 by 97cm). **£525-550** *CSK*

A box of Meccano Dinky Toys, Ships of the British Navy, No. 50, c1938, 16in (41cm) long. **£150-200** *BAf*

A Diarama, showing a half model of a clipper and lighthouse, by a sailor, c1860, 25¼in (64.5cm) wide. **£300-350** *DHo*

A schooner rigged pond yacht, Sea King, finished in green, black and varnish, late 19thC, hull measurements 14½ by 51in (37 by 129.5cm). **£1,100-1,200** *CSK*

A clockwork model Jupiter Ocean Pilot boat, by Sutcliffe, in mint condition, c1960, 9½in (24cm) long. **£65-85** *BAf*

A silver pocket flask, given by Wallace Hartley, Bandmaster on RMS Titanic to a Mrs Florence L. Ware, a 2nd class passenger, who survived the sinking. **£4,250-4,750** *ONS*

A gaff rigged pond yacht, with masts, sails, booms and rigging, early 19thC, 72 by 66½in (182.5 by 169cm). **£950-1,000** *CSK*

CROSS REFERENCE
Toys ⟶ p444

Shipping Ephemera

A commemorative postcard for sinking of the Titanic, showing ship, John Phillips and Captain Smith, published by Bragg. **£70-75** *VS*

A bookmark advertising Caledonian Railway and Steamers, 1906. **£15-18** *COB*

A seaman's Voyage Discharge Book, 1901. **£10-15** *BAf*

SILHOUETTES

Lady Rogerson Matthews, by J. Thomason of Dublin, on plaster, broken trade label, hammered gilt metal frame, 18thC, 3½in (9cm) high.
£1,250-1,400 *CSK*

A watercolour and gouache silhouette, 14 by 10½in (36 by 26cm).
£110-120 *PSC*

A silhouette on plaster, by John Miers, not labelled, 7 by 6in (17.5 by 15cm).
£250-300 *PSC*

An officer, by John Smith, on plaster, trade label, hammered gilt metal frame, 18thC, 3½in (9cm) high.
£875-900 *CSK*

A set of three groups of cut paper silhouettes of one family, parents and grandmother, 4 older children and 5 children including baby, 14 by 22in (36 by 56cm).
£600-700 *TER*

Lady Louisa Dalrymple Hamilton, by Lady Louisa Kerr, cut out with watercolour background, signed and dated August 9, 1847, in wood frame, 13in (33cm) high.
£1,000-1,200 *CSK*

A silhouette, by Mrs Beetham, painted on glass with wax backing, c1790, 6½in (16cm) high.
£200-225 *TER*

Papageno dancing in the woods playing pipes, by Lottie Reiniger, signed with initials and inscribed, in wood frame, 9¼in (23cm).
£300-360 *CSK*

Lottie Reiniger was the inventor of the animated silhouette film and is also credited with the first full length cartoon.

> CROSS REFERENCE
> **Portrait**
> **Miniatures** ⟶ p343

The Rev. Thos Weeks, by John Miers, on plaster, original label, 8 by 7in (20 by 17.5cm). **£300-350** *PSC*

A silhouette of 5 different heads, by Hubert Leslie, wood frame, 4in (10cm) high. **£230-260** *CSK*

Winston Churchill, cut-out and hand torn, by Suzanne Hayward-Young, signed, rectangular wood frame, 11in (28cm) high. **£225-250** *CSK*

This silhouette is believed to have been cut during a debate in the House of Commons.

A cut paper bronzed silhouette, 9¼ by 8in (24 by 20cm). **£100-135** *PSC*

Mrs John Ward, by Augustin Edouart, inscribed Mrs John Ward/9th October 1827/Clare Villa/Cheltenham, in wood frame, 11in (28cm) high. **£800-840** *CSK*

Frances Knowles Bresselier with her spaniel, by William James Hubard, and 2 others, 5 and 7in (12.5 and 17.5cm). **£500-525** *CSK*

A cut paper bronzed silhouette, 5¾ by 5in (14.5 by 12.5cm). **£90-95** *PSC*

A silhouette in watercolour, 4¼in (11cm) diam. **£60-65** *PSC*

A lady, by Mrs Isabella Beetham, painted on convex glass with verre églomisé border, unbroken trade label, turned wood frame, 3½in (9cm) high. **£5,500-5,750** *CSK*

Mrs Charles Austen, by John Miers, on plaster heightened with bronze, unbroken trade label no.12, black wood frame, 3in (8cm) high. **£2,400-2,600** *CSK*

Thomas Smythe, by John Miers, on plaster, unbroken trade label no.7 Liverpool, inscribed with the sitter's name, hammered brass frame, 18thC, 3½in (9cm) high. **£1,250-1,400** *CSK*

SMOKING

At the turn of the century more women began smoking than ever before. Consequently, cigarette holders soon became popular fashion accessories for both men and women. Cases were often elaborately decorated with precious metals or intricately carved.

The finest examples of cigarette holders came with small leather cases and boxes, which, if they survived, enhance the value of the holder.

A Continental gilt lined cigarette case, 3½in (9cm) long. **£360-390** *CSK*

l. A pewter cigarette case, with Tatiana design, 4 by 2¼in (10 by 6cm) **£50-60**
r. A silver Russian pre-Revolution cigarette case depicting Tatiana and The Demons, c1895, 4¼ by 3¾in (11 by 9.5cm). **£500-550** *ARE*

A Continental white metal, slightly curved gilt lined cigarette case, with enamelled lid, 3¾in (9.5cm). **£1,200-1,400** *CSK*

A Continental terracotta pug tobacco jar, 19thC. **£400-550** *DMT*

An acorn rustic style terracotta tobacco jar, English, late 19thC. **£250-300** *DMT*

A Bakelite blue tinted cigarette case, inlaid with silver ferns, rushes and bird and applied with initials, the interior incorporating an ivory notepad and pencil, 4in (10cm). **£300-325** *CSK*

A cased set of 2 pipes, cigarette and cigar holders and silver vesta case, c1907, 6 by 5in (15 by 12.5cm). **£100-120** *DP*

A brass matchbox, English, c1885, 3¾in (9.5cm) square. **£30-40** *TER*

Cigarette and Cigar Holders

A silver and amber cigarette holder, in silver case, 1895, 2in (5cm) long.
£40-50 *DP*

A Japanese ivory cigar holder, c1900, 3in (7.5cm) long.
£40-45 *DP*

A carved bone cigarette holder, c1895, 6in (15cm) long.
£30-35 *DP*

A carved Meerschaum cigar holder, 3¼in (8cm) long.
£40-50 *DP*

A carved amber cigarette holder, c1920, 5in (12.5cm) long.
£30-40 *DP*

An amber and gold mounted cigarette holder, 5¾in (14.5cm) long.
£30-35 *DP*

An ivory dragon head cigarette holder, 4in (10cm) long.
£30-40 *DP*

A carved Meerschaum cigar holder, c1910, 4⅓in (11cm) long.
£30-40 *DP*

A Bakelite twisted cigarette holder, c1920, 3¼in (8cm) long.
£5-10 *DP*

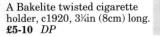

A Japanese carved ivory cigarette holder, signed, 4⅓in (11cm) long.
£50-60 *DP*

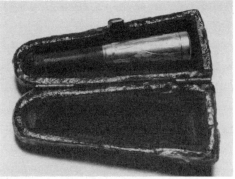

A silver cigarette holder, c1910, 2½in (6cm) long.
£10-15 *DP*

A gold mounted plastic cigarette holder, c1910, 5in (12.5cm) long.
£20-30 *DP*

An Art Deco plastic cigarette
holder, c1930, 5¼in (13cm) long.
£5-10 *DP*

An ivory cigarette holder, engraved with a
monkey, 3½in (9cm) long.
£30-40 *DP*

An amber and coloured plastic cigarette holder,
6in (15cm) long.
£10-15 *DP*

A Bakelite twisted cigarette
holder, c1925, 4¾in (12cm) long.
£20-30 *DP*

A plastic cigarette holder,
c1950, 4in (10cm) long.
£5-10 *DP*

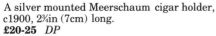

**MAKE THE MOST OF
MILLERS**

Condition is absolutely vital when
assessing the value of any item.
Damaged pieces appreciate much
less than perfect examples.
However, a rare, desirable piece
may command a high price even
when damaged.

A yellow plastic cigarette
holder, c1930, 3½in (9cm) long.
£5-10 *DP*

A silver mounted Meerschaum cigar holder,
c1900, 2¾in (7cm) long.
£20-25 *DP*

Two Meerschaum, amber and
silver cigarette holders, with
case, 1904, 4in (10cm) long.
£50-60 *DP*

An engraved amber and silver
mounted cigar holder, 3¼in
(8cm) long.
£30-40 *DP*

A cigarette holder decorated with roses,
c1940, 3¾in (9cm) long.
£10-15 *DP*

A Chinese carved ivory
cigarette holder, 4⅛in (11cm)
long.
£30-40 *DP*

Tampers

A brass leg shaped tamper, 2¾in (7cm) long.
£10-15 *NM*

Tampers were made from a variety of materials and used to push down or tamp tobacco in pipe bowls.

Four tampers in the form of figures, 2 to 2¾in (5 to 7cm) high.
£10-15 each *NM*

Two chrome/silver tampers, 1½ and 1¾in (4 and 4cm) high.
£10-15 each *NM*

Two brass hand-shaped tampers, 2⅜in (6cm) high.
£10-15 each *NM*

Three brass tampers in the form of figures, 2¼ to 2¾in (6 to 7cm) high. **£10-15 each** *NM*

Three brass head-shaped tampers, 2½in (6cm) high.
£10-15 each *NM*

A brass head shaped tamper, 2in (5cm) high.
£10-15 *NM*

A brass tamper shaped as a South African coin, 2⅜in (6cm) high.
£10-15 *NM*

A brass claw-and-ball tamper.
£10-15 *NM*

A glass hand-shaped tobacco tamper or sugar crusher, c1820, 5½in (14cm) high.
£150-185 *MJW*

A brass horse's head shaped tamper, 2½in (6.5cm) high.
£10-15 *NM*

A brass tamper shaped as the head of a man, 2⅜in (6cm) high.
£10-15 *NM*

Two brass tampers shaped as figures, 2¾in (7cm) high. **£10-15 each** *NM*

Two brass tampers shaped as a female figure and a bust. **£10-15 each** *NM*

A brass tamper in the form of a jockey, 2¼in (6cm) high. **£10-15** *NM*

Two brass head-shaped tampers, 2½in (6cm) high. **£10-15 each** *NM*

Two brass tampers as figures of Napoleon, 2¼in (6cm) high. **£10-15 each** *NM*

CROSS REFERENCE
Cigarette Cards → p194

SNUFF BOXES

A Georgian silver mounted tortoiseshell snuff box, the lid applied with a mother-of-pearl coat-of-arms, 3in (7.5cm) long. **£600-650** *CSK*

A papier mâché snuff box, early 19thC, 3¾in (9.5cm) diam. **£2,700-3,000** *CSK*

A China Trades gilt lined snuff box, 2½in (6cm) long. **£320-340** *CSK*

A papier mâché snuff box, the cover painted with a scene of a soldier visiting his lover, early 19thC, 3½in (9cm) long. **£500-550** *CSK*

An enamel and gilt metal mounted snuff box, commemorating the battle of Kunersdorf, the interior with a portrait bust of Elizabeth I, Empress of Russia, 18thC Birmingham, 3¼in (8cm) long. **£1,400-1,600** *CSK*

The battle of Kunersdorf was fought between Frederick the Great, and a Russian and Austrian army under Saltnikof, on 12th August 1759.

Three Victorian lacquered papier mâché snuff boxes.
£10-22 each *VB*

A ceramic walnut shaped snuff bottle, with silver top, Birmingham 1945.
£75-80 *WIL*

A gilt lined snuff box, nielloed with bands of scrollwork, N. Motokhov, Moscow, 1852, 3½in (9cm) long.
£450-475 *CSK*

A Victorian snuff box, with original painting on lid, 3in (7.5cm) long.
£50-60 *FMN*

A papier mâché snuff box, the interior inscribed Nach Vernet, 19thC, 3½in (9cm) diam.
£200-220 *CSK*

SOVEREIGN HOLDERS

Three metal sovereign/money holders.
£12-60 each *VB*

A Continental gilt lined snuff box, base and sides guilloche enamelled, with enamelled lid, London import marks, 3in (7.5cm) long.
£600-625 *CSK*

A leather purse sovereign holder.
£15-20 *VB*

SPORT

Although some fishing equipment can be expensive the highest prices seem to be reserved for golfing memorabilia. The world record for a golf club is over £90,000. Golf balls, especially the feather type, made from compressed goose down, are also highly prized. This year racquet game items, as well as pre-war skiing equipment, have been included.

The most interesting items to appear recently for sale and which obtained high prices are the Lonsdale belts awarded to Henry Cooper, the ex-British Heavyweight Boxing Champion. Remember that other collectables, especially ceramics can have their values greatly enhanced if they have a sporting connection. Use the cross reference boxes to locate where they are in this guide.

Archery

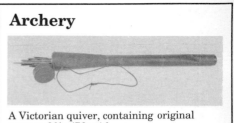

A Victorian quiver, containing original arrows, 30in (76cm) long.
£55-85 *WAB*

Athletics

A silver plate on oak athletics trophy, Charterhouse Athletics Sports, 1882, 7½in (19cm) high.
£25-35 *WAB*

American Football

A 1943 NFL Championship Game programme, Chicago Bears-v-Washington Redskins, the Bears defeated Washington 41-21, near mint condition.
£400-500 *S(NY)*

A 1947 All-America Conference Championship programme, New York Yankees-v-Cleveland Browns at Yankee Stadium, near mint condition.
£350-450 *S(NY)*

AAFC programmes are very scarce as the League was only operational for 2 years.

Badminton

A green tile depicting a game of battledore or shuttlecocks, 19thC, 8 by 12in (20 by 30.5cm).
£75-125 *WAB*

A badminton racquet, 26½in (67.5cm) long.
£8-15 *WAB*

A 1972 USC National Championship Football ring.
£1,000-1,500 *S(NY)*

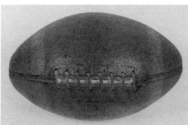

A double lined American football.
£10-20 *WAB*

Baseball

A 125 Louisville Slugger
baseball bat, 34in (86cm) long.
£12-15 *AHL*

A catcher
baseball glove,
11in (28cm)
long.
£12-15 *AHL*

A set of Babe Ruth's underwear
in box, c1930.
£400-450 *S(NY)*

A 1936 Yankees brown bat, bears the facsimile
signatures of 20 members of the World
Champion '36 Yankees team.
£1,200-1,500 *S(NY)*

CROSS REFERENCE
Colour Section ——➤ p346

A Joe DiMaggio game bat,
35in (89cm) long, 34oz.
£4,000-4,500 *S(NY)*

Basketball

A 1962 Bill
Sharman
advertising piece,
Hall of Fame
Series by
Spalding.
£400-450 *S(NY)*

Boules

Two French wood and nails boules,
early 19thC. **£80-100 each** *DMT*

Billiards

A Victorian
automatic billiards
scorer, in mahogany,
chrome and brass,
by George Wight &
Co. London, 9½in
(24cm) wide.
£30-45 *WAB*

A set of boules, in case, 6 by 9in
(15 by 22.5cm). **£75-85** *MofC*

Bowls

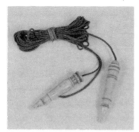

A Victorian bone bowls marker.
£15-20 *WAB*

A silver plated bowls trophy, 3¼in (8.5cm) high.
£25-35 *WAB*

Silver ended presentation bowls with canvas and leather case, 10½in (26cm) long.
£35-55 *WAB*

Boxing

Two silver gilt Lonsdale belts for the Heavyweight Championship of Great Britain, presented to Henry Cooper, hallmarked Sheffield 1961 and 1964, and Mappin & Webb maker's marks, 36in (92cm) long.
£12,000-13,000 each *S*

Four fight tickets for the Heavyweight Championship of the World, September 6, 1892, John L. Sullivan-v-Jas. J. Corbett.
£5,000-5,500 *S(NY)*

A 9ct gold Lonsdale belt for the Heavyweight Championship of Great Britain, presented to Henry Cooper, Sheffield 1936, made by Mappin & Webb, 36in (92cm) long, in case.
£26,000-28,000 *S*

These belts were the property of Henry Cooper who won the Heavyweight Championship of Great Britain 3 times.

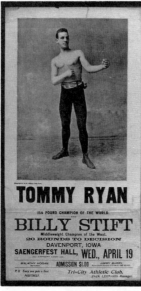

A fight poster for Ryan-v-Stift 1897. **£1,200-1,500** *S(NY)*

A gate card 9/25/1962, for Heavyweight Championship 1962, Patterson-v-Liston.
£250-300 *S(NY)*

Sonny Liston won the championship this night on a first round knockout.

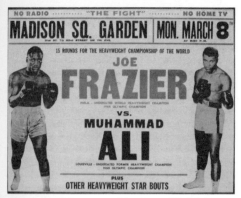

An on site fight poster, Frazier-v-Ali, Madison Square Garden, March 8, 1971.
£1,000-1,500 *S(NY)*

A cricket bat presented by Mr Paul Marples to The Renshaw Cricket Club, 1875, 34½in (88cm) long.
£125-185 *WAB*

A Hammonds cricket bat, autographed, c1935, 34in (86cm) long.
£15-25 *WAB*

Cricket

A Victorian cricket shield, mounted with silver trophy shields, all to F. Napper, 1890-98, 10in (25cm) high.
£75-125 *WAB*

A John Wisden Cricketers' Almanack, published by J. Whitaker and Sons, 1941, original limp cloth.
£280-320 *CSK*

A set of brass topped cricket stumps, 30in (76cm) long.
£35-45 *WAB*

A Staffordshire blue and white Metropolitan scenery meat dish, showing Eton School playing cricket at Windsor Castle, c1850, 19 by 15¼in (48 by 38.5cm).
£740-780 *S*

> CROSS REFERENCE
> **Ceramics**
> **Blue and White** ⟶ p85

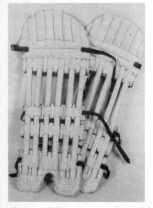

A pair of Victorian cricket pads, 25in (64cm) long.
£45-85 *WAB*

A photo-mechanical process print from an action photograph of Ranjitsinhji, by George W. Bedlam, 1 September 1905, the mount signed by George Bedlam in pencil and Ranjitsinhji in ink, framed and glazed, 27½ by 21in (70 by 53cm).
£950-1,000 *CSK*

- The value of sporting equipment, especially cricket bats and tennis racquets, can be greatly enhanced if they are signed by a famous sporting personality.
- Be wary of signed items (see autograph section) as it is very hard to prove their authenticity.

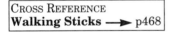

Gubby Allen's photograph album of 'The Bodyline' tour of Australia, New Zealand and America 1932-33, containing over 320 photographs. **£8,750-9,500** *DN*

CROSS REFERENCE
Walking Sticks ➤ p468

A walking stick, the handle carved in the shape of Spofforth, the Demon Bowler, late of Derbyshire, c1890. **£350-400** *S*

Fencing

A fencing mask, c1920, 13in (33cm) high. **£16-18** *AHL*

A selection of fencing foils, 42in (106.5cm) long. **£10-15 each** *WAB*

A sabre, 41in (104cm) long and a foil 42in (106.5cm) long, c1930. **£16-18 each** *AHL*

Croquet

Two Cassiobury croquet mallets, 37in (94cm) long. **£10-20 each** *WAB*

Four red bands on the handle mean that this mallet came from a set of 8.

A croquet mallet, with brass bands on lignum vitae, 29in (73.5cm) long. **£35-65** *WAB*

Cycling

A cyclist's leather racing helmet, 10in (25cm) long. **£15-20** *WAB*

Football

A leather football, c1930.
£10-20 *WAB*

A pair of football boots, c1960.
£10-20 *WAB*

A framed handkerchief
featuring West Bromwich
Albion football team, F.A. Cup
Final 1931, 17 by 16in (43 by
40.5cm).
£35-65 *WAB*

A pair of football boots, c1930.
£20-25 *AHL*

An English football, mid-19thC.
£75-125 *WAB*

Golf

A boxed wrapped set of 11
Ocobo gutta-percha golf balls,
stamped James B Halley, 76
Finsbury Pavement, London
EC, c1895, **£4,000-4,500** and
a similar box containing 12 golf
balls in very good condition.
£6,500-6,700 *S*

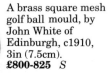

A brass square mesh
golf ball mould, by
John White of
Edinburgh, c1910,
3in (7.5cm).
£800-825 *S*

A hand hammered gutta-percha
golf ball, in fair condition,
c1870.
£950-975 *S*

A McEwan putter, with
thorn head and hickory
shaft, c1855.
£700-750 *S*

A square mesh gutty golf ball
mould, ball size 27, by John
White & Co. Edinburgh, in
perfect condition, c1895, 3¾in
(9.5cm) high.
£1,200-1,300 *S*

A late deep faced rut iron, shaft
split, c1900.
£300-325 *S*

A giant scared head driver, with persimmon head and hickory shaft, by James Sherlock of Stoke Poges, c1920, 53½in (135cm) long.
£1,600-1,700 *S*

This club was supposed to have been made for a member who accused Sherlock of never making a club 'man enough' for him, but in fact made by Sherlock as an advertising gimmick to hang in his shop.

A long nosed brassie, by Jack Morris of Hoylake, with beech head and hickory shaft, c1885.
£500-550 *S*

A long nosed putter, by Robert Forgan, c1885. **£600-650** *S*

A Simplex patent lofter, with torpedo shaped head, hickory shaft and American leather cloth grip, in used condition, c1900.
£1,650-1,750 *S*

A McEwan of Musselburgh long nosed short spoon, with beech head and hickory shaft, c1880.
£900-950 *S*

A long nosed long spoon, with beech head, hickory shaft and rams horn insert to leading edge, by Tom Morris of St Andrews, c1880, 45in (114cm), and a smooth faced iron, c1905.
£1,350-1,450 *S*

An unnamed rut iron, with a 5½in hosel and hickory shaft, c1830.
£2,000-2,250 *S*

A Dunn one-piece driver, by Bridgeport Gun & Implement Company, from one piece of hickory, in original condition, c1905.
£850-875 *S*

A long nosed short spoon, with beech head and hickory shaft, by Hugh Philp of St Andrews, c1835.
£9,500-10,000 *S*

An Artisan Golfers Association Northern Section Sunday Challenge Shield, winners' inscribed shields variously hallmarked 1918-31, 21½in (55cm) high, in maroon velvet lined box.
£1,800-1,900 *S*

A Dunlop plaster figure with golf ball head, in reasonable condition, 20thC, 16in (40cm) high.
£475-525 *S*

A Parker Brothers 'The Popular Game of Golf' table game, American, c1900, 14 by 21in (35.5 by 53cm).
£730-760 *S*

A golfing Hole in One coin-in-slot machine, requiring great skill to obtain your chewing gum, c1955, 11¾ by 7½in (30 by 18cm). **£600-625** *S*

24 Rules of Golf for Perrier Water, 3rd edition, by Charles Crombie, enclosed in a folder, each print and folder bears the Perrier Water embossed stamp, c1927.
£740-780 *S*

A Royal Ashdown Forest Golf Club Challenge Shield, presented by the officers of the First South Western Mounted Brigade, hallmarked London 1915, 22 by 17in (56 by 43cm).
£900-950 *S*

A spelter golfing figure, on a marble base, with replacement club, 8½in (21cm) high.
£275-300 *S*

A white metal cigarette case and a set of 25 Players cigarette cards, 1939.
£130-160 *S*

A studio photograph of old Tom Morris, autographed by himself, dated 1902, 5¼ by 4in (13 by 10cm).
£2,250-2,450 *S*

Hockey

A hockey trophy, c1932.
£20-30 *WAB*

A hockey stick, 32in (81cm) long.
£10-15 *WAB*

Ice Hockey

A complete set of 51 cards, Parkhurst Hockey Set, 1961/62.
£660-680 *S(NY)*

A Northland hockey stick, used by Gordie Howe, autographed twice by Howe, near mint condition, mid-1970s.
£1,400-2,500 *S(NY)*

A hockey stick, used by Marcel Dionne, early to mid-1970s.
£240-250 *S(NY)*

Hurling

A hurling stick, 35in (89cm) long.
£10-15 *WAB*

Lacrosse

Two lacrosse sticks, 43in (109cm) long.
£16-18 each *AHL*

Skiing

A pair of ski's, c1960, 38in (96.5cm) long.
£38-40 *AHL*

A pair of wooden ski's, c1930, 38in (96.5cm) long.
£75-80 *AHL*

Rugby

A rugby ball, 10½in (26cm) long.
£15-25 *WAB*

Table Tennis

An Edwardian table tennis bat, 10¾in (27cm) long.
£10-20 *WAB*

Tennis

Two lawn tennis measures,
4 and 5in (10 and 12.5cm) diam.
£20-35 *WAB*

A desk tidy, comprising a brass
tennis net suspending a small
gong engraved with players, an
inkwell in the form of a tennis
ball, and a giant paper clip in
the form of a tennis racquet,
c1890, 8in (20cm) high.
£575-625 *CSK*

A tennis racquet, 1920s,
26½in (67.5cm) long.
£25-45 *WAB*

A mahogany racquet press, with
brass fittings, R. Whitty,
Liverpool, leather strap
missing, c1890, 27¾in
(70.5cm) long.
£70-75 *AHL*

A Regulation tennis racquet
and 'The Grip' press, by
F.H. Ayres Ltd, c1920-1925.
£15-25 *WAB*

STANHOPES

- **Stanhopes were made from a variety
  of materials - bone, wood, metal and
  even plastic.**
- **Made specifically for the souvenir
  market.**
- **Named after the Earl of Stanhope,
  who invented the tiny lens inside.**
- **David Brewster had the idea of
  putting photographs inside, thus
  producng the first 'Stanhope', c1855.**
- **Most items found today date from
  after the 1890s, but items were still
  produced until the 1960s.**

Four metal bookmarks, with
views of Southsea, Alton, Great
Malvern and Killarney, 3½ to
4½in (8.5 to 11cm) long.
£25-50 each *PC*

Two rosaries, 9½
and 12in long,
(23.5 and 30.5cm)
long.
£20-30 each *PC*

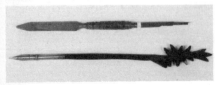

Two wooden dip pens.
£20-25 each *VB*

Two needle cases,
2¾in and 3½in
(7 and 8.5cm) long.
£35-45 each *PC*

l. A brooch, with a view of
Bowness, 1½in (3.5cm) diam.
r. An ivory pincushion, with
views of Edinburgh, 1¾in
(9cm) diam.
£35-45 each *PC*

A walking stick, incorporating a
pen, with a view of a lady with a
parasol, 32½in (82cm) long.
£100-130 *PC*

A selection of charms with
views of towns, including a
church with the Lords Prayer, ½
to ¾in (1 to 2cm) high.
£15-25 each *PC*

A pipe with a deer skin stem,
and a wooden pipe, 5½in
(13.5cm) and 4½in (11cm) long.
£35-50 each *PC*

l. A button hook, with views of
Llandudno, 3¼in (8cm) long.
£40-50
r. A 9ct gold watch key, with
views of Paris.
£75-85 *PC*

A selection of miniature Irish
bogwood Stanhopes, made in
France, 1¼ to 1¾in (3 to 4.5cm)
long. **£15-25 each** *PC*

A gold metal cross, with the
Lord's Prayer, 1¾in (4cm) long.
£25-35 *PC*

A selection of manicure sets, 2½
to 3½in (6.5 to 8.5cm) long.
£20-30 each *PC*

A watch and chain, 12½in
(31.5cm) long.
£45-55 *PC*

Two penknives:
l. With a view of the Eiffel
Tower, Paris.
r. With a nude view, Souvenir of
Habana.
£35-45 each *PC*

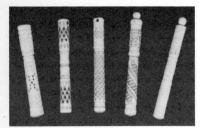

A selection of needle holders, 3½ to 4½in (8.5 to 11.5cm) long.
£25-35 each   *PC*

A selection of late Victorian miniature Stanhopes, in bone, ivory and bog oak, 1in (2.5cm) long.   **£12-25 each**   *VB*

TAXIDERMY

A mahogany and glazed case containing a stuffed fox, stoat, pheasant and birds, 35½ by 30¾in (90 by 78cm).
£180-200   *BIR*

A mounted stag's head, with 14 points, 1933.
£220-240   *P(O)*

TEA CADDIES

A George III mahogany marquetry tea caddy, 5in (12.5cm) high.
£580-600   *Mit*

A fruitwood tea caddy, 4in (10cm) wide.
£35-40   *SAD*

A japanned tea canister, some damage and rusting, mid-19thC.
£230-250   *WIL*

A Victorian walnut dome lidded tea caddy, inlaid with Tunbridge ware decoration, fitted interior with 2 small boxes and a glass mixing bowl, 12in (30.5cm) wide.
£380-400   *GAK*

A George II silver tea caddy, probably by John Newton, London 1731, 4in (10cm) high, 7oz.   **£650-675**   *CAG*

A walnut tea caddy with sarcophagus shaped lid, the fitted interior with 2 boxes and mixing bowl, early 19thC, 15in (38cm) wide.   **£380-400**   *GAK*

CROSS REFERENCE
Treen ———————➤ p463
Tunbridgeware ➤ p465

A George IV rosewood tea caddy, in the shape of a twin pedestal sideboard, with original glass bowl, c1820, 18½in (47cm) long.
£1,100-1,200 *AMH*

A Sheraton period tea caddy, c1780, 8¼in (21cm) high.
£350-400 *AMH*

TELEPHONES

A British candlestick telephone, type No. 150, complete with bell set type No. 25, c1928, 13in (33cm) high.
£350-380 *OTC*

A candlestick telephone, type No. 2, complete with bell set, No. 25, c1912.
£400-500 *OTC*

A candlestick telephone, c1907.
£100-150 *COB*

A telephone type No. 232, with bell set No. 26, c1937.
£150-200 *OTC*

A Belgian desk telephone, c1940.
£150-170 *OTC*

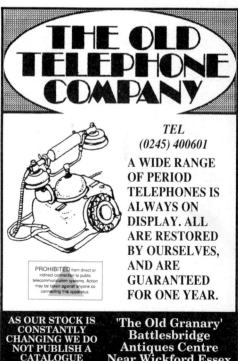

A Danish desk telephone, type No. D08, c1908.
£350-400   *OTC*

A Danish telephone, type No. D30, dated 1930.
£170-210   *OTC*

A desk telephone, type 332, made by Siemens Bros, 1950s.
£70-80   *OTC*

A British telephone, type 312, c1954.   **£100-120**   *OTC*

A desk telephone, probably Hungarian, made by Siemens & Halske in Germany for export, c1956.   **£180-220**   *OTC*

A Queen's Silver Jubilee telephone in Balmoral blue, with wall mounted bell set, 1977.   **£130-150**   *OTC*

A Belgian wall phone, red with gold transfer and black hand set, c1953.
£110-120   *OTC*

A red desk telephone, type No. 332, c1950s.
£320-350   *OTC*

A Belgian telephone, with accompanying cow bell set, 1940s.
£170-190   *OTC*

A GEC Muraphone
from the SS Canberra,
c1961. **£160-180** *OTC*

A GEC Muraphone desk
telephone, from SS Canberra,
c1961. **£100-120** *OTC*

A bronze telephone notice, c1930.
£50-60 *COB*

CROSS REFERENCE
Shipping ⟶ p387

Shipping ⟶ p387

A desk telephone, type 232,
c1935, with American walnut
bell set type 1AC, c1924, both
made by GEC at Coventry,
wired together.
£250-300 *OTC*

A grey German desk telephone,
1960s. **£30-40** *OTC*

A Swedish desk telephone, by
Ericsson, c1957.
£80-100 *OTC*

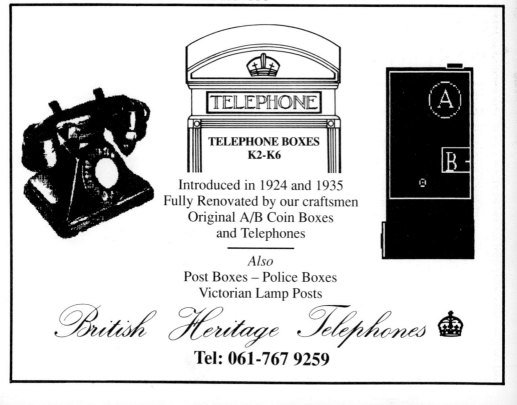

TEXTILES

The variety of collectable textiles available to the collector is enormous. Early needlework and samplers can be expensive if in good condition. However, items of lace and costumes can still be found at reasonable prices making it possible to equip the home with linens and decorative lace at very reasonable prices.

Costume collecting is very popular, with smaller items, notably underwear, gloves, shoes, etc., highly sought after. This is because they are easier to look after and do not require as much storage space as ballgowns and Victorian dresses. Designer costumes and haute couture from the '40s and '50s are also increasing in popularity.

Black Victorian mourning dress has never been particularly desirable with collectors. Always check for fading, repairs, and moth damage, all of which will reduce the value of your collectable.

Babywear & Children's Wear

A pale pink silk and embroidered net baby jacket, c1900.
£30-40 *LB*

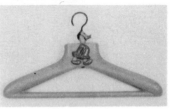

A child's plastic coat hanger, c1950, 12in (30.5cm) wide.
£3-7 *LB*

Bonnets

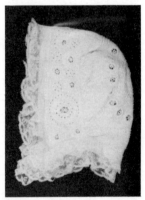

A Victorian white work and broderie anglais baby's bonnet, trimmed with lace.
£45-55 *LB*

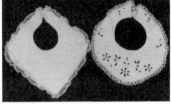

Two Edwardian baby's bibs, lawn and broderie anglaise.
£6-15 each *LB*

A child's petticoat, c1900.
£15-20 *LL*

A child's wooden coathanger, c1930, 10in (25cm) long.
£3-7 *LB*

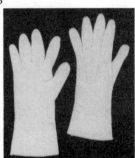

A pair of child's chamois leather gloves.
£10-15 *LB*

A Victorian quilted baby's bib.
£25-35 *LB*

An American silk lace trimmed bonnet, with Mississippi Babywear label, c1920. **£50-70** *LB*

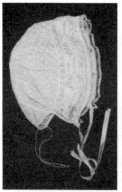

An Ayrshire ware bonnet,
c1880.
£35-50 *LB*

A lawn and lace bonnet,
c1900. **£25-35** *LB*

Christening Robes

A christening gown with
valence lace insertions,
19thC. **£65-85** *LB*

A cutwork christening robe,
c1900.
£85-100 *LB*

A late Victorian cotton
christening robe, 41in (104cm)
long.
£70-80 *LL*

Dresses

A lawn christening robe, with
slip, 19thC.
£45-65 *LB*

A christening robe, 40in
(101.5cm) long.
£95-120 *LL*

A child's bridesmaid outfit, with
hat and shoes, c1930.
£60-70 *LB*

A child's whitework dress,
c1860, 22in (56cm) long.
£45-55 *LL*

A child's lawn dress, c1920.
£20-30 *LB*

A baby's silk hand embroidered
jacket and hat.
£40-45 *PAR*

An Edwardian child's cutwork
dress. **£20-25** *LB*

An early Victorian baby's
embroidered lawn and
lace dress.
£45-55 *LB*

A baby's lawn
dress, c1920.
£18-25 *LB*

Shoes

A pair of
Victorian child's
leather shoes,
5in (12.5cm) long.
£30-40 *LB*

**MAKE THE MOST OF
MILLERS**

Condition is absolutely vital when
assessing the value of any item.
Damaged pieces appreciate much
less than perfect examples.
However, a rare, desirable piece
may command a high price even
when damaged.

A pair of Victorian child's cream
satin shoes.
£20-30 *LB*

A pair of Victorian baby's
beadwork shoes, 5in (12.5cm)
long. **£35-45** *LB*

A pair of Chinese baby's shoes.
£30-45 *LB*

A tin, decorated with a lady and gentleman, 1930s, 9in (22.5cm) wide. **£5-6** *AL*

A Rowntree's Coronation souvenir tin, with medal attached, 5½in (14cm) diam. **£20-25** *TER*

A biscuit tin, decorated with a bus, c1950, 9¼in (23cm) square. **£8-10** *AL*

A Bluebird toffee tin, 9½in (24cm) wide. **£6-8** *AL*

An Edward Sharp toffee tin, decorated with the Silver Fox train, 5½in (14cm) wide. **£20-25** *TER*

A tea tin, 4½in (11.5cm) high. **£4-5** *AL*

A Fancy Biscuit tin, with label, 6½in (16.5cm) wide. **£3-5** *AL*

A Mazawattee tea tin, c1910, 5½in (14cm) high. **£25-30** *TER*

A Pontefract Cakes tin, c1920, 5in (13cm) wide. **£3-5** *AL*

A Sharp's Toffee tin, with guarantee leaflet, c1950, 5½in (14cm) wide. **£5-6** *AL*

A tea tin, 4¼in (11cm) high. **£3-4** *AL*

A Victory V lozenges tin, c1920, 7in (18cm) high. **£10-12** *AL*

A garniture of clock tins, to hold 16lbs of Victory V cough sweets, invented by Jack Haythorne Thwaite, 10½ and 11in (26.5 and 28cm) high. **£125-175** *WAB*

An unbranded tin, 6½in (16.5cm) high. **£25-45** *WAB*

Three sporting advertising tins, 3 to 4in (7.5 to 10cm) wide. **£25-85 each** *WAB*

A McVitie & Price tin, decorated with Victoria Cross episodes, 5¼in (13cm) high. **£125-225** *WAB*

A Huntley & Palmer's clock tin, 11in (28cm) high. **£175-275** *WAB*

Three miniature Rowntree's sweet tins, 1½ to 2in (3.5 to 5cm) high. **£35-85 each** *WAB*

A pair of Huntley & Palmer's Worcester vase tins, 10¼in (26cm) high. **£150-250** *WAB*

A money box tin, with key, representing Queen Mary's doll's house, 3in (7.5cm) wide. **£15-25** *WAB*

A Henderson's log cabin biscuit tin, 4¾in (12cm) high. **£150-250** *WAB*

A Russian tobacco tin, c1890, 6½in (16cm) wide. **£15-25** *WAB*

A Keen's mustard tin, decorated with 'The Rivals', 7in (17.5cm) square. **£45-75** *WAB*

A Hignett's Golden Butterfly Cigarettes tin, 7½in (19cm) long.
£25-45 *WAB*

A Fry's chocolate drum-shaped tin, 3in (8cm) diam.
£30-45 *WAB*

A Coca-Cola sign, from a U.S. Diner, 1950s, 4in (10cm) diam.
£160-180 *COB*

A Carr's Scotch Oaten biscuits advertising plaque.
£130-140 *MAW*

A cardboard and tin Coca-Cola advertising sign, 1950s.
£20-25 *COB*

An unbranded cottage tin, 6¼in (16cm) long.
£35-65 *WAB*

A motor race marshal's vest, 1960s.
£40-50 *COB*

A Chad Valley Happy Days tin money box, 5¾ by 4in (15 by 10cm).
£12-18 *WAB*

Two card shop advertising displays for Chivers Jams.
£35-40 *MAW*

A Rowntree's Grace Darling tin, 11¾in (30cm) long.
£25-35 *WAB*

A Guinness lamp, with box.
£6-7 *COB*

A tinplate limousine, with 4 opening doors, folding rear seats, folding indicators, electric lights and front steering, motor missing, 1930s, 19½in (49cm) long. **£900-950** *S*

A Carette Sedanca de Ville, with opening rear doors and clockwork motor, light scratching, German, c1914, 14in (36cm) long. **£1,800-2,000** *S*

A Distler limousine, with clockwork motor, some rust, dent and scratches, German, c1930, 11¾in (30cm) long. **£575-600** *S*

A variation of a Smith & Cavey Minerva bus, some rust and paint loss. **£725-750** *S*

A Märklin hand painted tinplate four-seater open touring car, with steering wheel adjusting front wheels, cast lamp, clockwork motor driving rear wheels, German, c1905, 8in (20cm) long. **£7,000-7,500** *S*

A Carette lithographed tinplate limousine, with opening rear doors, clockwork motor driving rear wheels, German, c1911, 15¾in (40cm) long. **£6,000-6,500** *S*

A Lehmann Deutsche Reichspost van, with opening rear doors and spring motor, discolouration to roof, German, 1930s, with original box. **£3,000-3,250** *S*

A Chad Valley Green Line double-decker bus, with clockwork motor, English, 1950s, in a No. 10006 London bus box. **£1,600-1,700** *S*

A Distler 'Fares Please' bus, with 3 passengers and moving conductor, clockwork motor, German, c1928, 9in (22.5cm) long. **£1,800-1,900** *S*

A Carette rear entrance tonneau saloon, one tyre missing, paint loss and scratching, German, c1908, 12in (30.5cm) long. **£3,500-3,750** *S*

An Ingap tinplate clockwork motorcycle and rider, slight scratching, Italian, c1930, 7½in (19cm) long.
£720-740 *S*

An Ingap clockwork motorcycle and rider, slight scratching, Italian, c1937, 8in (20cm) long.
£700-750 *S*

A Paya tinplate motorcycle and rider, Spanish, c1940, 11in (28cm) long, with 3 smaller motorcycles.
£625-650 *S*

A Tipp fire engine, with 4 firemen and extending ladder, bell replaced, German, 1930s, 23in (58cm) long. **£1,500-1,700** *S*

A Bing clockwork 'Shell' tanker, paint chipped, German, early 1920's, 10½in (26cm) long.
£1,800-1,900 *S*

A Tipp clockwork Royal Mail van, with front steering, rear opening doors, German, 1920s.
£2,250-2,500 *S*

A Tipp 'APC' petrol tanker, with clockwork motor, some rust and scratches, German, c1925, 9½in (24cm) long.
£1,500-1,700 *S*

A Tipp tinplate clockwork motorcyclist with pillion passenger, battery operated headlamp, German, c1926, 9½in (24cm) long. **£900-950** *S*

A pair of Philipp Niedermeier racing motorcyclists, c1960, 6½in (16cm) long. **£500-550** *S*

A Tipp clockwork 'Shell' tanker, slight paint loss, German, 1920s, 9¼in (23.5cm) long.
£2,800-3,200 *S*

A J.M.L. tinplate clockwork motorcyclist and torpedo shaped sidecar, French, c1928, 8in (20.5cm) long.
£1,000-1,100 *S*

An Ingap clockwork motorcyclist, Italian, with mechanism operating rear wheel, paintwork chipped, c1938, 8in (20cm) long.
£750-800 *S*

A Nomura Toys Cadillac convertible tinplate car, Japanese, early 1950's, 13¼in (34cm) long. **£900-950** *S*

A Spot-On presentation car set, by Tri-ang, comprising a Triumph TR3, Bentley Sports Saloon, Jaguar 3.4 litre, BMW Isetta and Austin A40, c1959, in original box. **£450-500** *CSK*

A McLoughlin Bros. Bulls and Bears Great Wall Street Game, complete, c1883, 15½ by 12in (39 by 30.5cm). **£10,000-11,000** *CNY*

A tinplate clockwork paddle boat, 'Emma', with zinc plate hull, paint loss and damage, German or French, c1895, 22in (56cm) long. **£9,000-10,000** *S(NY)*

A Marusan tinplate friction drive Cadillac, electric headlights, Japanese, c1950, 12¾in (32cm) long. **£1,600-1,700** *S*

A Tipp tinplate double garage, with opening double doors, German, 1920s, 11 by 10in (28 by 25cm). **£125-150** *S*

A Lehmann painted and lithographed tinplate spring-motor 'Mandarin' Chinese sedan chair, No. EPL No. 565 in original box. **£2,000-2,250** *CSK*

A Dinky Toy/Hornby Series 28/1 part set of 4 delivery vans, with contemporary addition of another van and a truck, c1935, in original trade box. **£6,000-6,500** *CSK*

A Gama electric Cadillac, German, and a Japanese tinplate Lincoln, both c1950. **£1,750-2,000** *S*

r. A very rare Scalextric C70 Type 59 Bugatti racing car, 1963, 5in (12.5cm) long. **Est. £2,500-3000** *CSK*

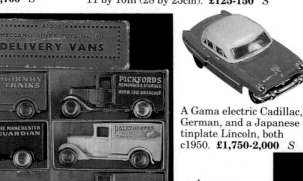

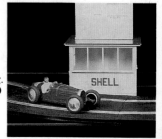

A gold mohair bear, 'Fido', hard stuffed with wood shavings, with growler, c1920, 16in (41cm) high. **£150-200** *TED*

A plush Sooty bear, unjointed, c1960s, 14in (35cm) high. **£10-20** *TED*

A mother bear, holding twins, English, 15in (38cm) high **£200-300** *TED*

A Steiff Alfonzo replica bear of the 1908 original, c1990, 13in (33cm) high. **£250-275** *TED*

This is an actual size replica of the original, owned by a Russian princess, which fetched a world record price of £12,100 in 1989.

A Merrythought mohair bear, kapok filled, with button in right ear and oversewn claws, c1935, 15½in (39cm) high. **£200-300** *TED*

A Tunbridge ware pin box, with sliding pincushion top, c1900, 3½ by 2in (8 by 5cm). **£35-40** *HAY*

A Tunbridge ware stationery box, with view of Eridge Castle, c1870. **£500-600** *AMH*

A Lamont Tartan ware stationery box, with fitted interior, 9 by 6in (22.5 by 15cm). **£385-400** *LBL*

A Tartan ware rattle, or bird scarer, in poor condition, 8in (20cm). **£135-155** *LBL*

A Victorian Tartan ware souvenir box, 2⅓ by 3½in (6 by 9cm). **£35-40** *HAY*

A Tartan ware stationery box, with painted panel of Balmoral Castle, stamped C. Stiven & Sons, Laurencekirk, 10 by 6in (25 by 15cm). **£685-725** *LBL*

A McLean Tartan ware box, with photograph of Brown's Terrace, Mauchline, 7in (17.5cm) long. **£165-175** *LBL*

A Prince Charlie Tartan ware notebook, with painted panel of the Scott Monument, 3½in (9cm). **£125-135** *LBL*

Three Victorian Tartan ware whist markers. **£60-70 each** *HAY*

A Tartan ware album containing lithographic views of The Trossachs, 4 by 6in (10 by 15cm). **£145-155** *LBL*

A Tunbridge ware writing slope, with a view of Tonbridge Castle, c1870, 14¾in (37.5cm) wide. **£1,300-1,400** *AMH*

Two agate watch keys, with steel or ormolu mounts.
£100-200 each *BER*

A Breguet 18ct gold openface watch, dial and movement signed, No. 4333, case numbered, c1925, 45mm diam.
£1,800-2,200 *S(NY)*

A Swiss gentleman's 18ct gold pocket watch, with musical quarter repeat cylinder, c1830.
£3,000-4,000 *BER*

r. An 18ct gold half-hunter keyless jewelled fob watch.
£425-450 *CSK*

A silver and mother-of-pearl triangular Masonic watch, Tempor Watch Co, Genève, c1920, with a silver mystery watch. **£2,000-2,500** *S(NY)*

A Cartier 9ct gold roulette wheel watch, 1938, 41mm diam.
£5,000-5,500 *S(NY)*

An 18ct gold openface keyless lever chronograph pocket watch, signed Mappin & Webb, c1902.
£650-675 *CSK*

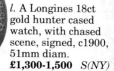

l. A Longines 18ct gold hunter cased watch, with chased scene, signed, c1900, 51mm diam.
£1,300-1,500 *S(NY)*

An Art Nouveau silvered metal openface tourbillon watch, c1915, 56mm diam.
£2,000-2,500 *S(NY)*

A Swiss miniature pendulum clock, c1920, 3in (7.5cm) high.
£100-125 *BER*

A 9ct gold engine-turned purse watch, with Swiss jewelled movement, the square case with cabochon thumbpiece, Glasgow import marks for 1930. **£425-450** *CSK*

A Viennese lady's desk clock, hallmarked silver and lapis lazuli with gold birds, 3½ by 2¼in (9 by 6cm).
£400-600 *BER*

An Ekco transistor radio, in working order, 1958, 4 by 7¾in (10 by 19.5cm). **£15-25** *RMV*

A Champion valve radio, with Bakelite case, FM only, 1961, 12½in (32cm) wide. **£20-35** *RMV*

A McMichael TM54 405 line TV, BBC only, 1952, 18in (46cm) wide. **£35-50** *RMV*

A Fleetwood plastic globe transistor radio, with chrome finish controls, 1960s, 6in (15cm) diam. **£50-75** *RMV*

A Philips 342A 'Music Maid' AC mains valve radio, pre-set tuning clock/alarm/radio, in Bakelite case, 1954, 12½in (32cm) wide. **£25-50** *RMV*

A GEC BT302 slimline television, with 13 channels, 17in (43cm), in bow fronted wooden cabinet, 1959. **£30-50** *RMV*

An Ekco U29 AC/DC valve radio, with Bakelite case, 1946, 12in (31cm) wide. **£30-60** *RMV*

An Icom World clock, cast metal base, plastic globe and liquid crystal display, 7½in (19cm) high. **£40-50** *RMV*

A Bush TU22 television, BBC 405 lines, 9in (23cm) screen, with Bakelite case, 1950, 15in (38cm) square. **£150-250** *RMV*

l. A Sobell 439 'Jelly Mould' valve radio receiver, with painted Bakelite case, 1949, 9in (23cm) wide. **£30-50** *RMV*

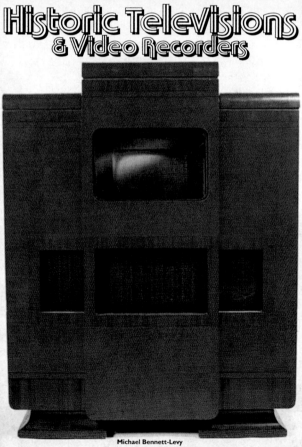

An Omega gold
calendar and
moonphase
wristwatch.
£1,800-1,900 *C*

A Patek Philippe
steel waterproof
automatic backwind
wristwatch.
£1,800-1,900 *C*

A Universal Watch Co.
gold single button
chronograph wristwatch,
1920s, 39mm diam.
£2,500-2,750 *C*

An Audemars
Piguet gold
wristwatch,
18 jewels.
£4,500-4,750 *C*

A Cartier gold
lady's wristwatch,
signed movement.
£1,800-1,900 *C*

A Patek Philippe
lady's 18ct pink
gold watch, with
bracelet, c1945.
£3,500-4,000
S(NY)

An Audemars Piguet
18ct gold 'star wheel'
automatic wristwatch,
36mm diam, with black
leather strap.
£4,500-5,000 *C*

A Patek Philippe
lady's 18ct pink gold
wristwatch, with
bracelet, c1960.
£2,500-3,000 *S(NY)*

A Bertolucci 'Pulchra'
stainless steel quartz
calendar wristwatch,
with moonphase.
£675-700 *S*

A Rolex Prince 9ct two-
colour gold duo-dial
wristwatch, 15 jewels,
1930, 42mm long.
£3,500-3,800 *S*

r. A Vacheron
Constantin white gold
automatic calendar
wristwatch, the signed
movement with gold
rotor and 36 jewels.
£1,250-1,350 *C*

l. Tibet, PWB 170, from the Pop Swatch Collection 1992. **£35-45** *Bon*

Louis Louis Swatch watch, GR 106, Stucchi, GN107, Versailles, 1990. **£170-180** *Bon*

r. A Chicchirichi Swatch watch, GR 112, American Easter Special, 1992, with special 'egg-box' packaging. **£100-110** *Bon*

Marmorata Swatch watch, GB 119, Blake's, late 1987. **£90-100** *Bon*

Lots of Dots, GZ 121, collector's Swatch watch No. 2, with original packaging, 1992. **£140-150** *Bon*

Sign of Samas Swatch watch, GX 105 watch, Paris Costes, late 1988. **£85-100** *Bon*

Calfatti Swatch watch, GK 105, Vienna Deco, late 1987. **£90-110** *Bon*

Twelve Flags Swatch watch, GS101, Skipper, mid-1984. **£200-215** *Bon*

Putti Swatch watch, PWK 168, designed by Vivienne Westwood, Pop Swatch Collection 1992. **£90-100** *Bon*

Sloane Ranger Swatch watch, GX 104, Maybridge, late 1988. **£100-110** *Bon*

Navy Berry Swatch watch, SCR 100, Chronograph Collection, mid-1991. **£110-120** *Bon*

r. Mark Swatch watch, GM 106, Franco, GG 110, Colour of Money, mid-1991. **£130-140** *Bon*

A boulle candle holder/seal tray, retailed by Aspreys.
£225-265 *DAB*

A cased knife and fork, with mother-of-pearl handles, Sheffield 1905. **£150-175** *DAB*

A brass hand paperweight, 19thC.
£100-135 *DAB*

A Mordan triple pencil, mid-19thC.
£125-160 *DAB*

A glass and silver stamp moistener.
£100-140 *DAB*

A Waterman's 25th Anniversary letter opener, hallmarked Chester 1908.
£250-285 *DAB*

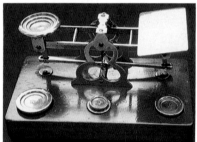

A pair of Mordan postal scales.
£200-265 *DAB*

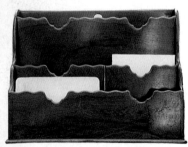

A figured rosewood stationery rack, 19thC. **£250-300** *DAB*

A Continental inkwell, c1920.
£60-80 *BAT*

A Mordan card dispenser shoe, Chester 1909.
£100-135 *DAB*

An olivewood cart inkwell.
£125-165 *DAB*

r. A dog's head inkwell and pen holder, 19thC.
£150-175 *DAB*

l. A Parker Duofold Senior pen and pencil set, with Duofold nib and unusual imprint, 1927 pattern.
£325-350 *Bon*

l. A Parker silver pearl Oversize Vacumatic pen and pencil set, with two-colour arrow nib and original price stickers, c1935, with box.
£425-450 *Bon*

r. A Wahl Eversharp Burmah green Oversize Doric pen and pencil, with No.10 adjustable nib, c1937.
£420-450 *Bon*

l. A red Mont Blanc 246 pen, with No.6 nib, 1940s.
£190-210 *Bon*

l. A Parker blue/black pearl Duofold Senior pen, with 'N' nib, c1945.
£220-240 *Bon*

l. A Mont Blanc 264-F pen, with No.6 nib, 1940s.
£180-200 *Bon*

r. A Mont Blanc Red EF Masterpiece pen, with 4810 nib, 1920s.
£280-300 *Bon*

r. A Parker silver/red Brickwork Victory pen, with 'N' nib, lacking tip, c1935.
£210-225 *Bon*

r. A Parker Lapis Lucky Curve Senior pen, with Duofold nib, c1927.
£280-300 *Bon*

l. A Parker Lapis Senior Duofold pen, with Duofold nib, c1930.
£320-340 *Bon*

r. A Conway Stewart Cracked Ice Executive 60 pen, with wide cap band and Duro nib, 1950s.
£150-170 *Bon*

l. A Parker brown/black Victory MkI pen, with 'N' Parker nib, c1946.
£180-190 *Bon*

l. A Pullman Lapis Automatic pen, with Pullman nib, c1934.
£660-720 *Bon*

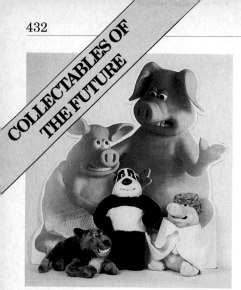

In 1993 Buckingham Palace opened its doors to the public for the first time and a number of commemorative items were produced in limited editions, including the mints, chocolates, first day cover and coin shown here. Already, some items are no longer available. **Mints/chocolates £3 each, 1st day cover £2, coin £5**

A collection of soft toys inspired by the British television commercial advertising the benefits of electricity. Their appeal, combined with their association with a famous advertising campaign, makes it likely that the toys will be sought after long after the adverts have ceased to be broadcast. **Large soft toys as shown, £20, small toys £10**

A Jelly Belly Bean machine, a refillable glass topped container which doubles as a savings bank and requires a coin to be inserted before it releases any beans. **£53 filled**

COLLECTABLES OF THE FUTURE

No-one knows what is going to be collectable in the future, but a good rule of thumb is to look for items that have a combination of innate appeal and an association with a notable person or event, and preferably are in limited supply. Disposable items will, by their very nature, be in short supply in future so any that survive will be highly sought after. Collect the original item, if it becomes popular cheaper imitations may soon appear on the market.

Above all remember: collect what you like and you won't be disappointed, the added bonus will come if your collectable suddenly becomes the one that everyone wants.

A John 'Greenshoots' Major Toby jug, from the Kevin Francis series, by Peggy Davies, one of a limited edition of 150 Midshipmate Fiddlers, in the style of the earliest Toby jugs, 9in (22.5cm) high. **£150** *ZKF*

Two disposable cameras. If any survive intact with their packaging they are likely to become highly collectable in the future, especially older models that become obsolete as they are replaced by updated versions. **£4-6**

Two tubes of M&M's chocolates with M&M Christmas figures. The M&M figures also come in a variety of sporting poses and are sure to have collectable value in years to come. **£1.50 filled**

Beadwork

An American Indian beadwork bag, c1880, 6in (15cm) square. **£35-40** *PSC*

A Victorian beaded bag, 6in (15cm) high. **£60-65** *SAD*

A beadwork bag, c1920. **£20-40** *LB*

A Victorian beaded bag, with jet frame and handle, 10in (25cm). **£50-55** *SAD*

An Edwardian beadwork bag, with a metal frame, 7in (18cm) square. **£40-60** *LB*

A beadwork bag, c1920. **£30-40** *LB*

An American Indian beadwork bag, c1930, 5in (12.5cm) high. **£25-30** *PSC*

An Edwardian beadwork tea cosy, 15in (38cm) long. **£35-65** *LB*

Costume

An embroidered wall pocket, c1830, 13in (33.5cm) high. **£130-140** *PSC*

A pair of Edwardian fine lawn divided leg bloomers. **£28-38** *LL*

A straw boater, c1920. **£28-30** *AHL*

A Victorian nightdress, 47in (119cm) long.
£40-50 *LL*

A heather tweed suit, with braid trimmed pockets, labelled in nape Chanel, c1960s.
£800-850 *CSK*

A late Victorian cotton camisole.
£15-25 *LL*

A yellow silk/satin ballgown, with bead trim to bodice, c1890.
£250-350 *CC*

A mushroom coloured silk brocade dress, with floral design and pagoda sleeves, c1850. **£400-500** *CC*

A green silk dress, with net over dress and heavy bead trim, weighted hem and black sash, c1910.
£200-300 *CC*

A silver grey silk cut velvet gown, with floral motif, side fastening, c1900. **£150-250** *CC*

A green gauze over white cotton two-piece dress, with black silk trim to sleeve and hemline, c1880.
£100-200 *CC*

An Edwardian lace blouse.
£30-50 *LB*

An Edwardian satin skirt.
£30-50 *LB*

An Edwardian lawn blouse.
£45-55 *LL*

A Victorian petticoat, 37in
(94cm) long.   **£40-55** *LL*

A selection of doyleys, 10 to 12in
(25 to 30.5cm) diam. **£3-6 each** *LB*

Doyleys

A Victorian
doyley, 11in
(28cm) diam.
£4-5 *LL*

A carricknacross
lace doyley,
6½in (16cm) wide,
and a filet lace
doyley, 8in (20cm)
square.
£3-5 each *LL*

An Irish crochet doyley, 6½in
(16cm) wide.   **£4-6** *LL*

A set of 4 doyleys, each embroidered with a
nursery rhyme, 8in (20cm) diam. **£20-25** *LB*

CROSS REFERENCE
**Children's
Ceramics** ⟶ p91

Handkerchiefs

A handmade lace handkerchief, 11in (28cm) square.
£15-25 *LL*

A silk handkerchief, with machine lace edging, 12in (30.5cm) square.
£25-30 *LB*

An early Victorian lawn and whitework handkerchief.
£40-50 *LB*

A Honiton lace hankerchief, c1900, 10in (25cm) square.
£15-25 *LB*

A Victorian needlepoint handkerchief, 12 by 14in (30.5 by 35.5cm).
£20-30 *LB*

A Honiton lace handkerchief, 11in (28cm) square.
£15-30 *LL*

Lace

A needlepoint lace fichu, 19thC.
£35-45 *LB*

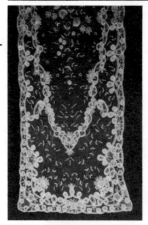

A lace runner, early 1900, 60in (152cm) long.
£45-55 *LL*

A Brussels handmade lace dress front, 15½in (39cm) long.
£20-25 *LL*

- **Never pin lace to a backing for display purposes as the pins will rust and stain the lace.**
- **Store lace flat between sheets of acid free tissue paper.**
- **Do not display needlework in direct sunlight as the colours will soon fade and the threads weakened.**

A pair of Normandy lace pillow cases, 28in (71cm) long.
£100-200 *LB*

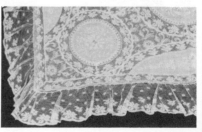

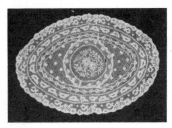

A set of 6 Normandy lace mats.
£60-80 *LB*

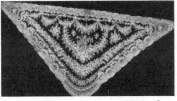

A Brussels appliqué lace triangular
wedding veil of 1860s, 50in (127cm)
deep and long.   **£625-650** *CSK*

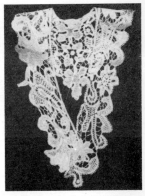

A Branscombe handmade lace
collar, early 1900.
£15-25 *LL*

Quilts

A 'Meadow Lily' quilt, appliquéd
with stems, leaves and
flowerheads on printed cotton,
the ground quilted, American,
mid-19thC, 88 by 74in (223.5 by
188cm).   **£575-625** *CSK*

A patchwork reversible coverlet,
with large panels of printed
cotton fabrics, English, c1850s,
94½ by 75½in (240 by 192cm).
£300-330 *P*

A pair of Honiton lace cuffs,
19thC, 9in (22.5cm) long.
£30-50 *LB*

A Mennonite quilt, with signed
squares, American, Lancaster
County, c1870.
£325-350 *AI*

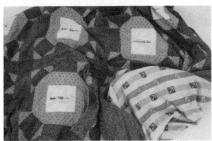

An American blue and white quilt.
£260-285 *AI*

Samplers

A sampler, by Ann Woolnough, some damage, 1797, 20½ by 18½in (52 by 47cm), framed and glazed.
£1,000-1,200 *CSK*

Silkwork

A silkwork picture, c1740, 8¼in (20.5cm) square.
£225-250 *PSC*

TILES

A Wedgwood brown tile, printed 'November', 6in (15cm) square.
£15-18 *TER*

A sampler, the World with all the Modern Discoveries, worked in black and coloured silks, framed and glazed, c1800, 18 by 25in (46 by 64cm).
£875-925 *CSK*

A silkwork picture, replaced glass, 10½ by 7in (26.5 by 17.5cm).
£250-275 *PSC*

A silkwork picture, with history on the reverse, c1820, 8½ by 7½in (21 by 18.5cm).
£550-600 *PSC*

A sampler, with alphabets and a verse, by Marion Murray, 1845, 16 by 12in (40.5 by 30.5cm).
£460-480 *CSK*

A silkwork picture, memorial to Shakespeare, 13 by 10in (33 by 25cm).
£300-335 *PSC*

Two Dutch Delft hand painted tiles, c1870, 5in (12.5cm) square.
£10-15 each *TER*

A Minton printed brown tile, 'Taming of the Shrew' by Moyr Smith, 6in (15cm) square. **£30-35** *TER*

A Minton printed tile designed by Moyr Smith, 6in (15cm) square. **£50-55** *TER*

Two Minton brown and ochre printed tiles, 'In Glasgow Tolbooth', and 'Cymbeline' by Moyr Smith, 6in (15cm) square. **£30-35 each** *TER*

A Minton printed tile, 'Merchant of Venice', by Moyr Smith, initialled MS. **£30-35** *TER*

A Minton tile, in gilt frame, c1810, 8in (20cm) square. **£90-95** *SAD*

TINS, SIGNS & ADVERTISING

A metal standing display from a pub, late 1950s. **£90-120** *COB*

Coca Cola

A bottle opener. **£6-10** *COB*

A glass advertising sign, 1960s. **£20-30** *COB*

A pub sign, The Roebuck, Ansells, 32 by 44in (81 by 111.5cm). **£100-120** *AL*

CROSS REFERENCE
Ceramics
Carlton Ware ⟶ p90

A promotional bottle, c1960, 19¼in (49cm) high. **£30-40** *AA*

Signs

A French enamel
chronometer,
39in (99cm) high.
£350-385 *REL*

A Pratt Ware advertising
plaque, 11½ by 9¼in
(29 by 23cm).
£1,700-1,800 *WIL*

An enamel advertising
sign for Sunlight soap.
£250-300 *SRA*

An enamel advertising sign, Frederick
W. Fitt. **£150-200** *SRA*

Tins

A Huntley & Palmers biscuit
tin, the first to be litho printed,
8½in (21cm) long. **£95-145** *WAB*

A Don
Confectionery
tin, in the
form of a
draughtboard
with draughts,
13 by 6½in
(33 by 20cm).
£35-55 *WAB*

CROSS REFERENCE
Toys & Games ⟶ p444

A Huntley & Palmers
biscuit tin, made in the
form of the F.A. Cup,
15in (38cm) high.
£350-550 *WAB*
*This giant version was
one of only 16 made.*

An unbranded tin, 'The smallest Rabbit in our class', 5¼ by 5in (13 by 12.5cm).
£15-25 *WAB*

A Hignett's 'Pilot' Flake tobacco tin, 6 by 3¼in (15 by 8.5cm).
£20-30 *WAB*

A Thorne's World's Premier Toffee tin, 5½in (14cm) diam.
£15-25 *WAB*

A Squadron Leader Curly Cut Tobacco tin, 4¼ by 3¼in (11 by 8cm).
£15-25 *WAB*

A Cadbury's chocolate tin, with Queens Victoria, Alexandra and Mary on reverse, 8in (20cm) wide. **£8-10** *TER*

An unbranded tin, Punch & Judy, 6in (15cm) diam.
£25-35 *WAB*

An unbranded tin, 'The Nipper', 6in (15cm) diam.
£15-25 *WAB*

Two Lyons Assorted Toffieskotch tins, 11in (28cm) high.
£425-450 *WIL*

A McVitie & Price Jaffa Cakes Express tin, c1980, 7½in (19cm) long.
£10-20 *WAB*

A Huntley & Palmers Gladstone bag tin, 8 by 6in (20 by 15cm).
£30-45 *WAB*

A Cadbury's chocolate tin, showing decoration on underside, c1910, 6½ by 4¼in (16 by 10.5cm).
£10-12 *AL*

A Huntley & Palmers 'The Rude Tin', c1920, 8in (20cm) diam.
£30-45 *WAB*

TOILETRIES
Nail Buffers

A selection of silver nail buffers, 1885-1915.
£15-35 each *VB*

An unbranded commemorative tea tin, Coronation of Edward VIII, c1936.
£15-30 *WAB*

A Huntley & Palmers biscuit tin, c1905, 7in (17.5cm) high.
£30-35 *TER*

Three silver nail buffers, 1900-20.
£14-22 each *VB*

Powder Compacts

An unopened Coty powder box, with design by Lalique, c1935, 2¾in (7cm) diam.
£12-15 *TER*

A painted metal powder compact, 1920s, 3in (7.5cm) diam.
£20-30 *BAT*

A frosted glass powder bowl, with painted and gilded decoration, c1920, 5in (12.5cm) diam.   **£40-60** *BAT*

A painted metal powder compact, c1920, 3in (7.5cm) wide.
£10-15 *BAT*

A French glass powder bowl, c1920, 4in (10cm) diam. **£40-60 BAT**

A lacquered powder compact, c1920, 3in (7.5cm) diam. **£40-60 BAT**

An Art Pottery powder bowl and cover, signed L. Dage, 6in (15cm) diam. **£40-60 OCA**

TOOLS

A mariner's saw, 17in (43cm) long. **£35-45 MofC**

A plane, c1730, 9½in (24cm) long. **£60-68 SAD**

A vineyard spade, c1880. **£20-25 MofC**

CROSS REFERENCE
Horticultural & Farm Implements ———▶p248

A leather tool case, with fittings, c1920, 13½ by 10½in (34 by 26cm). **£40-45 AHL**

An ebony and brass wood scorer, c1850, 7in (17.5cm) long. **£30-35 SAD**

A brace and bit, c1720, 14in (35.5cm) long. **£35-40 SAD**

MAKE THE MOST OF MILLERS

Price ranges in this book reflect what you should expect to *pay* for a similar example. When selling, however, you would expect to receive a lower figure. This will fluctuate according to a dealer's stock and saleability at a particular time, etc. It is always advisable, when selling a collectable, to approach a reputable dealer or an auction house which has specialist sales.

A bull nose rabbit plane, c1725, 5in (12.5cm) long. **£50-55 SAD**

TOYS

The value of all toys is seriously affected by condition, probably more so than any other field of collectables and antiques. The survival and condition of the original packaging, as well as the toy itself, entice serious collectors to pay high prices. Any toy that moves, or has moving parts, is desirable, but remember, if it moves it can break, so particular attention should be paid to originality of parts.

Fakes, unfortunately, are common amongst toy collectors. Tinplate toys, lead soldiers and figures have all received their fair share of attention from fakers. The packaging, if present, can be a good indicator of a reproduction, as this is more difficult to produce and age convincingly. Some of the rarer die-cast toys, especially from the pre-war period, should be carefully checked for authenticity. However, repainting an item does not necessarily mean the model itself is new although it does seriously affect its value. If in doubt about the authenticity of your item seek advice from reputable dealers, auctioneers and your fellow collectors.

A wood and printed paper toy theatre, with shaped proscenium arch, tin footlight holders, recovered with painted canvas, and some hand coloured sets, 28in (71cm) wide.
£740-780 *CSK*

A French pewter doll's dinner set, c1910.
£180-200 *ChL*

A wooden jigsaw puzzle, c1930.
£30-35 *ChL*

A Celluloid clown, c1930, 6in (15cm) high.
£15-25 *KOH*

An American cast iron swan chariot pull-along toy, c1885, 10½in (26cm) long.
£4,700-5,000 *S(NY)*

A musical bisque headed marotte, with conical body containing the musical movement activated by twirling the turned wooden handle, impressed OR, French, c1890, 16in (41cm) high.
£575-625 *S*

CROSS REFERENCE
Dolls ⟶ p138

A wooden long.
scooter, c1900,
24in (61cm)
£50-65 *MofC*

A George Robey pin jar,
Prime Minister of Mirth,
made for him for
publicity, German,
6⅓in (16cm) high.
£80-100 *BCO*

Die-cast

A rubber and wood
hand puppet, pours
milk into a cup, c1930,
9⅜in (24cm) high.
£25-35 *KOH*

A Bing vertical live steam
engine, with double acting
vertical single cylinder, spirit
fired burner, whistle, 13in
(33cm) high.
£200-240 *WAL*

A Mettoy saloon car, c1950, 8in (20cm) long.
£65-70 *ChL*

A Triang coach, good condition,
1960s, 30in (76cm) long.
£100-120 *COB*

A Prameta No. 2 clockwork chrome-finish
Mercedes Benz 300 Saloon, in original box with
key, c1952.
£600-640 *CSK*

Corgi

Three Minic toys: a lorry,
dustcart and a tanker, c1930-
50, 4½in (11cm) long.
£20-75 each *ChL*

A Minic open top car, c1930,
4½in (11cm) long.
£40-45 *ChL*

A Corgi Gift Set No.1
'Carrimore' Car Transporter,
with 4 cars, Ford Consul
Saloon, Vauxhall Velox Saloon,
Hillman Husk, and 2.4 Litre
Jaguar Saloon, in original boxes
contained in original set box.
£350-375 *CSK*

A Corgi Gift Set No.23
Chipperfields Circus Models,
with No.426 Booking Office, in
original box, 1963.
£375-400 *CSK*

A Corgi Mini-Cooper S Monte-
Carlo, painted red and white,
No.339, 1967, with special
leaflet, in original box.
£170-190 *CSK*

Dinky

A Dinky pre-war No.43 RAC Hut, Motor Cycle Patrol and
Guides, in original set box.   **£575-600** *CSK*

A Dinky Toys Private Automobiles
Gift Set No.2 with Packard Super 8
Tourer, Oldsmobile Sedan, Lincoln
Zephyr Coupé, Buick Viceroy
Sedan and Chrysler Royal
Sedan, in original green and
blue mottled set box with Harrods
price label 7/6 to base, c1947.
£1,500-1,600 *CSK*

Disney

A Mickey Mouse Pelham limited edition puppet.
£70-80   *COB*

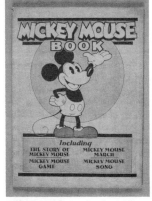

A Mickey Mouse book, with drawings by Walt Disney Studio, story and game by Bobette Bibo, 1930.
£7,750-8,000   *S(NY)*

A Mickey Mouse radio, 1970s.
£10-15   *COB*

A Mickey and Minnie Mouse train, c1930.
£260-280   *ChL*

Games & Puzzles

A Wills's Woodbine cricket game, 4 by 6in (10 by 15cm).
£20-30   *WAB*

A selection of bone and ivory tee to tums, with box, early 19thC, 2in (5cm) high.
£15-28   *VB*

A selection of popular puzzles, 5¼ by 4in (13 by 10cm) each.
£8-12 each *WAB*

A Victorian solitaire board, with marbles, 7¼in (18cm) diam.
£35-45 *WAB*

A set of brass and ebony dominoes, in tortoiseshell box, c1860, 5½ by 3½in (14 by 9cm). **£250-300** *CAI*

A Victorian figured walnut games compendium containing chessman, draughts and various card games, 14½ by 11in (37 by 28cm).
£925-950 *GAK*

A 'Piggy-Wig' puzzle game, 14 by 10in (36 by 25cm).
£20-30 *WAB*

A mahjong set, 10 by 7in (25 by 17.5cm).
£45-85 *WAB*

Two whist counters:
l. In 2 coloured woods, 18thC.
£25-30
r. With ivory markers decorated with jewelled insects, c1785.
£60-70 *SAD*

A Toulmin & Gale games compendium, the coramandel wood case containing ivory, coramandel and rosewood inlaid chequer board, 2 sets of bone and ivory dominoes, bezique board, ivory whist markers, ivory draughts and staunton pattern chessmen, drawer containing bone and bamboo mahjong set, 12½in (32cm) wide.
£720-740 *S*

A set of mini skittles, in a pierced bone holder, early 19thC.
£45-55 *VB*

A solid whist marker, with pointer, 20thC, 1¾in (5cm) diam.
£15-18 *HAY*

The Game of Foot-It, 10½ by 7¼in
(26 by 18cm).
£20-30 *WAB*

A set of Victorian mini
dominoes, contained in a trunk .
£35-45 *VB*

Robots

A piston robot, c1950,
12in (31cm) high.
£75-80 *ChL*

Cribbage Boards

An Edwardian rosewood and sycamore inlaid cribbage
board, 8¾in (22cm) long.
£20-25 *HAY*

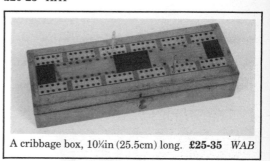

A cribbage box, 10¼in (25.5cm) long. **£25-35** *WAB*

An oak cribbage board, c1892,
26in (66.5cm) long. **£25-30** *SAD*

A Horikawa battery
operated
lithographed tinplate
Fighting Robot,
finished in dark grey,
with gears on the
head and firing gun
in the chest, slight
rusting, c1960,
11in (28cm)
high, in original box.
£200-225 *CSK*

A Nomura battery operated lithographed tinplate Sky
Patrol spaceship, with rotating machine gunner in open
turret, mystery action and blinking jet engines, in
original box, c1960, 13in (33cm) long. **£260-280** *CSK*

Rocking Horses

A late Victorian rocking horse, with leather saddle and bridle, original paintwork.
£1,400-1,500 *CK*

> **For a further selection of Rocking Horses please refer to *Miller's Collectables Price Guide, Vol IV, pp450-453*.**

A tricycle horse, c1880, 30in (76cm) long. **£625-650** *ChL*

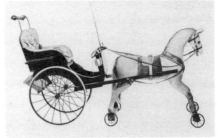

A Victorian child's horse and trap.
£740-780 *WIL*

A rocking horse, probably by Ives Bros., sold by Gamages, original paintwork, c1900.
£975-1,000 *CK*

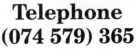

Stuffed Toys

A plush cat, with green glass eyed and plastic whiskers, c1940. **£18-20** *CK*

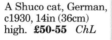

A Herman monkey, German, c1930, 14in (35.5cm) high. **£70-75** *ChL*

A Merrythought elephant, with nylon fur, marked, 1960s, 12½in (32cm) long. **£28-30** *CK*

A Shuco cat, German, c1930, 14in (36cm) high. **£50-55** *ChL*

A French rabbit, c1930, 8in (20cm) high. **£70-75** *ChL*

A stuffed dog, c1930, 8in (20cm) high. **£70-75** *ChL*

A Shuco 'yes/no' monkey, German, c1930, 14in (36cm) high. **£170-180** *ChL*

Pyjama Cases

A Scottie dog, with glass eyes and red felt tongue, possibly by Deans, 16in (40.5cm) long. **£20-22** *CK*

A brown tipped beige mohair dog pyjama case, probably by Chiltern, c1920, 17in (43cm) long.
£30-35 *TED*

A similar bear, rather than a dog, would be worth £100-150.

A French dog pyjama case, c1920, 15in (38cm) long.
£45-50 *ChL*

A Steiff 'Tige' Boston bull terrier, c1912, 16in (41cm) long.
£410-430 *CSK*

'Tige' was the long established companion of the famous American comic character 'Buster Brown', the creation of R.F. Outcault, and together they had a great many unbelievable adventures.

Steiff

The Steiff Company was formed by Margarete Steiff and produced toys from about 1877 until the present day. Over the years the company has become famous for the production of teddy bears. Look for the Steiff button, usually in a teddy bear's left ear, to ensure it is an authentic Steiff toy.

A Steiff velvet Bambi, with button in the ear, 1950s, 5in (12.5cm) high.
£30-35 *CK*

Two Steiff dachshund puppies, with black and white glass eyes, c1955, 5½in (14cm) long.
£30-35 each *CK*

Two Steiff squirrels, 1950s, 5in (13cm) high.
£30-35 each *CK*

A Steiff hen, with yellow, green, red and orange felt feathers, white label, 1117, c1910, 7in (17.5cm) high.
£700-725 *CSK*

A Steiff parrot, c1950, 10in (25cm) high.
£50-55 *ChL*

A Steiff elephant, c1950, 8in (20cm) high.
£35-40 *ChL*

A Steiff leopard, with eyes that glow in the dark, 1930s.
£280-300 *CK*

A Steiff cocker spaniel, with jointed head, black and white plastic eyes and button in the ear, 8in (20cm) long.
£30-35 *CK*

A Steiff elephant, with glass eyes, plastic tusks and felt pads, 1960s, 3½in (9cm) high.
£25-30 *CK*

A pair of Steiff bulldog puppies, with plastic eyes, 1960s, 5in (12.5cm) high.
£35-40 each *CK*

A Steiff hedgehog, with glass eyes, 1960s, 4½in (11cm) high.
£25-30 *CK*

An early Steiff kangaroo, c1913, 14in (36cm) high.
£420-450 *CSK*

A Steiff reindeer, c1950, 11in (28cm) high.
£40-45 *ChL*

Two Steiff puppies, one sitting, with brown glass eyes, 3in (7.5cm) high, the other standing, with black and white glass eyes, 6in (15cm) long, both c1955.
£30-35 each *CK*

Teddy Bears

A Chelsea Lion artist collector's bear, 12in (30.5cm) high.
£100-110 *ChL*

An English teddy bear, c1920, 30in (76cm) high.
£225-250 *ChL*

Two Schuco teddy bear scent bottles, one yellow, one gold plush, heads lift to reveal glass bottles, German, c1925, 5in (12.5cm).
£275-300 each *S*

Two Schuco teddy bears, c1920, 3½in (9cm) high:
l. With blue bead eyes. **£45-50**
r. With yellow metal eyes.
£90-100 *CK*

A teddy bear, with rigid body, marked Farnell Alpha Toys, c1925, 4in (10cm) high.
£45-50 *CK*

A sheepskin bear, made during World War II, with a hand knitted siren suit, 14in (36cm) high.
£20-30 *TED*

A brown 'Berlin' teddy bear, c1950. **£45-60** *COB*

A mohair teddy bear purse, in good condition, maker unknown, 1920s, 9in (23cm) high. **£300-400** *TED*

Three Steiff teddy bears: *l. & r.* Mohair, with white or yellow bead eyes, c1907, 3½in (9cm) high. **£150-200 each** *c.* White mohair, glass eyes, 1905, 5½in (14cm). **£280-300** *CK*

A Schuco lilac mohair scent bottle teddy bear, head lifts to reveal scent bottle, German, 1930s, 3½in (9cm) high. **£200-300** *TED*

Because of its unusual colour, this bear is worth more than a gold version.

A Steiff teddy bear, c1930, 10in (25cm) high. **£125-150** *ChL*

An English bear, with Rexine pads, c1930, 14½in (37cm) high. **£65-70** *CK*

A Joy Toys mohair teddy bear, Australian, 1930s, 12in (30.5cm) high. **£150-250** *TED*

A Schuco yes/no teddy bear, his tail moves his head up and down and from side to side, 1955, 9in (23cm) high. **£200-300** *TED*

A French teddy bear, c1930.
£110-120 *ChL*

A Pedigree teddy bear, with
label reading 'Made in England
expressly for Saks Fifth
Avenue', c1955, 28in (71cm) high.
£350-450 *TED*

An Alpha Farnell brown mohair
teddy bear, with red and blue
label on seam of left arm, 1950s,
10in (25cm) high.
£150-250 *TED*

An English bear, non-jointed,
with square pads, white glass
eyes, 1940s, 12in (30.5cm) high.
£25-30 *CK*

A Farnell golden plush covered
teddy bear cub, with orange and
black glass eyes, squeaker
inoperative, 17in (43cm) high.
£575-600 *CSK*

A cotton plush panda carnival
bear, stuffed with wood shavings,
1950s, 30in (76cm) high.
£20-40 *TED*

A Chad Valley teddy bear, with
button on chest, 1920s, 21in
(53cm) high.
£300-400 *TED*

A Steiff Jackie bear, replica of
1953 original, 7in (17.5cm) high.
£75-85 *TED*
*The replica was made in a
limited edition of 12,000 and is
now sold out. .*

Tinplate

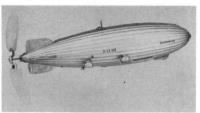

A Tippco clockwork lithographed airship, 'Hindenburg', Registration No. D-LZ 129, with original suspension, string wound on card, in original box, c1936, 11in (28cm) long.
£900-940 *CSK*

A Hercules racing car, with hollow lithographed tyres, the driver with lithographed helmet, American, 1920s, 19in (48cm) long. **£700-900** *S(NY)*

A Bing clockwork four-funnel battle cruiser, repainted, masts replaced, flags missing, c1912, 32½in (82cm) long.
£1,600-1,700 *CSK*

Two Japanese cadillacs, c1960:
l. A Yonezawa saloon, battery operated, 17¾in (45cm) long.
£900-930
r. A Bandai gold cabriolet, with flocked seats and lithographed control panel.
£850-875 *S*

An Arnold clockwork 'Mac 700' motorcycle, lithographed in red and silver, with key, in rare original box, 1954.
£1,100-1,200 *CSK*

A Schuco Elektro Radiant 5600 Vickers Viscount airliner, lithographed in BOAC livery, battery operated, with remote control and instructions, 16in (41cm) long, 19in (48cm) wingspan, in original box.
£540-580 *CSK*

A Schuco Elektro-Construction 6065 tipper lorry, red and grey painted tinplate and plastic, battery operated, remote control in original box, c1955.
£975-1,000 *CSK*

A Wells Brimtoy clockwork mobile field gun, mounted on the back of a four-wheeled lorry, gun with sprung breech, WWII.
£45-50 *WAL*

A George Carette lithographed limousine, good overall condition, German, c1910, 15¾in (40cm) long.
£3,000-3,500 *S(NY)*

A Mettoy clockwork and battery operated searchlight vehicle, light complete with lens and bulb. **£35-40** *WAL*

A Japanese car set, 1950, 10in (25cm) long.
£20-25 *ChL*

A Frog Mark IV Interceptor fighter plane.
£225-250 *W*

A Mettoy clockwork four-door saloon 'Staff Car', WWII.
£90-100 *WAL*

A Chad Valley clockwork single- decker bus.
£60-70 *WAL*

A seaside bucket, by Chad Valley Toys, c1950, 8in (20cm) high. **£20-25** *ChL*

A French clockwork aeroplane, c1920, 13in (33cm) long.
£70-75 *ChL*

A Schuco racing car, c1930, 5½in (14cm) long.
£85-90 *ChL*

A Märklin R-101 airship, with battery operated motor, lacks gondola and one engine, German, c1930, 15½in (39cm) long.
£320-340 *S*

Toy Trains

The Victorians were the first to make toy wooden trains designed to be pushed across playroom floors. Soon after clockwork mechanisms were fitted making them sought after by children of all ages.

The value of toy trains varies enormously making them a collectable to suit most budgets. The toy trains produced at the turn of the century by companies such as Märklin, Bing, Lionel, Carette and Bassett Lowke were priced at the high end of the market and have increased in value significantly over the years.

Frank Hornby's trains on the other hand, were priced and designed to appeal to the mass market. As the founder of Meccano, his company created a wonderful range of affordable railways and trains, including the famous Dublo. Hornby also made Dinky toy cars designed to complement the toy train sets which soon became collectables in their own right.

A 3-rail electric model of the LNER (ex GER) Raven Atlantic 4-4-2 locomotive and tender, No. 727, finished in LNER livery, 18¼in (46.5cm) long.
£375-400 *CSK*

A Bing clockwork lithographed tinplate LNER 4-4-0 locomotive and tender, No. 4390, c1925.
£375-400 *CSK*

A Hornby series Southern No. 2 corridor coach brake composite, in box, c1939.
£170-190 *CSK*

A Hornby Princess Elizabeth locomotive, finished in LMS maroon, complete with original wooden case. **£1,850-2,000** *AH*

A Hornby series electric SR L1
Class E220 locomotive and
tender, in original box, c1938.
£2,250-2,500 *CSK*

A Bing for Bassett-Lowke
3-rail electric 0-4-0 L&NER
No. 112 tank locomotive, in
green livery, c1929.
£225-250 *CSK*

A Hornby Dublo 2711 BR 4-6-2
'Golden Fleece' locomotive and
tender, in original red and
white striped picture box.
£185-200 *CSK*

A Hornby 2245 BR E3002 Bo-Bo pantograph
electric locomotive, in original red and white
striped picture box. **£520-560** *CSK*

A Hornby series electric 20 volt
E120 Great Western 0-4-0 tank
locomotive, c1935.
£375-400 *CSK*

A Bassett-Lowke 3-rail electric GWR Castle
Class 4-6-0 locomotive and tender, No. 4079,
'Pendennis Castle', with copy of the original
invoice and relevant Autumn 1950 catalogue.
£1,400-1,500 *CSK*

A 3-rail electric LNER N2
condensing tank locomotive,
No. 4751, in black livery, by
V. Reader.
£800-825 *CSK*

An Exley Caledonian bogie
suburban non-corridor 3rd class
brake end, c1965.
£150-170 *CSK*

A Bassett-Lowke special order 3-rail electric North British Railway Atlantic 'Hazeldean' locomotive and matching 6-wheel tender, locomotive built as one of a small run in 1960s. **£640-680** *CSK*

A 2-rail electric model of the SR King Arthur Class 4-6-0 locomotive and tender, No. 754, 'The Green Knight', in SR livery and lining, with Bassett-Lowke Railway label. **£350-375** *CSK*

A Hornby series electrically lit No. 4E Wembley station and 2 ramps, last style, in original box, c1939. **£350-370** *CSK*

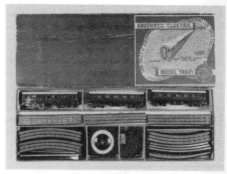

A Trix Southern Railway model electric train set, No. 5/375, in original box, c1938. **£440-480** *CSK*

A Hornby series GWR No. 2 corridor coach brake 3rd, in original box, c1939. **£340-380** *CSK*

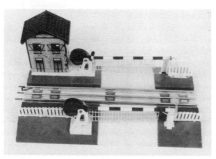

A JEP tinplate level crossing, c1935, 13 by 8in (33 by 20cm). **£35-45** *CA*

A Hornby Dublo D2 wooden City Station outfit, for building as terminal station and through station. **£800-850** *CSK*

Soldiers

A Heyde 58mm set of Wild Indians, in original box, 1930.
£285-300 *CSK*

A Britain's set No.2096, Pipes and Drums of the Irish Guards, first version metal drums, 1954.
£440-480 *CSK*

A collection of Lineol personality figures, comprising: Hess, with movable arm, Erich Ludendorff, General von Mackensen, General von Seeckt, Göring, and Hitler, with open raincoat and movable arm (arm missing), c1934.
£680-700 *CSK*

A Britain's set No.1641, Mechanical Transport and Air Force equipment, in original box, 1939.
£560-600 *CSK*

A Britain's set No.136, Russian Cavalry Cossacks, 1930.
£240-280 *CSK*

A Britain's set No. 1527, Band of the RAF, 1946-47 version.
£260-280 *CSK*

A Britain's set No.2074, 1st King's Dragoon Guards, 1960.
£140-160 *CSK*

A Britain's set No.182, 11th Hussars, Prince Albert's Own, dismounted with officer, 1948.
£160-180 *CSK*

A Britain's set No.123, The Bikanir Camel Corps, first version camels with detachable men, in original box, 1901.
£300-330 *CSK*

A Britain's set No.2067, The Sovereign's Standard of the Lifeguards and Escort, 1953.
£220-250 *CSK*

A Britain's set No.39, Royal Horse Artillery Gun Team, first version with seated gunners, 1895-1906.
£525-575 *CSK*

TRAYS

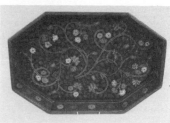

A wooden hand painted tray,
Russian, c1690.
£70-75 *SAD*

An original tip tray from the
Playboy Club, with a picture of
Marilyn Monroe, 4½in (11.5cm)
diam. **£35-40** *AAM*

A wooden tray, decorated
with butterflies wings,
1930s. **£100-120** *DaD*

TREEN

Treen is the generic term given to small
objects made of wood. These objects, usually
everyday household and domestic items, were
beautifully crafted and some of the earlier
pieces can be extremely valuable. Favourites
with collectors are the early fruit shapes,
especially apples and pears.

This year two extremely popular areas of
treen are being featured. They are Mauchline
ware and Tunbridge ware.

Mauchline ware (pronounced Mocklin ware)
was produced in the small Scottish town of
Mauchline, near Ayr, which gave its name to
a wide range of Scottish souvenir ware. The
industry was at its peak during the 1860s and
continued until 1933 when the factory burnt
down.

Tunbridge ware comes from the Tunbridge
Wells area of Kent. It was produced using
long strips of coloured wood formed into a
picture or design. The strips were glued
together and cut crossways to produce
decorative veneers which were applied to a
vast range of goods and souvenir items. Some
of the earliest known pieces date back to the
17thC, but the peak of popularity was in
Victorian times, around 1850-60.
Unfortunately by the turn of the century the
industry had virtually finished.

An Austrian tube lined ceramic
tray, with silver plated mount,
c1900, 15¼in (39cm) wide.
£300-500 *ASA*

A Flemish carved oak pedestal,
17thC, 32in (81cm) high.
£300-350 *SAD*

A pair of Edwardian wooden
shoe trees, 9in (23cm) long.
£10-15 *HAY*

A hand hewn bowl, 17thC,
10in (25cm) diam.
£125-150 *SAD*

A hand carved casket, 17thC,
with later lid, 14in (36cm) long.
£125-150 *SAD*

A Regency mahogany cheese coaster,
15½in (39cm) wide. **£200-250** *JAC*

An oak biscuit barrel, with silver plated mounts, c1900, 6in (15cm) high.
£25-30 *HAY*

A Victorian turned ebony throat spray, containing glass bottle, 5½in (14cm) high. **£20-25** *HAY*

A collapsible mahogany drinking cup, 20thC, 4in (10cm) high.
£20-25 *HAY*

Mauchline Ware

An Edwardian watch stand, with photographic ware view, 4in (10cm) high.
£25-30 *HAY*

Two transfer ware napkin rings, early 20thC, 2in (5cm) diam.
£5-10 each *HAY*

A needle case, with transfer ware view of Bournemouth, c1900, 3½in (9cm) long.
£20-25 *HAY*

A thread box, with transfer ware view of Pendennis Castle, Falmouth, early 20thC, 3¼in (8cm) diam.
£20-25 *HAY*

A sycamore cradle, early 20thC, 4½ by 3in (11 by 7.5cm).
£30-35 *HAY*

l. A transfer ware beaker, with view of Burn's cottage, 2½in (6cm) high.
r. A photographic ware thimble holder, early 20thC.
£20-30 each *HAY*

A Victorian box, with photographic ware view of Loch Katrine, 3¼in (8cm) wide.
£20-25 *HAY*

Two needle cases, 4 and 3½in (10 and 8.5cm) high, and a box, containing a medicine glass, c1900, 3in (7.5cm) high.
£15-20 each *HAY*

A Douglas fir transfer ware box, early 20thC.
£20-25 *HAY*

This box was made from wood from Drummond Castle Gardens.

A wool container, with transfer ware view, early 20thC, 3¾in (9cm) diam.
£30-35 *HAY*

Two Victorian sycamore boxes, with transfer ware views, 4 and 3⅛in (10 and 8.5cm) wide.
£15-20 each *HAY*

A thimble holder, shaped as a saucepan, with transfer ware view, c1900, 4in (10cm) high.
£25-35 *HAY*

A Victorian black lacquer pen and pencil holder, with a message 'To A Friend', 4in (10cm) high.
£20-25 *HAY*

A needle holder, early 20thC, 3¼in (8cm) long.
£15-20 *HAY*

A box, with transfer ware picture of Cawdor Castle, early 20thC, 4½in (11cm) wide.
£20-25 *HAY*

An egg timer, with photographic ware view, early 20thC, 3¼in (8cm) high.
£20-25 *HAY*

Tunbridge Ware

An Edwardian brush, 7in (17.5cm) long.
£20-25 *HAY*

A papier mâché spectacle case, c1850, 7in (17.5cm) wide.
£260-270 *AMH*

A pencil box, with a pheasant and a squirrel, c1840, 8¾in (22cm) long.
£425-450 *AMH*

Three thread winders, c1855, 2½in (6cm) wide.
£65-75 each *AMH*

A box, decorated with an emperor moth, c1860, 3¾in (9cm) wide.
£140-150 *AMH*

A box, c1870, 5in (12.5cm) wide.
£140-150 *AMH*

A card box, with 'keyhole' view, c1870, 5in (12.5cm) wide.
£225-250 *AMH*

A visiting card box, with a butterfly in tesserae, c1840.
£130-150 *VB*

A work box, with view of Battle Abbey gatehouse, c1870, 13in (33cm) wide.
£1,300-1,400 *AMH*

A notebook with pencil, c1870, 4in (10cm).
£220-225 *AMH*

A box, inscribed 'A Present from Hastings', c1870, 4in (10cm) long.
£110-130 *VB*

An inkstand, c1840, 6in (15cm) wide.
£600-650 *AMH*

A triple compartment stamp box, c1920, 19in (50cm) wide.
£70-80 *VB*

Two pin cushions, c1880.
£30-40 each *VB*

A bodkin holder, c1890, 3in (7.5cm) long.
£70-95 *VB*

A box, inscribed 'Needles', c1850, 2½ by 1½in (6 by 3.5cm).
£75-85 *VB*

A pin wheel, c1870, 2in (5cm) diam.
£35-45 *VB*

Three Tunbridge ware items:
l. A waxer
c. A cotton reel
r. An emery, c1860.
£30-45 each *VB*

A push-up pencil, c1880.
£100-125 *VB*

A dip pen, c1860.
£80-100 *VB*

A stickware tape measure,
marked E. Nye, c1850.
£65-85 *VB*

A compass and thermometer, by
Hollamby, c1870, 7in (17.5cm)
high.   **£400-500** *VB*

Two thimble holders,
c1850-70.
£55-75 each *VB*

A box, inscribed
'Needles', c1870.
£75-85 *VB*

A stickware perfume case, with
cut glass scent bottle, c1840, 2in
(5cm) high.
£170-180 *VB*

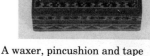

A waxer, pincushion and tape
measure, c1860, 2in (5cm) high.
£75-85 *VB*

A box, with a picture of a dog,
c1860, 3½in (9cm) wide.
£180-200 *AMH*

A letter opener, and a
bookmark, c1900.
£15-30 *VB*

A cotton winder, c1850,
2in (5cm) diam.
£50-60 *VB*

WALKING STICKS

A walking stick with plastic
handle, c1905.
£550-660 *ARE*

A shooting stick, with chrome and
leather seat, c1930, 34in (86cm) long.
£25-30 *AHL*

An ivory parasol, with
handle carved in the
form of an elephant's
head, being ridden by
a monkey dressed as
a jockey, late 19thC.
£575-600 *CSK*

An black silk umbrella, with
tassel, silver mount and neck,
35¾in (91cm) long.
£50-55 *AHL*

A black umbrella, with silver
mount and neck, c1900, 35½in
(90cm) long.
£35-40 *AHL*

A silver tipped
walking stick,
c1920, 32½in
(82cm).
£30-35 *AHL*

WATCHES

A Rolex
stainless steel
and pink gold
anti-magnetic
chronograph
wristwatch,
3.5cm diam.
£3,600-3,800 *C*

A Meylan two-tone 18ct gold
and enamel shutter clip watch,
case signed Verges Frères,
c1925. **£3,600-3,800** *S(NY)*

A Jaeger LeCoultre Art Deco
18ct gold Reverso wristwatch,
signed and numbered, with
maker's presentation box,
certificate of origin guarantee
and book of instruction, 2.6 by
3.8cm. **£9,000-10,000** *C*

A Cartier gold square Tank
Chinois wristwatch, c1930
£5,000-6,000 *S(NY)*

A Jaeger LeCoultre 18ct gold
wristwatch, dial signed Cartier,
1967. **£2,200-2,600** *S(NY)*

A Ulysse Nardin gentleman's 9ct gold wristwatch, 3cm diam.
£150-165 *TRU*

A Swiss 18ct chronograph wristwatch, with subsidiary dials, c1940.
£180-200 *TRU*

Swatch

A Nero, GB722, signed by Jasper Conran, together with a letter of authenticity.
£440-480 *Bon*

A Blue Matic, SAN 100, with limited edition packaging and Electra book, 1991. **£180-200** *Bon*

An Olympia II, GZ 402, limited edition, special 1990.
£240-280 *Bon*

Watch Holders

A Victorian boxwood watch holder, 5½in (13.5cm) high.
£40-45 *BER*

A carved wooden watch holder, in shape of a longcase clock, 14in (35.5cm) high.
£85-95 *BER*

A German carved wood watch holder, 6in (15cm) high.
£140-180 *BER*

A Victorian marble watch holder, 9in (22.5cm) high.
£75-85 *BER*

A wooden watch holder, with poker work, in shape of long case clock, 13¼in (33.5cm) high.
£50-60 *BER*

A Victorian ivory watch holder, 4¼in (10.5cm) high. **£65-75** *BER*

A Victorian inlaid ivory watch
holder, 11½in (29cm) high.
£240-280 *BER*

A porcelain watch holder, with
pink and green hand painted
decoration, 5in (12.5cm) high.
£35-45 *BER*

A brass watch holder, with
wooden base, 9¼in (23.5cm) high.
£220-260 *BER*

A Victorian cast iron
watch holder, 10½in
(26.5cm) high.
£230-260 *BER*

A porcelain watch
holder, with
Bournemouth crest,
6½in (16.5cm) high.
£70-85 *BER*

A Victorian watch
holder, modelled as a
brass frying pan,
6in (15cm) high.
£55-65 *BER*

A brass watch holder,
11⅛in (29cm) high.
£35-45 *WAB*

A green porcelain watch
holder, decorated with gold
birds, 6¼in (15.5cm) high.
£50-65 *BER*

A porcelain fob
watch holder,
with red and gilt
decoration, 4¾in
(12cm) high.
£25-35 *BER*

A metal watch holder,
with mirror back, 4⅜in
(11cm) high.
£65-75 *BER*

An Art Nouveau chrome
watch holder, 8½in
(21.5cm) high.
£20-30 *WAB*

Watch Keys

Three agate watch keys, with steel and ormolu mounts.
£100-200 each *BER*

An agate and metal watch key, 2in (5cm) high.
£100-200 *BER*

Two Breguet gold ratchet watch keys, ¾in (2.5cm) long.
£25-30 *BER*

Three watch keys, 1½in (3.5cm) long.
£3-5 *BER*

A gold watch key, 1in (2.5cm) long.
£25-35 *BER*

WRITING

The first self-filling pen was invented by J.J. Parker in 1823, but it was not until further refinements were completed that it became known as the fountain pen. Victorian and Edwardian fountain pens are the most popular to collect. Particular makers to note, apart from Parker, are Mabie Todd, Mont Blanc, Sheaffer, Dunhill-Namiki, Wahl-Eversharp, Swan and Waterman. Look out for replacement parts and check that fountain pens are in working order as replacements and repairs can be very costly.

Other areas of interest are inkwells, writing slopes and just about anything to do with postage and letters.

A pistol-shaped watch key, 1¾in (4.5cm) long.
£100-120 *BER*

A silver pen wiper, c1885.
£25-30 *VB*

An oak letter box, c1870, 25in (63.5cm) wide.
£350-400 *JAC*

A gilt card holder, on a marble base, English, c1880.
£250-350 *DMT*

A boulle blotter, from Asprey, c1870, 15in (38cm) wide.
£600-650 *AMH*

An Underwood typewriter.
£10-20 *WAB*

Two sets of postal scales, 4in (10cm) and 3¼in (8cm) high.
£25-35 *NM*

A brass letter rack and stamp box, c1910.
£45-55 *DUN*

A pen set, souvenir from the Grand Tour, c1820, 8¾in (22cm) wide.
£175-210 *ARE*

A mahogany desk compendium, by Love & Barton of Manchester, 19thC.
£450-480 *BIR*

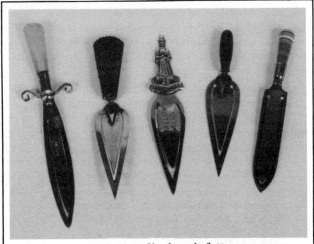

A selection of bookmarks/letter openers, c1900.
£10-30 each *VB*

A selection of pencil lead holders, c1900.
£2-4 each *VB*

A selection of pen nib and pencil lead holders, c1900.
£2-10 each *VB*

A brass mounted letter box, c1880, 12⅛in (31.5cm) high.
£160-190 *DUN*

A bronze letter clip, c1890, 6in (15cm) long.
£50-60 *DUN*

A Vienna bronze letter climp, in the shape of a hare, c1900, 13in (33.5cm) long.
£200-250 *DUN*

Inkwells

A silver inkwell, Birmingham 1913, 5in (12.5cm) diam.
£180-200 *DEL*

An Art Deco glass inkwell and pen stand, c1920, 4in (10cm) high.
£125-165 *MJW*

A brass tortoise inkwell, c1880, 6in (15cm) wide.
£200-240 *DUN*

Two travelling inkwells.
£20-30 each *VB*

A brass and glass inkwell, on onyx base, with lid opening either side, Betjemann patent, 8in (20cm) square.
£400-460 *MJW*

A brass jockey cap inkwell, c1880, 5in (12.5cm) high.
£350-385 *MJW*

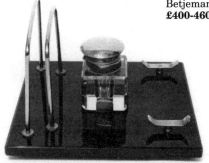

An inkwell and letter rack, with brass fittings, on black glass stand, c1930.
£80-90 *DEL*

A silver plated inkwell stand, with pen rest and a pair of cut glass inkwells, January 1919.
£220-260 *DEL*

A turned walnut inkwell,
c1890, 3¾in (9cm) diam.
£55-65 *TER*

Pens

A lacquered holder and
dip pen, c1920.
£12-16 *VB*

A silver plated inkwell, with
pen rest and cut glass well, on
horseshoe shaped base.
£140-150 *DEL*

A silver plated Buddha inkwell,
4¼in (11cm) high.
£360-390 *ARE*

- **Check carefully that the pen or pencil functions correctly - repairs, if indeed possible, can be very costly.**
- **Look closely for repairs, especially forced or glued replacement parts, as these can be expensive to rectify.**

A sycamore and mahogany pen
and inkwell set, c1920, 3in
(7.5cm) diam. **£15-20** *HAY*

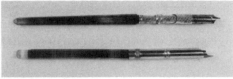

Two travelling dip pens.
£8-11 each *VB*

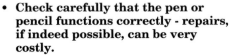

An Italian olive wood pen holder, 20thC, 6¼in
(15.5cm) long. **£10-15** *HAY*

Two Victorian agate dip pens.
£30-40 each *VB*

Two wooden dip pens. **£10-16 each** *VB*

A Victorian Tartan ware
reversible propelling pencil/dip
pen. **£35-45** *VB*

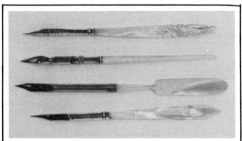

A selection of mother-of-pearl
dip pens.
£15-35 each *VB*

DIRECTORY OF SPECIALISTS

(A&A) Arms & Armour
(A&C) Arts & Crafts
(A&M) Arms & Militaria
(AD) Art Deco
(ADC) Art Deco Ceramics
(ADJ) Art Deco Jewellery
(Ae) Aeronautica
(AN) Art Nouveau
(Au) Automobilia
(B) Boxes
(Ba) Barometers
(BC) Baby Carriages
(BH) Button Hooks
(Bk) Books
(BM) Beer Mats
(Bot) Bottles
(BP) Baxter Prints
(Bu) Buttons
(C) Costume
(Ca) Cameras
(CaC) Card Cases
(CC) Cigarette Cards
(Ce) Ceramics

(Co) Comics
(Cns) Coins
(Col) Collectables
(Com) Commemorative
(Cor) Corkscrews
(D) Doulton
(DHF) Dolls House
    Furniture
(Do) Dolls
(DS) Display Stands
(E) Ephemera
(F) Fishing
(Fa) Fans
(G&CC) Goss & Crested
    China
(G) Glass
(Ga) Games
(GC) Greeting Cards
(Go) Golfing
(Gr) Gramophones
(H/HP) Hairdressing &
    Hat Pins
(I) Inkwells

(J) Jewellery
(Ju) Jukeboxes
(K), Kitchenalia
(L&K) Locks & Keys
(L&L) Linen & Lace
(LB) Le Blond Prints
(M) Metalware
(Ma) Matchboxes
(MB) Money Boxes
(O) Oriental
(OAM) Old Amusement
    Machines
(P) Pottery
(PB) Perfume Bottles
(PL) Pot Lids
(PM) Papier Mâché
(PMem) Police Memorabilia
(Po) Postcards
(R) Radios
(R&C) Rugs & Carpets
(Ra) Railwayana
(RH) Rocking Horses
(S) Silver

(S&MI) Scientific &
    Medical Instruments
(SC) Scottish Collectables
(Scr) Scripophily
(Sew) Sewing
(Sh) Shipping
(SP) Staffordshire Pottery
(Sp) Sporting
(St) Stereoscopes
(T&MS) Tins & Metal Signs
(T) Textiles
(Ta) Tartanware
(TB) Teddy Bears
(Te) Telephones
(Ti) Tiles
(To) Toys
(TP) Torquay Pottery
(Tr) Treen
(TW) Tunbridge Ware
(TV) Televisions
(W) Watches
(Wr) Writing
(WS) Walking Sticks

London

A. J. Partners (Shelley),
J28 Gray's-in-the-Mews,
1-7 Davies Mews, W1.
Tel: 071-629 7034/723 5363
(ADC)

Abstract, Kensington
Church Street Antique
Centre, 58-60 Kensington
Church Street, W8.
Tel: 071-376 2652
(ADJ)

Academy Costumes Ltd.
(Hire only),
25 Murphy Street, SE1.
Tel: 071-620 0771
(T, C)

Act One Hire Ltd., 2a
Scampston Mews,
Cambridge Gardens, W10.
Tel: 081-960 1456/1494
(T, C)

Andrews, Frank,
10 Vincent Road, N22.
Tel: 081-881 0658 (home)
(G)

Antique Textile Company,
100 Portland Road,
Holland Park, W11.
Tel: 071-221 7730
(T, C)

Anything American, 33-35
Duddenhill Lane, NW10.
Tel: 081-451 0320
(Ju)

Baddiel, Colin, Gray's
Mews, 1-7 Davies Mews,
W1.
Tel: 071-408 1239/
081-452 7243
(T)

Baddiel, Sarah, The Book
Gallery, B12 Gray's Mews,
1-7 Davies Mews, W1.
Tel: 071-408 1239/
081-452 7243
(Go)

Bangs, Christopher, SW11.
Tel: 071-223 5676
(M)

Barham Antiques,
83 Portobello Road, W11.
Tel: 071-727 3845
(B)

Barometer Fair, at
Cartographia Ltd.,
Pied Bull Yard, Bury
Place, Bloomsbury, WC1.
Tel: 071-404 4521/4050
(Ba)

Beverley & Beth,
30 Church Street, NW8.
Tel: 071-262 1576
(AD, Gl)

Blanchard, Sophia,
Alfie's Antique Market,
Church Street, NW8.
Tel: 071-723 5731
(T)

Boston, Nicolaus,
Kensington Church Street
Antiques Centre, 58-60
Kensington Church Street,
W8.
Tel: 071-376 0425
(P)

Bridge, Christine,
78 Castelnau, SW13.
Tel: 081-741 5501
(G)

British Commemoratives,
1st Floor, Georgian
Village,
Camden Passage, N1.
Tel: 071-359 4560
(Com, G&CC)

Brittania, Stand 101,
Gray's Antique Market,
58 Davies Street, W1.
Tel: 071-629 6772
(D)

Button Queen,
19 Marylebone Lane, W1.
Tel: 071-935 1505
(Bu)

Cameron, Jasmin,
Stand J6, Antiquarius,
131-141 King's Road, SW3.
Tel: 071-351 4154
(Wr)

Capon, Patrick,
350 Upper Street,
Islington, N1.
Tel: 071-354 0487/
081-467 5722
(Ba)

Casimir, Jack, Ltd.,
The Brass Shop, 23
Pembridge Road, W11.
Tel: 071-727 8643
(M)

Cekay Antiques,
Gray's Antique Market,
58 Davies Street, W1.
Tel: 071-629 5130
(WS)

Chelsea Lion,
Steve Clark,
Tel: 081-658 1599
(Do, To)

Chenil Galleries, Enigma
Z2, Pamela Haywood Z3,
Persifage Z5, Forthergill
Crowley D11-12, 181-183
King's Road, SW3.
Tel: 071-351 5353
(T, C)

Childhood Memories,
Teapot Arcade,
Portobello Road, W11.
(Do)

Clark, Gerald, Antiques,
1 High Street,
Mill Hill Village, NW7
Tel: 081-906 0342
(SP)

Classic Collection,
Pied Bull Yard,
Bury Place, WC1.
Tel: 071-831 6000
(Ca)

Classic Costumes Ltd.,
Tel: 081-764 8858/
071-620 0771
(T, C)

Collector's Shop, The,
9 Church Street, NW8.
Tel: 071-706 4586
(D)

Cropper, Stuart,
Gray's Mews,
1-7 Davies Mews, W1.
Tel: 071-629 7034
(To)

Dauphin Display Cabinet
Co., 118 Holland Park
Avenue, W11.
Tel: 071-727 0715
(DS)

David, 141 Gray's Antique
Market, Davies Street, W1.
Tel: 071-493 0208
(Cor, K, PMem)

De Fresne, Pierre,
'Beaux Bijoux',
Q9/10 Antiquarius,
135 King's Road, SW3.
Tel: 071-352 8882
(ADJ)

Decodence (Bakelite)
(Gad Sassower), Shop 13,
The Mall,
Camden Passage, N1.
Tel: 071-354 4473
(AD)

Dollyland, 864 Green
Lanes, Winchmore Hill,
N21.
Tel: 081-360 1053
(Do)

Donay, 35 Camden
Passage, N1.
Tel: 071-359 1880
(Ga)

Donohoe, L25/7, M10/12
Gray's Mews,
1-7 Davies Mews, W1.
Tel: 071-629 5633/
081-455 5507
(S)

East Gates Antiques,
Stand G006,
Alfie's Antique Market,
13-25 Church Street, NW8.
Tel: 071-724 5650
(G)

Eureka Antiques, Geoffrey
Vanns Arcade,
105 Portobello Road, W11.
(Saturdays)
(Ta, CaC, J)

Field, Audrey,
Alfie's Antique Market,
13-25 Church Street, NW8.
Tel: 071-723 6066
(L&L)

Fobbister, Rosemary,
Stand 28, The Chelsea
Antique Market,
245-263 King's Road, SW3.
Tel: 071-352 5581
(PM)

Gallery of Antique
Costume & Textiles,
2 Church Street,
Marylebone, NW8.
Tel: 071-723 9981
(T, C)

Gee, Rob, Flea Market,
Camden Passage, N1.
Tel: 071-226 6627
(Bot, PL)

Georgian Village,
First Floor, Islington
Green, N1.
Tel: 071-226 1571/5393
(Bot)

German, Michael,
38B Kensington Church
Street, W8.
Tel: 071-937 2771
(A&A, WS)

Gerwat-Clark, Brenda,
Alfie's Antique Market,
13-25 Church Street, NW8.
Tel: 071-706 4699
(Do)

Goldsmith & Perris, Stand
327, Alfie's Antique
Market, 13-25 Church
Street, NW8.
Tel: 071-724 7051
(S)

Gosh Comics, 39 Great
Russell Street, WC1.
Tel: 071-636 1011
(Co)

Harbottle, Patricia,
Geoffrey Vann Arcade,
107 Portobello Road, Wll.
(Saturdays)
Tel: 071-731 1972
(Cor)

Harrington Bros., The
Chelsea Antique Market,
253 King's Road, SW3.
Tel: 071-352 1720
(Bk)

Heather's Teddys, World
Famous Arcade,
177 Portobello Road, W11.
Tel: 081-204 0106
(TB)

Hebbs, Pam,
5 The Annexe,
Camden Passage, N1.
(TB)

Hogg, David, S141,
Gray's Antique Market,
Davies St., W1.
Tel: 071-493 0208
(BH)

Horne, Jonathan,
66B & C Kensington
Church Street, W8.
Tel: 071-221 5658
(SP)

Howard, Derek,
Chelsea Antique Market,
245-253 King's Road, SW3.
Tel: 071-352 4113
(S&MI)

Howard, Valerie
131E Kensington Church
Street, W8
Tel: 071-792 9702
(P)

Ilse Antiques,
30-32 The Vaults,
The Georgian Village,
Islington, N1.
(Ti)

Jaertelius, Monica, The
Mall, Camden Passage, N1.
Tel: 081-546 2807
(Bu)

Jag, Unit 6, Kensington
Church Street Antiques
Centre, 58-60, Kensington
Church Street, W8.
Tel: 071-938 4404
(ADC)

Jessops, 65 Great Russell
Street, WC1.
Tel: 071-831 3640
(Ca)

Keith, Old Advertising,
Unit 14, 155a Northcote
Road, Battersea, SW11.
Tel: 071-228 0741/6850
(T&MS)

King & Country, Unit 46,
Alfie's Antique Market,
13-25 Church Street, NW8.
Tel: 071-724 3439
(Go)

Lassalle, Judith,
7 Pierrepont Arcade,
Camden Passage, N1.
Tel: 071-607 7121
(Wed & Sat)
(RH)

Latford, Cliff,
Photography, G006,
Alfie's Antique Market,
13-25 Church Street, NW8.
Tel: 071-724 5650, and at
Colchester
Tel: 0206 564474
(Ca)

London Silver Vaults,
Chancery House,
53-65 Chancery Lane, WC2.
Tel: 071-242 3844
(S)

Maskerade, Antique
Centre, Kensington
Church Street, W8.
Tel: 071-937 8974
(J)

Memories, 18 Bell Lane,
Hendon, NW4.
Tel: 081-203 1772/202 9080
(Po)

Miller, Jess, PO Box 1461,
W6.
Tel: 081-748 9314
(F)

Moderne, Stand 5,
Georgian Village,
Camden Passage, N1.
(Bu)

Murray Cards
(International) Ltd.,
51 Watford Way,
Hendon Central, NW4.
Tel: 081-202 5688
(E, CC)

New Century, Art Pottery,
69 Kensington Church
Street, W8.
Tel: 071-376 2810
(ADC)

Noelle Antiques,
S26 Chelsea Antiques
Market, 253 King's Road,
SW3.
Tel: 071-352 5581
(BH)

Norman, Sue, Stand L4
Antiquarius,
135 King's Road, SW3.
Tel: 071-352 7217
(C)

Old Amusement Machines,
Tel: 071-889 2213/
0782 680667
(OAM)

Oosthuizen, Jacqueline
First Floor, Georgian
Village,
Camden Passage, N1.
Tel: 071-226 5393/
352 5581
and
23 Cale Street, SW3.
Tel: 071-352 6071
(SP, TP)

Oosthuizen, Pieter G. K.,
16 Britten Street, SW3
Tel: 071-352 1094/1493
(A&M)

Ormonde Gallery,
156 Portobello Road, W11.
Tel: 071-229 9800/
042482 226
(O)

Past and Present Toys,
862 Green Lanes,
Winchmore Hill, N21.
Tel: 081-364 1370
(TB, To)

Past and Present,
York Arcade, Unit 5,
Camden Passage, N1.
Tel: 071-833 2640
(ADC)

Patrician, 1st Floor,
Georgian Village,
Camden Passage, N1.
Tel: 071-359 4560/
435 3159
(ADC, I, PB)

Pieces of Time,
Gray's Mews,
1-7 Davies Street, W1.
Tel: 071-629 2422
(W)

Pinchin, Doug, Dixon's
Antique Centre,
471 Upper Richmond Road
West, East Sheen, SW14
Tel: 081-878 6788/948
1029
(D)

Powell, Sylvia, Decorative
Arts, 18 The Mall,
Camden Passage, N1.
Tel: 071-354 2977
(Ce)

Pleasures of Past Times,
11 Cecil Court,
Charing Cross Road, WC2.
Tel: 071-836 1142
(Bk, GC)

Relic Antiques,
248 Camden High Street,
NW1.
Tel: 071-485 8072
(K)

Reubens, 44 Honor Oak
Park, Brockley, SE23.
Tel: 081-291 1786
(S&MI)

Rotation Antiques,
Pierrepont Row
Fleamarket, Camden
Passage, N1.
Tel: 071-226 8211
(ADC)

Scripophily Shop,
Britannia Hotel,
Grosvenor Square, W1.
Tel: 071-495 0580
(Scr)

Stateside Comics plc,
125 East Barnet Road, N4
Tel: 081-449 5535
(Co)

Thimble Society of London,
The Bees, S134 Gray's
Antique Market,
58 Davies Street, W1.
Tel: 071-493 0560
(Sew)

Top Ten Comics,
9-12 St Anne's Court,
Soho, W1.
Tel: 071-734 7388
(Co)

Trio (Theresa Clayton).
Gray's Mews, 1-7 Davies
Mews, W1.
Tel: 071-629 1184
(PB)

Ursula, P16, 15 & 14,
Antiquarius,
135 King's Road, SW3.
Tel: 071-352 2203
(H/HP)

Vintage Cameras Ltd.,
254 & 256 Kirkdale,
Sydenham, SE26.
Tel: 081-778 5416/5841
(Ca)

Walker, Pat, Georgian
Village, Camden Passage,
N1.
Tel: 071-359 4560/
435 3159
(Do)

West, Mark J.,
Cobb Antiques,
39B High Street,
Wimbledon Village, SW19.
Tel: 081-946 2811/540
7982
(G)

Weston, David, Ltd.
44 Duke Street St James's,
SW1.
Tel: 071-839 1051/2/3
(S&MI)

White, John, Alfie's
Antique Market,
13-25 Church Street, NW8.
Tel: 071-723 0449
(ADC)

Wilcox, Norman, Alfie's
Antique Market,
13-25 Church Street, NW8.
Tel: 071-724 5650
(R)

Wynyards Antiques,
5 Ladbroke Road, W11.
Tel: 071-221 7936
(Tr)

Yesterday Child, Angel
Arcade, 118 Islington High
Street, N1.
Tel: 071-354 1601/
0908 583403
(Do)

Young, Robert, Antiques,
68 Battersea Bridge Road,
SW11.
Tel: 071-228 7847
(P)

Yvonne, K3 Chenil
Galleries, 183 King's Road,
SW3.
Tel: 071-352 7384
(Fa)

Zeitgeist, 58 Kensington
Church Street, W8.
Tel: 071-938 4817
(A&C, AN)

Avon

Barometer Shop, 3 Lower
Park Row, Bristol.
Tel: 0272 272565
(Ba)

Bath Dolls' Hospital &
Teddy Bear Clinic,
2 Grosvenor Place,
London Road, Bath.
Tel: 0225 319668
(Do)

Bristol Dolls' Hospital,
50-52 Alpha Road,
Southville, Bristol.
Tel: 0272 664368
(Do)

China Doll, The,
31 Walcot Street, Bath.
Tel: 0225 465849
(Do, DHF)

Dando, Andrew,
4 Wood Street, Bath.
Tel: 0225 422702
(P)

Gibson, Gloria,
2 Beaufort West, London
Road, Bath BA1 6QB.
Tel: 0225 446646
(B)

Great Western Toys,
Great Western Antique
Centre, Bartlett Street,
Bath.
(To)

Jessie's Button Box,
Great Western Antique
Centre, Bartlett Street,
Bath.
Tel: 0272 299065
(Bu)

Linford, Carr,
10-11 Walcot Buildings,
London Road, Bath.
Tel: 0225 317516
(CaC)

Marchant, Nick, 13 Orwell
Drive, Keynsham, Bristol.
Tel: 0272 865182
(M)

Pugh, Robert & Carol,
Bath.
Tel: 0225 314713
(P)

Saffell, Michael & Jo,
3 Walcot Buildings,
London Road, Bath.
Tel: 0225 315857
(T&MS)

Scott's, Bartlett Street
Antiques Centre,
Bartlett Street, Bath.
Tel: 0225 625335
(Ce)

Somervale Antiques,
6 Radstock Road,
Midsomer Norton, Bath.
Tel: 0761 412686
(G, PB)

Winstone Stamp Company,
S82 Great Western
Antiques Centre,
Bartlett Street, Bath.
Tel: 0225 310388
(CC, Ra)

Bedfordshire

Sykes, Christopher,
Antiques, The Old
Parsonage, Woburn.
Tel: 0525 290259
(Cor, S&MI, M)

Berkshire

Asquiths of Windsor,
10 George V Place,
Thames Avenue, Windsor.
Tel: 0753 854954/831200
(TB)

Below Stairs, 103 High
Street, Hungerford.
Tel: 0488 682317
(K)

Boxes From Derek
McIntosh,
10 Wickham Road,
Stockcross, Newbury.
Tel: 0488 38295
(B)

Mostly Boxes,
92 & 52b High Street,
Eton, Windsor.
Tel: 0753 858470
(B, I, TW)

Buckinghamshire

Cars Only, 4 Granville
Square, Willen Local
Centre, Willen, Milton
Keynes.
Tel: 0908 690024
(To)

Foster, A. & E.,
Little Heysham,
Forge Road, Naphill.
Tel: 024 024 2024
(Tr)

Neale, Gillian A.,
The Old Post Office,
Wendover.
Tel: 0296 625335
(Ce)

Cambridgeshire

Cambridge Fine Art Ltd.,
Priest House, 33 Church
Street, Little Shelford.
Tel: 0223 842866/843537
(BP)

Cheshire

Avalon, 1 City Walls,
Northgate Street, Chester.
Tel: 0244 318406
(Po)

Dé Jà Vu Antiques,
Hatters Row, Horsemarket
Street, Warrington.
Tel: 0925 232677
(Te)

Dollectable, 53 Lower
Bridge Street, Chester.
Tel: 0244 44888/679195
(Do)

Eureka Antiques,
7a Church Brow, Bowdon.
Tel: 061-926 9722
(CaC, J, Ta)

Nantwich Art Deco &
Decorative Arts, 87 Welsh
Row, Nantwich.
Tel: 0270 624876
(AD)

Rayment, Derek, Antiques,
Orchard House, Barton
Road, Barton, Nr Malpas.
Tel: 0829 270429
(Ba)

Cornwall

Millcraft Rocking Horse
Co., Lower Trannack Mill,
Coverack Bridges, Helston.
Tel: 0326 573316
(To, RH)

Cumbria

Bacchus Antiques,
Longlands at Cartmel.
Tel: 044 854 475
(Cor)

Ceramic Restorers,
Domino Restorations,
129 Craig Walk,
Windermere.
Tel: 05394 45751
(Ce)

Derbyshire

Norman King,
24 Dinting Road, Glossop.
Tel: 04574 2946
(Po)

Spurrier-Smith Antiques,
28b, 39-41 Church Street,
Ashbourne.
Tel: 0335 43669/42198
(M)

Devon

Bampton Telephone &
General Museum of
Communication and
Domestic History,
4 Brook Street, Bampton.
(Te)

Hill, Jonathan 2-4 Brook
Street, Bampton.
Tel: 0398 31310
(R)

Honiton Lace Shop,
44 High Street, Honiton.
Tel: 0404 42416
(L&L)

Dorset

Chicago Sound Company,
Northmoor House,
Colesbrook, Gillingham.
Tel: 0747 824338
(Ju)

Lionel Geneen Ltd.,
781 Christchurch Road,
Boscombe, Bournemouth.
Tel: 0202 422961
(O)

Mitton, Mervyn A.,
161 The Albany,
Manor Road,
Bournemouth.
Tel: 0202 293767
(PMem)

Old Button Shop,
Lytchett Minster.
Tel: 0202 622169
(Bu)

Old Harbour Antiques,
The Old Harbour, 3 Hope
Square, Weymouth.
Tel: 0305 777838
(Sh)

Yesterday's Tackle &
Books, 42 Clingan Road,
Southbourne.
Tel: 0202 476586
(F)

Essex

Basildon Baby Carriages,
83 Tyefields, Pitsea,
Basildon.
Tel: 0268 729803
(by appointment only)
(BC)

Blackwells of Hawkwell,
733 London Road,
Westcliff-on-Sea.
Tel: 0702 72248
(DHF)

East Gates Antiques,
91a East Hill, Colchester.
Tel: 0206 564474
(G)

G. K. R. Bonds Ltd.,
PO Box 1, Kelvedon.
Tel: 0765 71711
(Scr)

It's About Time,
863 London Road,
Westcliff-on-Sea.
Tel: 0702 72574
(Ba)

R. F. Postcards, 17 Hilary
Crescent, Rayleigh.
Tel: 0268 743222
(Po)

Waine, A., Tweedale,
Rye Mill Lane, Feering,
Colchester.
(ADC)

Old Telephone Co., The
Granary Antiques Centre,
Battlesbridge, Nr.
Wickford.
Tel: 0245 400601
(Te)

Gloucestershire

Acorn Antiques,
Sheep Street,
Stow-on-the-Wold.
Tel: 0451 831519
(Ce)

Cotswold Motor Museum,
The Old Mill,
Bourton-on-the-Water.
Tel: 0451 21255
(Au)

Greenwold, Lynn,
Digbeth Street,
Stow-on-the-Wold.
Tel: 0451 30398
(J)

Lillian Middleton's
Antique Dolls Shop,
Days Stable, Sheep Street,
Stow-on-the-Wold.
Tel: 0451 31542
(Do)

Park House Antiques,
Park Street,
Stow-on-the-Wold.
Tel: 0451 30159
(Do, DHF, TB)

Samarkand Galleries,
2 Brewery Yard,
Stow-on-the-Wold.
Tel: 0451 832322
(R&C)

Specialised Postcard
Auctions, 25 Gloucester
Street, Cirencester.
Tel: 0285 659057
(Po)

The Trumpet, West End,
Minchinhampton,
Nr. Stroud.
Tel: 0453 883027
(Col)

Hampshire

Art Deco China Centre,
62 Murray Road, Horndean.
Tel: 0705 597440
(ADC)

Cobwebs, 78 Northam
Road, Southampton.
Tel: 0703 227458
(Ae, Au, Sh)

Evans & Partridge
Auctioneers,
Agriculture House,
High Street, Stockbridge.
Tel: 0264 810702
(F)

Gazelles, 31 Northam
Road, Southampton.
Tel: 0703 235291
(AD)

Goss & Crested China
Ltd., 62 Murray Road,
Horndean.
Tel: 0705 597440
(G&CC)

Millers of Chelsea Ltd.,
Netherbrook House,
Christchurch Road,
Ringwood.
Tel: 0425 472062
(P)

Romsey Medal Centre,
5 Bell Street, Romsey.
Tel: 0794 512069
(A&M)

Toys Through Time,
Fareham.
Tel: 0329 288678
(Do)

Hereford &
Worcester

Barometer Shop,
New Street, Leominster.
Tel: 0568 3652
(Ba)

BBM Jewellery & Coins,
(W. V. Crook), 8-9 Lion
Street, Kidderminster.
Tel: 0562 744118
(I, J, Cns)

Button Museum,
Kyrle Street, Ross-on-Wye.
Tel: 0989 66089
(Bu)

Radiocraft, 56 Main Street,
Sedgebarrow, Evesham.
Tel: 0386 881988
(R)

Hertfordshire

Ambeline Antiques,
By George Antique Centre,
St. Albans.
Tel: 0727 53032/
081-445 8025
(H/HP)

Coombs, P.,
87 Gills Hill Lane, Radlett.
Tel: 0923 856949
(Ca)

Forget Me Not,
By George Antique Centre,
23 George Street,
St. Albans.
Tel: 0727 53032/
0903 261172
(J)

Oriental Rug Gallery,
42 Verulam Road,
St Albans.
Tel: 0727 41046
(R&C)

Isle of Wight

Nostalgia Toy Museum,
High Street, Godshill.
Tel: 0983 730055
(To)

Vectis Model Auctions,
Ward House,
12 York Avenue,
East Cowes.
Tel: 0983 292272
(To)

Kent

Amelia Dolls,
Pantiles Spa Antiques,
The Pantiles,
Tunbridge Wells.
Tel: 0892 541377/0342
713223
(Do)

Amherst Antiques,
23 London Road,
Riverhead, Sevenoaks.
Tel: 0732 455047
(Tr)

Antiques & Interiors,
22 Ashford Road,
Tenterden.
Tel: 05806 5422
(PM, T)

Beaubush House Antiques,
95 High Street, Sandgate,
Folkestone.
Tel: 0303 49099
(SP)

Blackford, Rowena, at
Penny Lampard's,
Antique Centre,
31 High Street, Headcorn.
Tel: 0622 890682/861360
(AD, K)

Burman, Valerie,
69 High Street,
Broadstairs.
Tel: 0843 862563
(ADC)

Candlestick & Bakelite,
PO Box 808, Orpington.
Tel: 081-467 3743
(Te)

Collectables, PO Box 130,
Rochester.
Tel: 0634 828767
(Col)

Dolls House Workshop,
54a London Road,
Teynham.
Tel: 0795 533445
(DHF)

Falstaff Antiques Motor
Museum,
63-67 High Street,
Rolvenden, Nr. Cranbrook.
Tel: 0580 241234
(Au)

Hadlow Antiques,
No. 1 The Pantiles,
Tunbridge Wells.
Tel: 0892 29858
(Do)

Heggie, Stuart,
58 Northgate, Canterbury.
Tel: 0227 470422
(Ca, St, R)

Kirkham, Harry,
Garden House Antiques,
118 High Street,
Tenterden.
Tel: 05806 3664
(F)

Kollectomania,
4 Catherine Street,
Rochester.
Tel: 0634 45099
(Ma)

Lace Basket,
1a East Cross, Tenterden.
Tel: 05806 3923
(L&L, H/HP)

Lampard, Penny,
28 High Street, Headcorn
Tel: 0622 890682
(K)

Magpie's Nest, 14 Palace
Street, Canterbury.
Tel: 0227 764883
(Do, DHF)

Old Saddlers Antiques,
Church Road, Goudhurst,
Cranbrook.
Tel: 0580 211458
(J, M)

Page Angela Antiques,
Tunbridge Wells.
Tel: 0892 22217
(P)

Reeves, Keith & Veronica,
Burgate Antiques,
10c Burgate, Canterbury.
Tel: 0227 456500/
0634 375098
(A&M)

Roses, 60 King Street,
Sandwich.
Tel: 0304 615303
(Col)

Serendipity,
168 High Street, Deal.
Tel: 0304 369165/366536
(Ce)

Stevenson Brothers,
The Workshop,
Ashford Road, Bethersden,
Ashford.
Tel: 0233 820363
(RH)

Strawsons Antiques,
33, 39 & 41 The Pantiles,
Tunbridge Wells.
Tel: 0892 30607
(TW)

Sturge, Mike,
39 Union Street,
Maidstone.
Tel: 0622 54702
(Po)

Up Country,
Old Corn Stores,
68 St. John's Road,
Tunbridge Wells.
Tel: 0892 23341
(K)

Variety Box, 16 Chapel
Place, Tunbridge Wells.
Tel: 0892 31868/21589
(BH, G&CC, Fa, G, H/HP,
Sew, S, TW)

Lancashire
A. S. Antiques, 26 Broad
Street, Pendleton, Salford.
Tel: 061-737 5938
(AD)

British Heritage
Telephones, 11 Rhodes
Drive, Unsworth, Bury.
Tel: 061-767 9259
(Te)

Bunn Roy W. Antiques,
34-36 Church Street,
Barnuldswick, Colne.
Tel: 0282 813703
(Ce, SP)

Lister Art Books,
22 Station Road, Banks,
Southport.
Tel: 0704 232033
(Bk)

Old Bakery The,
36 Inglewhite Road,
Longridge, Nr. Preston.
Tel: 0772 785411
(K)

Leicestershire
Charnwood Antiques,
Coalville, Leicester.
Tel: 0530 38530
(BP)

Jessups of Leicester Ltd.,
98 Scudamore Road,
Leicester.
Tel: 0533 320033
(Ca)

Williamson Janice,
9 Coverdale Road,
Meadows Wiston,
Leicester.
Tel: 0533 812926
(Ce, D)

Lincolnshire
20th Century Frocks,
Lincolnshire Art Centre,
Bridge Street, Horncastle.
Tel: 06582 7794/
06588 3638
(T)

Junktion, The Limes, Fen
Road, Stickford, Boston.
Tel: 0205 480087/480431
(To, T&MS)

Legends Rocking Horses,
Yew Tree Farmhouse,
Holme Road,
Kirton Holme, Boston.
Tel: 020 579 214
(To, RH)

Middlesex
Albert's Cigarette Card
Specialists, 113 London
Road, Twickenham.
Tel: 081-891 3067
(CC)

Ives, John, 5 Normanhurst
Drive, Twickenham.
Tel: 081-892 6265
(Bk)

Norfolk
Bluebird Arts,
1 Mount Street, Cromer.
Tel: 0263 512384/78487
(Po)

Howkins, Peter,
39, 40 & 135 King Street,
Great Yarmouth.
Tel: 0493 844639
(J)

Kensington Pottery,
Winstanley Cats,
1 Grammar School Road,
North Walsham.
Tel: 0692 402962
(Ce, P)

Pundole, Neville,
PO Box 6, Attleborough.
Tel: 0953 454106/
0860 278774
(ADC)

Trains & Olde Tyme Toys,
Aylsham Road, Norwich.
Tel: 0603 413585
(To)

Yesteryear Antiques,
24d Magdalen Street,
Norwich.
Tel: 0603 622908
(Ce, D)

North Humberside
Marine Art Posters
Services, 42 Ravenspur
Road, Bilton, Hull.
Tel: 0482 874700/815115
(Sh)

Northamptonshire
Shelron, 9 Brackley Road,
Towcester.
Tel: 0327 50242
(Po)

Nottinghamshire
Breck Antiques,
726 Mansfield Road,
Nottingham.
Tel: 0602 605263
(Ce)

Keyhole The, Dragonwyck,
Far Back Lane, Farnsfield,
Newark.
Tel: 0623 882590
(L&K)

Reflections of a Bygone
Age, 15 Debdale Lane,
Keyworth.
Tel: 06077 4079
(Po)

Vennett -Smith, T.,
11 Nottingham Road,
Gotham.
Tel: 0602 830541
(E,Po)

Vintage Wireless Shop,
The Hewarths, Sandiacre,
Nottingham.
Tel: 0602 393138
(R, TV)

Oxfordshire
Clockwork & Steam,
The Old Marmalade
Factory, 27 Parkend
Street, Oxford.
Tel: 0865 200321
(To)

Comics & Showcase,
19-20 St. Clements Street,
Oxford.
Tel: 0865 723680
(Co)

Key Antiques, 11 Horse
Fair, Chipping Norton.
Tel: 0608 3777
(M)

Manfred Schotten,
Crypt Antiques,
109 High Street, Burford.
Tel: 099 382 2302
(Go)

R.A.T.S., Unit 16,
Telford Road, Bicester.
Tel: 0869 242161/40842
(T&MS)

Strange Peter, Restorer,
The Willows, Sutton,
Oxford.
Tel: 0865 882020
(Do)

Teddy Bears,
99 High Street, Witney.
Tel: 0993 702616
(TB)

Thames Gallery,
Thameside,
Henley-on-Thames.
Tel: 0491 572449
(S)

Shropshire
Antiques on the Square,
2 Sandford Court,
Church Stretton.
Tel: 0694 724111
(ADC)

Manser, F. C., & Son Ltd.,
53 Wyle Cop, Shrewsbury.
Tel: 0743 51120
(CaC, Fa, S)

Nock Deighton,
Saleroom Centre, Tasley,
Bridgnorth.
Tel: 0746 762666
(F)

Rocking Horse Workshop,
Ashfield House,
The Foxholes, Wem.
Tel: 0939 32335
(RH)

Scot Hay House Antiques,
7 Nantwich Road, Woore.
Tel: 063 081 7118
(K)

Stretton Models,
12 Beaumont Road,
Church Stretton.
Tel: 0694 723737
(To)

Summers, Roger,
17 Daddlebrook,
Hollinswood, Telford.
(BM)

Tiffany Antiques, Unit 3,
Shrewsbury Antique
Centre, 15 Princess Howe,
The Square, Shrewsbury.
Tel: 0270 257425
and
Unit 15, Shrewsbury
Antique Market,
Frankwell Quay
Warehouse, Shrewsbury.
Tel: 0270 257425
(Col, K)

Vintage Fishing Tackle
Shop & Angling Art
Gallery,
103 Longden Coleham,
Shrewsbury.
Tel: 0743 69373
(F)

Staffordshire

Gordon The 'Ole
Bottleman, 25 Stapenhill
Road, Burton-on-Trent.
Tel: 0283 67213
(Bot)

Midwinter Antiques,
13 Brunswick Street,
Newcastle-under-Lyme.
Tel: 0782 712483
(T)

Somerset

House, Bernard G.,
Mitre Antiques,
Market Place, Wells.
Tel: 0749 72607
(Ba)

London Cigarette Card Co.
Ltd., Sutton Road,
Somerton.
Tel: 0458 73452
(CC)

Spencer & Co., Margaret,
Dept AD, Chard Road,
Crewkerne.
Tel: 0460 72362
(RH)

Yesterday's Paper,
40 South View, Holcombe
Rogus, Wellington.
Tel: 0823 672774
(Co)

Suffolk

Crafers Antiques, The Hill,
Wickham Market.
Tel: 0728 747347
(Ce, SP, Sew)

Hoad, W. L., 9 St. Peter's
Road, Kirkley, Lowestoft.
Tel: 0502 587758
(CC)

Surrey

Burns, David,
116 Chestnut Grove,
New Malden.
Tel: 081-949 7356
(S&MI)

Church Street Antiques,
15 Church Street,
Godalming.
Tel: 0483 860894
(ADC, Com)

Dorking Dolls House
Gallery, 23 West Street,
Dorking.
Tel: 0306 885785
(Do)

Nostalgia Amusements,
22 Greenwood Close,
Thames Ditton.
Tel: 081-398 2141
(Ju)

Sheppard Press, Unit 2,
Monk's Walk, Farnham.
Tel: 0252 734347
(Bk)

Victoriana Dolls, Reigate.
Tel: 0737 249525
(Do)

West Street Antiques,
63 West Street, Dorking.
Tel: 0306 883487
(A&M)

Wych House Antiques,
Wych Hill, Woking.
Tel: 04862 64636
(K)

Sussex

Barclay Antiques,
7 Village Mews, Little
Common, Bexhill-on-Sea.
Tel: 0797 222734
(TW)

Sporting Memories Ltd.,
5 High Street, Petworth
Tel: 0798 42377
(Sp)

Bartholomew, John &
Mary, The Mint Arcade,
71 The Mint, Rye.
Tel: 0797 225952
(Po)

Beech, Ron, Brambledean
Road, Portslade, Brighton.
Tel: 0273 423355
(Ce, PL)

Bygones, Collectors Shop,
123 South Street, Lancing.
Tel: 0903 750051/763470
(Col, Po)

Chateaubriand Antique
Centre, High Street,
Burwash.
Tel: 0435 882535
(Cor, O, L&L)

Dolls Hospital, 17 George
Street, Hastings.
Tel: 0424 444117/422758
(Do)

Ginns, Ray & Diane,
PO Box 129,
East Grinstead.
Tel: 0342 326041
(SP)

Keiron James Designs,
St Dominic's Gallery,
4 South Street, Ditchling.
Tel: 0273 846411
(TB)

Lingard, Ann,
Rope Walk Antiques, Rye.
Tel: 0797 223486
(K, Ti)

Old Mint House, Pevensey.
Tel: 0323 762337
(P)

Pearson, Sue, 13½ Prince
Albert Street, Brighton.
Tel: 0273 29247
(Do, TB)

Recollect Studios, Dept. M,
The Old School, London
Road, Sayers Common.
Tel: 0273 833314
(Do)

Rin Tin Tin,
34 North Road, Brighton.
Tel: 0273 672424/733689
(eves)
(Col, T&MS)

Russell, Leonard,
21 King's Avenue, Mount
Pleasant, Newhaven.
Tel: 0273 515153
(Ce, Com)

Sussex Commemorative
Centre, 88 Western Road,
Hove.
Tel: 0273 773911
(Ce)

Trains, 67 London Road,
Bognor Regis.
Tel: 0243 864727
(To)

V.A.G. & Co.,
Possingworth Craft
Centre, Brownings Farm,
Blackboys, Uckfield.
Tel: 0323 507488
(A&M)

Verrall Brian R. & Co.,
The Old Garage,
High Street, Handcross,
Haywards Heath.
Tel: 0444 400678
(Au)

Wallis & Wallis, West
Street Auction Galleries,
Lewes.
Tel: 0273 480208
(A&M, To)

Tyne & Wear

Ian Sharp Antiques
(Maling Ware), 23 Front
Street, Tynemouth.
Tel: 091-296 0656
(Ce)

Warwickshire

Arbour Antiques Ltd.,
Poet's Arbour,
Sheep Street,
Stratford-upon-Avon.
Tel: 0789 293453
(A&M)

Art Deco Ceramics,
Stratford Antique Centre,
Ely Street,
Stratford-upon-Avon.
Tel: 0789 297496/297244
(ADC)

Bowler, Simon, Smith
Street Antique Centre,
Warwick.
Tel: 0926 400554
(O)

Central Antique Arms &
Militaria, Smith Street
Antique Centre,
7 Smith Street, Warwick.
Tel: 0926 497864
(A&M)

Fab, 130 Queens Road,
Nuneaton.
Tel: 0203 382399
(Col)

Jazz, Civic Hall,
Rother Street,
Stratford-upon-Avon.
Tel: 0789 298362
(ADC)

Lions Den,
31 Henley Street,
Stratford-upon-Avon.
Tel: 0789 415802
(ADC, P)

Midlands Goss &
Commemoratives,
Warwick Antique Centre,
22 High Street, Warwick.
Tel: 0926 495704
(Ce, Com, G&CC)

Paull, Janice, 125 Warwick
Road, Kenilworth.
Tel: 0926 55253
(P, LB)

Rich Designs,
11 Union Street,
Stratford-upon-Avon.
Tel: 0789 772111
(ADC)

Time Machine,
Paul M. Kennelly,
198 Holbrook Lane,
Coventry.
Tel: 0203 663557
(To)

West Midlands

Doghouse The,
309 Bloxwich Road, Walsall.
Tel: 0922 30829
(K)

Moseley Railwayana
Museum, Birmingham.
Tel: 021-449 9707
(Ra, To)

Mr Morgan, F11 Swincross
Road, Old Swinford,
Stourbridge.
Tel: 0384 397033
(TB)

Nostalgia & Comics,
14-16 Smallbrook,
Queensway City Centre,
Birmingham.
Tel: 021-643 0143
(Co)

Railwayana Collectors
Journal, 7 Ascot Road,
Moseley, Birmingham.
(Ra)

Sawyer, George,
11 Frayne Avenue,
Kingswinford.
Tel: 0384 273847
(Po)

Walton & Hipkiss,
111 Worcester Road,
Hagley, Stourbridge.
Tel: 0562 885555/886688
(Au)

Wiltshire

Coppins of Corsham
Repairs, 1 Church Street,
Corsham.
Tel: 0249 715404
(J)

Expressions, 17 Princess
Street, Shrewsbury.
Tel: 0743 51731
(ADC)

Oxley, P. A., The Old
Rectory, Cherhill, Calne.
Tel: 0249 816227
(Ba)

Relic Antiques, Lea,
Malmesbury,
Tel: 0666 822332
(T&MS)

Wells, David, Salisbury
Antique & Collectors
Market, 37 Catherine
Street, Salisbury.
Tel: 0425 476899
(Po, To)

Yorkshire

Barnett, Tim, Carlton
Gallery, 60a Middle Street,
Driffield.
Tel: 0482 443954
(ADC)

British Bottle Review,
2 Strafford Avenue,
Elsecar, Nr. Barnsley.
Tel: 0226 745156/
0709 879303
(Bot)

Camera House,
Oakworth Hall,
Colne Road, Oakworth.
Tel: 0535 642333
(Ca)

Clarke, Andrew,
42 Pollard Lane, Bradford.
Tel: 0274 636042
(To)

Crested China Company,
Station House, Driffield.
Tel: 0377 47042
(G&CC)

Danby Antiques,
65 Heworth Road, York.
Tel: 0904 415280
(B)

Echoes, 650a Halifax Road,
Eastwood, Todmorden.
Tel: 0706 817505
(T)

Haley, John & Simon,
89 Northgate, Halifax.
Tel: 0422 822148
(To, MB)

Hewitt, Muir, Halifax
Antiques Centre,
Queens Road,
Gibbet Street, Halifax.
Tel: 0442 366657
(ADC)

In Retrospect,
2 Pavement, Pocklington,
York.
Tel: 0759 304894
(P)

Memory Lane,
69 Wakefield Road,
Sowerby Bridge.
Tel: 0422 833223
(TB)

National Railway Museum,
Leeman Road, York.
Tel: 0904 621261
(Ra)

Rouse, Sue,
The Dolls House,
Gladstone Buildings,
Hope Street,
Hebden Bridge.
Tel: 0422 845606
(Do)

Sheffield Railwayana
Auctions,
43 Little Norton Lane,
Sheffield.
Tel: 0742 745085
(Ra)

Spencer Bottomley,
Andrew,
The Coach House,
Thongsbridge, Holmfirth.
Tel: 0484 685234
(A&M)

Windmill Antiques,
4 Montpelier Mews,
Harrogate.
Tel: 0423 530502
(B, M, RH)

Scotland

AKA Comics & Books,
33 Virginia Street, Glasgow
Tel: 041-552 8731
(Co)

Black, Laurance,
45 Cumberland Street,
Edinburgh.
Tel: 031-557 4543
(Ta)

Bow Well Antiques,
103 West Bow, Edinburgh.
Tel: 031-225 3335
(Gr, SC)

Edinburgh Coin Shop,
2 Polwarth Crescent,
Edinburgh.
Tel: 031-229 3007/2915
(A&M)

Koto Buki, The Milestone,
Balmedie, Aberdeen.
Tel: 0358 42414
(O)

Maxtone Graham, Jamie,
Lyne Haugh, Lyne Station,
Peebles.
Tel: 0721 740304
(F)

Millars, 9-11 Castle Street,
Kirkcudbright.
Tel: 0557 30236
(ADC)

Miller, Jess, PO Box 1,
Birnam, Dunkeld,
Perthshire.
Tel: 03502 522
(F)

Now & Then Classic
Telephones, 7/9 Cross-
causeway, Edinburgh.
Tel: 031-668 2927/
0592 890235
(Te)

Stockbridge Antiques,
8 Deanhaugh Street,
Edinburgh.
Tel: 031 332 1366
(Do, T)

Toys & Treasures,
Wendy B. Austin-Bishop,
65 High Street, Grantown
on Spey, Morayshire,
Tel: 0479 2449
(Do)

Whittingham Crafts Ltd.,
8 Pentland Court, Saltire
Centre, Glenrothes, Fife.
Tel: 0592 630433
(RH)

Wales

Ayers, Brindley John,
45 St. Anne's Road,
Hakin, Milford Haven,
Pembrokeshire.
Tel: 06462 78359
(F)

Biffins, Ty Newydd,
Gwalchmai Uchaf,
Anglesey.
Tel: 0407 720550
(Po)

Corgi Toys Ltd.,
Kingsway,
Swansea Industrial Estate,
Swansea.
Tel: 0792 586223
(To)

Forbidden Planet,
5 Duke Street, Cardiff.
Tel: 0222 228885
(Co)

Gibbs, Paul,
25 Castle Street,
Conwy.
Tel: 0492 593429
(BH, ADC, Ti)

Howards Antiques,
10 Alexandra Road,
Aberystwyth, Dyfed.
Tel: 0970 624973
(P)

MacPherson, Stuart &
Pam, A.P.E.S.,
Ty Isaf, Pont y Gwyddel,
Llanfair T.H., Abergele,
Clwyd.
Tel: 074 579 365
(RH)

Victorian Fireplaces,
(Simon Priestley),
Ground Floor,
Cardiff Antique Centre,
69/71 St Mary Street,
Cardiff.
Tel: 0222 30970/226049
(Ti)

Watkins, Islwyn,
1 High Street/29 Market
Street,
Knighton, Powys.
Tel: 0547 520145/528940
(P)

Williams, Paul,
Forge Antiques,
Synod Inn,
Llandysul, Dyfed.
(T)

**If you would like your name and
address to feature in our Directory
of Specialists, please write to
Miller's Publications, The Cellars,
5 High Street, Tenterden, Kent, TN30
6BN, or telephone our Advertising
Department, on 0580 766411.**

DIRECTORY OF MARKETS & CENTRES

London

Alfie's Antique Market,
13-25 Church Street, NW8.
Tel: 071-723 6066
Tues-Sat 10-6pm

Angel Arcade, 116-118
Islington High Street,
Camden Passage, N1.
Wed & Sat

Antiquarius Antique
Market, 131/141 King's
Road, Chelsea, SW3.
Tel: 071-351 5353
Mon-Sat 10-6pm

Antiques & Collectors
Corner, North Piazza,
Covent Garden, WC2.
Tel: 071-240 7405
9-5pm every day

Bermondsey Antiques
Market, Corner of Long
Lane & Bermondsey
Street, SE1.
Tel: 071-351 5353
Friday 5am-2pm

Bermondsey Antiques
Warehouse, 173
Bermondsey Street, SE1.
Tel: 071-407 2040/4250
9.30-5.30pm, Thurs 9.30-
8pm, Fri 7-5.30pm.

Bond Street Antiques
Centre, 124 New Bond
Street, W1.
Tel: 071-351 5353
Mon-Fri 10-5.45pm,
Sat 10-4pm

Camden Antiques Market,
Corner of Camden High
Street & Buck Street,
Camden Town, NW1.
Thurs 7-4pm

Camden Passage Antique
Centre, 12 Camden
Passage, Islington, N1.
Tel: 071-359 0190
Stalls Wed 8-3pm (Thurs
books 9-4pm), Sat 9-5pm

Chelsea Antiques Market,
245-253 King's Road, SW3.
Tel: 071-352 5689/9695/1424
10-6pm

Chenil Galleries,
181-183 King's Road, SW3.
Tel: 071-351 5353
Mon-Sat 10-6pm

Corner Portobello Antiques
Supermarket, 282, 284,
288, 290 Westbourne
Grove, W11.
Tel: 071-727 2027
Fri 12-4pm, Sat 7-6pm

Cutler Street Antiques
Market, Goulston Street,
Nr Aldgate End, E1.
Tel: 071-351 5353
Sun 7-2pm

Crystal Palace Collectors
Market, Jasper Road,
Westow Hill,
Crystal Palace, SE19.
Tel: 081-761 3735
Wed 9-4pm, Fri 9-5pm, Sat
9-4pm, Sun 11-4pm

Dixons Antique Centre,
471 Upper Richmond Road
West, East Sheen, SW14.
Tel: 081-878 6788
10-5.30pm, Sun 1.30-
5.30pm, Closed Wed.

Franklin's Camberwell
Antiques Market,
161 Camberwell Road,
SE5.
Tel: 071-703 8089
10-6pm, Sun 1-6pm

Georgian Village Antiques
Market, 100 Wood Street,
Walthamstow, E17.
Tel: 081-520 6638
10-5pm, Closed Thurs.

Georgian Village,
Islington Green, N1.
Tel: 071-226 1571
Wed 10-4pm, Sat 7-5pm

Good Fairy Open Market,
100 Portobello Road, W11.
Tel: 071-351 5950/221 8977.
Sats only 5-5pm

Gray's Antique Market,
58 Davies Street, W1.
Tel: 071-629 7034
Mon-Fri 10-6pm

Gray's Mews,
1-7 Davies Street, W1.
Tel: 071-629 7034
Mon-Fri 10-6pm

Gray's Portobello,
138 Portobello Road, W11.
Tel: 071-221 3069
Sat 7-4pm

Greenwich Antiques
Market, Greenwich High
Road, SE10.
Sun 7.30-4.30/Sat June-Sept

Hampstead Antique
Emporium, 12 Heath
Street, Hampstead, NW3.
Tel: 071-794 3297
10-6pm, closed Mon & Sun.

Jubilee Market,
Covent Garden, WC2.
Tel: 071-836 2139
Open Mon

Kensington Church Street
Antiques Centre, 58-60
Kensington Church Street,
W8. 10-6pm

The London Silver Vaults,
Chancery House, 53-65
Chancery Lane, WC2.
Tel: 071-242 3844
9-5.30pm, Sat 9-12.30pm

The Mall Antiques Arcade,
359 Upper Street,
Islington, N1.
Tel: 071-354 2839
Tues, Thurs, Fri 10-5pm,
Wed 7.30-5pm, Sat 9-6pm

Northcote Road Antiques
Market,
155a Northcote Road,
Battersea, SW11.
Tel: 071-228 6850
10-6pm, Sun 12-5pm

Peckham Indoor Market,
Rye Lane Bargain Centre,
48 Rye Lane, Peckham,
SE15.
Tel: 071-246 3639
Tues-Sat

Pierrepoint Arcade,
Camden Passage, N1.
Tel: 071-359 0190
Wed & Sat

Portobello Road Market,
W11.
Sat 5.30-5pm

Rochefort Antique Gallery,
32/34 The Green,
Winchmore Hill, N21.
Tel: 081-886 4779/363 0910

Roger's Antiques Gallery,
65 Portobello Road, W11.
Tel: 071-351 5353
Sat 7-4pm

Steptoes Yard West
Market, 52a Goldhawk
Road, W12.
Tel: 071-602 2699
Fri, Sat & Sun

Streatham Traders &
Shippers Market, United
Reform Church Hall,
Streatham High Street,
SW16.
Tel: 071-764 3602
Tues 8-3pm

Wimbledon Market,
Car Park, Wimbledon
Greyhound Stadium,
Plough Lane, SW19.
Tel: 07268 17809. Sun.

Willesden Market,
Car Park, White Hart
Public House, Willesden,
NW10.
Tel: 081-569 3889

World Famous Portobello
Market,
177 Portobello Road &
1-3 Elgin Crescent, W11.
Tel: 071-221 4964
Sat 5-6pm

York Arcade,
80 Islington High Street,
N1.
Tel: 071-833 2640
Wed & Sat 8-5pm

Avon

Bartlett Street Antique
Centre,
5-10 Bartlett Street, Bath.
Tel: 0225 466689
Mon-Sat 9.30-5pm,
Wed Market 8-5pm

Bath Antiques Market,
Guinea Lane,
off Lansdown Road, Bath.
Wed 6.30-2.30pm

Bristol Antique Market,
St Nicholas Markets,
The Exchange,
Corn Street, Bristol.
Tel: 0272 224014
Fri 9-3pm

Clifton Antiques Market,
26/28 The Mall, Clifton,
Bristol.
Tel: 0272 741627
10-6pm, Closed Mon

Great Western Antique
Centre, Bartlett Street,
Bath.
Tel: 0225 424243
Mon-Sat 10-5pm,
Wed 8.30-5pm

Bedfordshire

Dunstable Antique Centre,
38a West Street,
Dunstable.
Tel: 0582 696953

Woburn Abbey Antiques
Centre, Woburn.
Tel: 0525 290350
11-5pm Nov to Easter,
10-5.30pm Easter to Oct

Berkshire

Hungerford Arcade,
High Street, Hungerford.
Tel: 0488 683701
9.30-5.30pm, Sun 10-6pm

Reading Emporium,
1a Merchant Place
(off Friar Street),
Reading.
Tel: 0734 590290
10-5pm

Twyford Antiques Centre,
1 High Street, Twyford.
Tel: 0734 342161
Mon-Sat 9.30-5.30pm,
Sun 10.30-5pm,
Closed Wed

Buckinghamshire

Amersham Antique
Collectors Centre,
20-22 Whieldon Street,
Old Amersham.
Tel: 0494 431282
Mon-Sat 10-6pm

Antiques at Wendover,
The Old Post Office,
25 High Street, Wendover.
Tel: 0296 625335
Mon-Sat 10-5.30pm,
Sun 11-5.30pm

Bell Street Antiques
Centre, 20/22 Bell Street,
Princes Risborough.
Tel: 08444 3034
9.30-5.30pm, Sun 12-5pm

Market Square Antiques,
20 Market Place, Olney.
Tel: 0234 712172
Mon-Sat 10-5.30pm,
Sun 2-5.30pm

Olney Antiques Centre,
Rose Court, Olney.
Tel: 0234 712172
10-5.30pm, Sun 12-5.30pm

Tingewick Antiques
Centre, Main Street,
Tingewick.
Tel: 0280 847922
10.30-5pm every day

Winslow Antique Centre,
15 Market Square, Winslow.
Tel: 0296 714540/714055
10-5pm

Cambridgeshire

Collectors Market,
Dales Brewery,
Gwydir Street (off Mill
Road), Cambridge.
9.30-5pm

Fitzwilliam Antiques
Centre, Fitzwilliam Street,
Peterborough.
Tel: 0733 65415

Willingham Antiques &
Collectors Market, 25-29
Green Street, Willingham.
Tel: 0954 60283
10-5pm, Closed Thurs

Cheshire

Davenham Antique
Centre, 461 London Road,
Davenham, Nr. Northwick.
Tel: 0606 44350
Mon-Sat 10-5pm,
Closed Wed

Nantwich Antique Centre,
The Old Police Station,
Welsh Row, Nantwich.
Tel: 0270 624035
10-5.30pm, Closed Wed

Melody's Antique
Galleries, 30-32 City Road,
Chester.
Tel: 0244 328968
Mon-Sat 10-5.30pm

Stancie Cutler Antique &
Collectors Fairs, Nantwich
Civic Hall, Nantwich.
Tel: 0270 624288

Cornwall

New Generation Antique
Market, 61/62 Chapel
Street, Penzance.
Tel: 0736 63267
10-5pm

Waterfront Antique
Complex, 1st Floor,
4 Quay Street, Falmouth.
Tel: 0326 311491
9-5pm

Cumbria

Carlisle Antique & Craft
Centre, Cecil Hall, Cecil
Street, Carlisle.
Tel: 0228 21970
Mon-Sat 9-5pm

Cockermouth Antiques
Market, Courthouse, Main
Street, Cockermouth.
Tel: 0900 824346
10-5pm

Derbyshire

Derby Antique Centre,
11 Friargate, Derby.
Tel: 0332 385002
Mon-Sat 10-5.30pm

Derby Antiques Market,
52-56 Curzon Street,
Derby.
Tel: 0332 41861
Mon-Sat 9-5pm, closed Wed.

Glossop Antique Centre,
Brookfield, Glossop.
Tel: 0457 863904
Thurs-Sun 10-5pm

Devon

The Antique Centre on the
Quay, Exeter.
Tel: 0392 214180
10-5pm

The Antique Centre,
Abingdon House,
136 High Street, Honiton.
Tel: 0404 42108
Mon-Sat 10-5pm

Barbican Antiques Centre,
82-84 Vauxhall Street,
Barbican, Plymouth.
Tel: 0752 266927
9.30-5pm

Dartmoor Antiques
Centre, Off West Street,
Ashburton.
Tel: 0364 52182
Tues 9-4pm

Dorset

The Antique Centre,
837-839 Christchurch
Road, East Boscombe,
Bournemouth.
Tel: 0202 421052
Mon-Sat 9.30-5.30pm

Barnes House Antiques
Centre, West Row,
Wimborne Minster.
Tel: 0202 886275
10-5pm

Bridport Antique Centre,
5 West Allington, Bridport.
Tel: 0308 25885
9-5pm

Gold Hill Antiques &
Collectables,
3 Gold Hill Parade,
Gold Hill, Shaftesbury.
Tel: 0747 54050

Sherborne Antique Centre,
Mattar Arcade,
17 Newlands, Sherborne.
Tel: 0935 813464
9-5pm

R. A. Swift & Son,
St Andrews Hall,
4c Wolverton Road
(off Christchurch Road),
Bournemouth.
Tel: 0202 394470
Mon-Fri 9-5.30pm

Wimborne Antique Centre,
Newborough Road,
Wimborne.
Tel: 0202 841251
Thurs 10-4pm, Fri 8.30-
5pm, Sat 10-5pm, Sun
9.30-5pm

Essex

Abridge Antique Centre,
Market Place, Abridge.
Tel: 0992 813113
10-5pm, Thurs 10-1pm

Battlesbridge Antiques
Centre, The Green,
Chelmsford Road, Battles-
bridge, Nr Wickford.
Tel: 0268 764197

Essex Antiques Centre,
Priory Street, Colchester.
Tel: 0206 871150
10-5.30pm

Grays Galleries Antiques
& Collectors Centre,
23 Lodge Lane, Grays.
Tel: 0375 374883
10-5.30pm

Kelvedon Antiques Centre,
139 High Street, Kelvedon.
Tel: 0376 570896
Mon-Sat 10-5pm

Maldon Antiques &
Collectors Market, United
Reformed Church Hall,
Market Hill, Maldon.
Tel: 07872 22826
1st Sat in month

Trinity Antiques Centre,
7 Trinity Street,
Colchester.
Tel: 0206 577775
9.30-5pm

Townsford Mill Antiques
Centre, The Causeway,
Halstead.
Tel: 0787 474451
10-5pm, inc Sun

Gloucestershire

Antique Centre,
London House,
High Street,
Moreton-in-Marsh.
Tel: 0608 51084
10-5pm

Charlton Kings Antique
Centre, 199 London Road,
Charlton Kings,
Cheltenham.
Tel: 0242 510672
9.30-5.30pm

Cheltenham Antique
Market, 54 Suffolk Road,
Cheltenham.
Tel: 0242 529812
9.30-5.30pm

Cirencester Antique
Market, Market Place,
Cirencester.
Tel: 071-262 5003. Fri

Gloucester Antiques
Centre, Severn Road,
Gloucester.
Tel: 0452 529716
9.30-5pm, Sun 1-5pm

Cotswold Antiques Centre,
The Square,
Stow-on-the-Wold.
Tel: 0451 31585
10-5.30pm

Painswick Antique Centre,
New Street, Painswick.
Tel: 0452 812431
10-5pm, Sat 9.30-5.30pm,
Sun 11-5.30pm

Tewkesbury Antique
Centre, Tolsey Hall,
Tolsey Lane, Tewkesbury.
Tel: 0684 294091
9-5pm

Windsor House Antiques
Centre, High Street,
Moreton-in-Marsh.
Tel: 0608 50993
10-5.30pm, Sun 12-5.30pm

Hampshire

Creightons Antique
Centre,
23-25 Bell Street, Romsey.
Tel: 0794 522758
9-6pm

Folly Antiques Centre,
College Street, Petersfield.
Tel: 0730 64816
10-5pm, Thurs 10-1pm

Kingsley Barn Antique
Centre, Church Lane,
Eversley, Nr Wokingham.
Tel: 0734 328518
10.30-5pm, closed Mon

Lymington Antiques
Centre, 76 High Street,
Lymington.
Tel: 0590 670934
10-5pm, Sat 9-5pm

Squirrel Collectors Centre,
9 New Street, Basingstoke.
Tel: 0256 464885
10-5.30pm

Hereford & Worcester

The Galleries Antiques
Centre, Pickwicks,
503 Evesham Road,
Crabbs Cross, Redditch.
Tel: 0527 550568
9.30-5pm, inc Sun

Hereford Antique Centre,
128 Widemarsh Street,
Hereford.
Tel: 0432 266242
9-5pm, Sun 1-5pm

Leominster Antiques
Market, 14 Broad Street,
Leominster.
Tel: 0568 2189
10-5pm

Worcester Antiques
Centre, Reindeer Court,
Mealcheapen Street,
Worcester.
Tel: 0905 610680/1
10-5pm

Hertfordshire

Antique & Collectors
Market, Market Place,
Hemel Hempstead.
Tel: 071-624 3214
Wed 9-2pm

Bushey Antiques Centre,
39 High Street, Bushey.
Tel: 081-950 5040

By George Antiques
Centre, 23 George Street,
St Albans.
Tel: 0727 53032
10-5pm

The Herts & Essex
Antique Centre,
The Maltings, Station
Road, Sawbridgeworth.
Tel: 0279 722044
Tues-Fri 10-5pm, Sat &
Sun 10-30-6pm, closed Mon

St Albans Antique Market,
Town Hall,
Chequer Street, St Albans.
Tel: 0727 44957
Mon 9.30-4pm

Humberside

New Pocklington Antiques
Centre, 26 George Street,
Pocklington, Nr York.
Tel: 0759 303032
Mon-Sat 10-5pm

Kent

The Antiques Centre,
120 London Road,
Sevenoaks.
Tel: 0732 452104
9.30-5.30pm, Sat 10-5.30pm

Beckenham Antique
Market, Old Council Hall,
Bromley Road,
Beckenham.
Tel: 081-777 6300
Wed 9.30-2pm

Bromley Antique Market,
Widmore Road, Bromley.
Thurs 7.30-3pm

Burgate Antiques Centre,
10 Burgate, Canterbury.
Tel: 0227 456500
Mon-Sat 10-5pm

Castle Antiques Centre,
1 London Road,
Westerham.
Tel: 0959 562492
Mon-Sat 10-5pm

Cranbrook Antiques
Centre, 15 High Street,
Cranbrook.
Tel: 0580 712173. 10-5pm

Folkestone Market,
Rotunda Amusement Park,
Marine Parade,
Folkestone.
Tel: 0850 311391
Sun

Hythe Antique Centre,
5 High Street, Hythe.
Tel: 0303 269043/269643
10-4pm, Sat 10-5pm
Closed Wed & Sun.

Malthouse Arcade,
High Street, Hythe.
Tel: 0303 260103
Fri & Sat 10-6pm

Noah's Ark Antiques
Centre, 5 King Street,
Sandwich.
Tel: 0304 611144
10-5pm, closed Wed & Sun

Paraphernalia Antiques &
Collectors Centre,
171 Widmore Road,
Bromley.
Tel: 081-318 2997
10-5.30pm, Sun 10-2pm

Rochester Antiques & Flea
Market, Corporation
Street, Rochester.
Tel: 071 262 5003
Sat 8-1pm

Sandgate Antiques Centre,
61-63 High Street,
Sandgate.
Tel: 0303 48987
10-6pm, Sun 11-6pm

Tenterden Antiques
Centre, 66-66A High
Street, Tenterden.
Tel: 05806 5885
10-5pm, inc Sun

Thanet Antiques Trade
Centre, 45 Albert Street,
Ramsgate.
Tel: 0843 597336
9-5pm

Tudor Cottage Antiques
Centre,
22-23 Shipbourne Road,
Tonbridge.
Tel: 0732 351719
10-5.30pm

Tunbridge Wells Antique
Centre, Union Square,
The Pantiles,
Tunbridge Wells.
Tel: 0892 533708
Mon-Sat 9.30-5pm

Lancashire

Blackpool Antiques
Centre,
105-107 Hornby Road,
Blackpool.
Tel: 0253 752514
9-5pm, closed Sat

Bolton Antiques Centre,
Central Street, Bolton.
Tel: 0204 362694
9.30-5pm, inc Sun

Bygone Times, Times
House, Grove Mill,
The Green, Eccleston.
Tel: 0257 453780
8-6pm, inc Sun

Darwen Antique Centre,
Provident Hall,
The Green, Darwen.
Tel: 0254 760565
9.30-5pm, Sun 11-5pm,
closed Tues

GB Antiques Centre,
Lancaster Leisure Park,
Wyresdale Road,
Lancaster.
Tel: 0524 844734
10-5pm, inc Sun

Last Drop Antique &
Collectors Fair,
Last Drop Hotel,
Bromley Cross, Bolton.
Sun 11-4pm

Levenshulme Antiques
Hypermarket,
Levenshulme Town Hall,
965 Stockport Road,
Levenshulme, Manchester.
Tel: 061 224 2410
10-5pm

Memory Lane Antique
Centre, Gilnow Lane,
off Deane Road, Bolton.
Tel: 0204 380383
9-5pm, inc Sun

Preston Antique Centre,
The Mill, New Hall Lane,
Preston.
Tel: 0772 794498
Mon-Fri 8.30-5.30pm,
Sat 10-4pm, Sun 9-4pm

Royal Exchange Shopping
Centre, Antiques Gallery,
St Anne's Square,
Exchange Street,
Manchester.
Tel: 061 834 3731/834 1427
Mon-Sat 9.30-5.30pm

Walter Aspinall Antiques,
Pendle Antique Centre,
Union Mill, Watt Street,
Sabden, Nr Blackburn.
Tel: 0282 76311
9-5pm, weekends 11-4pm

Leicestershire

The Antiques Complex,
St Nicholas Place,
Leicester.
Tel: 0533 533343
9.30-5.30pm

Boulevard Antique &
Shopping Centre, The Old
Dairy, Western Boulevard,
Leicester.
Tel: 0533 541201
10-6pm, Sun 2-5pm

Oxford Street Antiques
Centre Ltd., 16-26 Oxford
Street, Leicester.
Tel: 0533 553006
Mon-Fri 10-5.30pm, Sun
2-5pm

Lincolnshire

Boston Antiques Centre,
12 West Street, Boston.
Tel: 0205 361510
9-5pm, closed Thurs

Eastgate Antiques Centre,
6 Eastgate, Lincoln.
Tel: 0522 544404
9.30-5pm

Hemswell Antique Centre,
Caenby Corner Estate,
Hemswell Cliff,
Nr Gainsborough.
Tel: 0427 668389
10-5pm, inc Sun

The Lincolnshire Antiques
Centre, 26 Bridge Street,
Horncastle.
Tel: 0507 527794
9-5pm

Portobellow Row Antiques
Centre, 93-95 High Street,
Boston.
Tel: 0205 369456
10-4pm

Talisman Antiques,
51 North Street,
Horncastle.
Tel: 0507 526893
10-5pm, closed Mon.

Stamford Antiques Centre,
The Exchange Hall,
Broad Street, Stamford.
Tel: 0780 62605
10-5pm

Talisman Antiques,
Regent House,
12 South Market, Alford.
Tel: 0507 463441
10.30-4.30pm, closed Thurs.

Merseyside

Hoylake Antique Centre,
128-130 Market Street,
Hoylake.
Tel: 051-632 4231
9.15-5.30pm

Middlesex

Hampton Village Antiques
Centre,
76 Station Road, Hampton.
Tel: 081-979 5871
10-5.30pm

The Jay's Antique Centre,
25/29 High Street,
Harefield.
Tel: 0895 824738
10-6pm, Wed 10-1pm

Norfolk

Angel Antique Centre,
Pansthorn Farmhouse,
Redgrave Road,
South Lopham, Nr Diss.
Tel: 037 988 317
9.30-6pm, inc Sun

Antique & Collectors
Centre, St Michael at Plea,
Bank Plain, Norwich.
Tel: 0603 619129
9.30-5.00pm

Cloisters Antiques Fair,
St Andrew's & Blackfriars
Hall, St Andrew's Plain,
Norwich.
Tel: 0603 628477
Wed 9.30-3.30pm

Coltishall Antiques Centre,
High Street, Coltishall.
Tel: 0603 738306
10-5pm

Fakenham Antique Centre,
Old Congregational Chapel,
14 Norwich Road, Fakenham.
Tel: 0328 862941
10-5pm, Thurs 9.5pm

Gostling's Antique Centre,
13 Market Hill, Diss.
Tel: 0379 650360
10-5pm, Thurs 10-7pm

Norwich Antiques &
Collectors Centre,
Quayside, Fye Bridge,
Norwich.
Tel: 0603 612582
10-5pm

The Old Granary Antique
& Collectors Centre, King
Staithe Lane, off Queens
Street, King's Lynn.
Tel: 0553 775509 10-5pm

Wells Antique Centre,
The Old Mill, Maryland.
Tel: 0328 711433
10-5pm, inc Sun

Wymondham Antique
Centre, No 1 Town Green,
Wymondham.
Tel: 0953 604817 10-5pm

Northamptonshire

Antiques & Bric-a-Brac
Market, Market Square,
Town Centre,
Wellingborough.
Tel: 0905 611321
Tues 9-4pm

Finedon Antiques Centre,
Church Street, Finedon,
Nr Wellingborough.
Tel: 0933 681260
9.30-5.30pm, Sun 2-5

The Village Antique
Market, 62 High Street,
Weedon.
Tel: 0327 42015
9.30-5.30pm, Sun 10.30-
5.30pm

Northumberland

Colmans of Hexham,
15 St Mary's Chare, Hexham.
Tel: 0434 603811/2
9-5pm

Nottinghamshire

Castle Gate Antiques
Centre, 55 Castle Gate,
Newark.
Tel: 0636 700076
9-5.30pm

Newark Antiques Centre,
Regent House,
Lombard Street, Newark.
Tel: 0636 605504
9.30-5pm, Sun 11-4

Newark Antique
Warehouse, Kelham Road,
Newark.
Tel: 0636 74869
8.30-5.30pm, Sat 10-4pm

Nottingham Antique
Centre, British Rail Goods
Yard, London Road,
Nottingham.
Tel: 0602 504504/505548
9-5pm, closed Sat

Top Hat Antiques Centre,
66-72 Derby Road,
Nottingham.
Tel: 0602 419143
9.30-5pm

Oxfordshire

Antique & Collectors
Market, Town Hall, Thame.
Tel: 0844 28205
8.30-3.30pm, 2nd Tues of
month

Cotswold Gateway Antique Centre, Cheltenham Road, Burford Roundabout, Burford.
Tel: 099 382 3678
10-5.30pm, Sun 2-5.30pm

Chipping Norton Antique Centre, Ivy House, Middle Row, Chipping Norton.
Tel: 0608 644212
10-5pm, inc Sun

Deddington Antique Centre, Laurel House, Bull Ring, Market Square, Deddington.
Tel: 0869 38968
Mon-Sat 10-5pm

Friday Street Antique Centre, 2 & 4 Friday Street, Henley-on-Thames.
Tel: 0491 574104
9.30-5.30pm, Sun 11-5pm

Goring Antique Centre, 16 High Street, Goring-on-Thames.
Tel: 0491 873300.
10-5pm, Sat 11-5pm, closed Wed pm

Henley Antique Centre, Rotherfield Arcade, 2-4 Reading Road, Henley-on-Thames.
Tel: 0491 411468

The Lamb Arcade, High Street, Wallingford.
Tel: 0491 35166/35048
10-5pm, Sat 10-5.30pm
Wed 10-4pm

Oxford Antiques Centre, The Jam Factory, 27 Park End Street, Oxford.
Tel: 0865 251075
Mon-Sat 10-5pm and 1st Sun every month

Oxford Antiques Market, Gloucester Green, Oxford.
Tel: 0865 242216
Every Thurs

Span Antiques, 6 Market Place, Woodstock.
Tel: 0993 811332
10-5pm, inc Sun, closed Wed

Shropshire

Cleobury Mortimer Antique Centre, Childe Road, Cleobury Mortimer, Nr Kidderminster.
Tel: 0299 270513
10-5pm, inc Sun, closed Thurs

Ironbridge Antique Centre, Dale End, Ironbridge.
Tel: 0952 433784
10-5pm, Sun 2-5pm

Pepper Lane Antique Centre, Pepper Lane, Ludlow.
Tel: 0584 876494   10-5pm

Shrewsbury Antique Market, Frankwell Quay Warehouse, Shrewsbury.
Tel: 0743 350916
9.30-5pm

Shrewsbury Antique Centre, 15 Princess House, The Square, Shrewsbury.
Tel: 0743 247704
9.30-5.30pm

St Leonard's Antiques, Corve Street, Ludlow.
Tel: 0584 875573
9-5pm

Stretton Antiques Market, 36 Sandford Avenue, Church Stretton.
Tel: 0694 723718
9.30-5.30pm, Sun 10.30-4.30pm

Telford Antique Centre, High Street, Wellington, Telford.
Tel: 0952 256450
10-5pm, Sun 2-5pm

Somerset

Bridgwater Antiques Market, Marycourt Shopping Mall, Bridgwater.
Tel: 0823 451433
Friday 9-5pm, Sat 10-5pm

County Antiques Centre, 21/23 West Street, Ilminster.
Tel: 0460 54151. 10-5pm

Dulverton Antique Centre, Lower Town Hall, Dulverton.
Tel: 0398 23522. 10-5pm

Guildhall Antique Market, The Guildhall, Chard.
Thurs 9-3pm

Oscar's Antique Market, 13-15 Market Square, Crewkerne.
Tel: 0460 72718
10-5.30pm

Taunton Silver Street Antiques Centre, 27/29 Silver Street, Taunton.
Tel: 071-351 5353
Mon 9-4pm

Staffordshire

The Antique Centre, 128 High Street, Kinver.
Tel: 0384 877441
10-5.30pm

Antique Market, The Stones, Newcastle-under-Lyme.
Tel: 071-624 4848
Tues 9-4pm

Barclay House Antiques, 14-16 Howard Place, Shelton, Stoke-on-Trent.
Tel: 0782 274747
9.30-6pm

Rugeley Antique Centre, 161-3 Main Road, Brereton, Nr Rugeley.
Tel: 08895 77166. 9-5pm

The Potteries Centre, Stoke-on-Trent Antique & Collectors Centre, Winton Square, Station Road, Stoke on Trent.
Tel: 0782 411249
9-6pm

Tudor of Lichfield Antique Centre, Lichfield House, Bore Street, Lichfield.
Tel: 0543 263951

Tutbury Mill Antiques, 6 Lower High Street, Tutbury, Nr Burton-on-Trent.
Tel: 0283 815999
9-5pm every day

Suffolk

The Barn, Risby, Bury St Edmunds.
Tel: 0284 811126
10-5pm, inc Sun

Clare Antique Warehouse, The Mill, Malting Lane, Clare, Nr. Sudbury.
Tel: 0787 278449
9.30-5.30pm

Debenham Antique Centre, The Forresters Hall, High Street, Debenham.
Tel: 0728 860777
10-5.30pm, Sun 2-5pm

Long Melford Antiques Centre, The Chapel Maltings, Long Melford.
Tel: 0787 79287
9.30-5.30pm

Old Town Hall Antiques Centre, High Street, Needham Market.
Tel: 0449 720773
10-5pm

Snape Antiques and Collectors' Centre, Snape Maltings, Snape.
Tel: 0728 888038
10-6pm, inc Sun

Waveney Antiques Centre, Peddars Lane, Beccles.
Tel: 0502 716147
10-5.30pm

Wrentham Antiques Centre, 7 High Street, Wrentham, Nr. Beccles.
Tel: 0502 75376
10-5.30pm, Sun 2-5.30pm

Surrey

Antiquarius Antique Centre, 56 West Street, Dorking.
Tel: 0306 743398
9.30-5.30pm

Antiques Arcade, 22 Richmond Hill, Richmond.
Tel: 081-940 2035
10.30-5.30pm, closed Wed

Antiques & Interiors, 64 Station Road East, Oxted.
Tel: 0883 712806
9.30-5.30pm

The Antiques Arcade, 77 Bridge Road, East Molesey.
Tel: 081-979 7954
10-5pm

The Antiques Centre, 22 Haydon Place, corner of Martyr Road, Guildford.
Tel: 0483 67817
10-4pm, closed Mon & Wed

Cambridge Parade Antiques, 229-231 Carshalton Road, Carshalton.
Tel: 081-643 0014
10-5.30pm

Dorking Antiques Centre, 17/18 West Street, Dorking.
Tel: 0306 740915
10-5.30pm

Duke's Yard Antique Market, 1a Duke Street, Richmond.
Tel: 081-332 1051
10-6pm, closed Mon

Farnham Antique Centre, 27 South Street, Farnham.
Tel: 0252 724475
9.30-5.30pm

Fern Cottage Antique Centre, 28/30 High Street, Thames Ditton.
Tel: 081-398 2281
10-5.30pm

Maltings Monthly Market, Bridge Square, Farnham.
Tel: 0252 726234
First Sat in month

The Old Smithy Antique Centre, 7 High Street, Merstham.
Tel: 073764 2306. 10-5pm

Reigate Antiques Arcade, 57 High Street, Reigate.
Tel: 0737 222654
10-5.30pm

Surrey Antiques Centre, 10 Windsor Street, Chertsey.
Tel: 0932 563313
10-5pm

Sutton Market, West Street, Sutton.
Tel: 081-661 1245
Tues & Sat

Victoria & Edward Antiques Centre, 61 West Street, Dorking.
Tel: 0306 889645
9.30-5.30pm

Wood's Wharf Antiques Bazaar, 56 High Street, Haslemere.
Tel: 0428 642125
Mon-Sat 9.30-5pm

Sussex East

Antique Market, Leaf Hall, Seaside, Eastbourne.
Tel: 0323 27530
Tues & Sat, 9-5pm

Bexhill Antiques Centre, Quakers Mill, Old Town, Bexhill.
Tel: 0424 210182/221940
10-5.30pm

Brighton Antiques Gallery, 41 Meeting House Lane, Brighton.
Tel: 0273 26693/21059
10-5.30pm

Brighton Market, Jubilee Shopping Hall, 44-47 Gardner Street, Brighton.
Tel: 0273 600574. 9-5pm

Chateaubriand Antiques Centre, High Street, Burwash.
Tel: 0435 882535
10-5pm, Sun 2-5pm

Cliffe Antiques Centre, 47 Cliffe High Street, Lewes.
Tel: 0273 473266
9.30-5pm

Cliffe Gallery Antique Centre, 39 Cliffe High Street, Lewes.
Tel: 0273 471877
9.30-5pm

The Collectors Market, The Enterprise Centre, Station Parade, Eastbourne.
Tel: 0323 32690

The Courtyard Antiques Market, 13, 15 & 17 High Street, Seaford.
Tel: 0323 892091
8.30-5.30pm

Foundry Lane Antiques Centre, 15 Cliffe High Street, Lewes.
Tel: 0273 475361
10-5pm, closed Mon

George Street Antiques Centre, 47 George Street, Old Town, Hastings.
Tel: 0424 429339
9-5pm Sun 11-4pm

The Hastings Antique Centre, 59-61 Norman Road, Hastings.
Tel: 0424 428561
10-5.30pm

Horsebridge Antiques Centre, 1 North Street, Horsebridge, Nr Hailsham.
Tel: 0323 844414
10-5pm

Kollect-O-Mania, 25 Trafalgar Street, Brighton.
Tel: 0273 694229
10-5pm

Lewes Antique Centre, 20 Cliffe High Street, Lewes.
Tel: 0273 476148
9.30-5pm

Mint Arcade, 71 The Mint, Rye.
Tel: 0797 225952
10-5pm

Newhaven Flea Market, 28 South Way, Newhaven.
Tel: 0273 517207/516065
Open every day

The Old Town Hall, Antique Centre, 52 Ocklynge Road, Eastbourne.
Tel: 0323 416016
9.30-5pm, Sun 10.30-5pm

Pharoahs Antiques Centre, 28 South Street, Eastbourne.
Tel: 0323 38655. 10-5pm

Prinnys Antique Gallery, 3 Meeting House Lane, Brighton.
Tel: 0273 204554
9.30-5pm

Seaford's Barn Collectors Market & Studio Book Shop, The Barn, Church Lane, Seaford.
Tel: 0323 890010
Tues, Thurs & Sat
10-4.30pm

Sussex West

Almshouses Arcade, 19 The Hornet, Chichester.
9.30-4.30pm

Antiques & Collectors Market, Old Orchard Building, Old House, Adversane, Nr Billingshurst.
Tel: 0403 783594
Every day

Copthorne Group Antiques, Copthorne Bank, Crawley.
Tel: 0342 712802
Mon-Sat 10-5.30pm

Eagle House Antiques Market, Market Square, Midhurst.
Tel: 0730 812718

Mamies Antiques Centre, 5 River Road, Arundel.
Tel: 0903 882012
Thurs-Sun, 9-5pm

Midhurst Antiques Market, Knockhundred Row, Midhurst.
Tel: 0730 814231
9.30-5pm

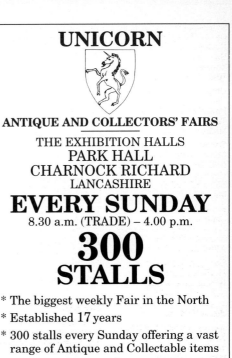

Shirley, Mostyns Antique Centre, 64 Brighton Road, Lancing.
Tel: 0903 752961
Mon-Fri 10-5pm

Petworth Antique Market, East Street, Petworth.
Tel: 0798 42073
10-5.30pm

Tarrant Street Antique Centre, Nineveh House, Tarrant Street, Arundel.
Tel: 0903 884307
9.30-5pm, Sun 11-5pm

Treasure House Antiques & Collectors Market, 31b High Street, Arundel.
Tel: 0903 883101
9-5pm

Upstairs Downstairs Antique Centre, 29 Tarrant Street, Arundel.
Tel: 0903 883749
10.30-5pm, inc Sun

Tyne & Wear

Antique Centre Newcastle, 8 St Mary Place East, Newcastle-upon-Tyne.
Tel: 091-232 9832
Tues-Sat 10-5pm

Blaydon Antique Centre, Bridge House, Bridge Street, Blaydon, Nr Newcastle-upon-Tyne.
Tel: 091-414 3535
10-5pm

Vine Lane Antique Market, 17 Vine Lane, Newcastle-upon-Tyne.
Tel: 091-261 2963/232 9832
10-5.30pm

Warwickshire

The Antiques Centre, High Street, Bidford-on-Avon.
Tel: 0789 773680
10-5pm, Sun 2-5.30pm, closed Mon

Antiques Etc.,
22 Railway Terrace, Rugby.
10-5pm, closed Tues & Wed

Dunchurch Antique Centre,
16/16a Daventry Road, Dunchurch, Nr Rugby.
Tel: 0788 817147
10-5pm, inc Sun

Leamington Pine & Antiques Centre, 20 Regent Street, Leamington Spa.
Tel: 0926 429679. 9-6pm

Meer Street Antiques Arcade, 10a/11 Meer Street, Stratford-upon-Avon.
Tel: 0789 297249

Meer Street Antiques Centre, Meer Street, Stratford upon Avon.
Tel: 0789 297249

Smith Street Antiques Centre, 7 Smith Street, Warwick.
Tel: 0926 497864
10-5.30pm

Spa Antiques Market, 4 Windsor Street, Leamington Spa.
Tel: 0926 22927
9.30-5.30pm

Stratford Antiques Centre, 60 Ely Street, Stratford-upon-Avon.
Tel: 0789 204180
10-5.30pm

The Old Cornmarket Antiques Centre, 70 Market Place, Warwick.
Tel: 0926 419119

Vintage Antique Market, 36 Market Place, Warwick.
Tel: 0926 491527.
10-5pm

Warwick Antique Centre, 20-22 High Street, Warwick.
Tel: 0926 495704
6 days a week

West Midlands

Birmingham Antique Centre, 141 Bromsgrove Street, Birmingham.
Tel: 021-692 1414/622 2145
Thurs from 9am

The City of Birmingham Antique Market, St Martins Market, Edgbaston Street, Birmingham.
Tel: 021-267 4636
Mon 6.30-2pm

Stancie Cutler Antique & Collectors Fair, Town Hall, Sutton Coldfield.
Tel: 0270 624288
Wed monthly, 11-8pm

Wiltshire

Antique & Collectors Market, 37 Catherine Street, Salisbury.
Tel: 0722 326033
9-5pm

The Avon Bridge Antiques & Collectors Market, United Reform Church Hall, Fisherton Street, Salisbury.
Tues 9-4pm

London House Antique Centre, High Street, Marlborough.
Tel: 0672 52331
Mon-Sat 9.30-5.30pm

The Marlborough Parade Antiques Centre, The Parade, Marlborough.
Tel: 0672 515331
10-5pm, inc Sun

Micawber's,
53 Fisherton Street, Salisbury.
Tel: 0722 337822
9.30-5pm, closed Wed

Yorkshire

The Ginnel, Harrogate Antique Centre, off Parliament Street, Harrogate.
Tel: 0423 508857
9.30-5.30pm

Grove Collectors Centre, Grove Road, Harrogate.
Tel: 0423 561680
10-4.30pm

Halifax Antiques Centre, Queen's Road/Gibbet Street, Halifax.
Tel: 0422 366657
Tues-Sat, 10-5pm

Malton Antique Market, 2 Old Maltongate, Malton.
Tel: 0653 692732
9.30-5, closed Thurs

Micklegate Antiques Market, 73 Micklegate, York.
Tel: 0904 644438
Wed & Sat, 10-5.30pm

Montpelier Mews Antique Market,
Montpelier Street, Harrogate.
Tel: 0423 530484
9.30-5.30pm

Treasure House Antiques Centre, 4-10 Swan Street, Bawtry, Nr Doncaster.
Tel: 0302 710621
10-5pm, inc Sun

West Park Antiques Pavilion, 20 West Park, Harrogate.
Tel: 0423 61758
10-5pm, closed Mon

York Antique Centre, 2 Lendal, York.
Tel: 0904 641445
Mon-Sat 9.30-5.30pm

Scotland

Bath Street Antique Galleries, 203 Bath Street, Glasgow.
Tel: 041-248 4220
10-5pm, Sat 10-1pm

Corner House Antiques, 217 St Vincent Street, Glasgow.
Tel: 041-248 2560 10-5pm

King's Court Antiques Centre & Market, King Street, Glasgow.
Tel: 041-423 7216
Tues-Sun

The Victorian Village, 53 & 57 West Regent Street, Glasgow.
Tel: 041-332 0808
10-5pm, Sat 10-1pm

Wales

Cardiff Antique Centre, 69-71 St Mary Street, Cardiff.
Tel: 0222 30970

Carew Market, Carew Airfield, on A477, Port Talbot.
Tel: 0639 886822. Sun

Jacobs Antique Centre, West Canal Wharf, Cardiff.
Tel: 0222 390939
Thurs & Sat 9.30-5pm

Offa's Dyke Antiques Centre, 4 High Street, Knighton, Powys.
Tel: 0547 528634/528940
Mon-Sat 10-5pm

Pembroke Antique Centre, The Hall, Hamilton Terrace, Pembroke.
Tel: 0646 687017
10-5pm

Port Talbot Market, Jubilee Shopping Hall, 64-66 Station Road, Port Talbot, Glamorgan.
Tel: 0639 883184
Mon-Sat

Swansea Antique Centre, 21 Oxford Street, Swansea.
Tel: 0792 466854
10-5pm

Channel Islands

Union Street Antique Market, 8 Union Street, St Helier, Jersey.
Tel: 0534 73805/22475
10-5pm

DIRECTORY OF COLLECTORS' CLUBS

This directory is in no way complete. If you wish to be included in next year's directory or if you have a change of address or telephone number, please could you inform us by October 31st 1994. Entries will be repeated in subsequent editions unless we are requested otherwise.

The Arms and Armour Society,
C/o Mr E J B Greenwood, Field House, Upper Dicker, Hailsham, East Sussex BN27 3PY.
Tel: 0323 844278

Badge Collectors' Circle,
C/o Mary Setchfield, 3 Ellis Close, Quorn, Nr Loughborough, Leics LE12 8SH.
Tel: 0509 412094

The Beswick Collectors' Circle,
PO Box 1793, Gerrards Cross, Bucks SL9 7YN.
Tel: 0753 882308

Association of Bottled Beer Collectors,
C/o David H Wilson, Thurwood, 5 Springfield Close, Woodsetts, Worksop, Nottingham S81 8QD.
Tel: 0909 562603

The British Beermat Collectors' Society,
C/o John F Feenan, 30 Carters Orchard, Quedgeley, Gloucester, Glos GL2 6WB.
Tel: 0452 721643

International Bond and Share Society,
C/o Michael Veissid, Hobsley House, Frodesley, Shrewsbury, Shropshire SY5 7HD.

Old Bottle Club of Great Britain,
C/o Alan Blakeman, 2 Strafford Avenue, Elsecar, Nr Barnsley, South Yorkshire S74 18AA.
Tel: 0226 745156

The British Button Society,
C/o Mrs K M Jenkins, 33 Haglane Copse, Pennington, Lymington, Hants SO41 8DR.
Tel: 0590 674044

The Buttonhook Society,
C/o Paul Moorehead, 2 Romney Place, Maidstone, Kent ME15 6LE.

Society of Caddy Spoon Collectors,
C/o Margaret Preston.
Tel: 0825 732681

Calculators Collectors' Club,
77 Welland Road, Tonbridge, Kent TN10 3TA..

Clarice Cliff Collectors' Club,
C/o Leonard R Griffin, Fantasque House, Tennis Drive, The Park, Nottingham NG7 1AE.

Susie Cooper Collectors' Group,
C/o Andrew Casey, PO Box 48, Beeston, Nottingham NG9 2RN.

Corgi Collector Club,
PO Box 323, Swansea SA1 1BJ.
Tel: 0792 476902

Disneyana Club,
31 Rowan Ray, Exwick, Exeter EX4 2DT.

Friends of Blue,
C/o Ron Govier, 10 Sea View Road, Herne Bay, Kent CT6 6JQ.

Goss Collectors' Club,
C/o Mr T Millward, 25 Sycamore Road, Awsworth, Nottingham NG16 2SQ.

The Oriental Ceramic Society,
The Secretary, 31b Torrington Square, London WC1E 7JL.
Tel: 071 636 7985

The Wedgwood Society of Great Britain,
C/o Dr W A M Holdaway, 89 Andrewes House, The Barbican, London EC2Y 8AY.

The Cartophilic Society of Great Britain,
C/o Alan Harris, 77 Carr Road, Calverley, Leeds LS28 5RJ.

The Cigarette Packet Collectors' Club of Great Britain,
C/o Mr Nat Chait, Nathan's Pipe Shop, 60 Hill Rise, Richmond, Surrey TW10 6UA.
Tel: 081 940 2404

The Antiquarian Horological Society,
C/o Marie Collins, New House, High Street, Ticehurst, East Sussex TN5 7AL.
Tel: 0580 200155

Costume Society,
Nigel Arch, C/o The State Apartments, Kensington Palace, London W8 4PX.
Tel: 071 937 9561

The British Numismatic Society,
C/o Mr Graham Dyer, The Royal Mint, Llantrisant, Pontyclun, Mid Glamorgan CF7 8YT.

The Royal Numismatic Society,
Mr Joseph Cribb, C/o Department of Coins and Medals, The British Museum, London WC1B 3DG.
Tel: 071 636 1555 extn 404

Comic Enthusiasts' Society,
C/o Denis Gifford, 80 Silverdale, Sydenham, London SE26 4SJ.

The Comics Journal,
C/o Bryon Whitworth, 17 Hill Street, Colne, Lancs BB8 0DH.
Tel: 0282 865468

Commemorative Collectors' Society,
C/o Steven Jackson, 25 Farndale Close, Long Eaton, Nottingham NG10 3PA.
Tel: 0602 727666

International Correspondence of Corkscrew Addicts,
C/o Donald Minzenmayer, Ambrose House, 29 Old Church Green, Kirk Hammerton, York YO5 8DL.
Tel: 0423 330745

Cricket Memorabilia Society,
C/o Tony Sheldon, 29 Highclere Road, Higher Crumpsall, Manchester M8 6WS.
Tel: 061 740 3714

The Doll Club of Great Britain,
C/o Mrs Jane Dunn, Unity Cottage, Pishill Bank, Henley on Thames, Oxon RG9 6HJ.

International Dolls' House News,
C/o June Stowe, PO Box 79, Southampton SO9 7EZ.
Tel: 0703 771995

Embroiderers' Guild,
C/o Mrs F Parsons, Apartment 41, Hampton Court Palace, East Molesey, Surrey KT8 9AU.
Tel: 081 943 1229

Ephemera Society,
C/o Mr Maurice Rickards, 12 Fitzroy Square, London W1P 5HQ.

Fan Circle International,
79a Alcoldale Road,
Westbury on Trym,
Bristol, Avon
BS9 3JW.

The Flag Institute,
C/o William Crampton,
10 Vicarage Road,
Chester CH2 3HZ.
Tel: 0244 351335

The Furniture History Society,
C/o Dr Brian Austen,
The Furniture &
Woodwork Collection,
The Victoria & Albert
Museum, London
SW7 2RL.
Tel: 0444 413845

The Hat Pin Society of Great Britain,
132 Hindes Road,
Harrow, Middlesex
HA1 1RR.

British Iron Collectors,
C/o Julia Morgan,
87 Wellsway, Bath,
Avon BA2 4RU.
Tel: 0225 428068

The Magic Lantern Society,
C/o L M H Smith,
Prospect, High Street,
Nutley, East Sussex
TN22 3NH.

British Matchbox, Label and Booklet Society,
3 Langton Close,
Norwich, Norfolk
NR5 8RU.

British Art Medal Society,
Philip Attwood,
C/o Dept of Coins and
Medals, The British
Museum, London
WC1B 3DG.
Tel: 071 323 8170
Extn 8227

The Psywar Society,
C/o Dr Rod Oakland,
21 Metchley Lane,
Harborne
Birmingham B17 0HT.
Tel: 021 426 2915

The Sylvac Collectors Circle,
174 Portsmouth Road,
Horndean, Hants
PO8 9HP.
Tel: 0705 591725

The Victorian Military Society,
C/o Ralph Moore-
Morris, 3 Franks Road,
Guildford, Surrey
GU2 6NT.
Tel: 0483 60931

British Model Soldier Society,
The Honorable
Secretary, 22 Lynwood
Road, Ealing, London
W5 1JJ.

Historical Model Railway Society,
59 Woodberry Way,
London E4 7DY.

The Hornby Railway Collectors' Association,
2 Ravensmore Road,
Sherwood, Nottingham
NG5 2AH.

The Matchbox International Collectors' Association,
C/o Stewart Orr,
The Toy Museum,
13a Lower Bridge
Street, Chester
CH1 1RS.
Tel: 0244 345297

Model Railway Club,
C/o Mr J E Geach,
Keen House,
4 Calshot Street,
London N1 9DA.

Train Collectors' Society,
C/o Joe Swain, Lock
Cottage, Station Foot
Path, Kings Langley,
Hertfordshire
WD4 8DZ.

The Trix Twin Railway Collector's Association,
C/o Mr C B Arnold,
6 Ribble Avenue,
Oadby, Leicester
LE2 4NZ.

The Vintage Model Yacht Group,
C/o Russel Potts,
8 Sherard Road,
London SE9 6EP.
Tel: 081 850 6805

British Association of Sound Collections,
C/o Alan Ward, National
Sound Archive,
29 Exhibition Road,
London SW7 2AS.
Tel: 071 589 6603

The City of London Photograph and Gramophone Society,
63 Vicarage Way,
Colnbrook,
Buckinghamshire
S13 0JY.

Hurdy-Gurdy Society,
C/o Doreen Muskett,
The Old Mill, Duntish,
Dorchester, Dorset
DT2 7DR.
Tel: 030 05412.

The Music Box Society of Great Britain,
C/o Alan Wyatt,
PO Box 299,
Waterbeach,
Cambridgeshire
CB4 4PJ.

The Cambridge Paperweight Circle,
C/o Roy Brown,
34 Huxley Road,
Welling, Kent
DA16 2EW.
Tel: 081 303 4663

Pewter Society,
C/o Dr John
Richardson, Hunters
Lodge, Paddock Close,
St Mary's Platt,
Sevenoaks, Kent
TN15 8NN.
Tel: 0732 883314

The English Playing Card Society,
C/o Major Donald
Welsh, 11 Pierrepont
Street, Bath, Avon
BA1 1LA.
Tel: 0225 465218

The Postal History Society,
C/o Michael Jackson,
PO Box 77,
Huntingdon,
Cambridgeshire
PE18 6TZ.
Tel: 0480 456254.

The Postcard Club of Great Britain,
C/o Mrs D Brennan,
34 Harper House,
St James's Crescent,
London SW9 7LW.
Tel: 071 733 0720

Scientific Instrument Society,
C/o Mr H A L Dawes,
PO Box 15, Pershore,
Worcs WR10 2RD.
Tel: 0705 812104

Silhouette Collectors' Club,
C/o Diana Joll, Flat 5,
13 Brunswick Square,
Hove, Sussex
BN3 1EH.
Tel: 0273 735760

The Silver Spoon Club,
C/o Mr & Mrs T R
Haines, Glenleigh
Park, Sticker,
St Austell, Cornwall
PL26 7JB.
Tel: 0726 652269

The Silver Study Group, The Secretary.
Tel: 081 202 0269

The Thimble Society of London,
C/o Bridget McConnel,
Grays Antique Market,
58 Davies Street,
London W1Y 1LB.
Tel: 071 493 0560.

The Tool and Trades History Society,
C/o Chris Hudson,
60 Swanley Lane,
Swanley, Kent BR8 7JG.
Tel: 0322 662271

Aeroplane Collection,
C/o Mr A Jenkins,
23 Dombey Road,
Poynton, Cheshire
SK12 1LT.

The Transport Ticket Society,
C/o Courtney Haydon,
4 Gladridge Close,
Earley, Reading,
Berkshire RG6 2DL.
Tel: 0734 579373

British Stickmakers' Guild,
C/o Brian Aries,
44a Eccles Road,
Chapel-en-le-Frith,
Derbyshire SK12 6RG.
Tel: 0298 815291

Wireless Preservation Society & CEM National Wireless Museum,
C/o Douglas Byrne,
52 West Hill Road,
Ryde, Isle of Wight
PO33 1LN.
Tel: 0983 567665

Writing Equipment Society,
C/o Maureen
Greenland,
4 Greystones Grange
Crescent, Sheffield
S11 7JL.
Tel: 0742 667140

INDEX TO ADVERTISERS

INDEX

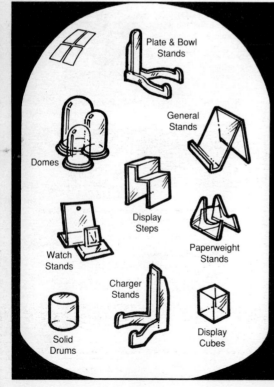

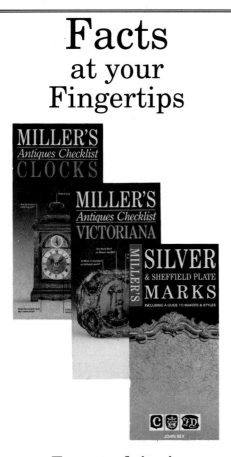